AGING PUBLIC POLICY:
BONDING THE GENERATIONS
SECOND EDITION

Theodore H. Koff
and
Richard W. Park

Jon Hendricks, Editor
SOCIETY AND AGING SERIES

D1166140

Baywood Publishing Company, Inc.
Amityville, New York

Library of Congress Catalog Card Number: 98-54620
ISBN: 0-89503-196-5 (CLOTH)
ISBN: 0-89503-195-7 (PAPER)

Library of Congress Cataloging-in-Publication Data

Koff, Theodore H.
   Aging public policy : bonding the generations / Theodore H. Koff
and Richard W. Park. - - 2nd ed.
      p. cm. - - (Society and aging series)
   Includes bibliographical references (p.   ) and index.
   ISBN 0-89503-196-5 (Cloth). - - ISBN 0-89503-195-7 (Paper)
   1. Aged- -Government policy- -United States.   I. Park, Richard W.
II. Title.   III. Series.
HQ1064.U5K64   1999
362.6'0973- -dc21   98-54620
                                    CIP

DEDICATION

To Yetta Koff and Inez Alexander, two women of different cultures
and backgrounds, who never met but shared common values
of honesty, decency, education and love of their children.
Each served to inspire us and through us, as teachers, they
have communicated to others their love and values.
They would have loved each other.

Nancy Alexander Koff
Theodore H. Koff

To the three generations of mothers who raised a crazy house
full of boys: May M. Schneider (Mamie), Marcella Hanisee (Donnie),
and Alma H. Park (Mom). These three marvelous ladies will always
be the spiritual center and sustenance for me and my brothers.
And to the mother of a new generation of Park boys:
my love and my support, Pamela.

Richard W. Park

Foreword

Public policies that affect the rapidly growing aged population in the United States have occupied center stage in the legislative, executive and judicial arenas for the past 50 years. Many policies have been established for the benefit of our millions of senior citizens—Social Security, Medicare, Medicaid, low-cost housing, senior centers and dozens of other programs. All of these have had significant impacts on U.S. residents, old and young.

When I was a teacher in the areas of public policy and aging programs, I longed for a book that would help me explain the processes by which programs for the aging are established by law and the administrative agencies of federal, state and local governments responsible for implementing these programs. What is known as the "aging network" is a complex system made up of thousands of local senior centers, more than 600 area agencies on aging, 50 state government units on aging, large and powerful national voluntary organizations that promote programs and benefits for the aging, and established activities and programs that reach millions of aged citizens.

Ted Koff and Richard Park have written the kind of book I needed. It carries the reader first through the policy process—how laws are made and the factors and forces which play a part in the establishment of laws. This is followed by a presentation of the historical background of aging policy in the United States and the role of various forces and interest groups in the policy process.

The authors have chosen four general program areas which illustrate the policy-making process in action: Social Security; health care for the elderly through Medicare and Medicaid, employment and retirement, and housing and social services. The forces and factors that have influenced the establishment and opera-tion of programs within these areas are described, and it is shown that one of the reasons well-intentioned programs often suffer from gaps and deficiencies is the incremental process that is characteristic to U.S. legislation.

The authors also look to the future and the unfinished business of establishing for this country a genuine policy on aging.

Students, both graduate and undergraduate, of gerontology and of public programs for the aged will find this book of great value. Political activists can gain from it an understanding of how laws are made. Persons entering the professions which touch on aging will find descriptions of existing programs and background material about them. The book is a practical resource for reaching a better understanding of the political and policy issues that indirectly, and frequently directly, affect services for the elderly.

In addition, the book contains convenient listings of the titles of the Older Americans Act, the activities and publications of the Federal Council on the Aging, the Committees of Congress which establish and provide funds for legally authorized programs, the major interest groups in the field of aging, and those of the various National Institutes of Health which have aging programs. A bibliography lists more than 200 relevant books, reports, articles and other publications.

This book represents a useful and important contribution to the field.

Charles I. Schottland
Former Commissioner of Social Security

Acknowledgments

No work of this scope can be done without the help of many individuals who care about the authors and the topic—or who welcome the opportunity of taking part in a marathon. Because of the devotion of these individuals, the task has been completed and the friendships remain.

I begin with a special word of appreciation to my associate, Richard Park, who enrolled in an undergraduate class I taught with no idea that it would lead to his seeking and receiving a graduate degree in long-term care administration and collaboration on this book as well as other publications and grant projects. He feigned alertness even after sitting through several years of my lectures and expanded classroom notes into content for this manuscript. He also learned to prepare a legislative history and to spend endless hours rummaging through the shelves of the university library.

Special thanks also are offered to Sandy McGinnis for her stability under pressure, good humor, and for balancing her responsible work load with the intricacies of piecing together revisions for the second edition of this book. And to Jai Larman, a graduate student whose labors on our behalf are appreciated. Jai is now working in the field of serving older persons, carrying on the tradition of his mentors and the mission of this book. Also special thanks to a long list of students who participated in the formulation of the ideas that make up this volume.

Theodore H. Koff
Tucson, Arizona

Have you ever had the experience of hearing someone speak or reading someone's words and saying to yourself "yes, that's just the way I would have said that (or wish I could have said that)?" Ted Koff has just this type of eloquence in his written and spoken words. Having said this and knowing that it is difficult to add even one word after Ted has said his piece, I do want to add my voice in chorus, thanking all of the above mentioned friends and helpers. Additionally, thanks are in order to my good friend and mentor, Richard Dickson, who provided me with an environment in which I was able to tie up my portion of the loose ends of this project.

Richard W. Park
Tucson, Arizona

Table of Contents

PART TWO: AGING POLICY DEVELOPMENT

PART THREE: MAJOR PUBLIC POLICIES
ON BEHALF OF THE ELDERLY

PART FOUR: THE ADVOCACY PROCESS IN
THE FIELD OF AGING: POLICIES FOR THE FUTURE

APPENDICES

List of Figures and Tables

LIST OF FIGURES

LIST OF TABLES

Introduction

In the beginning . . . is a good way to begin a book, but the subject of this one has no clear beginning. When did public policy begin in our society? What is public policy? Why is it an important subject about which to think, study, write or even get irritated? In the early years of the United States, when frontiersmen ruled by the force of their presence, there may not have been any public policy, at least none that was recorded. Policy may have determined that those with the fastest draw were right, the others were buried.

Today we have what has been referred to as a society of laws. We are governed by statutes that in their best form treat all persons equally and clearly spell out what is expected of our own behavior in society, of the government, and of others, as well as what constraints on our behavior have been imposed by law for the good of society. Laws govern almost every aspect of our society, and the absence of law may seem to endorse unacceptable behavior.

Other constraints on how we behave toward each other are not determined by law. A sense of decency, morality and respect for others guides us to behave in a way that represents ethical behavior quite apart from the law, although sometimes laws have been needed to establish certain ethical behaviors that were not being practiced by society at large.

Sometimes laws codify what are generally regarded as equitable principles. For example, we have enacted laws to assure that people will not be discriminated against because of their age, to provide that all people will have income to meet their basic needs, and to guarantee that health care will be provided to older people in need of such services. There is, in fact, a long list of laws that establishes a standard by which we as a society are expected to act toward older people in our society. It would be wonderful if everyone practiced throughout life all the things learned in kindergarten, as Fulghum reminded us in his best-selling book (1988, p. 4): "Share everything. Play fair. Don't hit people. Put things back where you found them. Clean up your own mess. Don't take things that aren't yours. Say you're sorry when you hurt somebody. Wash your hands before you eat. Flush.

Warm cookies and cold milk are good for you. Live a balanced life. Learn some and think some and draw and paint and sing and dance and play and work every day some. Take a nap every afternoon. When you go out into the world, watch for traffic, hold hands and stick together."

But our society has become too large, too diverse, too technical to live by the standards we learned in kindergarten or whatever "Golden Rule" we pursue in our own lives. We require public policies to guide the actions of government and of the people who reside in this country. However, we should not concede that all behavior must be directed by policies or that we cannot carry over into adulthood some of the moral lessons we learned when very young. In a sense it can be said that the statement of public policy should, in effect, restate the ideals of our kindergarten lessons for all to see and translate into adult terms.

This volume is about public policies that have the greatest influence on the lives of older persons and those that have been promulgated especially because of concern for older persons. Whether a policy is written on behalf of the entire population or specifically in response to the needs of a particular segment of the population (i.e., the elderly), public policies affect us all. Public policies are in a sense the way we share our concern for the welfare of the entire society. Providing societal assistance to any one segment of society sets the stage for everyone to work together to correct problems.

In addition to describing for a broad audience those policies that have the greatest impact on the older population, the book specifically addresses the evolution of policies as an outgrowth of developments in our society. The processes by which policies are introduced, debated and established, and the details of specific policies are all discussed. Some readers will want to know about public policies for the elderly because of a purely intellectual interest; others, especially persons who study the issues of aging or work in the field of gerontology, will want to learn how they can be in a better position to influence the formation of policies.

But what is public policy? Public refers to government, at any level. Policy refers to law. Public policies are the actions of governmental bodies that result in law. But, as mentioned earlier, there are public practices that are supported in the absence of any law. Are these also public policies although unstated? Is there a body of policy that is merely public practice?

We take the position that the absence of law is not law, that simply because a practice is not prohibited by law, it should not be construed as being supported by law. Prior to the passage of antidiscrimination laws, discrimination against older workers should not have been interpreted as representing public policy permitting such discrimination. Nevertheless, the absence of law, or of stated public policy, does have the effect of establishing that which is permissible or acceptable.

It is important that public policies represent standards for our lives as individuals and as a society that are based on ethical precepts and regard for the importance of every human being. Yet the ethics of our society and our regard for the rights of individuals have changed over the years in ways that require changes in public policies. Once established, policies should not be considered immutable; it is as important to understand the process for changing policies as it is to introduce new policies. Therefore it is especially important to know about the precedents of current laws and how they evolved into current policies.

Public policies may be the codification of public will or the response to a special interest group's desire for redress of a grievance. Policies may be advocated by elitists on behalf of the underprivileged or by the masses to express their own self-interest. Seemingly diverse political partners can be brought together for support of common goals. Social Security was developed in the 1930s as an outgrowth of an elitist-advocated policy to address the problems of a faltered economy. In the mid-1980s, massive public expression protected the Social Security program from an elitist approach to reducing Society Security benefits in order to rescue a faltering economy. The nature of the society, its people, values, and special interests all influenced the initial development of the program and all of these influenced proposed modification of the policy quite differently.

The potential for policy to be changed is ever-present and forces emerge both to argue for change and to defend the status quo. It is important to understand the history of a policy in order to appreciate expectations for change. This includes understanding the people and the groups whose presence influenced the development of the policy. For this reason people and policy will be considered inseparable and will be addressed together in this volume.

It has been said that those who have a high regard for sausage and the law should never watch either being made. While not admirers of sausage, we do have high regard for the law and, in spite of the admonition, we will take you through an exploration of how some of the laws affecting the elderly were made. It is our hope that this exploration, rather than converting sausage lovers, will inspire greater interest in the development of public policy on behalf of the elderly and make our readers more comfortable as well as more skillful in implementing their policy goals.

Through a large portion of this volume, and especially in those sections that describe the evolution of some public policy, the presentation of materials will be in the form of a legislative history. This means of conveying information has been selected because it illustrates, in a chronological sequence, the modification of a policy over time, the intervals of time between modifications and incremental adjustments to the primary policy. Many of the actors in the political process will be introduced through these historical renditions, including advocates from Congress, the bureaucracy and interest groups. The introduction to these various players will allow the reader to identify a particular policy with the names of persons or groups that have been instrumental in its enactment and subsequent alterations. This presentation should assist in communicating the dynamic process that is the evolution of public policy.

Is this a history book about public policies of special interest to the elderly or is this a book that instructs practitioners and students alike on how policies are formulated so that they can understand the process and intervene appropriately? Or is this book intended to identify the omissions in public policies and point to the need for change? Our response to this series of hypothetical questions is that the book is intended to be all of these, with priority given to helping students and practitioners in the field of aging participate fully in the policy process.

Understanding the policy process requires an appreciation of its roots in our unique constitutional form of government and the evolution of its history over the years. A record of the legislative history of a particular policy illuminates the trajectory of its development, enabling the reader to trace its events, know the history and be better prepared to contribute to its future. Accomplishments in some areas of public policy have been outstanding; in other areas they have been limited. Furthermore, any appraisal represents the point of view of the appraiser and is based on an expectation of the proper role of a government in regard to meeting needs of its people. We hope that reading this volume will help each reader establish a clear point of view and illustrate how it is possible to contribute to bringing your vision of the role of government in our society closer to a reality.

When we advocate on behalf of the issues related to the elderly in our society we also advocate for the human rights of all persons, irrespective of age or any other characteristic. There should be no age group that receives special consideration with regard to protection from hunger, homelessness and sickness; everyone is entitled to equal civil and human rights. All in this country should be afforded the opportunity for good health, a decent place to live, opportunities for employment and an income on which to live. To advocate on behalf of the elderly in no way conflicts with equally strong support of policies that benefit the needy of any age. Advocacy on behalf of the elderly may be most effective when united with coalitions that support policies that help all who are in need.

It is important to recognize that when we talk about "the elderly" the population for whom we are advocating has not yet been clearly defined, and if and when it is defined the definition probably will be provisional. That is because the terminology we use today will change tomorrow to reflect changing values or attitudes toward those considered to be in need of supportive public policies. Whether availability of services should be determined by need or be an entitlement will continue to be debated, as will the age at which aging services are made available.

We argue in favor of entitlement programs for the elderly and also recognize the need for programs that specifically rescue older individuals who have low or fixed incomes from the threat of poverty. If there were in the United States a national health care policy that recognized both acute and chronic care services and provided universal access to quality services, the issue of age would be irrelevant because Americans of all ages would have access to the health care they needed.

If there were an adequate family policy in this country that recognized the need for day care services for young children of working parents as well as the need for respite care services for frail elderly parents of working children there would be no need to place generations in competition for resources. It is important for us as a people and a country to find ways to support the family to carry out all their caring roles.

In this volume we refer to the people for whom we advocate as the elderly, older persons or people, the older population, aging members of society, the aging, older Americans, elderly constituents, the aging population, the aged, the disabled and probably several other terms that reflect the confusion that exists regarding just who it is for whom we advocate.

Is it the fifty-five-year-old who has just completed an application for the Job Training Partnership Act (JTPA) only to learn that the money for older workers had already been committed? Is it the fifty-nine-year-old who applied for housing for the elderly but was told that she was too young? Or is it the eighty-year-old highly qualified applicant for a position who has just been rejected for employment and told that the reason was an expectation that she could not meet the demands of the job?

Are all of these individuals "aging" or "elderly" or "older members of our society?" Perhaps they are, but that is unimportant. The real issue is whether we are committed to meeting the needs of individuals in our society who need public policies to serve them. Some of these individuals are older than others; some are close to retirement age or have retired. Some may be chronically ill at any age and some may be poor, hungry and homeless. For purposes of this volume we are concerned about all of these individuals, not merely persons who have reached a particular point on the age trajectory.

PART ONE:
THE POLICY PROCESS: RESPONDING TO HUMAN NEEDS THROUGH LAWS

This introductory section sets the stage for an understanding of the policy process by examining how our government evolved and illustrating stages and models of the policy process. While the focus of this volume is essentially on the policy process as it relates to the evolution of public policies on behalf of the elderly in our society, it is essentially the same in any content area. Having an understanding of the formation of policies in our society places an advocate for change in a strong position to defend the process and to demonstrate the value of a particular policy to our society.

Chapter 1: Constitutional Foundations

This chapter examines the founding of the American political system, the legislative process that it engendered and the expectations of the founding fathers for an American society. While we frequently wonder why it is so difficult for our government to pass a law, it is important to realize that an arduous system of checks and balances was devised deliberately to avoid concentrating too much power in any one segment of our government and thereby to avoid the tyranny the founding fathers feared as inherent in an autocratic government. The framework for the new form of government they devised was predicated on the values of federalism, the separation of powers, checks and balances, and the multiple interests of an extended republic. Each of these concepts will be described.

It is interesting to note that although we call our form of government a democracy, it was not viewed as such by the framers because they were opposed to a government that could be subject to the whims of the masses. Rather, they conceptualized a republic or representative government, and that form of government has continued from the inception of our Constitution.

Chapter 2: Making Policy in the United States

This chapter contributes to an understanding of the stages involved in the policy process, beginning with the identification of a problem and continuing through the implementation and evaluation of the policy. The several actors involved in this process (i.e., legislative bodies, the President, the courts and the bureaucracy) are also introduced.

Several models of the policy process are used to describe the ways in which policy-making is influenced. Four of these are described in the chapter: rationalism, interest group activity, elite preferences, and incrementalism.

Because a bill introduced into the Congress may have to go through 100 steps or decision points on its way to becoming a law, it is understandable that in a recent session only 6.4 percent of the legislation Congress considered was enacted into law. This chapter introduces the reader to the route taken by a bill as it is introduced into the Congress and its supporters struggle to have it pass. Obviously, the more responsive the bill is to an identified pressing community need or is favored by a strong and vocal constituency, the greater are its chances of surviving the maze of the legislative process and becoming law. Solving problems of the elderly is one identified community need.

On completing this chapter the reader should possess sufficient background in the policy process to be prepared to discuss and understand the framework through which policies for the elderly can be understood and efforts to intervene in the policy process in support of advocacy positions can be made productive.

Chapter 3: Historical Background to Aging Policy Development

This chapter reviews American policy responses to older persons since the mid-17th century. Those who might question the value of such an excursion into 200 years of history and its contribution to our current understanding of policy issues are reminded of the admonition inscribed on the entrance to the National Archives. "The Past is Prologue." Only if we remember our history will we have the wisdom to chart our future.

Our national search for societal responses to the needs of our elderly did not begin with our generation. The ancient scriptures pleaded "Do not cast us out in old age . . . do not forsake us when our strength fails," probably in an effort to discontinue practices prevalent when the number of elders was small and the onset of old age was considered to be far earlier than we view it today. This review serves as a reminder of the continuing search for a contemporary society that is at ease with its own aging as well as with its aging members.

PART TWO:
AGING POLICY DEVELOPMENT

Part Two discusses specific policies on behalf of the elderly, and evolves into an overview of the network of agencies created by the Older Americans Act, other federal agencies and special-interest groups, all designed to represent the needs and interests of older people in our society.

Chapter 4: The Aging Network

In Chapter 4, the "Aging Network" is defined. This is the term used to describe the inter-organizational structure fostered by the Older Americans Act (which gave rise to the Administration on Aging, the State Units on Aging and the Area Agencies on Aging). Its components and their roles in implementing programs, as well as influencing policy formation, are explained. Also included is a discussion of the somewhat disappointing performance of this aging network because completion of its mission, as described by federal policy, has not received adequate authority or funding. This lack of success has led to renewed discussion about the restructuring of the network and its position within the bureaucracy.

Chapter 5: Interest and Advisory Groups

Interest and advisory groups are presented as important parts of advocacy on behalf of the elderly. Chapter 5 first examines the advisory groups to the President, the Congress and the bureaucracy. These include the White House Conference on Aging, the Federal Council on The Aging (discontinued), and advisory groups to the states and the area agencies on aging that are mandated by law. Illustrations of the role of advisory groups in the policy process are provided, along with some comments regarding their weaknesses and the need for revisions that will involve the electorate more directly in the process. The roles of the special committees of the Congress, as well as of the congressional legislative committees, are described.

Interest groups on behalf of the elderly and the role of such groups in influencing the implementation of policy are also surveyed in this chapter. It is important to note that these groups may not realistically represent the interests of their members and that it may be politically immature to expect that such groups can control the voting behavior of the older persons they represent. The reasons older persons join advocacy groups are explored. Although membership may be for reasons other than political advocacy, the large numbers of members suggests a strong potential for influencing the political process.

PART THREE:
MAJOR PUBLIC POLICIES ON
BEHALF OF THE ELDERLY

Having dealt with processes related to the development of public policies in our democratic system of government and with the aging network and its advocacy capabilities, we next analyze some of the major public policies that immediately affect the elderly population. Emphasis is placed on the process that led to each policy, with references to material in earlier sections that provided a framework for the development of that policy. The major policies discussed are Social Security and other income maintenance programs, health policies (including Medicare and Medicaid), employment and retirement policies, and housing and social services.

Chapter 6: Social Security

This chapter is primarily devoted to Social Security, how and why it evolved and the changes implemented in its sixty-year history. This is essentially the major piece of legislation on behalf of older people in our society. It has had major impacts on the nation's economy, the role of the family, autonomy and dignity in aging, and the future of retirement programs for younger generations. Special attention is given to modifications in the law that have been responsive to societal changes. The politics as well as the programs of Social Security are discussed in this major case illustration of how the policy process has functioned during the past sixty years.

While Social Security is the primary income support program for the elderly, it is not the only one. Other programs, although in no way comparable in scope to Social Security, represent significant opportunities for many individuals, especially those with low incomes. Programs that are discussed include Supplementary Security Income (SSI), food stamps, surplus commodities distribution and tax advantages for the elderly. Questions are raised regarding the choice of public policies that support a variety of entitlement programs in lieu of an adequate income maintenance program that would permit older persons to purchase needed or desired services.

Chapter 7: Health Care Policies

The increasing age of the older population and the concurrent increase in the incidence of chronic illnesses has required a continuing examination of the public policies necessary to respond to the need. Consideration of Medicare and Medicaid presents an opportunity for additional case illustrations and examination of a process influenced by a Congress that is cautious in considering any major change. These programs demonstrate both the process of incrementalism and the significant impact of special interest groups.

Chapter 8: Coordinated System of Chronic Care

Chronic care is not limited to nursing homes, but includes a network of institutional and non-institutional services that respond to the needs typically associated with older persons. Major growth in the area of assisted living institutional settings as well as home health are noted as a growing response to less need for intensive nursing home care. Regulation of the quality of care provided, irrespective of the setting in which it is provided, continues to challenge the provision of chronic care services.

Chapter 9: Employment and Retirement

Policies that prohibit mandatory retirement because of age and policies that prohibit age discrimination in employment have been implemented but have not reversed a trend toward early retirement, perhaps because Social Security continues to penalize workers who continue full-time employment after becoming beneficiaries. This situation illustrates conflict between public policies and raises questions about whether the intention is to encourage or to discourage continuing employment of older workers. Special employment programs (i.e., Title 5 of the

Older Americans Act), training for employment (i.e., Job Training Partnership Act) and volunteer employment are shown as offering opportunities for continuing productivity on the part of older persons while also providing support of community services. In addition, this chapter examines policies related to the security and protection of funded retirement programs and the need to protect beneficiaries from the mismanagement or the default of programs from which they had anticipated retirement benefits. A policy intended to address this issue is embodied in the Employee Retirement Insurance Security Act (ERISA), which was enacted in 1974 to help regulate private pension plans.

Chapter 10: Housing and Social Services

Where people live and how they live are important to maintaining a satisfactory life style and good health. Where people live also influences their level of health and ability to care for themselves. Some people live independently while others may live in institutions. Many public policies have attempted to deal with issues ranging from provision of subsidized housing for the poor elderly and offering tax advantages to developers of housing for middle-income elderly to regulation of institutional care for the elderly. These policies are generally administered by the U.S. Departments of Housing and Urban Development and Health and Human Services.

PART FOUR:
THE ADVOCACY PROCESS IN
THE FIELD OF AGING:
POLICIES FOR THE FUTURE

As the numbers of older persons in our society has increased, so have the formal and informal structures established to represent the interests of this population. Special representation exists in both houses of the Congress, in the bureaucracy, in a surfeit of advisory groups, and in the office of the President. In addition, a wide array of special interest groups advocate on behalf of older people or in response to the perceived interests of this group. Rarely do all of these groups act in concert because the interests and needs of the older population cannot be neatly categorized according to a precise catalog of aging needs. Needs and concerns vary with the complexity of each individual's personality and many advocacy groups find themselves at odds with one another regarding how the elderly in our society can best be served.

Chapter 11: Bonding the Generations

The final chapter of the volume notes significant changes and enhancements over the past 200 years to public policies that respond to basic human needs. Nevertheless, the main thrust of the chapter is to emphasize how far our society remains from assuring the absence of poverty and the availability of adequate housing and health care for everyone. Changing societal perceptions of the needs of older persons have challenged the concept of entitlements to services by reason of age and argue for public policies that respond to need. Yet need-based eligibility may well result in the rationing of health care and lead to economics generating ethics rather than ethics guiding the use of available resources.

It is important to understand that no policy on behalf of the elderly responds solely to the elderly and that any advocacy on behalf of the elderly that does not respond to all who are in need is negligent. It appears likely that older people will feel better about themselves and all of us will feel better about our society when age is irrelevant and the basic needs of all persons are properly addressed.

PART ONE

The Policy Process:
Responding to Human Needs Through Laws

Constitutional Foundations

To begin our discussion of public policy-making in the United States and how it has influenced the lives of its aging members, it should be helpful to review briefly the founding of the American political system, the legislative process that it engendered and examples of policy determinations that illustrate how this process actually functions. Areas we will cover include: What were the expectations (i.e., the early concepts and visions) of the founding fathers for an American society? How was the Congress set up to function? How are laws passed by a legislature? What are some of the general concepts of the policy process? And finally, what are some of the general models of public policy-making in our governmental system? Examination of these questions should lead to an understanding of how the citizenry interacts with the decision-making environment of our government.

Throughout the volume, when reference is made to the "American Society" or other aspects of being "American," that reference is to the United States of America. We who live in this country are Americans but so are the Mexicans living in Mexico or the Canadians living in Canada. Although it may be egocentric to think of ourselves as being Americans without distinguishing ourselves as the Americans who live in the United States, we will continue to use the term for reasons of brevity and consistency, while disavowing any intention to minimize the equal status of other Americans.

GROWTH OF DEMOCRACY

Isn't it amazing that in the past 200 years when monarchies have tumbled, communism has failed as a national form of government, national borders have been disrupted, and governments have sought new ways to rule, the democracy practiced in the United States has flourished and thrived? Unquestionably there is much more to be achieved in order to assure every citizen of this country the equal rights and opportunities so eloquently expressed in the Declaration of Independence, but there should be no question that the opportunities present today are

3

available to many more persons than was the case when our government was initiated in 1781 (when the Constitution was ratified).

The growing strength of this society, measured in the way it responds to the needs of its people, has been an erratic, if uphill, continuing search for a more perfect union. There are many citizens who have not been served well and today there are some who continue to feel alienated from the mainstream of the American society. In a system that respects the rule of the majority, many minorities may be left without adequate representation. Political elections may not reflect substantial discussion of important issues that may be clouded or misrepresented by the activities of political manipulators who are more strongly motivated by the wish to have their candidate win than by a desire to help the electorate understand the issues and the differences between candidates. We rarely have an opportunity to vote on an issue in national politics. Rather, we select the party or candidate that we presume to have goals that are most consistent with our own beliefs. That is, those of us who actually vote.

Others may choose to express their displeasure by not voting, or feel that their vote will make no difference, or that voting has little to do with our form of democracy. Or they just do not care.

Our democracy has many imperfections, but what it "promises and delivers, ultimately, is the opportunity to do something about them" (Keefe et al., 1986, in prologue). Showing how we can do something about the needs of older persons in our society is the object of this volume.

Preceded by the development of a central government in 1774 (the First Continental Congress) and an armed rebellion initiated in 1775, the United States of America began to take form with the calling of the Second Continental Congress and formal approval of the Declaration of Independence on July 4, 1776, separating the colonies from Great Britain and proclaiming "an independence that had already been gained philosophically" (Ladd, 1991, p. 48).

The American revolution drew heavily on ideas that had roots in Europe in the 17th and 18th centuries when what came to be known as classical liberalism "developed as a protest against the then-dominant values, institutions and class arrangements of aristocratic society" (Ladd, 1991, p. 49). Six interrelated beliefs form the core of this political philosophy. They are individualism, freedom, equality, private property, government by popular choice, and limited government. This liberalism epitomizes what we now know and practice as American democracy. The opening statement of the Declaration of Independence, which reads:

> We hold these Truths to be self-evident, that all Men are created equal, that they are endowed by their Creator with certain unalienable Rights, that among these are Life, Liberty and the Pursuit of Happiness—

is central to our understanding of the evolution of policies based on belief:

> That to secure these Rights, Governments are instituted among Men, deriving
> their just Powers from the Consent of the Governed—

The reasons for seeking independence were cited in the Declaration of Independence, which specified that the King of Great Britain:

> . . . has forbidden his Governors to pass Laws of immediate and pressing
> Importance, unless suspended in their Operation till his Assent should be
> obtained; and when so suspended, he has utterly neglected to attend to them.

> He has refused to pass other Laws for the Accommodation of large Districts
> of People, unless those People would relinquish the Right of Representation
> in the Legislature, a Right inestimable to them, and formidable to Tyrants
> only.

> He has called together Legislative Bodies at Places unusual, uncomfortable,
> and distant from the depository of their public Records, for the sole Purpose
> of fatiguing them into Compliance with his Measures.

> He has dissolved Representative Houses repeatedly, for opposing with manly
> Firmness his Invasions on the Rights of the People.

> He has obstructed the Administration of Justice, by refusing his Assent to
> Laws for establishing Judiciary Powers.

> He has made Judges dependent on his Will alone, for the Tenure of their
> Offices, and the Amount and Payment of their Salaries.

> He has affected to render the Military independent of and superior to the Civil
> Power.

> For imposing Taxes on us without consent.

> For depriving us, in many Cases, of the Benefits of Trial by Jury.

Desire for liberty and democracy dominated the revolution of the colonies. The Declaration of Independence set forth the concept of liberty as the goal of the new society and the Constitution then established the means for attaining that liberty in a free society under a democratic form of government (Diamond, 1975).

Americans not only were the first people in recorded history to "bring forth" a new nation but they also were the first to found their government upon a central body of principles, clearly set forth in the preamble to their Declaration of Independence and in the preamble to their Constitution. "Those who declared independence and wrote the Constitution did not originate these principles, which were deeply rooted in classical history and philosophy, in Puritan theology, and, less formally, in the habits and practices formed by five generations of American experience. Nor did the 55 men who gathered in Philadelphia in May 1787 consult only their own convictions. They came with general instructions from both the Continental Congress and from their individual states and the people for whom these states spoke" (Commager, in Bowen, 1986, p. xv).

Those instructions were broad and simple: "to revise the Articles of Confederation to render the Federal Constitution adequate to the exigencies of government and the preservation of the Union—instructions echoed by all the states in essentially the same words" (Commager, in Bowen, 1986, p. xvi).

Commager has cited what he sees as the great inventions of the new republic in the writings of the constitution. These are:

- First, the Founding Fathers created a nation.
- Second, they created a government based on a federal system.
- Third, they wrote a Constitution for an entire nation and declared it the supreme law of the land.
- Fourth, they contrived an intricate network of checks and balances, frequent elections, division of authority among local, state and national governments and an independent judiciary.
- Fifth, they provided for the conversion of new territories into full-fledged states.
- Sixth, they established a separation of church and state.
- Seventh, they provided a subordination of the military to the civil authority.
- Eighth, they provided for democratic elections of all political offices.
- Ninth, they designated "the general welfare" as one of the primary objects of governmental responsibility.
- And tenth, they legalized revolution by authorizing the people to alter or abolish their government.

THE CONSTITUTIONAL BEDROCK

Today there are literally hundreds of power centers that function within our political system. It is clear that "national policy is likely to involve actions at a variety of levels and the participants in the process are drawn from various governmental and non-governmental institutions" (Chelf, 1981, p. 22). While the structure of our society and its political processes have been changed dramatically since the Constitution was written, there is no doubt that the structure of the governmental institutions they created has greatly influenced the ways our policies are made (Woll, 1974).

At the Constitutional Convention in 1786, Madison, Hamilton and the others made certain that the Constitution fragmented governmental power and established all manner of obstacles to prevent any one branch of government from dominating the policy process (Chelf, 1981). In order to avoid concentrating too much power in one place, power was divided among three branches of the national government (executive, legislative, and judicial), and between the nation and the states. It was the framers' firm belief that the "accumulation of all powers, legislative, executive, and judiciary, in the same hands . . . may justly be pronounced the very definition of tyranny" (Madison, Federalist No. 47).

The concepts which laid the groundwork for this new form of government were: federalism, separation of powers, checks and balances, and the multiple interests of an extended republic. The result of this constitutional framework has been a government that has often been described as being more prone to the prevention and delay of programs than to dynamic and bold initiatives designed to deal with critical issues (Chelf, 1981).

EXTENDED REPUBLIC

To fulfill their intention of setting up a *national* government that would allow for a great number of distinct parties and interests and would prevent the formation of an oppressive majority, the founders agreed to implement a "republic" (in which "the people" would elect representatives to govern on their behalf). They argued that the larger the republic, the more moderate would be the conflicts between competing factions (persons united by common passions or interest), because each representative would have to contend with many and varied factions within his own constituency and within the national government.

The framers further argued that an extended federal republic would be able to temper the influence of any one group united in a common cause since it would be superior to state governments, subsuming them all under its mantle. They contended that no one state, no matter how large, would be big enough to contain the variety of interests necessary to prevent oppressive majorities from using their legislative powers for their own benefit (Rossum and McDowell, 1981).

> Extend the sphere, and you take in a greater variety of parties and interests; you make it less probable that a majority of the whole will have a common motive to invade the rights of other citizens; or if such a common motive exists, it will be more difficult for all who feel it to discover their own strength, and to act in unison with each other (Madison, Federalist No. 10).

The founders' conception was thus to create a federal government that would be answerable to the multiplicity of interests contained in an extended republic. In such a nation-wide representative government a coalition of a majority of the whole society could seldom take place on any other principles than those of justice and the general good (Madison, Federalist No. 51).

In summary, an explanation of the extended republic concept found in Madison's manuscript notes to "Vices of the Political System in the United States" (April 1787) seems appropriate. He asks:

> Whenever . . . an apparent interest or common passion unites a majority what is to restrain them from unjust violations of the rights and interests of the minority, or of individuals? [His answer is that] . . . an enlargement of the

> sphere lessen[s] the insecurity of private rights, . . . not because the impulse of a common interest or passion is less predominant in this case with the majority; but because a common interest or passion is less apt to be felt and the requisite compositions formed by a great than by a small number. The Society becomes broken into a greater variety of interest, of pursuits of passions, which check each other, whilst those who may feel a common sentiment have less opportunity of communication and concert (Madison, in Meyers, 1973, pp. 82-92).

The issue of representation was critical in the debate that considered whether the government was to be founded on the people or on the states, on equal representation for all states or on proportionality (Keefe et al., 1986). The compromise that was reached called for the lower house to be based on population and the upper house tailored to respond to the concerns of the small states by providing for an equal number of members from each state.

SEPARATION OF POWERS

A second aspect of government that the framers considered important in order to preserve the nation's liberty was to make sure that the three departments of power (executive, legislative and judicial) were kept separate and distinct. The objective in creating separate power structures was to ensure that no one branch of government would monopolize governing power and that cooperation would be necessary for effective government (Oleszek, 1984). Such separation, however, was not intended to be absolute. Rather than creating three wholly independent centers of influence, the framers visualized a government consisting of three coordinated and essentially equal branches that would balance the others but not actually be isolated from them. "This 'balance of the parts' would consist in the independent exercise of their separate powers, and, when their powers are separately exercised, then in their mutual influence and operation on one another. Each part acts and is acted upon, supports and is supported, regulates and is regulated by the rest" (Wilson, in Rossum and McDowell, 1981, p. 69).

The reasoning behind this conception of a separation of powers came from the writings of the French philosopher Montesquieu. He insisted that:

> . . . when the legislative and executive powers are united in the same person or body . . . there can be no liberty, because apprehensions may arise lest *the same* monarch or senate should *enact* tyrannical laws to *execute* them in a tyrannical manner. . . . [And], were the power of judging joined with the legislative, the life and liberty of the subject would be exposed to arbitrary control, for *the judge* would then be *the legislator*. Were it joined to the executive power, *the judge* might behave with all the violence of *an oppressor* (Montesquieu, as quoted in Federalist No. 47).

The separation of powers was advocated by the framers not only to keep the government free of tyranny but also to make government more efficient. Separating the executive, legislative and judicial powers would make for a more productive government by allowing for different functions to be performed by agencies more specifically suited for the various tasks at hand (Rossum and McDowell, 1981). For instance, the role of an independent and powerful executive who could provide prompt execution of the laws and direct all the subordinate officers of the executive department was made possible by this separation of powers.

CHECKS AND BALANCES

Checks and balances are constitutional safeguards to prevent any of the powers in the new nation from becoming absolute since they are subject to being checked by another source of power.

As statements by James Wilson at the Constitutional Convention make clear, separating the powers of government did not mean that its institutions would be allowed to act independently of one another. Although each branch has its own constituency, providing it with a will of its own and the constitutional means to ward off any encroachments from the other branches, the Constitution also created overlapping powers among the branches of government. These overlapping powers provide the means to accomplish the checks and balances that the framers wanted to accompany the separation of powers. It was obviously felt that some safeguards would be needed to ensure that the balance of power among the three branches of government would not be upset by the exercise of power of any one (Chelf, 1981). According to Madison:

> . . . the powers of government should be so divided and balanced among several bodies of magistracy, as that no one could transcend their legal limits, without being effectually checked and restrained by the others (Federalist No. 48).

To achieve such restraint, the framers provided a coordinated system of checks and balances within the arrangement of separate government functions (Chelf, 1981). They made sure that:

> The magistrate in whom the whole executive power resides cannot of himself make a law, though he can put a negative on every law; nor administer justice in person, though he has the appointment of those who do administer it. The judges can exercise no executive prerogative, though they are shoots from the executive stock; nor any legislative function, though they may be advised by the legislative councils. The entire legislature can perform no judiciary act, though by the joint act of two of its branches the judges may be removed from their offices, and though one of its branches is possessed of the judicial power in the last resort. The entire legislature, again, can

exercise no executive prerogative, though one of its branches constitutes the supreme executive magistracy, and another, on the impeachment of a third, can try and condemn all the subordinate officers in the executive department (Madison, Federalist No. 47).

FEDERALISM

In addition to dividing power among the three branches of government, the framers adopted the concept of federalism in creating a form of government in which power is divided between the state and national levels of government. This arrangement complements the system of checks and balances in place at the national level. The state and national governments both derive their authority directly from the people, but the "supremacy" clause of the Constitution prohibits the states from passing any laws that could be deemed "unconstitutional." And, while there are certain distinct policy areas in which the federal government has sole power and responsibility (such as foreign policy or the coining of money) and others which are reserved to the states (the taxing of property or water use), there is still a considerable amount of overlap (Chelf, 1981). In general, those powers not granted to Congress remain with the states (Oleszek, 1984).

By dividing power between these two levels, the framers realized that they would be able to grant much more overall power to the federal structure than it would have been possible to entrust to either the federal or state governments alone (Rossum and McDowell, 1981).

> In a single republic, all the power surrendered by the people is submitted to the administration of a single government; and the usurpations are guarded against by a division of the government into distinct and separate departments. In the compound republic of America, the power surrendered by the people is first divided between two distinct governments, and then the portion allotted to each subdivided among distinct and separate departments. Hence a double security arises to the rights of the people. The different governments will control each other, at the same time that each will be controlled by itself (Hamilton or Madison, Federalist No. 51).

DEMOCRACY

As a final note, it is of interest to recall that the framers interpreted "democracy" quite differently from the way we envision it today. In the popular usage of the time, democracy was viewed in a very negative light, as a form of government subject to the whims of the masses. It was thought to be a volatile form of government in which the passions of the moment, fueled by local prejudices or sinister design, could incite the oppression of a minority by the majority of the people and ultimately betray the best interests of the people it was supposed to serve.

As they put together a new form of government, the framers strove to avoid any system in which the oppression of a monarch could be replaced by any other form of oppression. Believing federalism to best represent the wishes and protect the rights of all the people, they chose to establish a "republic," in which representatives of the people are elected to govern. To diminish any threat of oppression of a minority faction by a majority, they attempted to ensure that the republic encompass as many people as possible by having each representative chosen by a large number of citizens. Since each representative would be responsible to a variety of interests, it would be more likely that people of appropriate merit would be elected to office.

"Pure democracy," as practiced in ancient Greece and Rome, involved the immediate autocracy of the masses in a relatively small society. This form of government was assailed by Madison as seriously flawed:

> . . . a society consisting of a small number of citizens, who assemble and administer the government in person, can admit of no cure for the mischiefs of faction. A common passion or interest will, in almost every case, be felt by a majority of the whole . . . there is nothing to check the inducements to sacrifice the weaker party or an obnoxious individual. Hence it is that such democracies have ever been spectacles of turbulence and contention (Federalist No. 10).

The republic created by the framers was intended to be run by a small number of people elected by and responsible to the rest. Having later come to be known as "representative democracy," such a republic was designed to extend its powers over all the nation's citizens. More recently, "democracy" has been transformed through popular usage to mean "representative democracy," which is essentially the same as a "republic."

The Constitution that was ratified by nine of the 13 states in June of 1788 already had given rise to concerns that it did not adequately provide for safeguards against encroachment on civil liberties by the federal government. In December of 1791 the first ten amendments to the Constitution, or the Bill of Rights were formally adopted as part of the Constitution of the United States and have become the basis of this nation's law and policies related to human rights.

In subsequent years there have been a total of twenty-seven amendments to the Constitution, but the document remains a unique testament to the skill and dedication of the founding fathers in their creation of a form of government that for two centuries has served its people well. The 27th Amendment was formally accepted May 19, 1992 after it was ratified by 40 states, 202 years after it was proposed. The amendment limits Congress' ability to raise its own pay. Because of the importance of understanding the Constitution and its amendments in the study of policy formation for older Americans, the Bill of Rights is presented here.

THE BILL OF RIGHTS
Amendments

Article I

Congress shall make no law respecting an establishment of religion, or prohibiting the free exercise thereof; or abridging the freedom of speech, or of the press; or the right of the people peaceably to assemble, and to petition the Government for a redress of grievances.

Article II

A well regulated militia, being necessary to the security of a free State, the right of the people to keep and bear arms, shall not be infringed.

Article III

No soldier shall, in time of peace be quartered in any house, without the consent of the owner, nor in time of war, but in a manner to be prescribed by law.

Article IV

The right of the people to be secure in their persons, houses, papers, and effects, against unreasonable searches and seizures, shall not be violated, and no warrants shall issue, but upon probable cause, supported by oath or affirmation, and particularly describing the place to be searched, and the persons or things to be seized.

Article V

No person shall be held to answer for a capital, or otherwise infamous crime, unless on a presentment or indictment of a Grand Jury, except in cases arising in the land or naval force, or in the militia, when in actual service in time of war or public danger; nor shall any person be subject for the same offense to be twice put in jeopardy of life or limb; nor shall be compelled in any criminal case to be a witness against himself, nor be deprived of life, liberty, or property, without due process of law; nor shall private property be taken for public use, without just compensation.

Article VI

In all criminal prosecutions, the accused shall enjoy the right to a speedy and public trial, by an impartial jury of the State and district wherein the crime shall have been committed, which district shall have been previously ascertained by law, and to be informed of the nature and cause of the accusation; to be confronted with the witnesses against him; to have compulsory process for obtaining witnesses in his favor, and to have the assistance of counsel for his defense.

Article VII

In suits at common law, where the value in controversy shall exceed twenty dollars, the right of trial by jury shall be preserved, and no fact tried by a jury, shall be otherwise re-examined in any court of the United States, than according to the rules of the common law.

Article VIII

Excessive bail shall not be required, nor excessive fines imposed, nor cruel and unusual punishment inflicted.

Article IX

The enumeration in the Constitution, of certain rights, shall not be construed to deny or disparage others retained by the people.

Article X

The powers not delegated to the United States by the Constitution, nor prohibited by it to the States, are reserved to the States respectively, or to the people.

Making Policy in the United States

Legislation that has made its way through Congress and been enacted into law is a major source of public policy for our country, but it is not the only one. Although only members of Congress can actually introduce bills, public policy can be influenced at many other stages of the process by presidents, administrators of government agencies, and the courts.

Our institutions and levels of government are both independent and dependent. Congress cannot simply implement laws; they must be signed by the President. Bureaucrats can implement regulations, but these can be reversed by the Congress. Advocate groups cannot make policy, but they can have significant influence in the development of policy if they can generate sufficient institutional support. Additionally, as Lindblom has pointed out, the policy agenda may be influenced by a variety of sources.

> A policy is sometimes the outcome of a political compromise among policy-makers, none of whom had in mind quite the problem to which the agreed policy is the solution. Sometimes policies spring from new opportunities, not from 'problems' at all. And sometimes policies are not decided upon but nevertheless 'happen' (Lindblom, 1968, p. 4).

Furthermore, the complexity of merging interests and political resources may result in policies not intended at the initiation of the policy debate. For example, our Social Security program, especially its income replacement portion for retirees, has evolved from an effort initially intended to create jobs for younger workers during the depression. Figure 1 illustrates how the work of subgovernments is fed into the policy process of the formal institutions.

TYPES OF POLICY

Governments develop and implement different types of policies, which Denhardt (1991) has divided into four types. The first is regulatory policy

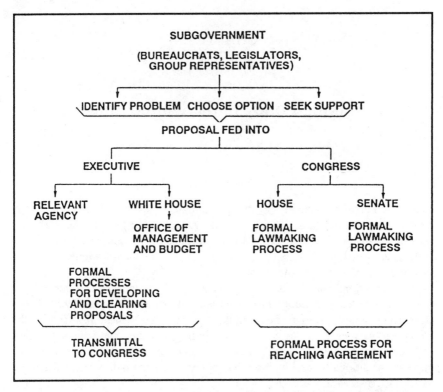

Figure 1. Feeding the Work of Subgovernments into Formal Institutions. **Source:** From *American Democracy: Institutions, Politics and Policies,* 2nd Edition by W. J. Keefe, H. J. Abraham, W. H. Flanigan, C. O. Jones, M. S. Ogul and J. W. Spanier. Copyright by The Dorsey Press, 1983 and 1986. Used with the permission of Brooks/Cole Publishing Company, Pacific Grove, CA 93950.

designed to limit the action of persons or groups so as to protect the general public. An illustration of this would be the regulation prohibiting discrimination in employment by reason of age. The next category is distributive policy, which uses general tax revenues to provide benefits to individuals or groups by funding services such as public libraries or entitlements. Redistributive policies take taxes from certain groups to pay for programs that benefit another group. The Older Americans Act and the Medicaid program represent legislation reflecting this kind of policy. Finally there are constituent policies that are intended to benefit the public generally or to serve the government. Foreign policy falls into this category but it might also include determination of where and how aging services are to be organized in the federal and state governments.

THE ACTORS IN THE POLITICAL PROCESS

In order to understand public policy, it is necessary to recognize who makes policy and how these policymakers use their power. Sometimes power is employed for the public good and at other times it is used to further some personal goal. Armand Hammer, the 20th century industrialist, had great power as a result of his wealth and need to be publicly recognized. Although he often used his resources in his self-interest, he also served his nation effectively in numerous roles that were performed behind the scenes and not publicly acknowledged. Wilbur Mills, as Congressman from Arkansas, used his power to impose a personal agenda on the Congress, which often meant that he opposed federal health insurance programs. Claude Pepper used the power developed over his long tenure as Congressman from Florida to advocate consistently for improvement of opportunities for older persons. Wilbur Cohen wielded great power because as a bureaucrat he was able to influence legislators, write proposed legislation, and detail regulations implementing Congressional actions. He had access to masses of information about programs and human needs that he was able to use effectively on behalf of older people.

Organizations may wield great power because of their wealth, numbers or societal acceptance of their mission. The American Association of Retired Persons has great power to advocate on behalf of older persons because of its large membership of older persons, its ability to communicate with them, and their elected officials. On the other hand, the Gray Panthers, although its membership is small, originally wielded a disproportionate amount of power because of the charismatic leadership of Maggie Kuhn and its espousal of the humanistic message of intergenerational understanding and support. The National Council on the Aging and the American Society on Aging have power because they represent providers of aging services who are in touch with the needs of the older persons using them.

The founders of this country organized a government designed to minimize power on the part of its components through division of power and a system of checks and balances. Theoretically, our government derives its power from the consent of the governed, but it also achieves power from alliances within the government as well from support generated by a variety of interest groups. Those who assume the mantle of advocacy often claim to abhor the concept of power as they do that of anarchy, but in order to succeed they must realize that power is an essential tool.

Power can be derived as much from the validity of an idea or the compassion aroused by a cause as from the influence of advocates, the wealth they represent or the numbers of persons who favor a proposal. In order to represent the needs of any segment of our population, supporters of any position need to know about power and advocacy. How important is it to have the support of a member of Congress? Does more power result from having support from the right member of Congress? Is it important to enlist the allegiance of one or more interest groups? Is one such group more important to a stated cause than others? To what extent does wealth represent power in a given situation, considering that access to it makes it possible to pay for media time, staff work or significant calls to policymakers?

One formal way to change national policy is to amend the Constitution. Consider the evidence of nearly 200 years. The first ten amendments, the Bill of Rights, were adopted by Congress in 1789 and ratified by the states in 1791. Since then, of nearly 6,000 amendments introduced in Congress, only twenty-three have passed both houses and been sent to the states. Seventeen have been adopted, making a total of twenty-seven amendments. (One of these, the 18th or Prohibition, has been repealed.) Two amendments have been approved since 1971, when voting for eighteen-year-olds was approved (Keefe et al., 1986, p. 24). In 1992, the amendment to limit the right of Congress to increase its salary was approved (202 years after it was proposed). Some changes take a long time. Currently, considerable attention is being given to proposed amendments guaranteeing equal rights, banning the desecration of the flag, balancing the budget, and ending busing to achieve racial equality in schools.

Obviously, changing the Constitution, which requires widespread voter support, is the most difficult way to change policy. Policy changes can more readily be achieved through the less cumbersome route of Congressional action through passage of laws that are consistent with the intent of Article 1 of the Constitution, which permits the Congress to make laws necessary for carrying out its powers. For example, Congress passed the Older Americans Act and the Medicare program in 1965 and modified it many times in order to respond to changes in our society. Policy also can be changed by issuance of regulations or rules for the operation of a specific program.

While the Constitution provides for the separation of powers between the federal government and the states, until recently there has been a distinct trend toward increasing the power of the federal government, especially since the presidency of Franklin D. Roosevelt (1933-45). Keefe et al. (1986) offers seven reasons for the growing domination of power at the federal level: the electoral success of political leaders committed to expanded federal power (in decline since the Presidency of Lyndon B. Johnson [1963-69]), widespread disillusionment with state governments, crises at the federal level as in wars and economic collapse, growth in population and social complexity, new sets of expectations of the American people, the expansion of national powers through court decisions, and the national government's superior financial resources. In contrast, the Reagan and Bush administrations recently have favored reduction in the size of the federal bureaucracy and strengthening the power of the states. Since 1996 there has been a significant devolution of power from the federal government to the states in the implementation of welfare reform. In 1996, the U.S. Congress passed the Personal Responsibility and Work Opportunity

Reconciliation Act (P.L. 104-193), designed to change open-ended entitlements to Aid to Families With Dependent Children (AFDC). A series of Block Grants will now be distributed from the federal to state governments in an effort to allow states broad freedom to design their own welfare programs. The most significant of the federal mandates to the states are that all recipients are required to work or prepare for work in exchange for benefits, that serious sanctions will apply to those who refuse to work, and that all aid will be capped at a lifetime maximum of five years. The role of the federal government continues to dominate, however, especially in such areas as health care, civil rights, income maintenance and aid to the poor. But, it was during the Clinton presidency that the responsibility for administering new welfare laws was transferred to states.

The major actors in the political process are described next. These include Congress, the bureaucracy, the courts, the presidency and the political parties.

THE CONGRESS

Despite the careful divisions of power and the checks and balances instituted to ensure against any overt abuses of authority, it is clear that the framers of the U.S. Constitution favored one branch of government—the legislative branch—over the others. Because of a general bias toward representative assemblies among the representatives at the Constitutional Convention, the Constitution makes Congress the primary policy-maker for the nation, naming it the *first* branch of government, assigning it "all legislative power" and granting to it many "explicit and implied responsibilities" (Oleszek, 1984, p. 2). In fact, Article I, which describes the functional powers of Congress, takes up almost half of the words in the document. The other two branches of government (executive and judiciary) are only briefly described in Articles II and III in terms of their framework and duties.

The protective measures of separation of powers and checks and balances were extended to the Congress through the establishment of a bicameral body, where legislative power is effectively checked through its division into a House of Representatives and a Senate. The House of Representatives consists of 435 members (the total authorized by statute) elected every two years. Representatives are elected from state districts apportioned according to population. Each state has at least one representative, and each representative has a fairly narrow constituency. The reapportionment of congressional districts occurs after each decennial census, with the redistribution of seats reflecting the changing population base of the nation, and its "changing political and economic centre of gravity" (Maidment and Tappin, 1989, p. 61).

The Senate, on the other hand, is allocated just two members per state. Senators are elected on a state-wide basis, giving them a much broader constituency than their counterparts in the House. Each senator has a six-year term of office, with one-third of all senators up for re-election every two years. Originally, the

Constitution specified that state legislatures were to elect senators, but since the 17th Amendment was adopted in 1913, they too have been selected by popular vote (Maidment and Tappin, 1989).

The dual representation provided by a divided legislature was intended to "encourage a more frequent renewal and recurrence to the government's first principles—i.e., the consent of the governed" (Rossum and McDowell, 1981, p. 71). While a consolidated legislature might at some point express an interest that might be contrary to the will of the people and distinct from it, a bicameral legislature was intended to reduce such legislative "weaknesses and mistakes" that could lead to "sudden fits of despotism, injustice, and cruelty" (Rossum and McDowell, 1981, p. 71).

Its two-house structure has not only served to fragment power in the legislature branch but has also provided many more points of access for those who wish to influence policy decisions (Chelf, 1981). Cooperation and consensus therefore are difficult to achieve. In recent times the situation has been aggravated by a lack of effective party and presidential leadership.

> Congressmen view themselves as being more closely attuned to their constituents than the president or their party leadership. Furthermore, they represent a variety of special and unique constituencies with widely differing interests. Finally, within the Congress power is widely dispersed among a number of highly individualistic committee and subcommittee chairmen (Chelf, 1981, p. 28).

While power traditionally was vested in committee chairpersons and party leadership, the recent growing influence of special interest groups and the independence of younger members have made leadership and direction in Congress nearly impossible (Chelf, 1981).

The framers had intended the Congress to be the primary agent for formulating and enacting policy in the government, and such was the case through the 19th century. In the 20th century, however, "legislatures have been challenged and eclipsed by executive and administrative branches that possess the specialization and technical expertise demanded by public service today" (Sharansky and Van Meter, 1975, p. 236). The many issues that congressional members must continuously juggle prevent them from being able to focus their skills in any one area. They must be generalists, and they often must rely on an executive agency's expertise in a given policy area. The policy-making role of the Congress is necessarily diminished by:

> . . . involvement of the federal government in an ever-growing number of problems, the increasing complexity of issues faced, the creation of more and more departments and agencies of government, and the fact that each member represents a constantly growing number of constituents (Chelf, 1981, p. 27).

Although various periods have been characterized as times of "presidential" or "congressional" governments, the dynamics of the relationship between these two branches has remained constant. "In short, the American political system is largely congressional *and* presidential government" (Oleszek, 1984, p. 5). The strategic importance of the interaction between the two branches in the policy-making arena is substantial. Despite somewhat lessened congressional power, "the strength and independence of Congress contrast sharply with the position of legislatures in other democratic countries" (Oleszek, 1984, p. 5).

For instance, in parliamentary governments, policy-making is a function of the prime minister and the cabinet, who are all elected members of the parliament and belong to the same party. Approval of policies takes place along party lines, since failure to support a party's position could lead to the resignation of the prime minister and possible replacement by the opposition party (Rushefsky, 1990).

In the United States, Congress and the President are separately elected, and each has independent policy-making authority. A stubborn Congress, even one in which both houses are of the same party as the President, may decide to go its own way on an issue and frustrate presidential prerogatives. The important position Congress holds in the policy-making process thus makes it imperative to understand how Congressional legislation becomes this country's public policy.

Congressional Committee System

In the words of Woodrow Wilson: "It is not far from the truth to say that Congress in session is Congress on public exhibition, while Congress in its committee rooms is Congress at work." Congressional committees are "the nerve ends of Congress . . . the gatherers of information, the sifters of alternatives, the refiners of legislation" (Kravitz, 1979, p. 123).

The power of the committees in Congress and weak central party leadership are characteristic of the decentralized power structure of this institution. According to Oleszek (1984), this aspect of Congress helps to define the decision-making process that affects the consideration of all legislation. Three other features of the Congressional process that also affect decision-making include: the existence of multiple decision points through which each piece of legislation must pass, the constant need for bargaining and compromise to gather a majority coalition of support to keep legislation moving past these decision points, and the two-year life cycle in which legislation must be passed once it has been introduced, since a bill automatically dies and must be re-introduced once a two-year Congressional term ends (Oleszek, 1984).

Committee Structures and Party Leadership

The committee structure of Congress is made up of three principal classes. Standing committees have permanently authorized staff and broad legislative mandates. Select or special committees are supposed to be temporarily authorized to operate for a specific period of time, or until a project for which they have been created is completed (their role is generally investigative rather than legislative). In the Senate, aging issues are the purview of the Senate Special Committee on Aging and in the House aging has been the focus of the House Select Committee on Aging. (See Appendix A for listing of committees relevant to aging policies.) Both committees are discussed in greater detail in Chapter 5. Joint committees, combining members from both chambers, usually conduct studies or are housekeeping in nature (conference committees are a special variety of joint committee, set up on an ad hoc basis to resolve differences in House and Senate versions of the same legislation). Although there are just sixteen permanent standing committees in the Senate and twenty-two in the House, the current committee system of Congress has more than 300 committees and subcommittees for both houses (Hardy and Schneider, 1985).

This extensive division of labor has resulted from the range of subject matter coming under Congressional consideration and from efforts to disperse committee leadership authority. Because of the tremendous demands on their time, members tend to specialize in particular policy areas and rely on their colleagues for information on areas outside their expertise. Although the committee system in general encourages gaining expertise through long association with a particular subject area, the level of specialization is much more pronounced in the House, where 435 Representatives cover the same range of issues handled by 100 Senators (Hardy and Schneider, 1985). Specialization in the committee system often causes broad issues to be subdivided for committee and subcommittee consideration. (The term "committee" will be used hereafter to encompass "subcommittee.")

The decentralized structure of Congress seems to invite special associations.

> . . . committees develop special relationships with pressure groups, executive agencies, and scores of other interested participants. These alliances, often called "subgovernments," "issue networks," or "sloppy large hexagons," dominate numerous policy areas. Committees, then, become advocates of policies and not simply impartial instruments of the House or Senate (Oleszek, 1984, p. 12).

The loyalty of members of Congress frequently becomes caught up in these special associations, often so greatly to the detriment of party affiliations that there may be little loyalty to party leadership. Furthermore, a number of highly individualistic committee chairpersons wield a great deal of power. Consequently, political parties have failed to play their intended role as a binding force to counter the fragmented committee system.

> Neither party . . . commands the consistent support of all its members . . . too many countervailing pressures (constituency, individual conscience, career considerations, or committee loyalty) also influence the actions of

representatives and senators . . . [Therefore] party leaders cannot count on automatic party support but must rely heavily on their skills as bargainers and negotiators to influence legislative decisions (Oleszek, 1984, p. 14).

Decision Points

A problem with the decision-making process in Congress results from the multiple decision points through which each piece of legislation must pass. The hurdles obstructing each bill's passage were well summed up by President Kennedy when he remarked: "It is very easy to defeat a bill in Congress. It is much more difficult to pass one." This process is so institutionalized that:

> Before a bill ever reaches the House or Senate floor, it is put through a series of rigorous tests, each of which may prove an insurmountable barrier . . . There are subcommittee and full committee votes. There is the matter of scheduling a bill for floor debate. And if a bill makes it that far in the process—and the majority of bills don't—there are intricate parliamentary procedures that opponents can use to prevent its consideration and passage . . . It is in short a process rife with potential pitfalls, and final approval by one House in no way assures that a bill will be enacted into law, since a similar process will have to be completed by the other body (Green, 1986, p. 37).

Many groups that have only minor influence in one chamber of Congress may have quite a bit of influence in the other, dramatically affecting eventual policy outcomes (Chelf, 1981). A bill might have to go through 100 specific steps or decision points in its progress from introduction through enactment into law, making it a wonder that *any* legislation finds its way through the congressional gauntlet (Oleszek, 1984).

Bargaining

In the process of moving legislation through Congress, majority coalitions must be formed to get past the various decision points and a considerable amount of bargaining occurs. Three techniques employed to get legislation through Congress by building majority coalitions are described by Oleszek (1984) as: logrolling, compromise, and non-legislative favors. Logrolling is basically an exchange of voting support between Congressmen, to whom not all bills under consideration are of equal importance. One member helps another by voting on a measure of great concern to the colleague but of little consequence for him/herself, and the favor is expected to be reciprocated in kind at some later date.

Compromise builds coalitions through negotiating the content of the legislation. Each side agrees to modify its program goals in order to make the legislation acceptable to the other.

Non-legislative favors for coalition building are generally used as bargaining tools by party leaders and may include such perquisites as appointments to prestigious committees, obtaining larger office space and staff, etc. In practice it is a way that party leaders can create personal obligations that can later be called due when a critical vote is needed (Oleszek, 1984).

Two-Year Congressional Term

The last factor in Oleszek's summary of the decision-making process of Congress is the two-year deadline for passage of legislation. Bills that have not found their way through the Congressional maze within that period automatically die and must be re-introduced in the next legislative session. In the last few weeks of a session many bills are passed without any debate or recorded votes in order to get them out in time.

However, it is not uncommon for some controversial bills to be introduced with no expectation of their being passed within a single congressional term. Legislation may initially be introduced simply to publicize an issue and generate interest. This action provides an important period of exposure designed to stimulate sufficient support for passage of a bill in a future session of Congress (Nickels, 1986).

How a Bill Becomes Law

We have described how the founding fathers of this government operationally defined the components of our system, how the primary policy-making body—the legislature—was structured, and how the decision-making process proceeds through the committee system of Congress. What follows is an extension of this journey into our governmental processes to explore how a bill finds its way through the congressional maze to become law.

The first step begins, naturally, with the idea for a bill. This may come from one or more of numerous sources—private citizens, interest groups, labor unions, corporations, the executive branch, Congressional committees, or individual members of Congress. Only a member of Congress can actually introduce legislation for formal consideration. Although it has been stated that as much as *half* of all legislation proposed in Washington is drafted completely or in part by interest groups (Deakin, 1966), a more recent estimate suggests the bulk of legislative proposals are generated by the President and the federal departments and agencies under him (Green, 1986). Such proposals emanate in part from the course charted by the President in his annual State of the Union Message and in part from the annual executive budget used as the basis for several appropriations bills and the annual executive economic report.

In order to be enacted, a bill must gain sufficient support from different groups at different stages, including (from the perspective of the House of Representatives): the relevant full committee and subcommittee, the party leadership, the House Rules Committee, the Committee of the Whole, the House, the Senate, the conference committee (if the same bill language is not agreed upon by both chambers), and the President. It is therefore no surprise that little legislation survives these rigors. For example, in the 98th Congress only 6.4 percent of the legislation considered was enacted into law (Nickels, 1986).

To have a bill introduced in the House, the bill is simply dropped in the hopper beside the house clerk's desk; in the Senate, members customarily present bills to the clerks at the presiding officer's desk for processing, although Senators occasionally introduce bills from the floor. The bills are then entered into each body's respective journal, the official record of its proceedings, and are assigned a legislative number. The following day the committee to which the bill has been referred will be noted in the *Congressional Record* and the bill subsequently is entered in that committee's Calendar of Business.

As noted in the previous section, it is in the committees of Congress that the work is actually done. It is here that the expertise of members comes into play, allowing them the "opportunity to advance, modify, or kill a pending piece of legislation" (Green, 1986, p. 39).

Bills are routed to those committees which have jurisdiction over the subject matter contained within the bill and from there are generally referred to the appropriate subcommittee. It is in the subcommittees that bills are closely examined to determine their merit as legislative proposals. A wide range of experts is often summoned to express opinions on the proposal under consideration. If the bill warrants a closer look, public hearings will be scheduled, after which the subcommittee will call for a "mark-up" session, where subcommittee members will decide whether a bill will be approved as worded, whether it needs to be amended or rewritten, or whether action on the bill should be postponed indefinitely (which will effectively kill it, in view of the time pressure created by two-year congressional terms).

If a bill is passed out of a subcommittee to the full committee, the full committee may decide either to hold its own hearings or to proceed directly to a mark-up session and a final vote. If the full committee decides a bill is worthy of consideration by the entire House or Senate, the bill may be reported out of committee with or without amendments.

Beyond this point, the rules for bringing a bill to the floor and the rules for debate and amending a bill differ considerably in the House and the Senate. In the House, a rule usually must be granted by the Rules Committee before a bill is sent to the floor. The Rules Committee (sometimes described as the "traffic cop" of the House) sets the time and terms of the floor debate rule, which may or may not grant permission to consider any amendments, the order in which they may be considered and the length of time they may be debated.

The Senate's process for bringing a bill onto the floor of the chamber is much more straightforward. The majority leader schedules bills for floor action and generally attempts to have a bill reach the floor by unanimous consent. Otherwise the bill must be brought to the floor through a motion for floor consideration, which usually results in debate. Extended debate may lead to a filibuster (the tactic characterized by uninterrupted speaking that can only be stopped by invoking "cloture"—a vote by 60 senators to end the debate). Understandably, a majority leader will be much more inclined to bring a bill to the floor if it can be considered without objection. An alternative is to negotiate substantive changes in a bill to meet any objections before offering it for floor consideration.

After floor consideration by the House or Senate, bills are sent on to the other chamber. The bill, which can technically be termed an "act" after passage by one house, must start its journey all over again in the other house. If amended by the second body, the bill must be returned to the originating house for concurrence in the amendments. If agreement cannot be reached, a conference committee, usually made up of the principal members from the committees of jurisdiction in each house, will be appointed to work out the differences. Once agreement is reached by the conference committee, its report is sent back to both houses for consideration. Then, after the House and Senate have accepted the agreement and the bill has been passed in identical form by both chambers, it is ready to be printed on parchment and delivered to the President.

> The President may approve the bill simply by signing it, or he may veto it. If Congress is in session and the President does not veto the measure within 10 days and return it with his objections, the Constitution provides that it become law anyway. If, however, Congress has adjourned "sine die" and the President fails to sign a bill, it is known as a "pocket veto" (Green, 1986, p. 45). (In essence, Congress has prevented the bill's return by virtue of its adjournment.)

If the bill is rejected (vetoed) by the President it requires a two-thirds vote of both houses to overturn the veto and pass the bill into law (see Figure 2).

The Line Item Veto Act of 1996 (Public Law 104-130), authorized the President to cancel discretionary budget authority, new entitlements, and limited tax benefits. When this authority became available on January 1, 1997, it changed the dynamics among all three branches of government. In response to presidential decisions to cancel certain provisions, Congress may change the way it drafts bills and committee reports. Lawsuits will bring these presidential and congressional actions before federal courts, raising a number of constitutional and statutory questions.

Similar issues have already been explored and resolved in the states that grant the governor an item veto. Legislators and legislative committees at the state level have used various tactics to counteract, blunt, and neutralize the governor's item veto power. How many of these legislative tactics can be applied by Congress to the "item veto" now available to the President? Having granted broad discretion to the President, will Congress now seek ways to circumscribe executive power? How are these tactics, often litigated in state courts, likely to be scrutinized by federal judges?

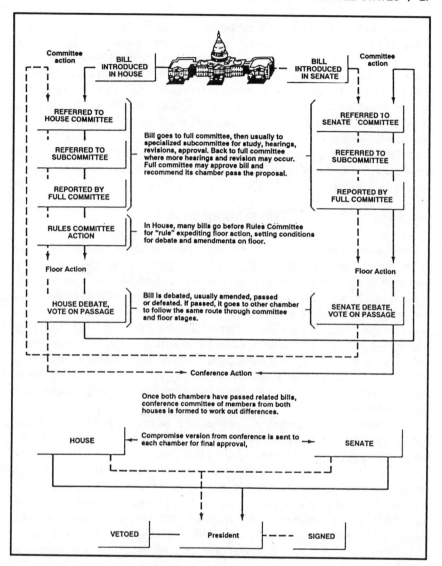

Figure 2. How a bill becomes law. This figure shows the most typical way in which proposed legislation is enacted into law. There are more complicated, as well as simpler, routes, and most bills never become law. Bills must be passed by both houses in identical form before they can be sent to the president. The path of a House bill is traced by a solid line, that of a Senate bill by a broken line. In practice most bills are introduced at roughly the same time in both chambers, though usually in somewhat different form. **Source:** Ladd, 1991, pp. 142-143. From *Congressional Quarterly Guide to Current American Government,* Washington, D.C.: Congressional Quarterly, Inc., Spring 1986, p. 145.

There are a number of basic differences between the item veto exercised in most states and the cancellation authority now available for the federal budgeting process. First, governors can delete items from a bill that is before them. Presidents, from George Washington to Bill Clinton, have had to sign the entire bill or veto the entire bill. The Line Item Veto Act does not alter that constitutional requirement. Presidents have no opportunity to strike particulars from a bill. The procedures in the Line Item Veto Act become available only *after* the President signs a bill into law.

At this time, a United States District Judge has determined that the Line Item Veto law as currently written is unconstitutional and this issue undoubtedly will require further review.

THE BUREAUCRACY

The bureau is the basic unit of the nation's administration, collectively known as the federal bureaucracy. While some governmental agencies function as bureaus they may also bear names such as office, administration or service. For example, the Social Security Administration and the Administration on Aging are two federal bureaus that are responsible for the administration of some of the major services for older persons. "The main federal bureaus, with their large ongoing program activities, have naturally become focal points for interest groups and, in turn, look to interest groups to help protect and maintain themselves" (Ladd, 1991, p. 220). Because bureaus have knowledge, access to interest groups, continuity and political savvy, they wield enormous power in policy-making and implementation.

The employees of government agencies (the bureaucracy) have substantial impacts on the policy process for two reasons: 1) Congress frequently delegates formal authority to agencies whose choices in the interpretation and implementation of legislation achieve the force of law, and 2) other actors in the political process often use government agencies as an important source of expert information. In fact, most of the legislation passed by Congress has been based upon administrative reports from government agencies that were intended as guides for Congressional decision-makers (Kelman, 1987). Recognizing these two factors, aging interest groups do not limit their advocacy efforts to contacts with legislators but also establish relationships with bureaucrats who may be able to influence the legislators or who have the authority to interpret the law through the issuance of regulations.

The support and the power of agencies in the federal bureaucracy are derived from their ability to mobilize political support and from their technical expertise. Political support may come from within the government by way of individual legislators or Congressional committees or from outside the government by way of private citizens or special interest groups. An agency's technical expertise is derived from the specialized nature of the programs it is charged with administering and from the skills of the administrators themselves (Sharansky and Van Meter, 1975).

Thus, even though the Constitution does not mention its powers, the bureaucracy has considerable authority.

> Theirs are the last hands to touch policy in the implementation stage. They have a more direct influence on the performance of government than any other group of officials . . . and have a substantial role in the formulation of policy. Executive and legislative officials often respond to administrators' program initiatives, or ask administrators to refine their own proposals for new programs (Sharansky and Van Meter, 1975, p. 289).

THE COURTS

Whenever a legislature passes a law that is signed by the chief executive it makes policy. Likewise, whenever a court rules it also makes policy, the scope of which depends upon the specificity of the law being challenged. The most important federal constitutional courts are the U.S. District Courts, the U.S. Courts of Appeals and the U.S. Supreme Court. There are ninety-four District Courts handling civil, criminal and bankruptcy cases and there are thirteen Courts of Appeal, constituting the intermediate appeals level of the federal court system. The Supreme Court stands at the apex of the judicial structure; it has nine members appointed by the President and primarily serves as the ultimate appeals court.

Today, the Supreme Court and the American court system have jurisdiction in some areas not typically found in the judiciaries of other countries: 1) interpreting the language of laws Congress has passed—laying down requirements based on the court's determination of what is demanded by a law, even if such a requirement is not explicitly stated in the statute; 2) appealing the decisions of administrative agencies—adjudicating rule-making decisions of general applicability or on an individual basis; 3) declaring laws that have been passed to be unconstitutional (Kelman, 1987).

The United States Supreme Court thus wields an enormous amount of influence on the policy process, with its greatest area of impact perhaps being its having the last word on the constitutionality of any piece of legislation.

> The Supreme Court is the final arbiter of whether an act of Congress, a presidential executive order or legislation passed by any of the fifty state governments, is constitutionally permissible (Maidment and Tappin, 1989, p. 25).

The court, however, is constrained in that it can only make decisions on policy questions that are brought to its attention through litigation. The jurisdiction of the Supreme Court is limited by the Constitution's requirement that the policy or program in question be brought to court as a "case or controversy." In recent years the formal authority of the judiciary has been greatly expanded, but the judiciary has also consciously limited its policy-making role. In particular the courts have avoided certain major "political" questions in areas such as taxation and international affairs (Sharansky and Van Meter, 1975).

THE PRESIDENCY

Finally, the impact on the policy process from the President's office is also very significant. It has been said that "in his constitutional grants of authority, the president is powerful beyond any other official in American government" (Lindblom, 1968, p. 71). The president, with his legal authority and extensive staff assistance, has the policy-making clout to equal, or even surpass that of Congress (Sharansky and Van Meter, 1975). In spite of this:

> Presidents did little to try to influence legislation . . . until Woodrow Wilson reinstituted the custom of oral delivery of the State of Union message and used the occasion to proclaim a legislative program for Congress. to consider . . . Since Wilson, Congress has come to expect the president to set its agenda with a legislative program and budget proposal to which it can then react . . comfort[ing] itself with the observation that the president only proposes, while Congress disposes (Kelman, 1987, p. 71).

Figure 3 identifies the varied duties of the President. These responsibilities are so broad and diverse that no one person could possibly accomplish them equally well.

Public support of the President tends to waver depending upon the issues. President Ronald Reagan enjoyed great popular support and was able effectively to take his message directly to the people through television addresses. However, when he campaigned to reduce Social Security benefits, strong objections from the American people quickly caused him to reverse his position. The most elusive aspect of presidential power is related to personality, to the incumbent's persuasiveness, commitment to ideals and political skill. Whereas President Reagan was very successful in making direct appeals to the people, President George Bush was considered to be more persuasive in personal conversations with legislators or heads of state. Bush was admired for his handling of international events like the Persian Gulf war but was seen as being less effective when dealing with domestic matters. Many Americans deplored his failure to address vigorously the national crisis resulting from inadequate health care coverage for the nation's citizens.

In his first term, President Bill Clinton mounted a major national initiative to overhaul the health care policy with a new national policy for all. The plan fell into disrepute when it emerged from secretive deliberations within the administration without having gained support from the Congress and the public. Perhaps the proposal was excessive in that it attempted a major reorganization of a national health program rather than incremental changes in areas that could generate national support.

Chief of State: The president is the ceremonial head of the American government.

Chief Executive: To the president falls the constitutional charge to "take care that the laws be faithfully executed."

Commander-in-Chief: He controls and directs the American armed forces.

Chief Diplomat: He has prime responsibility for the conduct of U.S. foreign policy.

Chief Legislator: The president is expected to play a large role "guiding Congress in much of its law-making activity."

Chief of Party: He has a partisan role as the leader of his political party.

Voice of the People: In the face of challenges, domestic as much as foreign, the president is expected to promote national security and tranquility.

Protector of Peace: In the face of challenges, domestic as much as foreign, the president is expected to promote national security and tranquility.

Manager of Prosperity: The president is now expected "to foster and promote free competitive enterprise, to avoid economic fluctuations . . . and to maintain employment, production, and purchasing power," in the words of the Employment Act of 1946.

World Leader: More than just chief diplomat of the U.S., he has broad responsibilities for the Western alliance and for international affairs globally.

Figure 3. Presidential responsibilities. **Source:** Ladd, 1991, p. 181. From Clinton Rossiter, *The American Presidency,* 2nd Edition, New York: New American Library, 1960, pp. 16-40.

The Clinton presidency also sought to contain the rapid growth in the Medicare and Medicaid programs and joined the national agenda of reducing taxes and bringing the national budget into balance.

POLITICAL PARTIES

The major functions of the political parties are to win elections and to organize the political structure of the Congress or local legislatures. Keefe et al. (1986) noted several additional roles of political parties, namely: to recruit and develop political talent, to develop issues and educate the public, to manage the election system, and to shape the direction of the government. However, when it comes to voting on policy, the parties and their memberships are relatively undisciplined, even though elected officials are subjected to intense pressure from party leadership to maintain party unity. While some party preferences are evident (i.e., on social welfare issues Democrats generally are liberal and Republicans conservative), "party lines collapse often enough to make party control over decision making less than reliable" (Keefe et al., 1986, p. 225). Figures 4 and 5

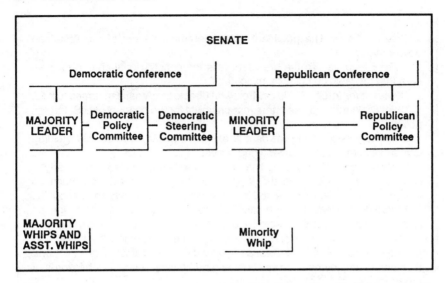

Figure 4. Party organization in the 101st Congress—Senate. **Source:** Ladd, 1991, p. 150.

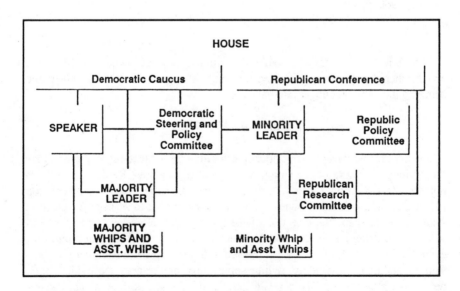

Figure 5. Party organization in the 101st Congress—House. **Source:** Ladd, 1991, p. 151.

illustrate a recent (1991) organization of the political parties within the Congress.

THE STAGES OF THE POLICY PROCESS

The many stages of creation of a policy will be described here in linear fashion to simplify and make understandable a very complex process. Description of the process is derived from *Public Policy in the United States: Toward the Twenty-First Century* by Rushefsky (1990) as adapted from Jones (1984). Figure 6 illustrates the phases of the process.

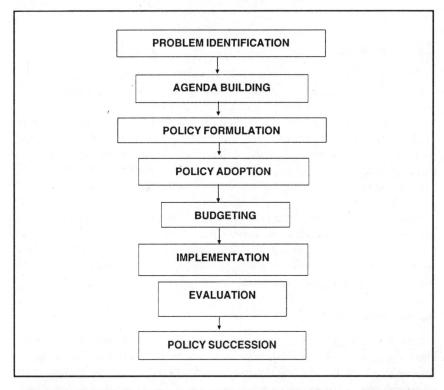

Figure 6. Steps in the policy process. **Source:** Adapted from *An Introduction to the Study of Public Policy,* 3rd Ed. by Charles O. Jones. Copyright © 1984 by Wadsworth, Inc. Adapted by permission of Brooks/Cole Publishing Company. Pacific Grove. CA 93950.

Problem Identification

The first stage is problem identification, during which an attempt is made to obtain government action on a problem or to have government recognize that an opportunity exists. A policy proposal is shaped by perception and definition of a problem or an opportunity by the various actors involved. Since each problem may be perceived and defined differently by different persons, this may lead to many diverse policy implications.

When there are many ways to explain an issue, it stands to reason that those persons who can best "define and frame the discussion of an issue will generally prevail in policy disputes" (Rushefsky, 1990, p. 4). The ways in which a problem is defined generally fall into several different categories. For instance, some problem definitions tend to rely on human interest narratives whereas others may focus on statistics to argue for public action or attempt to convey an understanding of a problem's underlying causes. Sometimes all three types of strategy may be combined in an attempt to gain the attention of policymakers (Rushefsky, 1990).

Agenda Building

Once a problem becomes a so-called "idea in good currency," the next step is getting it on the legislative agenda so that it can be seriously considered by policymakers. Rushefsky utilizes a model created by Kingdon (1984) to conceptualize the steps by which an issue gets on the agenda. In this model, a window of opportunity occurs when a problem, some potential solutions, and the political atmosphere are in accord. When all of these things coincide, an issue is easy to place on an agenda. For example, increased acts of terrorism against the United States resulted in quick passage of anti-terrorist legislation with limited display of partisan politics.

After this, the path an issue takes is determined by some peripheral factors. Resolution may be demanded by outside interest groups; political actors within government may attempt to mobilize widespread popular support through public appeals; or issues may emerge which political actors want quietly to advance without arousing potential opposition.

Policy Formulation

Once those in government have recognized an issue and have begun to consider it seriously, the next step is the formulation of a solution. This problem solving step in policy formulation includes the examination and evaluation of alternative courses of action, or policy analysis. Although the goal of this step is the "one best" solution of the problem under consideration, as Charles Lindblom noted in his 1959 article, "The Science of Muddling Through," there is a limit to our ability to evaluate all possible alternatives. Most of us do not have the time, the technical expertise, or sufficient information to tackle the potential universe of solutions. Consequently, the information used in seeking a solution to a problem is generally limited to the best possible data within certain predetermined limitations.

Policy Adoption

After formulating several policy proposals, one proposal may become the preferred one. Selecting a preferred option is a primary function of Congress, with legislation proceeding in a public and relatively open manner through subcommittees, committees, the floor of each house and then perhaps a conference committee before coming back to each house for a final vote.

However, a policy that has been "accepted by some person or group that has the power and authority to make decisions" can be adopted through bureaucratic, executive, or judicial action (Rushefsky, 1990, p. 9). In contrast to the open process of legislative policy adoption (where success requires agreement among at least two of three sets of actors: the legislative branch, the executive branch, and public opinion), policies adopted outside of the Congressional realm are subject to much less scrutiny. The President can directly adopt policies through issuing an "executive order" or making "executive agreements." An agency in the executive branch, with some limited public input and oversight of the Office of Management and Budget, is able to influence policy through the approval of regulations by the heads of agencies. In effect, an agency can change the intent of the legislation by the way it interprets the law. Finally, the judiciary can adopt policy through court orders backed by congressional action.

Budgeting

A policy cannot have much impact unless a program implementing it is funded. Budgeting directly affects program development, so it is fundamental to the policy process. The budgetary process involves many participants who attempt to influence it.

To begin with, the chief executive delineates program priorities through the executive branch budget annually presented to Congress. The President's budget, while strongly conveying the direction desired for government public program offerings, is simply a proposal. However, it often differs considerably from the goals of Congress and congressional leaders.

The congressional budgetary process that takes over after the introduction of the executive budget is quite elaborate. Budget or authorizing committees set overall targets for revenues and expenditures and establish limits on how much *can* be spent. Appropriations committees determine how much *will* be spent. In addition, many programs automatically receive funds each year without having to go through any committee review at all, making it difficult for new programs to obtain funding. For instance, a program for which budget authority for future spending has been appropriated in the past may be in conflict with an entitlement program that has set up legal obligations requiring payments to all those who meet eligibility requirements. Since entitlement programs make up approximately 46 percent of the federal budget, predetermined funding tends to tie the hands of legislators, frustrating their ability to fund other programs, no matter how worthy.

Implementation

The implementation stage of the policy process is critical. How a program is implemented by an authorized agency determines what impact it will have on the issue it was set up to address. According to Jones (1984), three activities are involved in the implementation stage: organization, interpretation and application.

To implement a program appropriately, an ongoing or newly created organization must have the resources to carry it out, personnel who are favorably disposed to the program, and a sense of how the problem is amenable to intervention (Mazmanian and Sabatier, 1983). In addition, the interpretation of the public policy embodied in the program often falls on the implementing agency or the bureaucracy, where staff members must write the rules that will ultimately define the effect of the law. Interpretation is especially important when the legislation passed is technically complex or of a controversial nature. Unfortunately, bureaucrats who are not elected officials may write rules that undermine the intent of the law or move into areas not intended by the original congressional legislation.

After the rules have been written, the final phase involved in implementing a policy is the establishment of program rules and public announcement that they are going into effect. Announcements of the impending implementation of new rules or rules changes must appear in the *Federal Register* and a period for public comment must be provided. The application of the rules that have been promulgated determines how the objectives of the program will be carried out.

Evaluation

Once a public policy has been successfully translated into an implemented program, its effectiveness can be judged in a systematic or a nonsystematic way. Systematic evaluation generally involves careful review of the program's results. Two agencies often involved at the federal level are the General Accounting Office and semi-independent Inspectors General. Nonsystematic evaluation involves more impressionistic, subjective comparisons, such as are achieved through legislative hearings and/or congressional staff investigations into how well a program is working.

Policy Succession

The final stage of the policy process, policy or program succession, determines whether a program is to be continued, modified or abandoned.

In addition, it is important to note that every policy proposal does not go through all the steps illustrated in Figure 6.

> Rather than start from the first stage and move systematically through the remaining stages, policies move in and out and back and forth between stages. Problem definition and formulation, for example, occur throughout all phases of the policy process . . . Many of the issues on the policy agenda are not new but are replays of old battles, and the replays are sometimes over different aspects of policy (Rushefsky, 1990, p. 19).

Models of the Policy Process

Several examples of the policy process have been formulated to demonstrate the operation of our governmental system. The four examples we will discuss have been selected as best capturing the complexities of the decision-making process discussed in previous sections. The conceptual differences they represent can be traced to the difficulty policy analysts have in isolating more than one aspect of the policy process at any one time (Kasschau, 1978). To one degree or another, each of them can be found in the policy process when it is viewed as a whole. The examples to be described include: rationalism—policy as the outcome of efficient planning and problem-solving, interest group activity—policy due to temporary group equilibrium, elite theory—policy as the result of elite preferences, and finally, incrementalism—policy due to minor changes to past policies and programs.

Current public administration literature (Fesler and Kettl, 1991) develops an approach comparable to the policy process illustrated above and extends it to the context of decision making, the expectation of administrators as well as elected officials. While no approach has achieved predominance, each has proved to be helpful for making decisions. Regardless of the approach used, two important characteristics must be identified and understood as having impacts on the policy process. These are the availability of information and the appreciation of the importance of political values. A policy cannot gain support unless its potential supporters have a common base of values. Both information and values constantly intermingle as policies are debated and implemented.

Rational Problem Solving

The rational model posits an ideal policy-making process in which the option chosen is the very "best one" possible. In other words, the rational actor has completed a comprehensive assessment of all relevant alternatives and found the one option that maximizes utility. This model assumes "that all relevant values of a society are known and that any sacrifice in one or more values that is required by a policy is more than compensated for by the attainment of other values" (Dye, 1978, p. 28). The policy ultimately chosen should be the one that will most "efficiently" attain the desired goal and "be relevant to expressed needs and efficient in implementation" (Kasschau, 1978, p. 13).

The bigger problem with this approach is that it seldom is adopted in government, and then is primarily used as a tool to discover the barriers to rational planning and problem solving within the existing policy process. A number of barriers to rational policy-making in our current governmental system have been suggested.

1. There are no societal values that are universally agreed upon.
2. Many conflicting values cannot be compared or weighed against one another.
3. Policymakers tend to maximize their own rewards rather than societal goals.
4. Policymakers will try to satisfy demands for progress by searching only until they find an alternative that "will work," not "the one best way."
5. Sunk costs in preexisting programs prevent consideration of alternatives.
6. The cost of information gathering, the availability of information, and the time involved in collection result in innumerable barriers to obtaining data on all of the possible policy alternatives.
7. The personal needs, ambitions, and inadequacies of policymakers prevent them from performing in a highly rational manner.
8. Uncertainty about the consequences of policy alternatives causes policymakers to stay as close as possible to previous policies (Dye, 1978, pp. 31-32).

Public welfare policies are one example of how rational policy-making is *not* utilized in our policy process. For years it has been reported that the requirements under which aid is received tend to discourage participants from seeking gainful employment or holding their family units together. Such approaches as providing training programs to teach the unemployed useful skills that could take them out of the welfare cycle have been a very long time coming. Even when a new welfare policy area seems to make perfect sense, there may be uncertainty about its consequences as well as reluctance to admit a mistake or scuttle a program that has considerable sunk costs.

Interest Group Activity

To what extent do the decision-makers rely upon the available empirical data base as opposed to obtaining information about aging problems from other "accurate" sources, such as family and friends, occasional chats with elderly constituents or clients, mass media reports, and the like (Kasschau, 1978, p. 13)?

Interest groups, known alternatively by their action-oriented moniker, "pressure groups," represent organizations that lobby policymakers on behalf of their particular concerns (Peters, 1986). This approach to policy-making is known as pluralism and recognizes both that American politics is open to competing interests and that there are many interests involved in making decisions. Influence on policy decisions flows upward from the masses (Kasschau, 1978).

The political environment, according to interest group theory, is framed by the struggle among various interest groups to influence public policy. Policy outcomes, therefore, "reflect the temporary equilibrium achieved among the competing demands of these groups. Decision makers are depicted as endlessly responding to group pressures and attempting to balance competing bids from multiple constituencies" (Kasschau, 1978, p. 14).

In a weak political party system, such as we have at present in the United States, the influence and power of these special interest groups is enhanced. A result of more citizens turning to interest groups to promote their concerns is the increasing fragmentation of our society and the increased difficulty of resolving conflicts.

Under the group theory hypothesis, where all meaningful political activity takes place in terms of group struggle, the demands upon policymakers are virtually constant. The larger the constituency of a political actor, the more diverse will be the interests represented. The more diverse the interests represented, the more latitude the politician has in choosing among those interests in forming needed majority coalitions to move legislation through Congress. "Thus, congressmen have less flexibility then senators who have larger and generally more diverse constituencies; and the president has more flexibility than congressmen and senators. Executive agencies [and political parties] are also understood in terms of their group constituencies" (Dye, 1978, p. 24).

The concept of the "potential" interest group is also important in understanding this model of the policy process. Mention often is made of the great potential force that older Americans, the great "gray lobby," can wield when legislation that negatively affects them is broached. This latent force causes many legislators to adopt a hands-off policy toward any issue that might offend their elderly constituents. It is quite possible that there are many other interests, similarly submerged just below the surface of our society, that could be activated by appropriate provocation. Even though these potential interest groups do not have direct access into the political process, "the possibility that they might organize . . . must always be taken into account by decision makers" (Woll, 1974, p. 37). This potential acts as an equalizing force, helping to maintain equilibrium among groups through the ever present threat of its latent force (Dye, 1978).

The countervailing forces of competing groups and overlapping group membership also help to maintain the equilibrium of groups in this model. Competing groups check the influence of any single group and balance each other's power. Groups are also held in check and must moderate their demands because their members may have other group affiliations. This factor will generally prevent "any one group from moving too far from prevailing values" (Dye, 1978, p. 25).

Not withstanding forces lined up to deter the domination of any one group, some very powerful pressure groups lobby the government. Indeed, "the groups that are best organized, and that have the most resources and access to government decision makers, exert the most power in the political system" (Woll, 1974, p. 42). It also has been noted that, although this model supports pluralism, interest groups often tend to be run by elites who dominate the decisions they make on behalf of their memberships (Woll, 1974).

A prominent example of the impact of interest groups on the policy process is that of the American Medical Association (AMA) on the continuing defeat of national health care legislation over the years. During the Roosevelt and Truman presidencies, the AMA gained a legend of invincibility by successfully opposing national health care proposals. Whether the defeat of these proposals was due entirely to the AMA or whether the conservative political climate and other political factors were equally responsible is open to debate. What is a certainty is that any consideration of a national health insurance package could not be proposed without taking into account the strong and vigorous opposition of the powerful AMA.

In the late 1950s and early 1960s, a change in the political environment caused by the increasing number of Americans aged fifty and older weakened the AMA's "legend of invincibility." Accompanying this increase in numbers was an increasing politicalization of the elderly (22% of the vote was cast by citizens aged 60 and over), which led to the development of self-interest and advocacy groups such as the National Council of Senior Citizens (Pearman and Starr, 1988). The effective result on the decision-makers of the emergence of these new interest groups was that sufficient pressure could finally be brought to bear to adopt limited national health insurance for the poor and the elderly—Medicaid and Medicare.

Some of the questions that could be asked of the current advocates for the elderly have been raised by Kasschau (1978): 1) Are legislators likely to be most responsive to the needs of the elderly community or should administrators in agencies actually dealing with aging programs be approached? 2) Do highly visible advocates accurately represent the needs of the elderly, or would some other group be more appropriate? 3) Is "senior power" an actual force in the political arena today or is it simply a "potential" threat in view of the large voter turnout among the over 65 age group? Groups advocating on behalf of the elderly have become more and more politically active in recent years and have strived to stimulate interest among their membership.

Elite Theory—Policy as Elite Preferences

Although this model theoretically is the opposite of the open system of "popular activism" postulated by interest group theory, Woll (1974) has commented on the infection of the interest group model by elitism. He suggests that the public masses are relatively silent, passive, and generally ill-informed and apathetic. A governing elite consisting of a chosen few individuals from the upper socio-economic strata who "know what is best for the rest" is really in charge and is assumed to be able to shape the public opinion of the masses on policy questions. Policies, furthermore, do not generally arise from the masses but rather are generated by persons in positions of authority and flow downward to the masses. In this model, public policy is thought to be a reflection of elite interests and values and not the demands of the people.

Dye notes that "public policy reflects the values of the elites, not the masses, and any changes in policy will be incremental" and "elites are not subject to much direct influence from the apathetic masses, and consequently tend to influence the masses more than the masses influence elites" (Dye, 1978, p. 26).

In the context of this model, it is crucial to the power of the elites to be able to keep certain issues off the government's agenda while placing others on it:

> The agenda does not represent the competitive struggle of relatively equal groups, as in the pluralist model, but . . . the systematic use of elite power to decide which issues the political system will or will not consider (Peters, 1986, p. 44).

For example, Wilbur Mills (D-Ark) was able to keep the implementation of a national health insurance program off the legislative agenda because he was chairperson of a powerful legislative committee. Although elites may control the political agenda, this does not necessarily mean that the policies they conceive are contrary to the "best interests" of the masses. In fact, the preferences of elites manifested in terms of enacted policies and programs may tend to show a great deal of sensitivity for the welfare of "the people" (Kasschau, 1978, p. 14).

Even if, as Woll (1974) has suggested, elitism is equated with our elected leadership, elites are ultimately responsible to the voting public. If their activities are to some extent governed by their own self-interest, the masses retain considerable power to check unreasonable policy decisions and make certain that those in power stay politically responsible.

Some of our most significant legislation has purportedly resulted from elitist action. The Social Security Act, Medicare and Medicaid, and civil rights legislation all fall under this category. All of these policies were the result of action and acquiescence on the part of the ruling and policy elites.

An example of policy elite action also is evident in the nonviolent struggle for racial equality led by Martin Luther King, Jr. The leadership of this extraordinary man culminated in the implementation of several important policies. As the result of a year-long boycott of the public buses led by King in Montgomery, Alabama in 1956 to protest racial segregation, the Supreme Court ruled that racial segregation in intrastate and interstate transportation was unlawful. After this victory, King organized the Southern Christian Leadership Conference (SCLC) which gave him a large base of operation and a national platform. King and SCLC were subsequently influential in the passage of the federal Civil Rights Act of 1964 and the Voting Rights Act of 1965 through significant campaigns such as the civil rights march on Washington in 1963 and antidiscrimination and voter registration drives in the early 1960s.

It is doubtful, however, that King and his followers could have succeeded without the acceptance and acquiescence of the established ruling liberal elites. These ruling elites wanted to ensure that those blacks who accepted the prevailing "rules of the game" and exhibited middle-class values would be able to participate in the benefits of our American system (Dye, 1978). This support in the upper echelons of our governmental system was the deciding factor that allowed King's advocacy to be translated into legislated public policy.

Incrementalism

There are times when innovative policy making is accomplished in our governmental system primarily because the conditions are right (as described in the section on the policy process under "agenda building"). Most of the time, however, policy decisions build on those that have come before, gradually effecting change over the years as the situation seems to warrant (i.e., as more becomes known about a problem, or as that problem changes). It is also often far easier to agree to modify an existing program incrementally to achieve a compromise among diverse factions than it is to attempt radically to redirect a policy or overhaul a program (Kasschau, 1978). This approach to policy making is known as "incrementalism." It is argued under this model that policymakers can never have complete information and full knowledge of the consequences of their actions and thus should not make sweeping policy changes, which could seriously upset the *status quo*.

It can further be argued that the system of American government was designed so that policy changes would, in fact, only be made on a slow and steady basis.

> One principal result of the necessity to form coalitions across a number of institutions is the tendency to produce a small, incremental change rather than a major revamping of policies. This might be described as policy-making by the lowest common denominator. The need to placate all four institutions of the federal government—as well as many smaller organizations of individuals within each—and perhaps state and local governments as well, means there can be little change from established commitments to clients and producers if the policy change is to be successful (Peters, 1986, pp. 20-21).

Causing policy making to be a tedious, deliberate task which requires quite a bit of time and effort to accomplish is one of the ways our system was designed to prevent tyranny by the majority (Rushefsky, 1990).

As we have noted, individuals "seldom look for the 'one best way,' but instead end their search when they find a way that will work" (Dye, 1978, p. 34).

> . . . in a pluralist political economy such as that of the United States, it is far easier to agree to continue the existing mesh of programs that provide something for nearly everyone than it is to engage in overall social planning (Kasschau, 1978, p. 16).

Social Security stands out as an example of incremental policy making. There have been numerous attempts over the years to create a whole new Social Security program for this country. Each time, despite powerful advocates and occasionally widespread support that often affects the tone of the debate, only technical adjustments have resulted (Achenbaum, 1986). The issue here is not that some of these ideas for radical change are not valid, but rather that no one is willing to attempt a major overhaul of what is seen as a major federal institution.

The "pattern of incremental reform has characterized Social Security policy making for fifty years" (Achenbaum, 1986, p. 6). Even the 1983 Amendments, which were fairly extensive in scope in order to buttress the system in a time of crisis and included such sweeping changes as gradually raising the age of entitlement to benefits and taxing the benefits of the wealthy, were made within the structure of the program. But while few openly oppose the fundamental structure or principles of Social Security, some of the changes that have been made in the program have been blatantly political, as when incremental increases in benefit levels appeared in Social Security checks shortly before elections from 1952 to 1974 (Achenbaum, 1986).

It may be that bolder steps will be required to solve Social Security problems. Incremental solutions, while they may be more politically palatable, may not be able to keep up with the needs of the changing times. An historical perspective must prevail for any sort of reforms to be truly successful, but the program should not, in Thomas Jefferson's terms, be treated as a "covenant, too sacred to be touched" (Achenbaum, 1986, p. 7).

Summary

It should be repeated that all of these models usually operate simultaneously in the policy making process, with one or the other assuming a dominant position from time to time. Any policy decision is likely to result from drawing upon all of the models. They have been presented separately to clarify their essential characteristics and help the reader understand the complexities of the policy process. When Social Security was created it was not a rational solution to a major problem of the Great Depression but a politically sound portion of a major package of policies promulgated by an elitist administration. Each time the Social Security law is revised it provides evidence of incrementalism or the ability to build upon what exists. Unquestionably, each revision has also displayed the influence of interest groups representing older persons, labor, the insurance industries, health care professions or myriad other groups having a special interest in public policies that relate to older persons. At the same time, policy changes have been implemented by elitists, either in the bureaucracy, the executive branch or the legislature.

When it was proposed to revise the Medicare program to provide coverage for the high cost of prolonged institutional care, home care and medications, an incremental approach was designed and named catastrophic coverage. Incremental change had been advocated by interest groups, but when elitists in the bureaucracy and legislature prepared the policy they stipulated a method of payment for the program that was a major revision of existing practices. The elitists misinterpreted the wishes and responses of the elderly, who vociferously rejected the catastrophic care policy, and the law was repealed in the subsequent session of Congress.

Public policy formation is complicated by multiplicity of participants in the process, the imposed system of checks and balances, and the complexity of political parties and interests in the Congress. In addition, constant pressure from the perceived power of the electorate at the polls or from special interest groups can be inhibiting and unpredictable. It appears that the founders attained their goal of minimizing the threat of governmental tyranny.

CHAPTER
3

Historical Background to Aging Policy

The primary public policies dealing with the elderly prior to the 20th century in the United States were far from national in scope. Although Thomas Paine first proposed national pensions in 1797 to help offset the destitution experienced by the country's indigent elderly, no national policies would actually be put into effect until the Civil War Veterans Pension Program in the latter part of the 19th century. In our country's colonial years, local relief policies took care of the poor aged and other "unfortunates." During the 17th century all of the colonies passed statutes tailored to meet specific needs and providing for the minimal relief of the destitute through a "poor rate" (tax) levied on all householders (Williamson et al., 1985). Such laws established secular and legal obligations to aid the less fortunate in addition to the recognized moral and religious obligations to give alms to the poor.

The conceptual basis for these laws had been brought to the colonies by the English settlers, who had been raised under the Elizabethan Poor Law of 1601 that recognized the responsibility of the state for the indigent members of its population. The colonists fully understood "that giving public relief to those who could not support themselves, or secure support from relatives, friends, or private philanthropy, was a proper function of local government" (Quadagno, 1984a, p. 422), but the way the elderly were treated varied with their status. Those who were wealthy and had influence were clearly venerated in their later years. Others who lacked strong ties to family, property, or occupation had to endure an old age characterized by deprivation and destitution (Haber, 1983). Lacking other means of support, "one common solution to old age dependency was to assign the person's property over to the community in exchange for care for life, usually through some boarding arrangement" (Quadagno, 1984a, p. 423). The social position of the elderly in early America, depended on their connections and not their age; those who were retired, childless, widowed, or poor more often than not found themselves segregated from society in their final years (Haber, 1983).

Informal "theories" or generalizations concerning the adequacy of social support for dependent elderly persons in the past are clearly not based on an informed understanding of the care that was provided the elderly under this country's poor laws. One such "theory" postulates a Garden-of-Eden-like existence for socially dependent elders before the onset of industrialization. But it was not the "evils" of industrialization that caused the elderly's "fall from grace." In fact, there has been no real change in our basic attitudes over time. Inconsistent treatment of the old has spanned human history from primitive society to the present day— "Old people were respected or despised, honored or put to death according to circumstance" (Minois, 1989, p. 11).

17th CENTURY

In colonial America of the 17th century, much of the population lived in small frontier communities in which isolation contributed to a feeling of solidarity among the residents. This strong sense of community encouraged acceptance of the concept of social responsibility for those in need in the community and suppressed inclinations toward individualism (Williamson et al., 1985). Fischer (1978) has noted that the elderly made up a relatively small proportion of the population (6% over age 60 and less than 2% over age 65) and the median age from 1625 to 1810 hovered around sixteen years of age. The general population was young and rural, with 90 percent living on farms, and the mean age at death in 1650 was fifty-two years for men and fifty for women.

Due to the agricultural economy of the time, many elderly had a farm to pass on to their children, property which often would be given to a son or a daughter in return for care in the parents' declining years. "The powers and privileges of old age were firmly anchored in the society. . . . In that world of high fertility and high mortality, where the population was very young and the odds against surviving to a ripe age were great, respect for age was enhanced by its comparative rarity" (Fischer, 1978, pp. 58-59).

In colonial America the elderly poor were lumped together with other categories of the impotent poor—the blind, the disabled and the mentally disabled. Institutional care of the destitute in an almshouse was not preferred (as it was in England) and was used only infrequently as a last resort. The typical form of relief was administered in a minimally intrusive way, so that: 1) an elderly widow who had her own home or had a place in the home of one of her children could receive relief in the form of a small pension; 2) those in serious economic straits could obtain a reduction or elimination of taxes; or 3) a neighbor or other member of the community could be paid to provide care in the event that an elderly resident became debilitated and had no close relatives to care for him or her (Williamson et al., 1985).

18th CENTURY

As towns began to grow in size toward the end of the 18th century, a subtle shift in attitude toward the dependent old began to take place. The elderly poor were not viewed as they had been in smaller communities, as neighbors or peers who had fallen on hard times and deserved support, but rather began to be vilified as rogues or vagabonds who were personally responsible for their economic condition (Williamson et al., 1985). While the aging patriarch might still be able to demand respect from his family and peers, power was shifting away from the old to the young men of the colonies. The agriculturally-based society had provided older persons with landholdings that gave them some vestige of power in their declining years. At the same time the "oral tradition" of education made contact with knowledgeable elderly advantageous. Without such assets, however, town-dwellers' last years could take quite another turn—into destitution and disrepute, since they were of little use to the community (Haber, 1983).

With the increase in urbanization in the latter part of the 18th century, the elderly in the cities were separated from the connections which had traditionally guaranteed their status:

> In leaving the farm, migrants also left behind the power and prestige inherent in the ownership of land and goods . . . Furthermore, in highly populated urban areas, authorities were far less able to demand a family's continued support of an aged pauper or threaten deportation to the original county of residence. The most common official response was to confine the needy elderly man or woman to an almshouse . . . [spending] their final years surrounded by the signs of their weakness and dependence (Haber, 1983, p. 27).

19th CENTURY

Early 19th century recommendations for relief marked a definite shift away from home relief to institutional relief in the almshouses and included: 1) curtailment of relief assistance to any able-bodied person between the ages of eighteen and fifty; 2) provision of assistance to the old, the blind, and other needy groups only in institutions, not in their own homes; and 3) providing that administration of relief should be dealt with at the county level, not by the town (Schneider, 1938). By the middle of the 19th century every town of any size had an almshouse, and by the end of the Civil War, a very large percentage of those receiving long-term care relief were in institutions (Rothman, 1971; Coll, 1969). One explanation of this trend toward institutionalization was the growing imperatives of a developing capitalist economy, which tried to get as much work as possible from labor for the lowest possible cost. It was believed that isolating dependents in institutions would free more people to participate fully in the work force and enable them to support their families on a lower income (Scull, 1977).

The numbers of elderly in America were increasing as well, with one-third of all native-born Americans surviving to age sixty by 1830 (Fischer, 1977). The average life expectancy at birth in 1850 was forty years, which would increase to forty-seven by the turn of the century (Soldo and Agree, 1988). Before 1810, the proportion of people over age sixty-five had remained less than 2 percent of the total population. After 1810, this proportion started to rise (to 3% in 1870 and 4% by 1900), as did the median age, which steadily advanced from age sixteen in 1810 to age nineteen by 1850 and to age twenty by 1870 (Fischer, 1977). This notable increase in the length of life and the number of older Americans in the early 19th century may perhaps be attributed to several factors, although it is not clear which had precedence: 1) improved diet and sanitation practices; 2) medical advances that included the conquest over smallpox; and 3) the change in the virulence of diseases itself (Fischer, 1977).

At the same time that the numbers of aged persons were increasing, however, their value to society seemed to be diminishing. In the context of a growing industrial society, various experts (charity workers, social theorists, doctors and businessmen) reinforced the popular conception of the uselessness of old age by focusing on elderly persons' general loss of traditional sources of prestige (parental authority, occupation and wealth). Old age began to be depicted as a constant battle against disease and dependence. These experts' advice on policy issues helped to further separate the elderly from their communities by depicting the majority of the old as having little left to contribute to the social welfare. Such shifts in attitude in the mid-19th century helped to bring about a dramatic change in the old-age relief policies of the United States, which were becoming more restrictive than ever before.

By the late 19th century even physicians despaired of being able to help the aged. The body of the elderly person was thought to be particularly susceptible to a variety of diseases which were often fatal and aging itself was identified as an incurable disease state (Haber, 1983). The best course of action for the elderly, according to these physicians, would be to simply withdraw from the work-a-day world and seek medical assistance and retirement in order to retain their precious vital energy:

> Thus, concerned doctors began to categorize the last segment of the life cycle as a period of disability and disease . . . Those who had become senile had indeed begun to suffer from a progressive and incurable illness (Haber, 1983, p. 81).

In spite of these negative views of aging, programs in the latter part of the 19th century were developed out of genuine concern to provide assistance to the frail and dependent elderly. Old age homes were put in place in order to give this population a refuge from the struggle for subsistence and provide an escape from the almshouse. Pension plans provided a means of avoiding poverty after one's working years were over. At the same time, these programs, based on age as they were, gave rise to some altogether new problems. Those who might have remained self-sufficient and employed were adversely affected by new measures which used age rather than actual condition or ability as the basis of application. The varied abilities of the elderly were not recognized by policies that separated assistance to the aging from that to the young and middle-aged. Pension plans were effectively used as a means of removing active elderly individuals from the labor market and, over time, age rather than individual needs or differences defined a person's place in society (Haber, 1983).

20th CENTURY

By the late 19th and 20th centuries, the effects of improvements in sanitation practices had dramatically accelerated the improvement in life expectancy in this country. In 1900 the average life expectancy at birth was forty-six years for males and forty-eight years for females (Soldo and Agree, 1988), approximately half of all native-born Americans were living to age sixty, and by 1920 the median age had risen to twenty-five years (Fischer, 1977). Public attitudes toward the elderly poor had become even less sympathetic and public policy less generous between the years of the Civil War and the end of the century (Achenbaum, 1978). The tenets of social Darwinism espoused by Herbert Spencer (who coined the phrase "survival of the fittest"), became very popular in the United States and may have been responsible in influencing this change in attitude (Duncan, 1908). Social Darwinism provided a "scientific" basis for many adherents of *laissez-faire* ideology, including the belief that the only remedy for poverty is self-help (Bremner, 1956). Social Darwinists eschewed any kind of relief efforts, even private charity, and believed that relief to the elderly poor would undermine incentives for the non-aged to work hard and be thrifty. The destitute elderly who decided to forgo relief and avoid the stigma of becoming public dependents were praised for their choice (Trattner, 1974).

Yet, despite such recommendations for self-sufficiency among the elderly, legislation establishing the Civil War Veterans pensions was enacted in 1861, providing a fairly successful program of support for many elderly in the post-Civil War era. This military pension plan had initially been restricted to the disabled and the diseased, but was subsequently amended over the years to provide benefits to all soldiers and their dependents who had served in the Union army (Olson, 1982). In a controversial decree in 1904, for instance, President Theodore Roosevelt helped to make the presumed incapacity associated with aging a standard part of pension law by including *every* aged veteran in the Civil War Veterans pension program. In 1907 applicants were divided into specific age categories, defining dependence according to age, such that:

> . . . the applicant, upon attaining the age of sixty-two, would be considered "disabled one-half in ability;" at sixty-five he became two-thirds incapacitated; and after seventy he reached total disability . . . Unless proven otherwise those beyond seventy would be considered overaged (Haber, 1983, p. 112).

The Civil War pension system constituted a major portion of the federal budget in the years between 1880 and World War I, and by 1900 two-thirds of the elderly were receiving these pensions (Lammers, 1983). Discussion about developing a federal pension system similar to the one introduced in Germany in 1889 took place around the close of the 19th century. It is perhaps ironic that the federal government was administering what was perhaps the largest old age pension program in the world in the form of military pensions while opposing a national social security program (Williamson et al., 1985). It may be that the Civil War pension program was so successful in covering a large number of the elderly population that it was partly responsible for the United States having a late start in introducing a federal social security system (Fischer, 1977). Other factors involved were strong traditional attitudes and a relatively lower proportion of elderly in the population (compared with other western industrialized nations).

The period from 1904-1918, which has been described as a progressive era in governmental activities, was a time when significant outpouring of social concern and interest in social reform was taking place. A few members of Congress started to call for some form of national response to the problem of old age dependency (Achenbaum, 1988). The real action during the first decades of the 20th century, though, was taking place not in Washington, but at the state and local levels. Private initiatives by individuals and their families were considered the elderly's primary line of defense against deprivation, while:

> . . . voluntary associations, religious groups, ethnic and fraternal organizations, as well as philanthropies, businesses, and unions complemented other private initiatives. States, municipalities and local communities attended to the needs of other citizens as part of their mandate to provide public health services, welfare relief, and protection for their own employees (Achenbaum, 1988, p. 27).

When the numbers of Civil War pensioners began to decline rapidly after 1910, state-level direct pension efforts became the predominant system of relief (Lammers, 1983). These state-level systems were poorly operated and were seemingly based on "the attitude that pauperism was a form of social disease and degeneracy." Towns and counties begrudged the assistance which they were obliged to give, as "the poor were [seen as] a population which floats between the almshouses, the jail, and the slums" (Stevens and Stevens, 1974, p. 5).

Prior to the 20th century, private enterprise showed little interest in providing benefits for retirees or establishing residential facilities for the aged. By 1910, only forty-nine companies had established pension plans, and only 2 percent of the elderly (65 years and older) were cared for in old age homes (Haber, 1983). There were still many elderly in the rural areas who could provide for themselves through their own labor, their own possessions, and their own families, but as more Americans began moving into and around urban areas and entering the industrial work force they found themselves subject to numerous age restrictions which had been written into employers' regulations which stated:

> ... the man or woman over sixty-five (or, at most, seventy) was beyond the age of usefulness. Regardless of actual physical state, this person had entered a stage distinctive for its weakness and dependence ... The laborer was no longer expected to continue to work until permanently disabled but merely until he attained a particular age. Mandatory retirement and the age-based pensions that justified it both reflected and furthered this transformation ... Regardless of health or abilities, all persons beyond sixty-five could be characterized as superannuated (Haber, 1983, pp. 108 and 124).

Additionally, the elderly were increasingly confronted with the problem of occupational segregation that accompanied urban and industrial growth, becoming "vastly under-represented in the fields of endeavor that would come to dominate modern America" (Haber, 1983, p. 32). Whereas two-thirds of men over age sixty-five had been in the labor force in 1890, by 1930 that proportion had declined to less than half, leaving 40 percent of the nation's elderly economically dependent (Lammers, 1983).

In a four-stage developmental model suggested by Achenbaum (1988) the historical eras of aging policy in America may be summarized sequentially as: 1) the gestational period (1797 to 1935); 2) the formative years (1935 to 1950); 3) federal expansion (1950 to 1972); and finally, 4) incrementalism and cost containment (1972 to present). The era previously described would fall into the "preliminary gestational period."

FORMATIVE YEARS (1935-50)

What Achenbaum (1988) calls the "formative years" saw the passage of the greatest single piece of legislation on behalf of the elderly population. The Social Security Act of 1935 made old age assistance and federally-based pension benefits a "right." Other federal legislation plans made during the Depression never saw the light of day due to the demands imposed by World War II. By 1940, two-thirds of all native-born Americans were surviving to age sixty (Fischer, 1977), and the problems of old age had become a legitimate item on the national agenda. Academics and scientists had finally begun organizing to study the problems of aging in order to help improve the lot of elderly Americans (Achenbaum, 1988).

Even so, old traditions always die hard, and Americans in the 1930s continued to persist in the belief that care of the indigent elderly should fall upon the individual's own family, private charity, or state and local welfare agencies (Kasschau, 1978). The prevailing social attitude in the first decades of the 20th century mirrored Madison's statement in *The Federalist (No. 41)*, in which he said that the role of the federal government in providing for the general welfare did not extend to providing for individual citizens. Similarly, President Warren G. Harding had observed that:

> Just government is merely the guarantee to the people of the right and opportunity to support themselves. The one outstanding danger of today is the tendency to turn to Washington for the things which are the tasks or the duties of the forty-eight commonwealths (Norton, 1943, p. 46).

The financial crash of 1929, however, drastically changed the prevailing attitude about federal noninvolvement in economic assistance programs. Under the burden of the "Great Depression," state and local government programs simply broke down. Like many middle class individuals, Dr. Francis Townsend, a physician from Long Beach, California, lost the financial security he had always enjoyed and became one of many people to relinquish the belief that those who sought government assistance were in some way unfit.

Dr. Townsend took advantage of this turn of events to advocate for an old age revolving pension program, calling for payments of $200 per month to persons sixty years of age or older, financed by a national tax of 2 percent levied on all commercial transactions. His plan generated a great deal of popular enthusiasm, so much that Townsend Clubs began appearing across the country, creating among the elderly an expectation of some form of federal help.

The role of the Townsend Movement in creating an atmosphere favorable for initiating a national pension plan is not entirely clear. One author suggests that the focused support of 1.5 million older persons in the 7,000 Townsend Clubs across the country helped to pressure legislators and the President to come up with a national old age security program (Holtzman, 1963). Other observers (Witte, 1962; Altmeyer, 1968; Pratt, 1976) gave the Townsend Movement much less credit for the passage of Social Security. Witte (1962) argued that the goal of the Townsend Plan was unattainable and actually made the passage of the Social Security Act more difficult.

But despite the serious misgivings of many legislators who felt that the federal government had no business meddling in what they believed to be the exclusive affairs of the states, the Social Security Act was passed in 1935, providing a landmark "national" response to the growing economic unease of the country's elderly. Its passage at this juncture in the American experience was practically mandated by: 1) the high unemployment and privations brought on by the Depression; 2) the inadequacy of private sector pension plan efforts which had been repeatedly pushed by President Herbert Hoover; 3) an increasing interest in national pension plan proposals and their political attractiveness to elected officials, thanks in part to the lobbying efforts of groups such as the Townsend Movement; and 4) the skillful maneuvering of President Franklin D. Roosevelt in steering policy choices toward a fairly conservative initial piece of legislation, which he supported in his role as an advocate for a Social Security program (Lammers, 1983).

After the establishment of this national system of old-age insurance, many Americans remained skeptical and suspicious of such federal government assistance, considering it to be a form of institutionalized welfare (Kasschau, 1978). In addition, one author (Haber, 1983) has theorized that the passage of Social Security in 1935 gave national credibility to the assumption that all old persons are overaged and outdated. The enactment of Social Security in her view was based on:

> . . . the notion that at sixty-five every worker would retire and collect a pension . . . This act served to rationalize the labor force . . . [and], in a period of massive unemployment, it removed the old from competition with the young and justified their jobless condition. Social reformers of the middle and late 19th century had stressed similar remedies for an overcrowded job market (p. 129).

FEDERAL EXPANSION PERIOD (1950-72)

During the years 1950-1972 the role of the federal government in programs for the elderly expanded considerably (Achenbaum, 1988). Congress repeatedly liberalized existing programs and made the federal government a factor in areas once considered the exclusive province of the private sector or state or local government. In the span of one momentous year, 1965, three *major* pieces of legislation were enacted: the Older Americans Act (OAA), Medicare, and Medicaid.

The Older Americans Act sought to spell out the nation's goals for its elderly and to provide and/or coordinate local assistance for needy elderly through a federally-mandated system (see Chapter 4). Medicare provided what many saw as the first step toward comprehensive national health care insurance. By targeting the elderly this national health care insurance plan would help to offset the health care costs of the segment of the population that tends to utilize the most health care services. Medicaid provided a "means tested" program of assistance to those persons who, regardless of age, were unable to pay for health care services for themselves. (See Chapter 7 for a discussion of Medicare and Medicaid.)

All of these programs have had difficulties in meeting the goals set for them: The Older Americans Act has not come close to attaining the goals it set for family and community-based elder care under its Title I; Medicare has become overburdened by inflated hospital and physician costs, due in some part to the spiraling use of ever more technologically-enhanced treatments; and Medicaid has resulted in the impoverishment of many people by making it necessary to "spend down" to become qualified for coverage under its strict eligibility rules.

With modernization and economic growth that came with industrialization, there had been a concomitant decline in birth rates that subsequently increased the proportion of the elderly in our society:

> The astonishing youthfulness of the American population [in colonial times] was caused more by high fertility than by high mortality. The families of early America produced great swarms of children; the median age was low primarily on that account . . . [Birth rates] fluctuated a little because of war and changing economic conditions, but were generally remarkable for their stability. Then, in the decade 1800-1810, fertility began to fall, and continued to do so for the next one hundred and fifty years. The trend reversed with the "baby boom" of the 1940s and 1950s, but resumed in the 1960s and 1970s. Changes in fertility and age composition have run together in American history.
>
> Fertility has changed first, with changes in age composition coming close behind, like a statistical shadow. Mortality and migration also had their effects, but not very great ones. Eighty percent of the change in age composition was caused by a falling birth rate, less than 20 percent by a fall in death rates (Fischer, 1977, pp. 27-28, 105).

By the middle of the 20th century the median age had risen to thirty years, where it remained, with some slight fluctuations through 1980. The average life expectancy at birth had increased from sixty-eight years in 1950 to approximately seventy years in 1960 and seventy-one years in 1970 (National Center for Health Statistics, 1989). According to Hudson and Strate (1985), "the effects of industrialization . . . also brought about major changes in the make-up and obligations of the family and other social groups. Most important [was] the shift in caretaking responsibility from the family to the state" (p. 569). The special status afforded the elderly in our society as citizens worthy of federal government assistance had been evident initially in the treatment that was granted to veterans in the decades following the Civil War and had now been institutionalized through the enactment of Social Security, The Older Americans Act, Medicare, and Medicaid.

INCREMENTALISM AND COST CONTAINMENT (1972-PRESENT)

The period since 1972 has been defined by Achenbaum (1988) as a time of purse-string tightening in federal government that continues today. The politics of incrementalism as well as cost containment prevail. Thus, while a diverse coalition of supporters has been cultivated and appeased through step-by-step amendments and enhancements to existing programs, stricter quality controls, revenue sharing, and regulations have become integral features of recent old age legislation. Such cost-containment proposals reflect the influence of powerful figures in the executive and congressional branches who had pledged to reduce the federal share of the burden of caring for the elderly, as well as of others who wanted at least to slow the increase in the growth of expenditures in programs for the fastest growing segment of our population.

Schwarz (1988) has contributed some additional understanding of the phenomenon of the purse-string tightening period and describes this era as a "reversal of the political ideology that had guided the nation for the prior fifty years, under both Democratic and Republican administration" (pp. 1-2). The prevailing attitude that the government could be used to further the public good was replaced with the idea that big government was the cause of all the financial difficulties of the nation and that we had to become more self-reliant rather than dependent on the government.

An image of failure had been implanted on the American mind, making it easy to transfer responsibilities away from the government. Yet during this same time period needs of Americans continued to grow along with the expectation that government could be more effective in meeting community problems than individuals. Schwarz (1988) added that there is a lesson to be learned for the twenty post-Eisenhower years, namely, that we are a caring society that should not be distracted by the rhetoric of the failure of government and should commit ourselves to having "a strongly activist government" (p. 191).

The proportion of elderly (65 years and older) in our society has steadily risen from less than 2 percent in colonial times to 12.8 percent today. In the future this proportion of elderly is expected to increase to over 20 percent of the population by 2030, when the "baby boom" generation reaches age sixty-five (AARP, 1996). Four-fifths or more of all native-born Americans are now living to age sixty, and the median age has started to rise again and is now approximately thirty-four years. The life expectancy from birth has increased from approximately forty-seven years for men and forty-nine years for women in 1900 to seventy-five years and seventy-eight years for men and women, respectively, in 1988 (National Center for Health Statistics, 1989). It is expected that this trend will continue, although at a much slower rate over the next seventy years, so that by 2060 life expectancy at birth will have reached approximately seventy-seven years for men and eighty-five years for women (Kingson et al., 1986). The graying of America is no longer in the making, it is upon us.

This gratifying extension of life may, however, be accompanied by the adverse situation of poor health and greater dependency in what has been described as "Trading Off Longer Life for Worsening Health" (Olshansky et al., 1991). With the removal of most infectious and parasitic diseases, "the mortality transition that occurred in this century redistributed the majority of all deaths to older ages" (Olshansky et al., 1991, p. 195).

Although life expectancy at birth has increased by twenty-eight years in the United States since the turn of the century, the trade-off has been substitution of the diseases of old age for the pain associated with death at early ages. These authors point out that:

> ... if all major fatal diseases are eliminated, people will still grow old and die. This occurs because major fatal diseases are symptoms of aging, not causes of aging ... that for many people who die after the age of 85, instead of dying from a specific disease, death will result from old age (p. 200).

The net effect of these changes in the population results in substantial increases in the size of the older population because the "largest gains in survival are occurring at the declining phase of the survival curve where the greatest numerical increases in the size of the older population are possible" (Olshansky et al., 1991, p. 201).

It has become a common expectation that the old will require specialized care and attention, but the problem with policies which offer such care is that much assistance simply helps to perpetuate the dependence of a large proportion of the elderly population (Haber, 1983). Furthermore, it is quite likely, in fact, that the characteristics of future cohorts of the elderly will be considerably different from their predecessors:

> For one thing, level of educational attainment will increase and substantially higher proportions will have completed at least some college. Second, it is probable that future cohorts will enjoy a greater degree of economic security ... it is also likely that future cohorts, especially the young-old, will enter old age in better health than their predecessors. Improvements and innovations in medical care and health resources, better lifetime health habits, and public health efforts targeted at disease prevention and health promotion may result in increases in "active life expectancy" and extensions of middle-aged physical and functional viability into the later years (Cutler and Hendricks, 1990, p. 177).

Yet historically the elderly have had little success in maintaining their prestige when they are retired on a pension so small that it does not provide for their needs or are put into a nursing home. Despite popular belief to the contrary, the lack of respect afforded the elderly today has not come about:

> ... simply because we live in a youth-oriented society or one that at some point came to detest the aged. Rather, over the course of a century, demographic and economic realities have combined with professional policies to enforce the powerlessness of old age. Once beyond 65, most persons are bureaucratically characterized as diseased and dependent. This age-based conception of senescence has a distinctive history. In the evolving scale and nature of society and its modes of organization lie our modern notion of what it means to be overaged (Haber, 1983, p. 129).

Binstock (1983) has stated that from the time of the Townsend Movement several stereotypes have gained wide public acceptance: 1) the aged are poor, frail, and are in need of public assistance and a more positive image; 2) the elderly are relatively important as a political force, and through advocacy they need to develop a sense of "senior power;" and 3) the disadvantages forced upon the elderly by mandatory retirement, the disabilities and frailties of old age and the prejudices of our youth-centered society have categorized the aged of our society as "deserving poor," giving them the right to all the help our wealthy American society can offer.

However, in recent years, the potential economic and social burdens that an aging population presents to industrialized nations has changed the societal perceptions of the elderly. Streib and Binstock (1990) tell us that as of the late 1970s these images have begun to be reversed, so that popular public axioms defining the image of the elderly now tend to stereotype them as prosperous, hedonistic and selfish, relatively well-off—poverty is seen as a thing of the past for this age group. Advocates for children are starting to blame the active voting power of the elderly for the sorry state of our nation's youth, i.e., the lack of adequate health care, nutrition, education and supportive family environments. Sharp reductions in programs for the elderly have been suggested as a way for our nation to regain its stature as a world-class power; and a proposal has even been made that persons in their late seventies or older should be denied life-extending care as a matter of public policy (Streib and Binstock, 1990).

Some of this change in perception has come about because of the rise in real median income experienced by the elderly in the 1980s, while income for the rest of society rose only slightly, stayed the same or fell. There also has been concern over the increasing costs and solvency of the federal Social Security system (see Chapter 6). Much has been made of the potential inability to carry on a program that depends on a pay-as-you-go system when the ratio of workers to elderly in another fifty years will be dropping to approximately two to one. We have been incredibly successful in meeting our goals for zero population growth, but we will literally be paying for this success in the future. As one article on the future of generational politics explains:

> Young workers today must pay well over 15 percent of their total salaries toward Social Security and Part A of Medicare. But 40 years from now, projections indicate that the share will be between 22 percent and 33 percent. Including the 75 percent taxpayer subsidy to fast-growing Part B of Medicare, that share will rise to 30 percent at a minimum. Under the Social Security Administration's "pessimistic" scenario, which some say is most likely, the combined costs of these programs would total 50 percent of payroll (which is another way of saying that sooner or later changes in our benefit provisions are inevitable) (Hewitt and Howe, 1988, pp. 10-11).

In the words of one recent historian, the social role of our elders and the contributions they can offer society through their experience and wisdom has been particularly contested in the historical societies of the west (Minois, 1989).

Certain parallels may be found in recent developments in African societies with strong oral traditions that have been permeated by books and writing, resulting in the diminished prestige of older persons:

> The power of the gerontocracy is henceforth demystified, and even attacked ... In the same way, the emergence of a type of democratic government and the progressive elimination of religion in politics are factors contributing to the demise of gerontocracy ... Western history from antiquity to the Renaissance is marked by fluctuations in the social and political role of the old. What we are seeing is not so much a continuous decline as a switchback evolution; the general tendency however is towards degradation (Minois, 1989, p. 7).

Our experience has also been somewhat cyclical—in America's colonial past local efforts were focused on caring for people in their homes, then efforts gradually became more and more centered on institutional forms of care, and finally we have come back around to a climate in which the home is again the caring environment of choice. A significant change from colonial times to today is that assistance efforts in the colonial era tended to be radically different from one locale to another, while today the country has nationally standardized care modalities in place. We have been the last western industrialized nation to provide such nationalized care for our elderly and disabled citizens and are still the only industrialized country without a comprehensive national health care plan. The following illustrates the major advances in aging that have occurred during the past century with a look ahead to changes anticipated by the year 2030 (adapted from The Benjamin Rose Institute, 1996).

1908: Average Life Expectancy—Forty-Seven Years

- The number of elderly in the United States was 3.1 million; the number of "oldest old" (age 85+) was 122,000.
- Government health insurance programs such as Medicare, Medicaid, and Social Security did not exist. People who outlived their financial resources were sent to poorhouses.
- Rehabilitation for common health conditions such as hip and knee problems and strokes was not conducted.

1995: Average Life Expectancy—Seventy-Five Years

- The number of elderly in the United States was 31.1 million; the number of "oldest old" (age 85+) had risen to 3 million.
- African Americans over age sixty-five numbered 2.6 million.
- Caucasian Americans over age sixty-five numbered 28.3 million.
- Hispanic Americans over age sixty-five numbered 1.1 million.
- Asian/Pacific Islander Americans over age sixty-five numbered 454,000.

- Native Americans over age sixty-five numbered 114,000.
- Half of all American seniors would have been in poverty without Social Security.
- Ways to curb public funding of Medicare, Medicaid, and Social Security began to be explored. Managed care and other approaches to health care were implemented more rapidly than the government could keep pace with.

2030: Average Life Expectancy—Seventy-Nine Years

- The number of elderly in the United States is projected to be 66 million, that of the "oldest old" (age 85+) is projected to be 8.1 million.
- African Americans over age sixty-five projected to number 7.8 million.
- Caucasian Americans over age sixty-five projected to number 56.6 million.
- Hispanic Americans over age sixty-five projected to number approximately 11 million.
- Asian/Pacific Islander Americans over age sixty-five projected to number 6 million.
- Native Americans over age sixty-five projected to number over 500,000.
- The demand for physicians' services is expected to increase by 129 percent.
- The ratio of dependent older people to caregivers will continue to rise.
- The number of Americans expected to be nursing home residents by 2000 is projected to be 2 million, and by 2030 that number is expected to double.

Estes believes that issues of individual and population dependency will be important in the twenty-first century. "As a social product, dependency is the result of a multitude of social forces, such as:

- social policies and practices that permit age discrimination and, until recently, mandatory retirement;
- lower incomes of retired persons that decline with age;
- high and growing out-of-pocket health costs that are not offset by Medicare;
- treatment of functional debility and chronic illness with acute medical care rather than rehabilitative and personal support;
- discrimination and exclusion of elders from multiple arenas of social life precipitated by loss of social contact through retirement, widowhood, and the death of friends;
- low self-esteem and lack of confidence resulting from the stigmatized status of older persons; and
- asymmetrical power relations between older persons and the professional caregivers who provide them with services.

There is also an important link between socially produced dependency and community care. The community long-term care "system" is more than a system for distributing services; it is a system of *social relationships* that reflects and bolsters the power inequities between experts and lay persons. This system of care may be deleterious, especially where the emphasis is on social management or control of older persons rather than on opportunities for participation, rehabilitation, and self-determination (1993).

Summary

Our national aging policies have thus evolved and grown to the point at which we are no longer asking whether we "should" provide care, but are rather asking "how much is enough?" Over the course of the 20th century aging policies have gradually covered more and more of the older population in more and more aspects of their lives. To conclude this section on the history of aging policy a summary covering the policy highlights of the last 100+ years in this country is presented. As can clearly be seen, the national commitment to aging policy fairly blossomed in the 1960s and 1970s. Whether the 1980s and 1990s will turn out to have been indicative of a continuing trend toward simple maintenance of aging policies that have been previously enacted, or whether innovations are germinating at this time and will bear fruit at a future date remains to be seen.

TOWARD A NATIONAL POLICY ON AGING: HISTORICAL HIGHLIGHTS

(Adapted from the National Association of State Units on Aging, July, 1985, pp. 115-116; and Achenbaum, 1988, p. 27)

1861: CIVIL WAR VETERANS PENSION legislation enacted covering disabled veterans of the war.

1907: AMENDMENTS TO THE CIVIL WAR VETERANS PENSION expanded its coverage to include all veterans and their dependents.

1917: FIRST STATE DEPARTMENT OF PUBLIC WELFARE was established in Illinois.

1920: THE CIVIL SERVICE RETIREMENT ACT was enacted to provide a retirement system for many government employees, including members of the U.S. Congress and those in the uniformed and civil services.

1935: THE SOCIAL SECURITY ACT was signed into law by President Franklin D. Roosevelt "to provide protection as a matter of right for the American worker in retirement." Major provisions of the act included "Old Age Assistance" and "Old Age Survivors Insurance."

1937: RAILROAD RETIREMENT ACT was enacted to provide annuities (pensions) for retired railroad employees and their spouses.

1940: The NATIONAL INSTITUTE OF HEALTH was created as a clearinghouse for studies on the aged and sponsor of "scientific" research on senescence.

1945: The first STATE AGENCY ON AGING, a "State Commission on the Care and Treatment of the Chronically Ill, Aged and Infirm," was established in the state of Connecticut.

1946: The HILL-BURTON PROGRAM was instituted (Public Law 79-482, Medical Facilities Survey and Construction Act) to provide funds for the planning, construction and equipping of nursing homes and hospitals.

1948: The TASK FORCE ON AGING was set up by the Federal Security Agency (predecessor of the Department of Health, Education and Welfare).

1950: The first NATIONAL CONFERENCE ON AGING was convened in Washington, D.C. under the sponsorship of the Federal Security Agency, attracting 861 delegates and becoming the prototype for the decennial White House Conference on Aging. President Harry S Truman approved a 77 percent increase in average Title II Social Security benefits.

The SOCIAL SECURITY ACT was amended to establish a program of aid to permanently and totally disabled and to broaden aid to dependent children to include a relative with whom an eligible child is living.

1953: The DEPARTMENT OF HEALTH, EDUCATION, AND WELFARE was established in April to replace the former Federal Security Agency.

1956: A SPECIAL STAFF ON AGING was assigned coordinative responsibilities for aging within the Office of the Secretary of HEW.

The HOUSING ACT of 1956 (Public Law 84-1020) was passed, including Section 404 on housing for the elderly and modifying public housing legislation to accommodate the special problems of the elderly.

1958: A bill calling for a WHITE HOUSE CONFERENCE ON AGING was introduced in Congress by Representative John E. Fogarty (D-RI).

The SMALL BUSINESS ADMINISTRATION was authorized through the Small Business Act and the Small Business Investment Act to provide loans to nursing homes.

1959: The HOUSING ACT was enacted, authorizing a direct loan program to non-profit rental projects for the elderly at low interest rates. Provisions of the act also reduced the eligible age for public low-rent housing to age 62 for women and age 50 for disabled individuals.

1960: SOCIAL SECURITY AMENDMENTS created many changes in the existing law, including: a) eliminating age 50 as a minimum to qualify for disability benefits: b) liberalizing the retirement test and the requirement for fully insured status; and c) extending public health care assistance to poor elderly through the creation of Medical Assistance for the Aged in the Kerr-Mills Bill.

1961: The first WHITE HOUSE CONFERENCE ON AGING was convened in Washington, D.C.

SOCIAL SECURITY AMENDMENTS lowered the retirement age for men from 65 to 62, increased minimum benefits, added categories of retired persons, increased benefits to older widows, and liberalized the retirement test.

1962: LEGISLATION was PROPOSED for a COMMISSION ON AGING by Senator McNamara (D-MI) and Representative Fogarty, calling for an independent three-member body to serve as the focal point within the federal government for developing national policy on aging. Only eight of more than 160 bills related to the aged and aging introduced in Congress were enacted.

1965: MEDICARE (TITLE XVIII) and MEDICAID (TITLE XIX) were signed into law as amendments to the Social Security Act by President Lyndon B. Johnson. Medicare established a health insurance program for the elderly financed through the Social Security System. Medicaid established a system of "Grants to States for Medical Assistance" for the poor of all ages, as determined by an eligibility "means test."

THE OLDER AMERICANS ACT OF 1965 was passed and signed into law as Public Law 89-73. Major provisions of the act included the establishment of an ADMINISTRATION ON AGING within the Department of HEW and grants to states for community planning, services and training, with STATE UNITS ON AGING to be established to administer the program.

The HIGHER EDUCATION ACT OF 1965 authorized "Community Service and Continuing Education Programs" to solve community problems in urban and suburban areas and expand available learning opportunities for adults.

1967: The OLDER AMERICANS ACT AMENDMENTS of 1967 (Public Law 90-42) extended its provisions for two years and directed the AoA to undertake a study of personnel needs in the aging field.

The AGE DISCRIMINATION IN EMPLOYMENT ACT (ADEA) was enacted to protect workers between the ages of 40 and 64.

THE ADMINISTRATION ON AGING was removed from the Office of the Secretary of HEW and placed in a newly created SOCIAL AND REHABILITATIVE SERVICE AGENCY (SRS) within the department.

1969: The OLDER AMERICANS ACT AMENDMENTS OF 1969 (Public Law 91-69) extended the act's provisions for three years and authorized the use of Title III funds to support AREAWIDE MODEL PROJECTS.

1971: The second WHITE HOUSE CONFERENCE ON AGING was convened in Washington, D.C.

1972: The NUTRITION PROGRAM FOR THE ELDERLY ACT (Public Law 92-258) was enacted. (It was redesignated as Title VII of the Older Americans Act, as amended in 1973).

1973: THE OLDER AMERICANS COMPREHENSIVE SERVICES AMENDMENTS of 1973 (Public Law 93-29) established AREA AGENCIES ON AGING under an expanded Title III authority, which also provided for grants for model projects, senior centers and multidisciplinary centers of gerontology. A new Title IX, "Older Americans Community Service Employment Act," was added, funding was authorized for Title VII nutrition projects, and the act's other provisions were extended for two years.

The FEDERAL COUNCIL ON THE AGING, also created under the 1973 amendments to the Older Americans Act, replaced the Advisory Committee on Older Americans in the Department of Health, Education and Welfare.

The DOMESTIC VOLUNTEER SERVICE ACT was passed and signed into law, establishing the Retired Senior Volunteer Program (RSVP) and Foster Grandparent programs to replace Title VI of the Older Americans Act, which was subsequently repealed.

THE COMPREHENSIVE EMPLOYMENT AND TRAINING ACT (CETA) was enacted "to provide job training and employment opportunities for economically disadvantaged, unemployed and underemployed persons, including those facing barriers to employment commonly experienced by older workers."

THE ADMINISTRATION ON AGING was returned to the Office of the Secretary of HEW, where it was quickly subsumed by the newly formed Office of Human Development.

Passage of the FEDERAL HEALTH MAINTENANCE ORGANIZATION ACT set the stage for a new payment mechanism for health care.

1974:   The NATIONAL INSTITUTE ON AGING was established by Congress "to conduct and support biomedical, social and behavioral research and training related to the aging process and the diseases and other special problems and needs of the aging."

The EMPLOYEE RETIREMENT SECURITY ACT (ERISA) was passed and signed into law to regulate private pensions.

AMENDMENTS TO THE OLDER AMERICANS ACT added a special TRANSPORTATION program under Title III "model projects."

The HOUSING AND COMMUNITY DEVELOPMENT ACT included provisions directing the Secretary of Housing and Urban Development to consult with the Secretary of HEW to ensure the acceptable provision of low-income housing for the elderly or handicapped, pursuant to the U.S. Housing Act of 1937.

SOCIAL SECURITY ACT AMENDMENTS authorized TITLE XX, "Grants to States for Social Services." Among the programs which could be supported under this provision were: protective services; homemaker services; adult day care services; transportation services;

training; employment opportunities; information and referral; nutrition assistance; and health support.

TITLE V OF THE NATIONAL HOUSING ACT OF 1949, the "Farm and Rural Housing" program, was expanded to include the RURAL ELDERLY as a special target group.

AMENDMENTS TO THE NUTRITION PROGRAM FOR THE ELDERLY ACT were signed into law as Public Law 93-351.

The NATIONAL HEALTH PLANNING AND RESOURCES DEVELOPMENT ACT provided for combining and redirecting the efforts of a number of federally supported state and local agencies (i.e., the Hill-Burton Program begun in 1946), the Regional Medical Program enacted in 1965, and the Comprehensive Health Planning Program of 1966. The new act established the Health Systems Agencies.

A PATIENT'S BILL OF RIGHTS was introduced to protect the rights of nursing home patients.

1975: THE OLDER AMERICANS ACT AMENDMENTS OF 1975 (Public Law 94-135) authorized the Commissioner on Aging to make grants under Title III to INDIAN TRIBAL ORGANIZATIONS. For the first time PRIORITY SERVICES (transportation, home care, legal services and home renovation/repair) were mandated. Amendments also made minor changes in Title IX, "Community Service Employment for Older Americans."

The AGE DISCRIMINATION ACT OF 1975 specifically excluded from its purview age discrimination in employment except as it related to participation in government-funded employment programs.

1977: THE OLDER AMERICANS ACT AMENDMENTS OF 1977 (Public Law 95-65) authorized changes in the Title VII nutrition program, primarily related to the availability of surplus commodities through the U.S. Department of Agriculture.

FEDERAL INSURANCE CONTRIBUTION ACT (FICA) taxes were increased by Congress to shore up Social Security financing.

1978: The COMPREHENSIVE OLDER AMERICANS ACT AMENDMENTS OF 1978 (Public Law 95-478) consolidated Titles III, V, and VII (social services, multipurpose centers and nutrition services, respectively) into one Title III. The amendments also redesignated the previous Title IX

(Community Service Employment Act) as Title V, and added a new Title VI, "Grants for Indian Tribes."

The CONGREGATE HOUSING SERVICES ACT authorized the Secretary of Housing and Urban Development to enter into contracts with local public housing agencies and with nonprofit corporations to provide congregate services programs that would promote and encourage maximum independence within a home environment for individuals capable of self-care.

THE AGE DISCRIMINATION IN EMPLOYMENT ACT AMENDMENTS OF 1978 reflected recommendations of the U.S. Civil Rights Commission, which argued that the Age Discrimination Act of 1975 had been interpreted to allow discrimination in employment, which was clearly not the intent of Congress. A provision to extend the act's coverage from age 65 to age 70 set the stage for abolishing mandatory retirement.

CHANNELING GRANTS PROGRAM were initiated to support the development of comprehensive, coordinated systems of community long-term care.

1980: Funding initiated a series of LONG TERM CARE GERONTOLOGY CENTERS based in university settings throughout the country.

The Department of Health, Education and Welfare was formally renamed the Department of Health and Human Services with the establishment of a separate Department of Education.

1981: The third WHITE HOUSE CONFERENCE ON AGING convened in Washington, D.C.

THE OLDER AMERICANS ACT AMENDMENTS OF 1981 (Public Law 97-115) extended its program for three years through September 30, 1984.

1982: The JOB TRAINING PARTNERSHIP ACT of 1982 replaced the CETA program and required each state to set aside 3 percent of its funds for employment programs for economically disadvantaged persons 55 years of age and older.

1983: DIAGNOSTIC RELATED GROUPS were established by Congress in an effort to control hospital costs under Medicare and thereby avert a funding crisis.

THE SOCIAL SECURITY AMENDMENTS OF 1983 created sweeping changes. 1) Coverage was expanded to cover all federal employees, and all current and future employees of private, non-profit, tax-exempt organizations while state and local governments were prohibited from terminating coverage. 2) Benefits were modified by shifting COLA increases to a calendar year basis and providing that if trust fund reserves fall below a certain fraction of benefit outlay (20 percent after December 1988) the COLA will be calculated on the lesser of the wage or price index increases. 3) Taxation of benefits was initiated (50 percent of benefits to be taxed for those whose income exceeds $25,000 for individuals and $30,000 for couples, with the additional tax revenue returning to the retirement trust fund). 4) Retirement age increases were instituted (65 to 67 years, gradually phased in between the years 2003 and 2027). 5) Payroll tax rate increases were accelerated (rising to 7.65 percent of earnings in 1990).

1984: THE OLDER AMERICANS ACT AMENDMENTS OF 1984 (Public Law 97-115) clarified the position of the state and area agencies on aging in coordinating community-based services and in maintaining accountability for the funding of national priority services (legal, access and in-home services), increased flexibility in administering programs by liberalizing transfer authority between Parts B and C of Title III, and reauthorized the act for three years, through September 30, 1987.

1986: AGE DISCRIMINATION IN EMPLOYMENT ACT AMENDMENTS OF 1986 eliminated mandatory retirement altogether, effective January 1987.

The TAX REFORM ACT OF 1986 established substantial disincentives to use pension or deferred compensation plan accruals for any purpose other than providing a stream of retirement income.

1987: The OLDER AMERICANS ACT AMENDMENTS OF 1987 (Public Law 100-175) significantly expanded some service components of state and area agency programs under Title III to target the special needs of certain populations. New services included in-home services for frail older individuals, long-term care ombudsman services, services to prevent abuse, neglect and exploitation of the elderly, health, education and promotion services, and outreach activities for those who may be eligible for benefits under the Supplemental Security Income, Medicaid and Food Stamp programs.

The ADMINISTRATION ON AGING was elevated from the Office of Human Development Services (OHDS) to the same level of authority as assistant secretaries and other commissioners within the Department of Health and Human Services, but was retained within its position at OHDS through 1988 while an internal study regarding AoA's status was completed.

The STEWART B. MCKINNEY HOMELESS ASSISTANCE ACT provided housing and other services for the homeless.

The OMNIBUS BUDGET RECONCILIATION ACT OF 1987 (OBRA) (PL 100-203) redefined nursing home requirements for care, staffing, training nursing aides and residents' rights.

1989: The ADMINISTRATION ON AGING was finally given equal status with the other assistant secretaries and commissioners. The Commissioner on Aging now reported directly to the Secretary of Health and Human Services, but because resources and funding for AoA remained under the control of OHDS, AoA had limited ability to utilize funds as it saw fit.

1990: The OLDER WORKERS BENEFIT PROTECTION ACT (PL 101-433) was designed to overturn the Public Employees Retirement System of Ohio versus Betts, in which the Supreme Court held that the ADEA does not protect older workers from discrimination in the area of employee benefits.

The OMNIBUS BUDGET RECONCILIATION ACT removed the Social Security Trust Funds from the Gramm-Rudman-Hollings deficit reduction calculations.

HOME HEALTH CARE AND ALZHEIMER'S DISEASE AMENDMENTS were designed to combat the major diseases and conditions that impair the independence of older Americans and their families, particularly Alzheimer's disease and related dementias.

The HOUSING ACT OF 1990 dealt with supportive services in housing for the elderly to enable elderly persons to live with dignity and independence by expanding the supply of supportive housing.

1991: The ADMINISTRATION ON AGING was reorganized as a separate operating component within the office of the secretary, reporting directly to the secretary.

The Administration on Aging introduced the ELDERCARE INITIATIVE with support for state units on aging as well as 12 National Eldercare Institutes.

1992: THE OLDER AMERICANS ACT AMENDMENTS OF 1992 (Public Law 102-375) extended the program through 1995 and introduced a new Title VII, Vulnerable Elder Rights Protection Activities.

1993: OBRA amendments affected ERISA by including specific requirements to protect dependent children.

1994: The White House Conference on Aging that was scheduled to be held by December 31, 1994 did not come about.

Specific amendments to clarify ERISA were enacted. ERISA, Section 404(c), was amended to allow an employer to shift responsibility for retirement plan investments to the participant.

1995: The Fourth White House Conference on Aging was convened in Washington, D.C. The Older Americans Act was not reauthorized but was continued as a Continuing Resolution.

1996: The Personal Responsibility and Work Opportunity Reconciliation Act (PRWORA) Public Law 104-193, changed open-ended entitlements to recipients of Aid to Families with Dependent Children (AFDC). Block grants will be available to states to design their own welfare programs. All aid will be limited to five years and recipients will be required to work or prepare for work in exchange for benefits.

The Older Americans Act remained a continuing resolution.

1997: On March 4, 1997, Senator Barbara Mikulski (D-MD) introduced S 390, the Administration's proposed bill to reauthorize the Older Americans Act.

SUMMARY OF PART ONE

Having started by describing the beginning—well, almost the beginning—of the formation of public policy in the United States, we have shown how the Constitution evolved from ideas harking back to other cultures and experiences. As such, it established the beginning of public policy in this country in the form of written codes that defined a form of government that has survived for over 200 years.

The first chapter set the stage for an understanding of the policy process, of the separation of powers among several levels of policymakers, of checks and balances to assure the best representation of the greatest numbers of the population, and of the significance of federalism and the struggle for power between the states and the federal government. Of greatest importance is the significance of the Constitution as the bedrock of the society of laws we cherish in this country.

The second chapter focused on the policy process itself and how the primary actors in the process—Congress, the President, the courts and the bureaucrats—each contribute to the multiple stages in the policy process. Making a difference in the policy is easier if the steps in the process are understood and observation of several models reveals possible options.

The third chapter provided a chronology of national policies related to the elderly, going back to the Civil War Veterans Pension program. Also considered is the changing of society's image of the elderly from the "deserving old" to "greedy geezers." Debate will continue regarding services to the elderly as entitlements or welfare for the needy and on whether policies will continue to expand to meet the increasing size and needs of the older population or remain mired in a period of minimal incrementalism and cost containment.

Thus, the first section of this volume has set the stage for an understanding of the policy process in our society as well as the background for an appreciation of the emerging policies on behalf of the elderly.

We are now at a transition point to the next section of this volume, where some of the major specific policies affecting the older population are detailed within the framework of a legislative history. Special attention will be given to the process, the models and the personalities involved. The collective contribution of the first three chapters should enable the reader to understand the history and process of the policies and the direction of their evolution. How the individual can contribute to the process and how the process of policy-making on behalf of the elderly can be taught to others will then become apparent.

PART TWO

Aging Policy Development

CHAPTER
4

The Aging Network

THE OLDER AMERICANS ACT

The Older Americans Act (OAA) has for a quarter of a century established stable federal policies for the elderly and provided an instrument for policy changes. Over the years since its inception in 1965 it has remained essentially the same, with the same format, similar titles and a similar statement of objectives. Yet because of the frequency with which it has been amended, thirteen times since 1965, the act has continued to expand its horizons and take on new responsibilities (see Appendix B).

Periodic congressional reauthorization of the act has offered opportunities to reexamine the changing demographics of the population and the varied interests of members of the Congress, advocacy groups and providers of services to the elderly. Dynamic changes have taken place over the years. Area agencies on aging were initiated, nutrition programs were developed, ombudsman and home-delivered programs were implemented, new groups were targeted for services and the positioning of the Commissioner on Aging in the administrative hierarchy has been tinkered with and sometimes changed.

Funding that has increased from an initial appropriation of $6,500,000 in 1965 to the 1998 appropriation of $1,293,168,000 (Table 1) has never been adequate to meet the expectations of the program or the varied needs of older persons in the society, however, funding has declined from a high of $1,334,762,000 in 1991.

The act has served our society primarily as an arena in which sometimes conflicting needs, especially those of the most needy, can be defined; the most pressing of those needs can be met; and an effort to balance our expectations of the provision of human services to respond to these needs with our readiness to pay for them can be attempted.

An initial expectation of the act was that its services would be an entitlement to persons who had reached a specified chronological age. The ability of an individual to pay for a wide range of services was not to be considered in the

Table 1. Older Americans Act Authorization Levels and Appropriations,
Fiscal Years 1966-1992

Fiscal Year	OAA Authorizations	OAA Appropriations
1966	$ 6,500,000	$ 6,500,000
1967	11,000,000	9,000,000
1968	16,950,000	16,930,000
1969	26,000,000	23,000,000
1970	37,000,000	18,860,000
1975	380,000,000	257,500,000
1980	1,235,000,000	908,320,000
1985	1,256,250,000	1,027,600,000
1990	1,667,889,000	1,260,344,000
1997	1,293,168,000	1,293,131,000
1998	1,405,250,000	

Source: Administration on Aging, http://www.aoa.dhhs.gov, 1998.

determination of eligibility. However, a very significant increase in numbers of the very old has created a vastly greater demand for intensive services, many of which need to be delivered at the home of the recipient rather than in senior centers or other community organizations.

At the same time, many interests are competing for federal financial support and there is a total absence of an adequately funded federal chronic care policy. In view of the very limited funding for the Older Americans Act ($1.3 billion compared with $211 billion for Medicare in 1997), a careful reassessment of the role of the act and its funding resources is essential, along with an exploration of ways to augment funding of the act with additional resources.

Periodic reauthorization and recommitment to the act have clearly demonstrated the practice of incrementalism as an instrument of policy development. In its evolution the act has received a high level of support, as evidenced by the margins of positive votes by the Congress at each reauthorization. Having been accepted as the major source of planning, funding and implementation of nutrition, social and employment services for the elderly, the act has resulted in the bureaucratic and service organizations referred to as the *aging network,* which we define as the network of federal, state and area agencies on aging along with its advisory and advocacy groups. The network has had its service mission broadened with each authorization, and there is no question that the act significantly represents major public policy related to the elderly.

Current expectations of the results of that policy can be understood best against a background of the incremental changes that have taken place over 13 authorizations and an understanding of the dynamic interrelationships among the Congress, the Administration and public and private advocacy groups.

On signing the Older Americans Act on July 14, 1965 President Lyndon B. Johnson declared:

> The Older Americans Act clearly affirms our nation's sense of well-being of all of our older citizens. But even more, the results of this act will help us to expand our opportunities for enriching the lives of all of our citizens in this country, now and in the years to come.
>
> This legislation is really the seed-corn that provides an orderly, intelligent and constructive program to help us meet the new dimensions of responsibilities which lie ahead in the remaining years of this century (Public Papers of the Presidents, 1965).

This message of expectation is complemented by the following statement of the National Association of State Units on Aging on the twentieth anniversary of the act in 1985.

> The Older Americans Act and its network of state and area agencies on aging make up one of our nation's most dynamic human service systems. That system has helped identify the complexity of the needs of older people and the multiple responsibilities involved in the delivery of a continuum of coordinated services (National Association of State Units on Aging, 1985, p. v).

An examination of some of the age-related changes from 1965 set the stage for a discussion of the Older Americans Act (Figures 7, 8, and 9).

	1995	2000	2025	2050	2075	2100
	In Millions					
65 Years and Over	34.2	35.4	60.8	74.1	83.7	89.9
75 Years and Over	15.1	16.8	25.1	39.3	45.9	50.6
85 Years and Over	3.8	4.4	6.3	14.7	16.9	20.1

Figure 7. Aged population/projected. **Source:** Social Security Administration, Office of Programs. Data from the Office of the Actuary, 1997.

In Years		
Year	Male	Female
1965	12.9	16.3
1980	14.0	18.4
1985	14.4	18.6
1990	15.0	19.0
1991	15.1	19.1
1992[1]	15.2	19.3
1993[1]	15.1	19.0
1994[1]	15.3	19.0
1995[2]	15.4	19.2
1996[2]	15.4	19.2
1997[2]	15.5	19.3
1998[2]	15.5	19.3
1999[2]	15.6	19.3

[1]Preliminary; [2]Estimated

Figure 8. Life expectancy at age 65/trends. **Source:** Social Security Administration, Office of Programs. Data from the Office of the Actuary, 1997.

Year	Persons in Millions	Percent of Total Elderly
1966	5.1	28.5
1970	4.8	24.6
1980	3.9	15.7
1985	3.5	12.6
1990	3.7	12.2
1991	3.9	12.4
1992	3.9	12.9
1993	3.8	12.2
1994	3.7	11.7

Figure 9. Elderly persons living below poverty level/trends. (Beginning in 1983, income estimates used for determining poverty level were based on improved measurement of interest income. Income estimates beginning in 1987 are based on revised methodology.) **Source:** U.S. Department of Commerce, Bureau of the Census, 1997.

Organization of the Act

A legislative history of the act illustrates clearly the uncertainties and difficulties accompanying the establishment of a major new public policy. In contrast to the reauthorizations of the act that have occurred routinely on a cycle of two, three or four years, passage of the act in 1965 represented the fulfillment of an effort initiated in 1950.

The far-reaching elements of the act set forth in its various titles, as currently amended, are summarized in Table 2. Table 3 describes the administrative units created to implement them.

The Older Americans Act (OAA)

To meet the diverse needs of the growing numbers of older persons in the United States, the Older Americans Act of 1965 (OAA), as amended, created the primary vehicle for organizing, coordinating, and providing community-based services and opportunities for older Americans and their families. All individuals sixty years of age and older are eligible for services under the OAA, although priority attention is given to those who are in greatest need. The Senior Community Service Employment Program (SCSEP), a part of the OAA currently administered by the U.S. Department of Labor, offers part- or full-time employment to low-income persons who are fifty-five years of age or older. In FY 1997, the OAA appropriation was approximately $830 million for programs administered by the Administration on Aging (AoA) (this figure does not include the SCSEP).

The Administration on Aging (AoA)

The OAA established the Administration on Aging, which is headed by an Assistant Secretary for Aging and is an agency of the U.S. Department of Health and Human Services. The AoA is the federal focal point and advocacy agency for older persons, as mandated by the OAA, and administers most OAA programs at the federal level. These programs provide assistance to older persons and their caregivers, as well as critical support services, such as nutrition and transportation, for older persons at risk of being prematurely or unnecessarily institutionalized. The AoA also administers programs that protect the rights of vulnerable and at-risk older persons and educates them and their communities about the dangers of elder abuse and consumer fraud. Other OAA programs offer older persons opportunities to enhance their health and serve their communities through employment and volunteer programs.

The National Aging Network

The AoA provides leadership, technical assistance, and support to the national aging network. Headed by a central office in Washington, D.C., AoA and its

Table 2. Titles of the Older Americans Act (FY1997)

Title I — Declaration of Objectives and Definitions
States objectives for older persons in our society and establishes a sense of mission.

Title II — Administration on Aging
Establishes the Administration on Aging and the Federal Council on the Aging, describes the role of the Commissioner on Aging, sets forth how the act is to be administered, adds a nutrition officer and studies the effectiveness of state long term care ombudsman programs.

Title III — Grants for States and Community Programs on Aging
Principal service authorization of the act.

    Part A — Organization of state and area agencies.
    Part B — Supportive services and senior centers.
    Part C — Congregate meals and home-delivered meals.
    Part D — In-home services for frail older individuals.
    Part E — Additional assistance for special needs.
    Part F — Disease prevention and health promotion.
    Part G — Supportive activities for caretakers.

Title IV — Research Training and Demonstration Projects

    Part A — Education and training.
    Part B — Research, Training and Demonstration Projects

Title V — Senior Community Service Employment
Also known as the "Older American Community Service Employment Act," Title V is administered by the Department of Labor.

Title VI — Grants to Indian Tribes
Provides Title III supportive and nutrition services to American Indians, Alaskan Natives and Native Hawaiians.

Title VII — Grants to States for Protection of Vulnerable Older Americans

    —Ombudsman services
    —Prevention of elder abuse
    —Insurance and benefit counseling.

Title VIII — Amendments to Other Laws
Calls for White House Conference on Aging

Table 3. Major Administrative Units of the Aging Network

Administration on Aging (AoA)
Administers provisions of the Older Americans Act except Title V. Advocates at the federal level on behalf of older citizens throughout the nation. Operates out of the Department of Health and Human Services (DHHS) with a central office in Washington, D.C. and ten regional offices across the nation.

State Units on Aging (SUA)
Agencies in the fifty states, the District of Columbia and the U.S. territories designated to serve as the focal point for all matters related to the needs of older persons within their respective areas. Each state unit must prepare a *state plan* that encompasses all the specific programmatic and financial commitments that it will administer, coordinate or supervise over a multi-year period.

Area Agencies on Aging (AAA)
Designated by each state unit on aging to develop and administer an *area plan* for services to the elderly in its planning and service area (PSA) in order to receive subgrants or contracts from the SUA's allotment under Title III of the Older Americans Act. The plan must contain provisions required by the act and commitments that the AAA will administer activities funded under Title III in accordance with all federal requirements.

regional offices across the country provide an aging network comprised of fifty-seven State Units on Aging (SUAs); more than 661 Area Agencies on Aging (AAAs); 222 tribal organizations representing 300 tribes; and thousands of service providers, senior centers, caregivers, and volunteers. Working in close partnership, the members of the aging network plan, coordinate and develop community-level systems of services designed to meet the needs of older persons and their caregivers.

State Units on Aging (SUA)

The AoA funds supportive home and community-based services provided by the SUAs, which are located in every state and U.S. territory. In addition to funding for critical nutrition and supportive services, SUAs receive financing for elder rights programs, including the long-term care ombudsman program, legal services, outreach, and elder abuse prevention efforts. Funding for programs is allocated to each SUA based on the number of persons over the age sixty in the state. Most States are divided into planning and service areas, so that programs can be tailored to meet the specific needs of older persons residing in those areas.

Area Agencies on Aging (AAA)

Nationally, more than 661 Area Agencies on Aging receive funds from their SUAs to plan, develop, coordinate, and arrange for services to assist the older persons who are in greatest need in each planning and service area. The AAAs also work closely with senior advisory groups made up of older members of each community. The AAAs contract with 27,000 service provider agencies and public and private groups to provide home and community-based care services, which include:

- Access Services—information and assistance; outreach; escort and transportation; and case management
- In-Home Services—home delivered meals; chores; home repair; modifications and rehabilitation; homemaker/home health aides; and personal care
- Community Services—congregate meals; senior center activities; adult day care; nursing home ombudsman services; elder abuse prevention; legal services; employment and pension counseling; health promotion; and fitness programs
- Caregiver Services—respite; adult day care; counseling and education. AoA also works to assist older persons with Alzheimer's disease and related disorders and to support caregivers by improving coordination between health care and community service systems.

Native Americans

The AoA awards funds to 222 tribal organization, representing more than 300 tribes in the United States, to assist older Native Americans, Alaskan Natives, and Native Hawaiians. Native Americans in general— and older Native Americans in particular—are among the most disadvantaged groups in the country. AoA's support provides home and community-based services in keeping with each client's cultural heritage and specific needs.

Discretionary Grants Programs

Demonstration projects test program initiatives in order to serve the elderly, especially vulnerable older persons, more effectively. Such projects lay the foundation for programs to be replicated nationally under the OAA. Some examples include home-delivered meals or congregate meals, the long-term care ombudsman program, legal services, home and community-based care, aging services infrastructure development, the home equity conversion program and elder abuse prevention.

AoA's discretionary grants have been instrumental in leveraging public, local, and private support for innovative programs that serve the elderly and disabled.

Although recent budget reductions have curtailed many discretionary programs, ongoing demonstration projects include the Eldercare Locator, a national toll-free information and assistance directory for caregivers and their families; Family Friends, a program made up of older volunteers who support chronically ill or disabled children and their families; and Senior Legal Hotline and Legal Assistance programs.

LEGISLATIVE HISTORY OF THE OLDER AMERICANS ACT

The major federal legislation on behalf of older Americans prior to 1965, the Social Security Act of 1935, helped to meet some of the needs of older Americans through its income security programs. Many serious needs had still not been addressed, however, primarily because there was no coordinated system at the federal level that could identify gaps in national programs. Two significant steps forward in dealing with the problems of the aging population were taken at the federal level in 1965, when the Older Americans Act and the Social Security Amendments establishing Medicare and Medicaid were enacted. (The Social Security Amendments are discussed in Chapter 6; Medicare and Medicaid in Chapter 7.)

The need for a centralized federal agency which could speak for the aged and focus full-time attention on the problems of aging had been considered in Congress since 1950. Between 1950 and 1960 at least fifty-three bills were introduced to either establish an agency on aging within the Department of Health, Education, and Welfare or to create a separate U.S. Commission on Aging.

The first National Conference on Aging, held in 1950 at the behest of President Harry S Truman, attracted more than 800 delegates from all over the country and directed national attention to the challenge of a rapidly growing older population (U.S. Senate, 1965). Connecticut had been the first state to set up a state unit on aging (in 1945), the Connecticut State Commission on the Care and Treatment of the Chronically Ill, Aged, and Infirm (Norman, 1982). In response to the National Conference, other states began to establish commissions or committees on the aged, and a special Committee on Aging and Geriatrics was created in the Federal Security Agency (succeeded in 1953 by the Department of Health, Education, and Welfare). The functions of this committee were to compile data from published material, to publish a national newsletter on aging (entitled "Aging"), to provide some technical assistance to states and localities, and to maintain relationships with voluntary organizations.

From 1950 to 1952 more than fifty major conferences on aging were held around the country, culminating in a general call for another national conference in 1952 (U.S. Senate, 1965). The Conference of State Commissions on Aging and Federal Agencies was subsequently held in Washington, D.C. in September 1952 under the auspices of the Committee on Aging and Geriatrics of the Federal Security Agency. Two years later expansion of activities related to aging by state governments prompted the 46th annual meeting of the Governors' Conference in July 1954 to authorize the Council of State Governments to conduct a year-long study of the problems of older citizens (U.S. Senate, 1965).

In 1955 the results of this study were published in a 176-page report entitled *The States and Their Older Citizens,* in which appeared a "Bill of Objectives for Older People" and a "Program of Action in the Field of Aging." The "Bill of Objectives" set out recommendations that in the years to come would be echoed time and again in subsequent legislation calling for a coordinating federal agency on the aged and eventually become the basis for Title I of the Older Americans Act of 1965.

In April of 1956, President Dwight D. Eisenhower appeared to respond to the study by establishing the Federal Council on Aging, a subcabinet committee comprised of representatives from all of the various departments involved with aging issues. This new council quickly called for another joint Federal-State Conference on Aging to be held in Washington, D.C. on June 5-7, 1956 (U.S. Senate, 1965).

The Committee on Aging and Geriatrics was reorganized as the Special Staff on Aging in 1956 but was not given any significant new authority or responsibility because the ineffectiveness of the group had become quite clear. It was taking no part in the formation of national policy, and its small staff increased very little over the years, despite the rapid growth of federal responsibility in problems concerning the elderly.

When Congress convened in January 1958, Congressman John E. Fogarty (D-RI) made sure that one of the first orders of business would be consideration of his bill calling for a White House Conference on Aging. The bill became law in August but, the conference was put off until 1961 to give the states time to hold preliminary state meetings that would help formulate a national agenda (NASUA, 1985). Fogarty's bill had set up plans for a national forum on aging which would bring together the most knowledgeable people in the field and create a "blueprint for action in aging." That year a subcommittee of the House Education and Labor Committee also held hearings on the need for a "Bureau of Older Persons," the creation of which a number of House members would actively promote in the years to follow.

In 1960, Congressman Thomas J. Lane (D-MA) introduced a bill establishing an Office of Aging which could serve as a clearinghouse for information, sponsor research and training programs, and provide clear leadership and direction in the coordination of federal, state, and local community action. Lane stated an incremental, improvisational approach to aging problems had resulted in duplicated and overlapping services that obscured many problem areas that had never been addressed (Congressional Record, August 24, 1960, p. 16,287).

The first White House Conference on Aging was held on January 9-12, 1961, following two years of intensive statewide meetings that were attended by more than 30,000 people. The conference yielded twenty specific recommendations for action that were the culmination of the experience of the decade of the 1950s and reiterated the need for a central federal agency that could provide information, guidance, and support to the rapidly growing number of organizations dealing with aging issues.

> In order to qualify for the grants to prepare for the Conference, many of the States [had] established units on aging. The creation of these organizations, even though some of them were only temporary, helped to build the State organizational strength. . . . By February 1960, every State had set up one or more official units to deal with the overall field of aging (Norman, 1982, p. 2).

It had become clear that states and communities wanted to carry out their roles in partnership with the federal government, but that the federal partner was not yet performing adequately (U.S. Senate, 1963). The various co-equal federal agencies responsible for aging issues were not willing to give up any of their authority to another agency.

The Federal Council on Aging, which had been elevated to the cabinet level in 1959 by presidential letter, was supposed to have coordinated the various departments through bringing together the secretaries in an ex officio committee, but this had not occurred.

> The budget of the council was small, financed by contributions from the participating departments and agencies, and the staff was made up of only two people, an executive secretary and an office secretary. The council had a history of meeting infrequently, and it never recommended a single piece of legislation. Cabinet members, involved in ever pressing matters of national and international concern regarded the council as a peripheral activity, and even a nuisance (U.S. Senate, 1961).

In its 1961 report, issued shortly after the First White House Conference on Aging, the Senate Subcommittee on Problems of the Aged and Aging recommended that Congress establish a U.S. Office of Aging within the Department of Health, Education, and Welfare, along with similar agencies at the state level. It was suggested that the following elements be included:

1. A statutory basis and more independent leadership.
2. Adequate funds for coordination and other assigned functions through a "line item" appropriation.
3. Responsibility for formulation of legislative proposals for submittal to Congress.
4. Responsibility for periodic reviews of and reports on the various programs, departments, and agencies working in behalf of older people to achieve their effective coordination and operation (Section 20, Federal Organizations and Programs, 1961 WHCOA).

The subcommittee felt that, in addition to these elements within an Office of Aging in HEW, the top-level position of an assistant secretary for aging should also be created to emphasize the importance of the work to be done in this field. The duties of the office would include: offering a clearinghouse for information related to problems of the aged and aging; assisting the secretary in all matters pertaining to aging; providing technical assistance and consultation to states and localities; preparing and publishing educational materials dealing with welfare of older persons; and gathering statistics in the field of aging.

The office would also administer grants to:

1. Provide planning assistance to each state to develop new programs, as well as improve and coordinate existing ones.
2. Initiate and operate demonstration programs to further the implementation of the "Declaration of Objective for Senior Americans" (which had been included as Title I of Senator Patrick McNamara's (D-MI) bill [SR 3807] from the 86th Congress creating Office of Aging within HEW).
3. Provide assistance to nonprofit groups to conduct training and research programs in the field of aging.

The members of the Subcommittee on Problems of the Aged and Aging maintained that:

> . . . there is presently no special agency [in the federal government] authorized by the Congress to be concerned full time with the total range of problems in this national area of public policy. The Nation's approach [to its senior citizens and to planning concerning the problems of the aged and aging] is fragmented, piecemeal, haphazard and without focus. [The voices of the elderly are muted in the many agencies of government.] The position of the programs [concerning the elderly] is relegated to a secondary role and low status.

> . . . The single most obvious fact about the problems of aging is that they concern in one way or another practically every department and agency of Government . . . the only efficient approach is an organic overall view (U.S. Senate, 1961, p. 167).

Legislation proposed in 1961 to take positive action on White House Conference recommendations included the resubmission of Senator McNamara's bill creating an Office of Aging in HEW. This proposal was dropped in the second session of the 87th Congress in favor of another bill on January 31, 1962, when Senator McNamara and Congressman Fogarty jointly presented a new proposal calling for an independent agency that would be named the U.S. Commission on Aging and would provide a bipartisan three-man commission appointed by the President and responsible to him. As a permanent, high-level commission, it would serve as the focal point within the federal government for developing national policy and for providing information, guidance, and support to public and nonprofit agencies with aging programs. It would sponsor and develop a balanced nationwide program to achieve the objectives set forth in its preamble and would be assisted by an advisory council of twenty members, including the heads of the departments concerned, three senators and three representatives, and representatives of an interdepartmental council.

The commission would also be authorized to provide planning and project grants to assist states in developing programs for the aged and would provide for federal sharing in the administrative costs of a state's planning and coordinating agency. Research, demonstration, and training grants to institutions and organizations would also be made available. This model's only major difference from Senator McNamara's previous bills for an Office on Aging was in calling for the commission to have independent status.

At hearings on HR 10014 (the Fogarty-McNamara bill) held in the General Subcommittee on Education on April 17-19, 1962, thirteen of fourteen witnesses clearly favored the commission form of organization. The major point at issue was whether a commission was needed or authority should continue to be vested in the Department of HEW and the Federal Council on Aging.

HEW strongly opposed establishing a new agency, and a compromise counterproposal was presented a month after the conclusion of the hearings. An administration bill introduced "without enthusiasm" and "by request" by Senator McNamara and Congressman Bailey (HR 11752) authorized $10 million a year for a five-year program of special project grants to be administered by the Secretary of HEW. At the same time, Assistant Secretary Wilbur Cohen of the Department of HEW announced that the Federal Council on Aging was being converted into the President's Council on Aging by executive order and would have greater stature and fiscal support. This announcement just when the House was considering action on the U.S. Commission on Aging was highly suspect.

The objective of the administration's proposal would be to support research, demonstration, and evaluation projects and to encourage and assist universities, professional schools and other appropriate institutions to step up training programs for professional and technical personnel needed to provide the broad range of services older persons require. No provision was made for federal financial support of state agencies or for an overall state plan, nor was there recognition that typical community agencies were being placed in unequal competition with universities, which were more experienced in the preparation of research proposals.

This bill gained no support and, subsequently, Congressman Barratt O'Hara (D-IL) introduced a similar one (HR 12799) that eliminated the grants to nonprofit organizations and reinstated the formula grants to the states that had been provided in the McNamara-Fogarty bill. The administration supported this as a substitute for its first bill, indicating that the Department of HEW was prepared to accept the grant provisions of the McNamara-Fogarty bill, but not the independent commission form of organization.

Despite the fanfare accompanying the announcement in May 1962 that the Federal Council on Aging was being resurrected as the President's Council on Aging, very few improvements had been made. Only one or two additional staff members were hired, and the secretaries of the various executive departments continued to give the council limited consideration or attention. It was soon acknowledged to be failing to perform the stimulating, coordinating functions that were expected of a dedicated office on aging (U.S. Senate, Report No. 8, 1963).

In December 1962 the Secretary of HEW's announcement that a Welfare Administration was being established in the department and that the Special Staff on Aging (renamed the Office on Aging) would be a part of it angered many advocates of greater attention to the needs of the aging. Nevertheless, despite repeated urging by members of Congress of both parties, the administration insisted the change be made. The special staff became responsible to the Secretary of HEW and through him to the President's Council on Aging (U.S. Senate, Report No. 124, 1965).

ANTECEDENTS OF THE OLDER AMERICANS ACT

On February 21, 1963, President Kennedy became the first president to deliver a special message to Congress concerning the elderly. His "Special Message on Aiding Our Senior Citizens" recommended the establishment of a federal agency that would provide a focus for the many and varied aging programs. In his message the President stated:

> Place and participation, health and honor, cannot, of course, be legislated. But legislation and sensible, coordinated action can enhance the opportunities for the aged. Isolation and misery can be prevented or reduced . . . Society, in short, can and must catch up with science.

> Public efforts will have to be undertaken primarily by the local communities and by the States. But because these problems are nationwide, they call for Federal action as well. I recommend legislation to establish a new five-year program of grants for experimental and demonstration projects to stimulate needed employment opportunities for our aged. The heart of our program for the elderly must be opportunity for and actual service to our older citizens in their home communities.

> The Federal Government can assume a significant leadership role in stimulating such action. To do this, I recommend a five-year program of assistance to State and local agencies and voluntary organizations for planning and developing services; for research, demonstration, and training projects leading to new or improved programs to aid other people; and for construction,

renovation and equipment of public and nonprofit multipurpose activity and recreational centers for the elderly (Public Papers of the Presidents: John F. Kennedy, 1963. GPO, 1964, pp. 188-201).

The President's request for enactment of a new Senior Citizens Act, largely based on the recommendations and findings of the 1961 White House Conference and related studies that significantly reflected the message McNamara and Fogarty had long been trying to get across, helped to provide extra ammunition and direction for their legislation.

On September 17, 1963, hearings began on the most recent version of Congressman Fogarty's bill, entitled the Older Americans Act of 1963. This bill (HR 7957) would have established an Administration of Aging in the Department of HEW and authorized federal grants to states and public or private nonprofit organizations for programs for the aging. Senator McNamara sponsored an identical bill in the Senate (S 2000) and thirteen other bills that were almost identical in nature and content were presented that year.

It would be several years, however, before such legislation would make its way into law, despite the popularity of its intentions. The House failed to act upon McNamara and Fogarty's bill in 1963 or 1964. Reintroduced once again by Fogarty on January 27, 1965, as HR 3708, it finally gained passage on the strength of the wide bipartisan support that had been gathering since the 1961 White House Conference on Aging. The problems facing the rapidly growing elderly population had at last been widely recognized as of far-reaching societal importance.

While the Older Americans Act of 1963 (HR 7957) was under consideration, the chairman of the Select Subcommittee on Education, Congressman John H. Dent (D-PA), noted that creation of an Administration of Aging within the Department of HEW continued to be a significant point of controversy. Fogarty and McNamara sought creation of this agency because they objected to the downgrading of the Special Staff on Aging from the Office of the Secretary to the Welfare Administration.

In an effort to take "aging" out of "welfare," Fogarty and McNamara proposed an Administration of Aging that would be a new unit within HEW, under the direction of a Commissioner of Aging. The commissioner would be appointed by the President, subject to confirmation by the Senate, and placed at a level equal to that of the Commissioner of Social Security and the Commissioner of Welfare. The intention was to ensure that this commissioner's power and authority would not be questioned when overlapping or interdepartmental disagreements arose. It also was proposed to establish a 16-member Advisory Committee on Older Americans, made up of members from outside of government and chaired by the commissioner.

The Administration of Aging would: 1) act as a clearinghouse of information on problems of aging and the aged; 2) advise the Secretary of HEW on matters concerning the aging; 3) administer grants under the act; 4) provide technical assistance to state and local governments; 5) develop and arrange for research and demonstration programs; 6) prepare educational materials and statistics on aging; and 7) stimulate the effective use of existing resources and services (Committee on Education and Labor, House Report No. 145, 1965).

Of the eighteen witnesses called at these hearings over September 17-19, 1963, only then Secretary of HEW Anthony Celebrezze was *not* in favor of creating a new operating agency in HEW. Celebrezze maintained that the Office on Aging coordinated all the programs in aging within the department, where more than half of all federal programs on aging were centered, worked with other federal agencies having programs in aging, and that the President's Council on Aging tied together the various programs through its interdepartmental committees. Central responsibility and organization remained in the Department of HEW under the control of the Commissioner of the Welfare Administration and the Office on Aging. It was obvious that the problem that had been plaguing a federal coordinating effort had not really been addressed.

> The measures taken with respect to coordinating, highlighting, and giving drive to a multiplicity of Federal programs in aging, have been sporadic, spasmodic, piecemeal, hesitant, and futile (U.S. Senate, 1963, p. 163).

Amendments to the Older Americans Act proposed in 1963 (and those of 1964 and 1965 that followed) responded to the problems of ineffective organization of federal programs on aging. First, establishment of an Administration of Aging provided with adequate personnel, funds, and authority necessary to devote full attention to identifying and solving aging problems was considered essential. The Administration of Aging was to be a specific high-level agency with the power and responsibility to take effective action. Second, funds authorized under the act for a five-year period were mainly to be used for grants to states for community planning, demonstration projects, training programs and related activities, with a smaller percentage to go to public or private nonprofit organizations for demonstration, research, and training projects in the field of aging.

In its final form, the Older Americans Act of 1965, HR 3708, was passed by a roll call vote in the House on March 31 with only one dissenter, Congressman Dave Martin (R-NE) who said that the bill had not been properly considered in committee and would cost the government billions of dollars. After minor amendments in committee, the Senate passed the act with a voice vote on May 27. The Senate amendments were agreed to by voice vote in the House on July 6, and the act was signed into law on July 14, 1965 as PL 89-73.

When the Administration on Aging replaced the Office of Aging in HEW, Congressman Dent remarked that it was "time to acknowledge the existence of these good citizens with an agency not associated with welfare . . . [and] with the authority and ability to speak on all matters of interest to the aged."

Upon signing the Older Americans Act into law, President Johnson, commented, "Under this program, every State and every community can now move toward a coordinated program of services and opportunities for our older citizens."

Wilbur J. Cohen, then Under Secretary of HEW, added that,

> With a strengthened unit of aging in every State, local concern for the aging can more readily be translated into action. The Act makes it clear that, in the long run, local communities must assume responsibility for providing services for their older citizens, but their efforts will be magnified by strong State units" (*Aging, No. 130,* U.S. Senate, 1965, p. 3).

IMPLEMENTATION OF THE OLDER AMERICANS ACT

The Administration on Aging (AoA) was organized into five offices: the Office of the Commissioner: the Office of State and Community Services; the Office of Program Policy and Information; the Office of Research, Demonstration, and Training; and an Office of Administration. Operations in the field were to be conducted by a regional staff in the ten regions of the department. William Bechill became the first Commissioner on Aging in November 1965.

The AoA administered three grant programs: under Title III—grant programs to aid states, communities, and nonprofit and public organizations in developing community planning, services, and training which could provide new approaches to meeting the needs of the elderly; under Title IV—grant programs for research and development that could provide new knowledge about the older population and their living conditions; and under Title V—grant programs for training personnel who can provide special services needed by the elderly.

To encourage closer coordination among federal agencies involved in aging programs, Commissioner Bechill was designated chairman of the Executive Committee of the President's Council on Aging. This interdepartmental council was supposed to keep the federal departments informed about developments in aging, to discuss proposed program operations, and to focus on areas where joint agency action was required. Additionally, a departmental committee on aging within HEW was to bring together the program planning of the different agencies, so that any gaps in service offerings to the elderly could readily be identified and action taken to fill them (U.S. Senate, 1966).

The Advisory Committee on Older Americans, created under Title VI of the Older Americans Act (OAA), provided for a committee of fifteen prominent citizens and leaders in the field of aging to advise the Secretary of HEW on his responsibilities under the act.

The Foster Grandparent Program came into being through a contract signed on June 30, 1965, between the Office on Aging and the Office of Economic Opportunity (OEO), and was put under the administration of the AoA. This program was designed to employ men and women over the age of sixty and having incomes below the poverty index to provide general care and attention to children who lacked the affection and companionship of a concerned adult. The OEO also initiated other programs for the elderly at the local level which were later incorporated into AoA-funded programs.

The Older Americans Act followed the lead of the Economic Opportunity Act of 1964 in its grouping of social service programs within a decentralized structure. As originally conceived, the OAA was to establish a coordinated and comprehensive system of services at the community level in order to create a more responsive service system. The original act established the Administration on Aging as the federal-level agency responsible for the administration of programs under the act and authorized state and community social services programs and research, demonstration, and training programs. The original legislation did not provide sufficient funds to carry out the broad policy objectives of the act, but it did provide a structure through which Congress could, and eventually did, expand aging services.

For readers who are interested in following the details of a classic example of policy developed through incremental change, a year-by-year account of various amendments to the Older Americans Act and internal organizational changes are included at the end of this chapter as a legislative history.

THE OLDER AMERICANS ACT: IS IT U.S. POLICY ON AGING?

The promise of an agency that would coordinate aging programs and policies at the federal level has never been realized. A struggle to create something even remotely resembling an independent authority that could act in that capacity has been continuous. Although the Administration on Aging was supposed to be a step in that direction, its placement within the Department of HEW deprived it of independent status. Its mandate to coordinate federal programs, advocate for the elderly, and influence the broad range of federal programs and policies has remained in force, although seriously compromised by location of the Administration on Aging within a federal department where reorganization appeared to take place whenever an opportunity arose for the AoA to gain some potential status and clout.

By 1967, the Department of HEW had placed the AoA under a subordinate administration, the Social and Rehabilitation Service (SRS), that included several welfare programs. This move displeased aging advocates, since one of the factors that motivated the call for a new Office of Aging in 1965 had been the placement of the previous office in the Welfare Administration of HEW. A connection between welfare and aging seemed to these advocates to detract from their efforts to elevate the status of the elderly in their communities and to separate advancing age from an association with "welfare."

When, through the 1973 amendments, Congress again moved AoA and made it solely responsible to the Office of the Secretary of HEW, HEW created the Office of Human Development Services (OHDS). Once again, AoA was incorporated into a bureaucratic structure, purportedly for its benefit but with the opposite effect.

Arguments during discussion of the 1978 amendments again raised the problem of the AoA's placement. Suggestions ranged from an independent office at the White House level to leaving it where it was. In the end the amendments did not change the law and AoA remained within OHDS.

Although reauthorization proceedings in 1981 once more raised the issue of AoA's weak status within OHDS, nothing was changed. After the 1984 hearings on reauthorization a bill passed in the House of Representatives proposed replacing AoA with an Office on Aging that would be headed by a Commissioner on Aging who would report directly to the Secretary of the DHHS. In a conference agreement, however, AoA was retained within OHDS but was to maintain a reporting relationship between the Commissioner and the office of the Secretary.

Then, in 1987, Congress elevated AoA to the same level of authority as the offices of assistant secretaries and other commissioners within the department by designating that the Commissioner on Aging would report directly to the Secretary.

After the passage of this amendment, however, the Secretary of HHS, citing various departmental interpretations of congressional intent regarding the status of the AoA, asked the Assistant Secretary of Management and Budget to review the effects of the recent amendments, "including use of AoA funds in consolidated research and evaluation activities." The AoA was to remain in its previous status within the OHDS structure until this study was completed, a situation that continued throughout 1988.

In 1989 the AoA finally achieved equal status with other HHS offices and the Commissioner on Aging has since reported directly to the Secretary. However, resources and funding continued to be under the control of the OHDS, limiting the ability of the Administration on Aging to utilize funds at its own discretion. In 1991 the Administration on Aging was made a separate operating component within the Department of Health and Human Services.

There is a consensus that the Older Americans Act has resulted in public policy that has successfully provided widely respected services that benefit all of society. Furthermore, it is perceived that the value of the act has increased over the years as activities related to it have become more focused and its budget has been increased. At the same time, there is concern that its enlarged scope and broader intentions have not been accompanied by adequate funding. Of necessity, this has required implementation of alternative policies and strategies that emphasize service to those in greatest social and economic need, a search for other sources of funds, and reductions in programs that would have long-range benefits through support of wellness.

In the absence of a national chronic care (or long-term care) policy, Older Americans Act activities, de facto, have become the nation's provider of many chronic care services, but without benefit of a clear national policy or appropriate funding. In fact, there are those who believe that AoA programs, however limited their response to the needs of homebound persons, have actually postponed the adoption of a viable national chronic care policy.

It is important that the Older Americans Act not become a disguised form of a national chronic care policy. Many concerned advocates of the AoA believe that this has already happened as amendments to the act have increasingly targeted services to persons who are frail, homebound and needy while minimizing wellness programs.

Despite a strong commitment to the basic premise that Older Americans Act programs are an entitlement for those who have reached age sixty (or 55 for Title V employment programs), there is disagreement as to whether all aspects of the act or only some portions are entitlements. Specifically, there is consistent questioning of whether costly home-delivered services should be provided to all who request or require such services.

Ultimately, the debate must focus on the amount of resources allocated to the act. Substantial waiting lists have developed for some of the most crucial services and funds have been transferred from wellness programs to make it possible to serve persons having increased dependency needs. It is apparent from these waiting lists and fund transfers that program funding has been far less than what would be required to respond adequately to the needs of older Americans.

Policymakers and providers confronted with obvious needs and limited resources have creatively sought other sources of funding. Cost sharing, means testing, targeting, sliding fee schedules, and private partnerships have evolved as alternative approaches to providing more than can be offered with limited core funding from the Older American Act. However, each of these approaches challenges a basic premise of the act, entitlement, and raises questions about its net effect on the quality and quantity of services for the very poor. There is concern lest the Older Americans Act provide a two-tiered system, one for the poor and another for the well-to-do, thereby acquiring some of the negative attributes of our national welfare system. At issue is the basic ability of the act to meet its changing and increasing role with regard to frail older persons unless there are major changes in its funding.

Given the act's potential to emerge as a powerful policy response to the aging of our population, it is disturbing that there has not been forceful advocacy for major adjustments to its funding. Each of the alternative approaches to financing of programs seems to compromise the crucial position that more money is needed from the federal government. There are those who argue that the country cannot afford more, that the deficit will not permit more, that taxes cannot be increased, etc.

Clearly, it will be difficult to generate major increases in funding and certainly no new monies of any consequence will be allocated unless both old and young persons advocate vigorously on behalf of caring for the elderly and supporting the Older Americans Act.

It is of no small consequence that Congress has not been deluged with requests for increasing support for the act. While a strong outpouring of support for increased resources will not necessarily produce all that is needed, it is incontestable that Congress will deal only with issues that have strong public support. Recent health care policy implementation has demonstrated how quickly Congress can react to public sentiment.

Why has there been relatively little public concern about the need for additional and appropriate funding to implement the programs of the act? Perhaps the lack of reaction is related to the fact that there is no relationship between the act and direct out-of-pocket costs to the taxpayer, as was the case when increased Medicare contributions were proposed. People may not be sufficiently aware of the value of the services provided by the act or they may not recognize just what important services are associated with the act. The primary advocates for increasing funding of the act have been provider organizations rather than masses of recipients of services, and perhaps provider advocacy is less effective than direct outpouring of concern from those designated to be served by the act.

Future reauthorization debates will continue to examine the changing complexion of the aging population, its service needs and the role of the aging network in response to those needs. Undoubtedly the special interests of members of Congress as well as the effective expression of advocacy groups and the Administration on Aging will have major impacts on policy changes. The dissolution of the U.S. House of Representatives Select Committee on Aging indicates the absence of a special interest presence in the House on behalf of issues on aging, resulting in limited advocacy and the lack of appropriations for existing legislation.

Reauthorization of the act in a form that will make it more effective will require coalescing of the many advocacy resources of older people—not merely representative groups—in support of increased funding.

A LEGISLATIVE CALENDAR OF THE
OLDER AMERICANS ACT

The following information concerning the changes in the Older Americans Act by year since its passage was adapted from various source materials, including the *CIS Index Legislative Histories,* the *U.S. Code Congressional & Administrative News,* and selected articles from the *Congressional Quarterly Almanac* and the *Congressional Quarterly Weekly.*

1965

The Older Americans Act of 1965 (PL 89-73), signed into law on July 14, passed in the House on March 31 with one dissenting voice and in the Senate on May 27 by a voice vote. This law created the Administration on Aging and replaced the Office of Aging in the Department of Health Education and Welfare.

1967

Signed into law as PL 90-42 on July 1, 1967, the Older Americans Act Amendments of 1967 provided an extension of the grant programs through fiscal 1972 and increased authorization of funds for fiscal years 1968 and 1969. These amendments also called for the Secretary of HEW to undertake a study of the needs for trained personnel in the field of aging and of the availability and adequacy of educational and training resources for those preparing to work in programs related to the objectives of this act. An increase in the federal contribution to states' Title III allotment was included, along with other minor and technical amendments to improve the act's workability. By extending programs and substantially increasing the authorizations of the OAA for fiscal years 1968 and 1969, Congress reaffirmed its support and gave recognition to the fact that the AoA was performing valuable functions worthy of increased appropriations.

In August 1967, however, a new Social and Rehabilitation Service (SRS) was created through a reorganization plan, uniting under a single executive both HEW's income support programs and its social service and rehabilitation programs. The AoA became a unit within SRS, with new responsibilities for providing services for the elderly that included overseeing services to the elderly poor under public assistance programs provided through state welfare agencies. Close attention to the implementation of the SRS was cautioned by the Senate Special Committee on Aging (U.S. Senate, 1967), with special emphasis on how this reorganization would affect the development of future social services for the elderly.

There was widespread concern over what many perceived as the downgrading of AoA under this realignment of federal welfare, rehabilitation and social programs. AoA had become one of five major divisions within SRS. The other divisions were: the Rehabilitation Services Administration, the Children's Bureau, the Medical Services Administration, and the Assistance Payments Administration. The AoA Commissioner, who had formerly reported directly to the Secretary of HEW, now had to report to the Administrator of SRS.

The two major questions raised by the reorganization were: did this move violate the intent of Congress when it passed the OAA of 1965, and did this new status for AoA reduce its potential leadership role in providing national visibility to vital public issues related to the elderly? The intention had been to have an administration and a commissioner of co-equal status with the other six major agencies of the Department of HEW. This was no longer the case. Linking AoA with a series of agencies whose fundamental concern was with welfare made AoA less readily visible as a distinct entity and deprived it of the advantage of being in a position of equality with the other major agencies in HEW.

One reason Congress had been motivated to create AoA had been a similar reorganization in December 1962 which had placed the former Special Staff on Aging under the Welfare Administration as the Office on Aging. Senator McNamara and Representative Fogarty at that time initially had pressed for an independent Commission on Aging within the Executive Office of the President but had been willing to substitute an Administration on Aging within HEW as the only politically achievable arrangement. They had, however, still expected AoA to be a strong independent agency, totally separate from agencies that provided welfare assistance or services and having direct access to the secretary.

John W. Gardner, Secretary of HEW, overruled those plans by reorganizing the department along lines he felt would be more efficient, demonstrating that a loss of administrative flexibility that former Secretary Celebrezze had feared when the Administration on Aging was authorized obviously had not taken place. In addition, this reorganization had occurred without any prior discussion with leaders in the field of aging, or even with members of the Advisory Committee on Aging.

At a Senate hearing in mid-September (which had been called to consider another matter) individual legislators and representatives of national organizations spoke out against the reorganization and plans were subsequently made for a major conference at which the reorganization could be discussed at length with HEW. It also was suggested that the next White House Conference on Aging should serve as a forum for discussing issues related to coordination of policies and programs dealing with aging.

1969

On September 17, 1969, the President signed into law (PL 91-69) the Older Americans Act Amendments of 1969. The main features of this bill were:

1. Creation of the Retired Senior Volunteer Program (RSVP), in which persons aged 60 and over were to provide community services, without compensation but with reimbursement for their meals, travel, and other out-of-pocket expenses.
2. Giving the Foster Grandparents Program, which had previously been administered by AoA with funds from the Office of Economic Opportunity, specific ongoing statutory authorization to be administered by AoA with its own funds. The program also was expanded to provide funding for persons over 60 to care for retarded and orphaned children. Like the RSVP program, Foster Grandparents was designed to provide service opportunities for older Americans, and together the two programs were packaged in the 1969 amendments as components of a "national older Americans volunteer program."

3. Authorizing $25 million to be distributed over three years for area-wide model community projects to be conducted through the Secretary of HEW.

In this year John B. Martin was appointed commissioner and served as the President's Special Assistant on Aging, for the first time giving the commissioner a voice in the highest counsels of government. Research and development activities on nutrition for older persons were emphasized during 1969, as directed by Congress. AoA became heavily involved in model cities activities, in cooperation with the Department of HUD, state and local governments and their aging agencies; and President Nixon issued a call for the 1971 White House Conference on Aging.

A serious problem on the horizon, though, was the cutback in appropriations for programs for the aging in the fiscal 1970 budget of the new Nixon administration. The funding proposed would support only about 700 projects under Title III, approximately 400 fewer than in fiscal 1969.

Funding for RSVP was not included in the 1969 amendments, but it was requested under the revised budget estimate of the new administration.

1970

In 1970 state plans were approved by the AoA in Indiana, Alabama, and Wyoming, the last three states to qualify for funds under the OAA of 1965. There was now an agency that could represent its elderly citizens (a state unit on aging) in every state. There was still deep concern, though, about the future of the Administration on Aging itself. The struggle for adequate appropriations for programs for the aging continued. The budget for fiscal 1971 submitted by the Nixon administration in early 1970 represented a $1 million cutback in funding, approximately 37 percent of the amount that was authorized for the OAA for 1969. New programs, such as RSVP, experienced considerable trouble getting off the ground. Other programs were forced to be maintained at earlier levels, and some were reduced sharply.

Reorganization moves within HEW that had raised additional concerns about the downgrading of AoA involved the decentralization of the Title V (Training) and Foster Grandparent programs to the ten Social and Rehabilitation Service (SRS) regional offices, where they would have to compete with other SRS programs for appropriations. Indeed, appropriations for both programs were severely cut back in the fiscal 1972 budget requests.

The Senate Special Committee on Aging again called for the White House Conference on Aging scheduled for 1971 to take up the question that had been debated at the 1961 conference, namely—what kind of federal agency should be established to administer programs for the elderly and serve as a symbol of national concern about the well-being of aged and aging Americans? The committee argued that this issue not only had not been resolved by the establishment of the AoA but that questioning about the role and capabilities of the AoA had intensified. Congress had intended AoA to be a strong advocate for the elderly, headed by a commissioner who would be appointed by the President and have direct access to the Secretary of HEW. None of these conditions was currently being met (U.S. Senate, 1970).

1971

The Areawide Model Project program, authorized by the 1969 Amendments to the OAA were implemented in 1971. This program was set up to provide grants to designated state agencies on aging on a discretionary basis. The grants were to fund the development and testing of innovative approaches to changing conditions that prevent or limit opportunities for older persons who wish to live independently and participate meaningfully in community life.

Congress struggled to obtain from the administration more adequate funding for the OAA and finally, through the combined efforts of bipartisanship and the 1971 White House Conference on Aging, was successful. While the Nixon administration had at first been willing to settle for $29.5 million for OAA activities, a $100 million appropriation was secured after the White House Conference demonstrated that the elderly were deeply dissatisfied—a $70.5 million victory for the elderly.

A bill (HR 17763) to amend the OAA of 1965 to provide grants to states to establish nutrition programs for the elderly introduced by Congressman Claude Pepper (D-FL) on May 21, 1970, was reintroduced on February 25, 1971 as HR 5017. On November 30th, a similar bill, introduced by Senator Edward M. Kennedy (D-MA) was passed in the Senate by an 89 to 0 roll-call vote. This bill authorized grants to states to establish nutrition projects providing meals to eligible persons aged sixty years and older, with preference given to projects that served the needs of the low-income elderly or minority groups. Funds for the program were to be allocated by the Department of HEW to the states on the basis of their proportionate share of the nation's population aged sixty and older. Having opposed this measure for two years, the Nixon administration was now ready to capitulate to overwhelming bipartisan congressional support.

1972

Concern about the future of the Administration on Aging continued in 1972. Members of the Senate Special Committee on Aging deplored the position to which it had fallen, believing that the current administration had presided over the protracted decline of the agency. Rather than becoming the strong national focal point which Congress had intended, it found itself to have no real clout in the federal bureaucracy.

Reorganization moves in HEW during the previous five years had reduced its program responsibility by fully two-thirds since 1970 and Congressional advocates again were calling for the establishment of an independent office on aging at the White House level which could formulate policy and monitor programs on aging. Legislators also advocated the creation of an advisory council to assist this high-level office and prepare an annual report on progress made in resolving issues concerning older Americans. Finally, they were demanding the re-elevation of the AoA by specifically requiring the Commissioner on Aging to report directly to the Secretary of HEW.

These demands were embodied in the Older Americans Comprehensive Services Amendments bill (HR 15657) presented to Congress in 1972. Other programs recommended by this legislation were an older Americans community service employment program that would enhance employment and service opportunities for persons aged fifty-five and older and a National Information Clearinghouse on Aging to collect, prepare, and distribute information regarding the needs of older Americans. However, the nutrition program that in 1971 had been put forth in S 1163 was the only action to pass as an amendment to the Older Americans Act in this year; PL 92-258 became the new Title VII in the OAA, but no funds were provided for its implementation during 1972.

On October 30, 1972, President Nixon pocket vetoed a much more extensive amendment bill (HR 15657). Designed to extend the OAA and strengthen the AoA, the Older Americans Comprehensive Services Amendments bill had passed by a vote of 351 to 3 on July 17th in the House, and by 89 to 0 in the Senate (as S 4044) on October 3. Because Congress had adjourned before the veto, it had lost the chance for a very likely override. Authorizations for all the programs funded under the OAA except the nutrition program had expired on June 30, 1972. It thus became necessary to administer the OAA programs under continuing resolutions until the next year's budget.

In order to pacify some of the unrest in Congress, the Nixon administration readily acknowledged the lack of a high-level spokesman for the elderly in government and tried to show how it had taken action to improve that situation. Elliot Richardson, Secretary of HEW, related how, soon after his inauguration, Nixon had appointed the Commissioner on Aging as his Special Assistant on Aging, giving him a direct line of communication, and had further strengthened the White House focus and coordination of aging concerns by the appointment of Dr. Arthur S. Flemming as Special Consultant on Aging to the President. The Domestic Council Cabinet Committee on Aging, chaired by the Secretary of HEW, which the administration had set up to coordinate government policy development as it affects the elderly, was also cited as evidence of increasing responsiveness to the needs of older Americans.

The Secretary also stated that the role and capacity of the Advisory Committee on Older Americans were to be expanded and that the Commissioner on Aging, as chairman, would report directly to the Secretary. Bertha Adkins, former Under Secretary of HEW would serve as vice-chairman of the committee. Furthermore, a Technical Advisory Committee on Aging Research, which would report directly to the chairman and vice-chairman of the advisory committee, would develop a comprehensive plan for aging-related research activities within HEW. Richardson also proposed that existing state agencies be strengthened and that new "substate" agencies on aging be created and required to develop better comprehensive area plans on aging.

1973

The Older Americans Comprehensive Services Amendments bill that Nixon had vetoed was reintroduced in the Senate on January 4, 1973 as S 50 and was approved on February 20 by a vote of 82 to 9. Companion legislation that had been introduced in the House on January 3, 1973 as HR 71 was passed on March 13 by a vote of 329 to 69, though at a funding level $600 million below that passed by the Senate. The President was said to have pocket vetoed the earlier bill because of excessive authorizations ($2 billion) and unnecessary new categorical programs. The final compromise version was worked out by the appropriate House and Senate committees and administration aides without a formal conference committee, and passed by Congress on April 18. On May 3, 1973 President Nixon signed the bill into law (PL 93-29).

The bill as passed had scaled down the authorization sums earlier approved by the House and Senate by about $1 billion, authorizing just $543.6 million for fiscal 1973-75. A mid-career training program (Title X) that had been passed in the Senate bill was dropped in the compromise bill. Although several members of Congress predicted an easy override of any Presidential veto of S 50, the Senate sponsor, Thomas Eagleton (D-MO) argued for the compromise, saying that the welfare of older Americans was more important than the political gains to be won by overriding a veto.

As enacted, the bill kept in place most of the provisions included in the 1972 bill (HR 15657). The bill that had been vetoed had a strong provision calling for strengthening the Administration on Aging through three fundamental changes:

1. AoA was to be returned to the office of the Secretary of HEW.
2. The Commissioner on Aging was to report directly to the Secretary of HEW.
3. The Secretary was to be prohibited from delegating any of the Commissioner's functions to any officer not directly responsible to the Commissioner without first submitting a delegation plan to Congress.

Of these three changes, the one specifying that the Commissioner on Aging report directly to the Secretary of HEW was deleted in the final compromise bill; the other two were passed into law. Other provisions of the Older Americans Comprehensive Services Amendments of 1973 established:

The Federal Council on the Aging, a 15-member body that would replace the Advisory Committee on Older Americans in HEW. Members appointed by the President with the advice and consent of the Senate were to advise and assist the President on matters relating to the interests of the elderly and to represent the elderly to the President and Congress in planning federal programs and policies.

Model Projects, a new program charged with developing solutions to problems of the elderly related to housing, pre-retirement counseling, continuing education, and social services for handicapped elderly.

National Information and Resources Clearinghouse, established to collect, analyze and distribute information on the needs of older Americans, and to develop a network of information and referral sources in the states and communities.

Multipurpose Senior Centers, a new Title V program that superseded the previous Title V authorization for the training of personnel in the aging field and authorized funding for the acquisition, staffing and renovation of multipurpose senior centers.

Title III Grants for State and Area Programs, to strengthen the role of the state agencies on aging and area agencies on aging as focal points in planning and developing service systems for providing comprehensive coordinated, community-based services for the elderly.

Title IV Grants for Training and Research, consolidating provisions relating to training (previously in Title V) with research in a new and revised Title IV and authorizing sums for grants for training and research and for funding gerontology centers and special transportation research projects.

Foster Grandparents, expanding the Foster Grandparent Program to include supportive services to children and adults in community settings, as well as services for institutionalized children. Funds for the National Older Americans Volunteer Program were authorized.

Nutrition Program, by designating the nutrition program authorized in PL 92-258 to be operated in coordination with other programs of aid to older Americans.

Older Americans Community Service Employment Program, by creating a new Title IX within the Department of Labor to aid persons aged 55 and older to secure employment.

Federal grants for programs to assist the elderly were extended and expanded through fiscal 1975 and Arthur S. Flemming became the third Commissioner on Aging.

In 1973 the AoA was removed from SRS and placed under the auspices of a new Office of Human Development (OHD) that was formed within the Office of the Secretary of HEW. This change presumably was to enable AoA to work closely with other OHD components whose responsibilities also involved serving AoA's target groups (low income and racial minority groups) (U.S. Senate, 1973 and 1974).

The new amendments provided the basis for a comprehensive coordinated system for the elderly, specifically in Titles III (grants for state and area programs) and VII (nutrition program). Title III authorized formula grants to the states to create substate or area level systems to coordinate untapped resources for the elderly within their boundaries. Each state was now required to develop a state plan showing how the state would be divided into distinct planning and service areas (PSAs) and which of these areas would be designated to develop area agencies on aging (AAA) within their boundaries.

Congregate meals, as well as home-delivered meals, were provided for under the new Title VII nutrition program. It was stated in the amendments that the Title VII programs were to provide supportive services coordinated with those of Title III and that all these services could be coordinated within the area agency on aging (AAA) under the Title III structure.

The National Older Americans Volunteer Program, Title VI of the OAA, supported such programs as RSVP and the Foster Grandparents Program. In October 1973, this title was repealed by the Domestic Service Act, and these volunteer programs were reauthorized and incorporated into one law, placing the legislative authority for all such programs under the auspices of an independent agency, ACTION, removing them from the Older Americans Act.

1974

The 1974 amendments to the OAA (PL 93-35) primarily extended the national nutrition program and authorized a special program for transportation services. Final passage was delayed almost five months in House-Senate conference committee negotiations over a provision included in the House bill but not the Senate's to ban unreasonable discrimination in federally-funded programs on the basis of age. They finally reached agreement on November 17; the House adopted the conference report by a 404 to 6 vote and the Senate adopted the report by a unanimous vote on November 20.

1975

By 1975 it was estimated that 70 percent of the older population in the country was covered by the 412 local area agencies created in 1965 but most of the programs funded under the 1973 extension of the OAA had expired June 30, 1975.

The Older Americans Act of 1975 (PL 94-135), signed into law by President Ford on November 28, 1975 contained the following major provisions:

Aid to Indians — The Commissioner on Aging was required to provide direct assistance grants to elderly Indians, setting aside basic assistance funds for the new programs based on the proportion of all American Indians over age 60.

Special Services — Priority was given for the use of grant funds to provide: 1) transportation services, 2) home services including home health care, 3) legal and tax counseling, and 4) programs to help the elderly repair and renovate their homes.

Personnel Training — The commissioner was authorized to make grants for short-term or university-based training programs for personnel who work with the elderly.

Community Service Employment — The community service employment program was amended to make it clear that national organizations, such as the National Council of Senior Citizens, could continue to carry out local employment programs. These programs were extended through fiscal 1978.

Volunteer Programs — Senior volunteer programs run by ACTION, including the Foster Grandparent Program, Retired Senior Volunteer Programs (RSVP), and the Senior Companions Program were extended through fiscal 1978.

Age Discrimination — Unreasonable discrimination on the basis of age in programs that receive federal funding was prohibited. The U.S. Commission on Civil Rights was required to identify unreasonable age discrimination in an 18-month study, and within one year of the commission's report, the HEW Secretary was to propose general regulations to implement the ban. The HEW regulations banning age discrimination were not to take effect before January 1, 1979.

Authority for basic grants to state and local AAAs was extended through fiscal 1978.

Because the OAA had been almost entirely rewritten in 1975, with establishment of the network of area agencies on aging one of the most important changes, no major overhaul appeared necessary in 1975. The area agencies were still in the process of being installed and having their functions more clearly defined. The state agencies on aging and the Administration on Aging had also been given new roles and responsibilities. Furthermore, funds for several of the programs authorized in 1973 had not yet been appropriated.

Considerable concern about the well-being of the AoA had already surfaced in committees deliberating possible changes in the OAA. Blaming the President for not having consulted with the Commissioner on Aging before proposing a 5-percent ceiling on Social Security cost-of-living increases, Congress refused to approve this proposal (U.S. Senate Report No. 94-255).

This failure to communicate was seen as evidence of the administration's disregard for the commissioner's office as an advocate for the elderly, and another review of the organizational position of the AoA in HEW was suggested. As noted in Senate Report No. 94-255 (June 6, 1975) of the Labor and Public Welfare Committee:

> The 1973 amendments to the Act lifted AoA out from the depths of the Social and Rehabilitation Service and placed it in the Office of the Secretary precisely for the reason that added visibility was required if the Commissioner and AoA were to do an effective job of representing the interests of the elderly. Now, AoA is apparently being submerged again—this time in the Office of Human Development (OHD). While no new action with respect to AoA's placement in OHD was decided upon in connection with this bill, it is a matter of continuing interest to the Committee (p. 16).

Differences between Congress and the administration over aging policy extended beyond the role of AoA as federal advocate for the elderly. The administration opposed several proposals for 1975 amendments. For example:

- The administration called for the termination of the training, gerontology centers, and multipurpose senior centers programs.
- HEW Secretary Casper Weinberger strongly opposed priority funding for "special services," urged that the measure to authorize direct funding of Indian tribes be deleted and requested that the Federal Council on the Aging study the proposed Age Discrimination Act.
- Under Secretary of Labor Richard F. Schubert opposed the extension of the Title IX Older Americans Community Service Employment Act, stating that funding for this sort of activity was already available under the Comprehensive Employment and Training Act (CETA).

Overwhelming bipartisan support for the conference bill detailing the 1975 amendments to the OAA soundly rejected these administration arguments and demonstrated clearly that a veto could very easily be overridden. With complaints over the high authorization levels and decrying the Age Discrimination Act in particular, President Ford signed the 1975 amendments into law.

1978

By 1978 there were 563 area agencies on aging and over 90 percent of the eligible population was now covered by an area agency on aging plan.

In the spring of that year Robert C. Benedict became the fourth Commissioner on Aging. Nelson H. Cruikshank, chairperson of the Federal Council on the Aging, was appointed as Special Assistant for Aging to President Carter and was followed in this position by Harold Sheppard at the close of the Carter administration. Neither President Reagan nor President Bush appointed anyone to this position.

The OAA was again substantially revised in 1978. The House passed its version of the amendments on October 4 (HR 12255) by a 361 to 6 vote, the Senate passed its version (S 2850) on October 6 and the amendments were signed into law October 18, 1978 as PL 95-478 by President Carter.

The amendments consolidated Title V, the administration of multipurpose senior centers, Title VII, nutrition services (previously under separate authorizations for congregate meals and home-delivered meals), and legal and ombudsman services under one title: Title III (grants for state and area programs). It was hoped that uniting social services, senior centers and nutrition services would eliminate duplication of community services and increase the visibility, political strength and significance of the area agencies on aging.

The amendments also enacted a new Title VI to provide direct grants to Indian tribes to develop social services, legal services, nutrition programs and ombudsman programs for Native Americans aged sixty and older.

Other major provisions of the 1978 amendments included:

Duties of the Commissioner — The Commissioner on Aging was authorized to review and comment on all federal policies affecting the elderly, required to advise, consult and cooperate with heads of other federal agencies with programs that serve the elderly. Heads of agencies were required to consult with the commissioner before establishing programs involving the elderly and the commissioner was required to prepare a study on the need for a separate legal services program under the OAA.

Federal Council on the Aging — The requirement that the Secretary of HEW and the Commissioner on Aging serve as ex officio members on the Federal Council of the Aging was abolished in order to make the council more independent. The council was authorized to have its own staff, appointed by the chairperson, and was required to conduct a study to examine the purposes and effectiveness of programs authorized by the OAA.

Aging Network Services — A continuum of care for the vulnerable elderly was required to be established as part of comprehensive and coordinated service systems. Each area agency on aging was required to establish, where feasible, a focal point for comprehensive service delivery in each community. A three-year planning cycle was mandated for area agencies and 50 percent of each area agency's social service allotment was required to be spent on programs associated with access, in-home services and legal services. State agencies were required to reserve $20,000 or 1 percent of their social services allotment, whichever was greater, to establish and operate long term care ombudsman programs.

Community Service Employment — Title IX was changed to Title V and the community service employment program for the elderly was extended for three years, through fiscal 1981. The income eligibility criterion was raised from the poverty index to 125 percent of that index.

Volunteer Programs — Volunteer programs (RSVP, Foster Grandparent/ Senior Companion programs) were extended under the Domestic Volunteer Service Act of 1973 for three years, through fiscal 1981.

White House Conference on Aging — A White House Conference in 1981 was authorized.

Racial and Ethnic Study — The U.S. Commission on Civil Rights was required to do a study on discrimination based on racial or ethnic background in any federal program involving older persons.

Age Discrimination — Persons claiming to be harmed by alleged violations of the Age Discrimination Act of 1975 were allowed to file civil suits, provided other remedies had first been exhausted.

The Older Americans Act was extended for three years, through fiscal 1981.

The House Education and Labor Committees had proposed a requirement that the Commissioner on Aging report directly to the Secretary of HEW, rather than to an assistant secretary in the Office of Human Development Services (OHDS), and this measure had passed in the House. The Senate Committee on Human Resources, although acknowledging that there was some concern about AoA's again being submerged within HEW, saw some merit in its continuing there for purposes of coordinating programs under the AoA with those administered by the Public Services Administration, the Developmental Disabilities Office, the Office of Child Development, the Office of Youth Development, and the Rehabilitation Services Administration.

In conference committee, the House receded from its position when the Secretary of HEW gave assurances that the commissioner would retain full access to the Secretary. The conferees agreed to monitor closely whether the commissioner was being given visibility appropriate to his position in HEW and being allowed to serve as a focal point for aging programs.

1981

In fiscal year 1980, there were 610 area agencies on aging across the United States, serving more than nine million older participants under approved area plans. Lennie Marie P. Tolliver, the fifth Commissioner on Aging, was sworn in in September of 1981. In this year the implementation of OAA provisions was principally carried out through the establishment of a national network on aging in which the Administration on Aging represented the federal level. The state agencies and area agencies on aging established under Title III provided the state and local community levels, with local community subcontractors implementing the programs (U.S. Senate, 1981).

Authorization for appropriations under the OAA amendments of 1978 having expired on September 30, 1981, a Senate bill (S 1086) introduced on April 30,

1981 eventually became the principal reauthorization measure. It was passed on November 2 by a 75 to 0 vote. The House bill incorporating the Older Americans Act Amendments of 1981 (HR 3046) was introduced on April 7, 1981, and was passed on November 20 by a vote of 379 to 4. Many components of the House bill had been incorporated into the Senate version during final consideration in conference committee.

A Reagan administration proposal (S 1121) introduced on May 6 and calling for consolidation of three separate authorizations for programs for the elderly into a block grant and merging home-delivered and congregate meal programs into a single authorization was eliminated from the final conference report. After approval by the Senate by a vote of 90 to 0 on December 11, and adoption by the House by voice vote on December 16, the Comprehensive Older Americans Act Amendments of 1981 were signed into law by President Reagan on December 29, 1981 as PL 91-115.

Major provisions under these amendments included:

Duties of the Commissioner on Aging — Language was retained that would require the Commissioner to report to the "Office of the Secretary" rather than to the Secretary of Health and Human Services (formerly HEW). Functions of the commissioner as they relate to the overall "common" functions in the HHS Department were clarified.

Nutrition Services — Separate authorizations for the congregate and home-delivered meal programs and supportive social services were retained. A new provision allowed states to transfer up to 20 percent of federal funds between their nutrition and social service programs.

Social Services — The provision that required area agencies to spend at least 50 percent of their social services funds on access, in-home and legal services was changed to require only that an "adequate portion" of their funds be spent on these services. The long term care ombudsman program (now including oversight of boarding homes) was retained in the 1978 amendments and a number of new services were included as allowable supportive services: employment services and education, crime prevention and victim assistance programs, and the installation of security devices and structural changes of elderly residences to prevent unlawful entry. An age definition for older Indians was eliminated from the Title VI program of grants to tribal organizations.

National Clearinghouse — Authorization for the National Information and Resource Clearing House for the Aging was eliminated.

All titles of the Older Americans Act were extended through 1984, with state and area agencies on aging planning requirements modified to allow each state the choice of two-, three-, or four-year planning cycles.

The 1981 amendment process was seen as a matter of fine-tuning the legislation as amended in 1978. Several factors were cited as reasons to delay a major overhaul of the act at this time, including: 1) the delay in the implementation of the regulations under the 1978 amendments (specifically those related to the states and area agency programs under Title III, for which final regulations were not published until March 30, 1980); 2) possible program recommendations that could evolve from the 1981 White House Conference on Aging, and 3) possible recommendations from several national studies being conducted on the operation of community aging programs.

The perennial issue of the organizational placement of the Administration on Aging in the Department of HHS surfaced again in 1981, largely because of a report on a General Accounting Office study requested by the Senate Special Committee on Aging to assess the relationship of AoA to the Office of Human Development Services. This report made clear that several activities (policy-making and non-policy-making) that had been vested by statute in the Commissioner on Aging, such as the functions of administering grants and contracts and financial management for grants, had been delegated to offices in OHDS not directly responsible to the commissioner. The Senate Special Committee had expected a study dealing only with the department's compliance with the OAA and the need to make any necessary corrections.

Although there continued to be concern that administrative decisions had gradually diminished the commissioner's authority in the Department of HHS, organizational positioning of the Administration on Aging in HHS also was seen as a very serious problem.

Having co-equal status with several other human service agencies made it difficult to argue that aging services should be given priority over other service groups. At the same time, it was felt that simply upgrading the AoA position would not necessarily affect its ability to advocate for more effective aging policies unless significant authority and sufficient staff to support the position were added.

The Clearinghouse for the Aging was eliminated in the 1981 amendments. Congress felt that, although the agency's record of effectiveness did not justify continued separate authorization, the commissioner should continue to use available agency funds to collect and disseminate information on aging needs and concerns.

1984

The OAA had now evolved from its origins as a program of small grants and research projects into a network of fifty-seven state units of aging, more than 660 area agencies on aging, and approximately 15,000 community organizations providing supportive social and nutritional services to older adults. In December

1984, Carol Fraser Fisk became the Acting Commissioner on Aging and in August 1986 was promoted to become the sixth Commissioner on Aging.

The expansion of services that had continued into the early 1980s slowed as Reagan administration policies reduced the size and scope of many federal programs. Between fiscal years 1981 and 1982, for example, Title IV funding for training, research, and discretionary programs was cut by almost 50 percent. In fiscal 1983, the administration proposed to eliminate the Senior Community Service Employment Program (Title V), but Congress refused to do so.

With authorization for appropriations under the Amendments of 1981 scheduled to expire on September 30, 1984, a Senate reauthorization bill (S 2603) was introduced on April 26, 1984, referred to the Committee on Labor and Human Resources, and finally passed in the Senate by voice vote on May 24. The House bill (HR 4785) introduced on February 8, 1984, eventually passed the full House on August 8 by a vote of 406 to 12. A number of provisions in the Senate version were incorporated into the final conference bill approved in the Senate by voice vote on September 26, 1984 and passed 393 to 2 in the House later that same day. On October 9, 1984 the President signed the legislation into law as PL 98-459.

Its major provisions were:

Administration on Aging — Although the House reauthorization bill would have replaced the AoA with an Office on Aging headed by a commissioner directly responsible to the Secretary of HHS, the conference agreement retained the AoA while restating requests for a direct reporting relationship between the commissioner and the Office of the Secretary and prohibiting the Secretary's delegating any of the commissioner's functions.

The intent was to assure that responsibility for federal aging policy be firmly placed in the AoA and not in the Office of Human Development Services and that the commissioner would have a reporting relationship with no official other than the Secretary.

Federal Council on the Aging — Selection of members was modified to better assure the independence of the council from the executive branch by requiring that a portion (5) of the members be appointed by the President, a portion (5) by the President pro tempore of the Senate, and a portion (5) by the Speaker of the House. Previously, the law had required the council to be composed of 15 members appointed by the President with the advice and consent of the Senate.

Supportive Social Service Programs — The amount allowed to be transferred between supportive and nutrition services was increased from 20 percent to 27 percent in fiscal 1985, to 29 percent in 1986, and to 30 percent in 1987. Provisions were included to emphasize that service priorities at state and area agencies should be geared toward aiding minority individuals and elderly victims of violence and abuse as well as providing supportive services to the families of Alzheimer's sufferers. Area agencies were also required to involve long-term care providers in service coordination and to involve their communities in dealing with the needs of the institutionalized.

Training, Research and Demonstration — The Commissioner on Aging was required to give special consideration to projects dealing with the recruitment and training of personnel and volunteers to assist Alzheimer's victims and their families.

Community Service Employment — A cap on federal funds that could be used for project administration was placed at 13.5 percent in fiscal 1986 and 12 percent in fiscal 1987. Labor Department regulations had previously limited spending on administrative expenses to 15 percent of an agency's funds.

Aid to Indian Tribes — Eligibility requirements for tribal organizations to receive funds for supportive and nutrition services were liberalized so that tribal organizations would be eligible if they represented at least 60 older Indians, rather than the 75 previously required.

Health Education Programs — A new title was created under the 1984 amendments, Title VII: Older Americans Personal Health Education and Training Program. This program required the Secretary of HHS to award grants to universities through the AoA to develop health education and training programs for the elderly. This title was never funded and was later dropped.

Amendments to the Age Discrimination in Employment Act (ADEA) — Protection against age discrimination was extended to U.S. citizens employed by U.S. employers in foreign countries and the provision of the ADEA allowing companies to force the retirement from executive or other high-level positions after age 65 if they were entitled to a retirement benefit of at least $27,000 was altered to provide a threshold of $44,000 a year.

The Older Americans Act Amendments of 1984 essentially "fine-tuned" the act again, without making major changes. Both Congress and the aging network perceived that the programs were being run efficiently and effectively, and growing concern for the size of the budget deficit made it clear that proposals to expand program services would almost certainly be rejected. Nevertheless, Congress was unwilling to accept an administration measure introduced as HR 5325 that proposed: 1) consolidation of various parts of the supportive and nutrition programs into a block grant to the states under Title III; and 2) transfer of the Title V Senior Community Service Employment Program from the Department of Labor to the AoA (which did not have the capacity to administer the program adequately) and discontinuing separate funding for Title V.

The revision of the selection process for members of the Federal Council on the Aging was an attempt to loosen the council's apparent close ties with the executive branch that had been demonstrated when it followed the administration's lead in: 1) supporting the shift of Title V to the Department of HHS; 2) opposing the elevation of the Commissioner on Aging to assistant secretary status in HHS; and 3) supporting the total consolidation of funding categories under Title III. Such an acquiescent attitude appeared to make the council functionally useless in the advisory capacity for which it had been created.

With the approach in 1985 of the twentieth anniversary of the Older Americans Act of 1965, much concern about the lack of development of a national aging policy under its auspices remained, even though progress had been realized in the gradual evolution of programs under the act. Bringing about of a truly coordinated and comprehensive system of services at the community level, with a strong focal point for aging policy at the federal level, would require Congress to go beyond making incremental reforms and return to furthering the goals set forth in 1965.

1986

Through the years, "the essential mission of the Older Americans Act remained very much the same: to provide a wide array of social and community services to those older persons in the greatest economic and social need in order to foster maximum independence. The key element in the program was to help maintain and support older persons in their homes and communities to avoid unnecessary and costly institutionalization" (U.S. Senate, 1986).

Targeting services more narrowly to certain subgroups of the elderly, as had been proposed in the 1984 reauthorization hearings, was consistently resisted by Congress. Funding problems had always forced the act's advocates to fight just to keep up with inflation. From 1983 through 1985, funding for OAA programs had increased at an annual rate that was less than the rate of inflation, but, despite efforts by the Reagan administration to cut domestic spending, the OAA had consistently received increased appropriations, even with some 1981 to 1982 program reductions. Although the new Title VII, Older Americans Personal Health Education and Training Program, had not as yet been funded, Title III programs continued to receive small increases in appropriations. An Older Americans Act Amendments of 1986 bill, HR 2453, increased the amounts authorized to be appropriated for fiscal years 1985, 1986, and 1987 for commodity distribution, increasing the per-meal reimbursement rate for USDA assistance to states for elderly meal programs. The Senate adopted the conference report of this bill by voice vote on March 13, 1986, and the House accepted it by a vote of 344 to 0 on March 18. This legislation was then signed into law (PL 99-269) by the President on April 1, 1986.

1987

The authorization of appropriations for the OAA of 1965, as amended, was scheduled to expire at the end of fiscal year 1987. The House set forth its plans for reauthorization of the act in 1987 when on May 28 it passed HR 1451 by a vote of

379 to 8. The Senate followed suit on August 6, passing an identically worded resolution (originally S 887) by a vote of 98 to 0. The final conference report was adopted by Congress on November 12, 1987, with both House and Senate overwhelmingly passing it by votes of 404 to 7 and 93 to 0, respectively. The major provisions of this act as signed into law by President Reagan on November 29, at PL 100-175, were:

Declaration of Objectives — An additional objective was added: protection of the elderly from abuse, neglect, and exploitation.

Administration on Aging — The status of the Commissioner on Aging was elevated within the Department of HHS so that he/she would now report directly to the Secretary, rather than to the "Office of the Secretary." The commissioner also was directed to create within the AoA a new Office for American Indian, Alaskan Native and Native Hawaiian Programs, to be headed by an associate commissioner. Data collection was expanded to increase the information on services provided by AoA to include the number of individuals served, the funds spent, the number of senior centers funded, and the effectiveness of state and area agencies on aging.

Federal Council on the Aging — The number of elderly persons (65 and older) on the council was increased from six of the 15 members to nine of 15 members and representation from Indian tribes was required.

Supportive Social Services — A number of new authorizations were added to Title III: 1) a new Part D, providing non-medical in-home services for the frail elderly (those with physical or mental disabilities, such as Alzheimer's disease, which threaten their ability to function independently); 2) a new Part E, providing services for unmet "special needs" such as transportation and outreach; 3) health education and promotion service activities under a new Part F; 4) area programs to prevent the abuse, neglect and exploitation of older persons under a new Part G; 5) outreach services to elderly potentially eligible for SSI, Medicaid, and Food Stamp programs; and 6) long-term care ombudsman services. State and area agencies had previously been responsible for programs in these areas, but specific separate authorizations of Title III funds for these services were now provided for the first time.

Other amendments included the stipulation that each state agency set a minimum percentage of funds to be used in three priority service areas: 1) access services (transportation, outreach, and information and referral); 2) in-home services (homemaker and home health aide, visiting and telephone reassurance, chore maintenance, and supportive services for families of Alzheimer's sufferers); and 3) legal assistance. Coordination of services was mandated on behalf of specific subgroups including: those with mental illness, Alzheimer's victims and their families, those with disabilities, and persons in need of community-based long-term care services.

A new provision required area agencies to conduct outreach activities to identify older Indians and, if their numbers were significant within the planning and
service area, to inform them of services offered. Other provisions were added to
clarify that Indians were now eligible to receive services under both Title III and
Title IV grant programs, as well as under Title VI.

Training, Research and Discretionary Programs — New demonstration
authorities allowed the commissioner to offer grants to: 1) universities or
colleges for health education and promotion programs; 2) provide volunteer
opportunities; 3) identify older persons eligible for but not receiving welfare
benefits; 4) demonstrate cooperative efforts between the state long-term
care ombudsman and state protection and advocacy agencies for the mentally
ill or developmentally disabled; and 5) demonstrate and advocate consumer
protection activities in long-term care, such as in-home non-medical care.
Funding of long-term care gerontology centers, previously supported at the
discretion of the commissioner, now was made mandatory.

Community Service Employment — An administrative cap was set at 13.5
percent of funds allocated, but a prior provision allowing the Secretary
of Labor to raise the cap to 15 percent, if necessary, was retained. A
new provision was added to exclude wages received by Title V enrollees
from consideration when determining eligibility for federal housing and
food stamp programs. A requirement that program participants be informed
about their rights under the Age Discrimination in Employment Act was also
included.

Native American Grants — Title VI was expanded to include a new Part B,
authorizing funds to be appropriated for a Native Hawaiians programs. Tribal
organizations were to be eligible for Title VI funds if they had at least 50 older
Indians, rather than the 60 previously required.

Older Americans Personal Health Education and Training Program — A
new Title VII, created under the 1984 amendments and never funded was
repealed. The amendment to Title IV (Training, Research and Demonstration
Programs) on health education and promotion was added to preserve this
title's intent.

1991 White House Conference on Aging — The President was to call a
conference in 1991 and to include on its agenda the development of recommendations for the coordination of federal policy with state and local needs
and a review of the status of recommendations adopted at previous White
House Conferences.

Consumer Index for Older Americans — A provision authored by Senator
John Melcher (D-MT) required the Secretary of Labor to develop an index of
consumer prices that would reflect the consumption expenditures of persons
aged 62 and older.

National School Lunch Act Amendment — Another provision from Senator Melcher permitted adult day care centers to receive reimbursement under the Child Care Food Program for persons 60 years or older or those chronically disabled.

The Older Americans Act Amendments of 1987 reauthorized the OAA for another four years, through fiscal 1991. Despite an increase in authorizations, OAA programs continued to be over-extended and under-funded, which prompted some area agencies on aging, the administration and some Congressmen (such as Thomas J. Tauke, R-IA) to advocate cost-sharing for certain services. Proponents argued that charging fees on the basis of ability to pay would make it possible to use the funds obtained to provide outreach services for low-income and minority populations. Congress rejected this proposal as being a thinly-veiled form of means-testing, though the Senate Committee on Labor and Human Resources asked the Government Accounting Office to study current state cost-sharing systems and report its findings by September 30, 1990.

The Reagan administration's fiscal year 1988 budget request for OAA programs was in the form of a generic appropriation of $2.2 billion for 26 separate discretionary programs within the Office of Human Development Services. The Congress viewed this as an attempt to make the Older Americans Act a "block grant" program and not only rejected the proposal but also authorized six additional appropriations under Title III.

Another attempt by the administration, this time to raise the age of eligibility for Title III programs from sixty to sixty-five years of age, also was roundly defeated by Congress on the grounds that: 1) it would decrease the amount of overall appropriations; 2) vulnerability cannot be measured by age alone; and 3) such an age change would have a negative impact upon minority elderly, whose life expectancy is lower than that of non-minorities.

Attempts continued to be made to elevate the position of the Commissioner in the DHHS in an effort to counteract what was viewed by a Senate report as the:

> . . . apparent inclination within the current structure to usurp both funding and resources intended by Congress to be used to support the Administration on Aging for other programs within the Office of Human Development Services . . . [The expectation was that] the Commissioner on Aging [would be] included in appropriate departmental decision making, . . . have independent access to the Secretary, and . . . function with the same level of authority as assistant secretaries and other commissioners within the Department (U.S. Senate Report No. 100-136, p. 49).

In January of 1989 George Bush was inaugurated as President of the United States. Joyce Berry was appointed acting commissioner in April 1989 and was subsequently sworn in as the seventh Commissioner on Aging thirteen months later, in March 1990.

Commissioner Berry assumed her office at a time of reduced federal resources, a presidential promise not to raise taxes and an increasing number of older persons in need of the services of the Older Americans Act. The Eldercare Initiative advocated by Berry was an attempt to accommodate these conflicting needs. A group of eldercare coalitions in communities throughout the country were established to seek increased local participation in programs for the elderly and encourage local providers to fund necessary services. State units on aging were allocated Title IV funds to stimulate the development of the local initiatives and twelve National Eldercare Institutes were funded to:

- Enhance the coalitions' capabilities to identify issues that need to be addressed in their communities.
- Help the coalitions develop strategies to implement in-home and community-based Eldercare agendas.
- Promote adoption of these agendas by segments of society that can build a broad base of support for Eldercare expansion.
- Offer analysis, synthesis and dissemination of useful materials, training, and consultation and technical assistance (Older Americans Report, 1992).

The institutes were funded for three years, after which they were expected to have found alternate sources of funding to maintain their programs. Representing a new approach on the part of the Administration on Aging, the Eldercare Initiative was designed to generate additional support for serving the elderly from individual communities throughout the country. If successful, it was expected to have increased awareness of the needs of the elderly and establish strong local commitment to the provision of services. However, part of the reason for creating it appears to have been a sense that the federal government was unable to increase its expenditures to meet the increasing needs of a growing population. On the other hand, there were many who argued that major modification of the budget process and reallocation of defense funding could make additional funds available for domestic services without forcing a choice between allocating additional federal funds or expanding the base of interest and support when both were needed, as was a national health care policy responsive to the chronic care needs of our oldest population. In the absence of such a policy, the Older Americans Act was cast in a major role as provider of home and community-based programs for the frail elderly without having been given concomitant financial resources to meet the growing need.

A 1990 General Accounting Office investigation of the AoA to determine whether its ability to provide services was hampered by budgetary organization and administrative constraints within HHS found that since 1965 the cost of mandated AoA services increased concurrently with an increase in the aged population without any concomitant increase in resources. In real terms, AoA resources actually declined from $650 million in 1980 to $460 million in 1990, a decrease of about 30 percent at a time of rising numbers and increasing expectations. The study also found a serious lack of data needed to determine whether needs of the older population were being met because a serious shortage of travel money prevented AoA staff from monitoring projects. There were shortages of staff, especially staff qualified to evaluate Older Americans Act programs. A particular need was for a staff nutritionist who could provide guidance to a very large nutrition program. The trends observed are made evident in Figures 10 and 11.

1991

Concern regarding the location of the AoA in the Department of Health and Human Services and how that positioning influences the effectiveness of the agency in its ability to carry out its mission had been long-standing. The AoA had sometimes been described as being "buried within the Office of Human Development Services since 1978" and it was widely believed that location in the hierarchy had a profound impact on the agency's ability to rise to its mission of becoming a focal point for all federal matters concerning the elderly.

A significant change took place when, on April 15, 1991, the Secretary of Health and Human Services, Dr. Louis W. Sullivan, announced that the Administration on Aging would become a separate operating component within the Office of the Secretary, reporting directly to the Secretary rather than, as previously, to the director of the Office of Human Development Services or later the Office of the Secretary. At the same time a new division was created, the Administration of Children and Families, charged with responding to the needs of other age groups.

It was recognized that repositioning of the AoA in HHS could result in meaningful change only if accompanied by sufficient operating funds to enable the AoA to implement its program. Additional funds would be necessary merely to provide the same level of support services that had been made available earlier through the Office of Human Development Services. The new arrangement did give the AoA the same organizational status in the department as that of the Social Security Administration, the Health Care Financing Administration, the Public Health Service and the Administration for Children and Families (U.S. Senate, 1991).

Although no reauthorization of the Older Americans Act occurred in 1991, Congress maintained the program through a "continuing resolution," extending it without altering either program or funding. It should be noted that the Older Americans Act was not singled out for delay but was caught up in widespread problems resulting from indecision regarding the federal budget. When reauthorization appeared to be imminent, Senator John McCain (R-AZ)

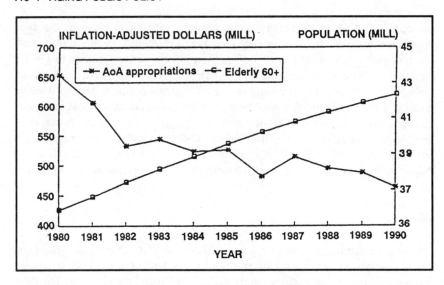

Figure 10. Trends in aging, 1980-90, AoA appropriations and aging population.
Source: U.S. House of Representatives Select Committee on Aging, 1991.

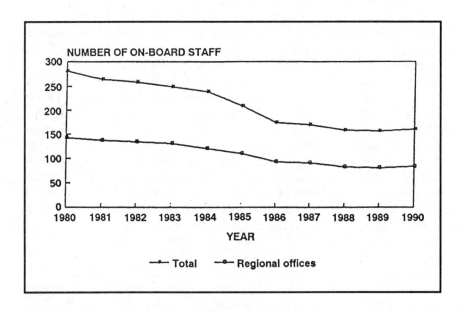

Figure 11. AoA staff, 1980-90. **Source:** U.S. House of Representatives Select
Committee on Aging, 1991.

introduced an amendment to remove the earnings test as part of the Social Security program and allow persons retiring at age sixty-five or older to continue to earn wages without any loss of Social Security benefits. This amendment was unrelated to the Older Americans Act, but procedures of the Senate permit the introduction of an amendment to bills introduced in the Senate. The Social Security earnings test had been revised several times and there appeared to be sufficient support for this further modification. The House of Representatives approved a revised amendment, but there was conflict in the Senate between those who supported it and those who were concerned that its passage would add to an already over-burdened federal budget. By mid-1992, reauthorization remained stalled by failure to advance the initiatives of the proposed amendments and indecision regarding when the next White House Conference on Aging should be held.

At the end of September 1992, through concerted efforts by advocates for the Older Americans Act, the McCain Amendment was defeated and the Older Americans Act Amendments of 1992 (PL102-375) were passed by Congress and signed by President Bush. These amendments reauthorized the act through 1995. Among the provisions was a rescheduling of the next White House Conference on Aging, which in 1992 had been indefinitely postponed by the Bush Administration.

1996

The 1991 reorganization of the Department of Health and Human Services raised the status of the Administration on Aging to be equal to that of the Social Security Administration, the Health Care Financing Administration, and the Administration of Families and Children. However, sufficient operating funds to implement the program did not accompany the status. In fact, the efforts to balance the budget in effect resulted in even less funding available for Older Americans Act activities. Appropriations for AoA FY 1997 totaled $830,168,000, compared with FY 1991 appropriations of $846,000,000 (less appropriation for Senior Community Service Employment).

The focus of public interest retreated from efforts to assist the elderly to efforts to balance the budget through cost containment. The 103rd Congress brought social legislation under close scrutiny, resulting in deep financial cuts to many federally funded social programs, not solely those for the aging.

The Older Americans Act was due to be reauthorized by the end of 1995. Efforts were made to revamp the OAA by giving block-grants to the states to provide services to the aging or to promote privatization of services, with emphasis on reducing the role of government.

To date the Older Americans Act has not been reauthorized; it remains a Congressional continuing resolution. The Senate Subcommittee of the Committee on Appropriations and the Senate Subcommittee on Aging of the Committee of Labor and Human Resources both examined proposed legislation and held numerous hearings. The House Subcommittee on Early Childhood, Youth and Families of the Committee on Economic and Educational Opportunities also held hearings on the Older Americans Act.

Advocacy on behalf of older persons has not been a high priority for congressional committees due to some extent to the disappearance of the House Select Committee on Aging. The result is that legislation relating to concerns of older Americans has simply not developed.

1997

Since the 104th Congress adjourned without having reauthorized the Older Americans Act, the 105th Congress sought the fourteenth reauthorization of the OAA. Senator Barbara Mikulski (D-MD) introduced S.390, the Administration's proposed bill, on March 4, 1997. Representative Matthew G. Martinez (D-CA) introduced H. R. 1671. Co-sponsors were Representatives Green (D-TX), and Filner (D-CA), and Senator Kennedy (D-MA). The proposals contained the same recommendations approved in legislative committee in the 104th Congress except for a proposal to the USDA to transfer cash in lieu of commodities to AoA and a proposal to transfer Title V (Senior Community Service Employment) from the Department of Labor to the AoA.

While the Older Americans Act is maintained as a continuing resolution, its funding for 1998 was approved with an increase of 4 percent over the previous fiscal year. This new budget will permit additional funds for home delivered meals, research and demonstration programs while maintaining other programs at the same funding level.

Table 4 summarizes the terms of commissioners who have served since the act was passed.

SUMMARY

It took more than twenty-seven years, from before the passage of the Older Americans Act until 1992, and required thirteen amendments of the act to establish the Administration on Aging as a discrete unit in the Department of Health and Human Services. Importantly, when this happened the Administration for Children and Families also was organized. This decision to create parallel organizations, rather than giving special status to the Administration on Aging made a significant statement regarding equity of responses to the needs of all age groups.

When we enhance the opportunities for older people we must do the same for younger persons.

The reauthorization process for the Older Americans Act provides an opportunity to reaffirm an intention to respond to the needs of this rapidly growing segment of our society. Clearly, a large majority of members of Congress support the act and can be expected to vote for its reauthorization. There is no indication of a movement to reverse the progress that has been made under the act since 1965. Yet funding to meet the needs of a growing population that also is growing older has never been sufficient to fulfill its declared mission.

The progress made over the years as a result of this act illustrates the incremental model of policy evolution. It also illustrates how relatively easy it is for policy makers to identify needs but how difficult it often is to provide the funds necessary to implement a program's intentions. The history of the Older American Act also illustrates the intrinsic duality of policy making, i.e., the authorization of programs and the authorization of funding for them are two different processes. Knowing of the need to address both issues is crucial to effective public policy activities.

Table 4. U.S. Commissioners on Aging

Nov. 1965-69	William D. Bechill
May 1969-73	John B. Martin
Jun. 1973-78	Arthur S. Flemming
Feb. 1978-81	Robert C. Benedict
Aug. 1981-84	Lennie-Marie P. Tolliver
Dec. 1984-86	Carol Fraser Fisk (Acting)
Aug. 1986-89	Carol Fraser Fisk
Apr. 1989-90	Joyce Berry (Acting)
Mar. 1990-93	Joyce Berry
Apr. 1993-96	Fernando Torres-Gil
Aug. 1996-97	Robyn Stone (Acting)
Apr.-Nov. 1997	Bill Benson, Acting Principal Deputy Assistant Secretary for Aging
Nov. 97-Present	Jeanette C. Takamura

CHAPTER
5

Interest and Advisory Groups

Interest and advisory groups are ubiquitous in our political system and are conspicuous parts of the aging network. They are located in the executive office, the bureaucracy, the legislature and in groups external to the government. They are recognized by government both because they contribute to the debate surrounding the development of policies responsive to the needs of older persons and because they clamor for benefits for their constituent interests. This chapter describes advisory groups functioning within governmental jurisdiction like the Federal Council on the Aging (FCA), discontinued in 1996, the White House Conference on Aging (WHCOA) and advisory groups to state units on aging and area agencies on aging as well as special interest groups that function outside of government (i.e., mass membership groups, provider groups and professional organizations). Within the government, the Senate Special Committee on Aging and the House Select Committee on Aging (discontinued in the 103rd session of Congress, 1993) had been significant advocacy groups, and have been mentioned in Chapter 2. All of these are considered advocacy groups on behalf of the elderly.

ADVISORY GROUPS

The aging network, established by the Older Americans Act of 1965 (OAA), includes a uniquely coordinated stream of agencies with significant participation from federal and state government (See Table 5). These include state and local community agencies. All participants in the network are charged with implementing services authorized by the act for people over the age of 60 years and they represent a relationship among the three levels of government that is not duplicated elsewhere. The federal government provides policies and funding, which are then augmented by the states through state plans and financing for implementation in local communities. In addition, a parallel structure of advisory groups

Table 5. Advisory Groups in the Aging Network

Governmental Level	Advisory Group
Federal The President and the Congress	White House Conference on Aging. The Federal Council on the Aging (discontinued in 1996).
State State Units on Aging	Advisory Groups to State Units or a Governor's Advisory Council or Commission
Local Area Agencies on Aging	Mandated Advisory Groups to the Area Agencies

serves at each level of government, providing an ongoing opportunity for citizen participation.

While clear organizational responsibilities have been defined for the administrative agencies, the expected interrelationships of the multiple advisory groups have not been clearly defined. Despite the value of having citizen advisory groups contribute to public policy in a democratic society, the potential positive impact of such groups may not be fully realized in the field of aging because of poorly defined relationships among groups and poorly stated expectations of the performance of advisory bodies. Often the relationship between an advisory group and its appointing authority are not sufficiently clearly established to ensure that the desired valuable contribution will be forthcoming.

It must be recognized that professional elitists may deliberately minimize the effectiveness of the advisory group function because they are uncomfortable with public expectations or legal requirements for advisory groups. Advisory groups sometimes may not have met society's expectations of performance because their value has been underestimated or because earlier advisory group recommendations regarding a national policy on behalf of the elderly have not been implemented.

The Older Americans Act of 1965 as amended over the years established a Federal Council on the Aging to advise the President and the Congress, a White House Conference on the Aging to advise the President, state advisory groups to the governor or the state office on aging (not mandated in the statutes), and advisory groups to each of 670 area agencies on aging. The composition of each of these groups is defined in the statutes and participants serve voluntarily by appointment.

No theoretical framework structures a uniform approach to the constitution and functioning of these approximately 720 advisory groups. Nor is there any mechanism to correlate activities at any one level of government with those at the other levels. Because there is no process by which the value of the national advisory groups can benefit from the cumulative contributions of the state and local advisory groups, the potential for advisory groups to achieve a concerted value through a program of integrated activities remains an unrealized goal.

While advisory groups are not unique to the aging network, the presence of a network of advisory groups in parallel with the administrative structure of Older Americans Act programs provides a unique opportunity for collaboration between citizen participation, congressional intent and bureaucratic implementation of programs. The unfulfilled opportunity for advisory group contributions on a national basis is disappointing, especially because it fails to replicate the successful administrative structure of Older Americans Act programs. Some ideas generic to all advisory groups are presented here to assist in strengthening the value of advisory groups.

In the aging network, as in other segments of our society, advisory groups can be classified as being either a task-oriented ad hoc group or a continuing (permanent) group set in place to review, question, and be consulted concerning the execution of programs and the policies that underlie them (Seidman, 1970).

Seidman also has pointed out that what government basically wants from advisory councils is not "expert" advice, but support. Council members may be expected to be missionaries for a program, perhaps lending respectability to one that is new or controversial (Seidman, 1970). But although advisory councils are inherently limited by their inability to enforce any decisions they make, their value does not rest only on their function as "window-dressing" to promote policies or programs. The usefulness of advisory councils has also long been recognized by the bureaucracy as bringing outside views to bear on new bureaucratic policies. Particularly in this era of increasing bureaucratic participation in policy-making, advisory councils can prove valuable in keeping bureaucrats in tune with public opinion (Fritschler, 1969).

This cannot be the whole story, however, for while advisory councils may provide one mode of access to the policy-making arena, they are not the sole avenue of expression through which affected individuals or groups can voice their concerns about federal programs or policies. Section 4 of the Administrative Procedures Act provides that (with some exceptions) public notice must be given of the opportunities available for interested persons to express their views on proposed agency rule-making before a final decision can be made. Councils therefore often merely formalize and legitimize arrangements which have already been established by earlier consultation (Seidman, 1970).

These functions constitute only a very small portion of either the many roles which advisory councils may perform or their reasons for being, however. A more complete listing includes:

1. Focusing public attention on a problem.
2. Conducting evaluations independent of government agencies.
3. Representing different viewpoints.
4. Utilizing expertise from the private sector.
5. Forestalling sudden, precipitous action (which is an important symbolic function for commissions/councils).
6. Increasing public pressure for action (Jones, 1984, p. 183).

If an advisory body is to put these stated purposes to good use, the internal make-up of a council becomes very important. To reflect the views of broad sectional, professional, economic, or social interests, a council should be acceptable to, and in good standing with, the organizations that represent those interests (Seidman, 1970). Furthermore, the ability of advisory groups to represent the views of a broad spectrum of the public can be successful only when a determined effort is made to include individuals who have divergent and even conflicting points of view (Fritschler, 1969).

The selection process for participation on an advisory council can help to ensure its broad scope and neutral integrity. Individuals may be attracted to service on advisory groups for any number of reasons, such as honor, prestige, influence, curiosity and opportunity for public service, but these may not be sufficient to qualify a person for membership (Seidman, 1970). Professional associations, federal agencies, and other interested groups can be called upon to help suggest people for council membership or recommend elimination of individuals from consideration. Such a selection process protects a council from attack on grounds that the membership was stacked against one or another particular interest (Fritschler, 1969).

Actually marshaling influence to initiate a change in policy brings in another set of factors, however. In order to move an issue from obscurity to the top of a government agenda, hard work, careful strategy and large portions of luck are necessary. The obstacles that stand in the way of change may be tremendous, and can . . . "range from the powerful inertia of tradition to forceful opposition from important individuals and groups who see some challenge to their fortunes in whatever policy change is contemplated" (Fritschler, 1969, p. 35). This is especially important in the aging network, where advisory groups can help to overcome these obstacles by bringing issues into focus and surfacing various viewpoints on a program or policy. They therefore can be a powerful force for positive change, making simultaneous presentation of viewpoints at the federal, state and local levels.

To illustrate this unusual opportunity, the Federal Council on the Aging, the White House Conference on Aging, both of which serve in an advisory capacity to the President and the Congress, and the advisory groups to state and area agencies on aging will be discussed. These are by no means the only advisory groups in the aging network but they do represent the major formally structured groups.

THE FEDERAL COUNCIL ON THE AGING

The Federal Council on The Aging was established by Congress in the Amendments to the Older Americans Act of 1973 and had as its purposes to:

1. Advise and assist the President on matters relating to the special needs of older Americans.
2. Review and evaluate, on a continuing basis, federal policies regarding the aging and programs and other activities affecting the aging conducted or assisted by all federal departments and agencies for the purpose of appraising their value and their impact on the lives of older Americans.
3. Serve as a spokesperson on behalf of older Americans by making recommendations to the President, to the Secretary, the Commissioner and to the Congress with respect to federal policies regarding the aging and federally conducted or assisted programs and other activities relating to or affecting them.
4. Inform the public about the problems and needs of the aging by collecting and disseminating information, conducting or commissioning studies and publishing the results thereof, and by issuing publications and reports.
5. Provide public forums for discussing and publicizing the problems and needs of the aging and obtaining information relating thereto by conducting public hearings, and by conducting or sponsoring conferences, workshops and other such meetings (from the Compilations of the Older Americans Act of 1965 and Related Provisions of the Law as Amended through September 30, 1985).

A history of the Federal Council on the Aging must begin with some background on its nominal precursor, the Federal Council on Aging (later designated as the President's Council on Aging). Although the original council was decidedly different in its purpose (it was an interagency coordinating body rather than an advisory body), it nonetheless handled some responsibilities that paralleled those of the current Federal Council on the Aging, such as providing annual reports to the President concerning all federal policies and programs dealing with the elderly. These two bodies actually coexisted for a time in the Department of Health, Education, and Welfare, and it was inevitable that one would wax while the other waned. The confusion that surrounded the delineation of the responsibilities of the two councils helped initiate the decline of the President's Council and its subsequent political demise.

1956-1962 (The Federal Council on Aging)

During President Eisenhower's administration, in 1956, concern for the problems of older persons in the country (a concern brought about by the marked extension in years of life expectancy and the lack of a coordinated public policy response to this phenomenon), resulted in the establishment of the Federal Council on Aging. It was initially put into place by a memorandum dated April 2, 1956 from President Eisenhower to the heads of various departments and agencies involved in aging policy. These department and agencies included the Treasury Department; the Department of the Interior; the Department of Agriculture; the Department of Commerce; the Department of Labor; the Department of Health, Education and Welfare; the Office of Defense Mobilization; the U.S. Civil Service Commission; the Office of Veterans Affairs; the Office of Housing and Home Finance; the Small Business Administration, and the National Science Foundation. The Federal Council was formulated in order to establish on a "broader and more permanent basis" the informal Interdepartmental Working Group on Aging, which had been initiated by various departments and agencies having special concerns in the field of aging. Representatives of these federal organizations made up an interagency council operating under the auspices of the Department of Health, Education, and Welfare. Its broad objective was to coordinate policy development, planning and programming so that departments and agencies could work together toward common goals with a minimum of duplication and wasted effort.

In 1959 the Federal Council on Aging was reconstituted at the cabinet level by a presidential letter dated March 7, 1959 to the Secretary of HEW, Arthur S. Flemming. This was done to strengthen the council's efforts to improve the effectiveness of federal programs in the field of aging. The council was now to be much more formally structured according to the President's design. The designated chairman was to be the Secretary of Health, Education, and Welfare, and membership was to include the Secretaries of Agriculture, Commerce, Labor, and the Treasury, and the Administrators of the Housing and Home Finance Agency and of Veterans Affairs. Other department and agency representatives who were not permanent members of the council were to be asked to participate when matters in their areas of responsibility came under consideration by the council.

1962-1973 (The President's Council on Aging)

On May 14, 1962 President John F. Kennedy abolished the Federal Council on Aging, establishing in its place the President's Council on Aging. The basic membership structure remained the same as the reconstituted Federal Council on Aging, with the exception that the chairperson of the Civil Service Commission was added as a new member. It seems clear that by reactivating the Council under an executive order with a new name more closely associating it with the chief executive, the President intended to give the council renewed political clout, backed up by the power of the executive office. The functions of the Council were reformulated under the executive order so that the broad objectives now were: 1) to study the overall federal responsibilities in the field of aging; 2) to identify those matters requiring coordinated action among departments and agencies; 3) to promote sharing of information on aging between federal agencies and between federal and state levels of government; and 4) to prepare a consolidated annual report to the President.

Despite this effort to invigorate the President's Council on Aging, a general decline in its activities that began in the autumn of 1965 can be attributed to the ignorance in Congress of the council's role and functions in the federal government.

Actually, the demise of the President's Council can be traced to the enactment of the Older Americans Act of 1965 (PL 89-73). This act had created a new agency (the Administration on Aging) within the Department of Health, Education, and Welfare to be headed by a Commissioner on Aging appointed by the President and confirmed by the Senate. Congress intended the new agency to serve as a focal point at the federal level for all matters concerning the aging. Although nothing about the President's Council or its staff was mentioned in the OAA, its intention was erroneously interpreted by some legislators, including those on the appropriations committee, as requiring the Commissioner on Aging and the newly created Administration on Aging to perform staff work for the President's Council on Aging. This misunderstanding led to the abolition of the council staff (which was functioning under the direction of the council's executive committee) because Congress subsequently refused to appropriate any more funds for it.

Language was included in the 1967 amendments to the Older Americans Act to rectify the situation and clarify responsibilities (i.e., . . . "The Secretary is authorized . . . to provide staff and other technical assistance to the President's Council on Aging"), but the damage had already been done. The Administration on Aging was able to provide only a fraction of the human resources needed to staff the executive committee fully and activity of the council steadily declined from this point on.

An undoubted source of much of the confusion during the period in 1965 when the President's Council was disabled was the Advisory Committee on Older Americans created by the Older Americans Act of 1965 (Section 701 of Title VII). Set up as a public advisory committee of the Office of the Assistant Secretary for Community and Field Services in the Department of Health, Education, and Welfare, its function was to advise the Secretary of HEW concerning national policies and programs to improve the well-being and status of the elderly. As a public advisory committee, its fifteen members were to be chosen by the

Secretary of HEW from persons outside of federal government who were knowledgeable in the field of aging, and the Commissioner on Aging was to serve as its chairperson. Members were to serve overlapping terms of three years, with meetings to be held on a quarterly basis. All administrative and staff support was to be provided by the Office of the Assistant Secretary for Community and Field Services.

In 1971, the White House Conference on Aging developed a broad range of issues, problems, and recommendations concerning the special needs of the elderly in this country. These went far beyond the scope of activities conducted by the Department of HEW and it became clear that a citizen advisory body tied to one specific department in the executive branch of the federal government could not accomplish the task at hand. However, instead of recognizing the usefulness of the President's Council on Aging as an appropriate coordinating body for federal aging programs and policies, legislators of both parties agreed upon a different tactic. When administration-sponsored amendments to the Older Americans Act were introduced in both houses of Congress on March 2, 1972, a provision was included to elevate the Advisory Committee on Older Americans from a departmental advisory committee to the stature and status of a presidential advisory group, and concurrently to discontinue the advisory group to the Administration on Aging.

1973-1996 (The Federal Council on the Aging)

The Advisory Committee on Older Americans was terminated by amendment to the Older Americans Act under the Older Americans Comprehensive Service Amendments of 1973 (PL 93-29) and its functions were designated to be absorbed by a newly created presidential advisory group, the Federal Council on the Aging. Further 1973 amendments to the Older Americans Act dealt the struggling President's Council another stunning blow, the repeal of Title VIII (which contained the language inserted in 1967 pertaining to the Council's staff). It has been suggested that many legislators may have been confused and erroneously concluded that the functions of the President's Council had been taken over by the new Federal Council on the Aging.

Thus, although the President's Council's identified function as a coordinator of interagency activity in aging issues had not been superseded by either the Advisory Committee on Older Americans or the new advisory council, it had in fact been rendered ineffectual. Although Commissioner John B. Martin stated in a memorandum dated January 8, 1971 that:

> The President's Council is an answer to the need for a mechanism to coordinate scattered federal activities in aging by improving communications between those who are carrying out these activities,

the Council remained essentially inactive after October 14, 1968, when the Executive Committee of the Council met for the last time.

On December 28, 1978 President Carter further modified the President's Council through an Executive Order. As had been the case with President Johnson's order in 1968, this order totally avoided addressing the problems plaguing the council and simply rearranged the membership. Finally, not long after a 1979 program analysis stressed the usefulness of reviving the President's Council as an active coordinating body, President Reagan issued an Executive Order which terminated the unlucky President's Council on Aging on August 12, 1982.

The difficulties encountered by the President's Council provide a useful lesson. The 1979 program analysis identified several difficulties which contributed to that body's eventual downfall. These included: 1) a lack of staff, which had hindered its ability to take any effective action; and 2) a lack of authority, which made it impossible for the President's Council to satisfy its mandated responsibility of interagency coordination, either through moral persuasion or coercion (Norman, 1982). According to Norman, these problems might have been corrected through a revised executive order, authorizing a small council that could form a nucleus for action and giving the council modest powers to enable it effectively to coordinate interagency activities. Such recommended reforms unfortunately did not occur. Some parallels can be drawn between this history and the current difficulties of the Federal Council on the Aging in meeting the objectives set out for it.

The Federal Council on the Aging was formally established on January 2, 1974. Unlike the Advisory Committee on Older Americans, which was set up to advise only the Secretary of HEW on matters concerning the elderly, the Federal Council's responsibility was to be much broader. As Senator Thomas Eagleton (D-MO) commented on October 12, 1972 from the floor of the Senate:

> . . . I want to emphasize that the term "advisory body" was deleted from the title in a conscious effort to make this body something more than the usual passive advisory council . . . We intend that the Federal Council on the Aging shall make vigorous efforts to serve as an advocate for older Americans across the whole range of the federal establishment (Congressional Record).

The Federal Council on the Aging (FCA), as the successor to the former departmental advisory body, continued to operate under the auspices of the Department of HEW, but in the Office of Human Developmental Services. The Council, like the advisory committee that preceded it, was to have fifteen members from outside the federal government. Their appointments were to be made by the President, with the approval of the Senate. (Appointment procedures were changed by amendments contained in the 1984 Reauthorization of the Older Americans Act so that the President now selected one-third of the members and Congress selected two-thirds in order to reflect the political spectrum better and to bypass delays that might be caused by the need for Congressional approval.) The members appointed were to be representative of rural and urban older Americans, national organizations with an interest in aging, business, labor, the general public (and were later expanded to include minorities, including members of Indian tribes). At least five persons (nine since the 1987 Reauthorization of the Older Americans Act) were required to be older persons. The chairperson of FCA was to be selected by the President from among the appointed members. The Federal Council on the Aging was mandated to meet at least quarterly and at the call of the chairperson. Various subsidiary units of FCA, to be chaired by members of FCA, were to be formed from year to year to deal with issues or problems as they were identified by FCA or the White House Conference on Aging or are mandated by Congress.

The most recent responsibilities of FCA are set forth in the Older Americans Act (as amended through 1987):

> The Council shall: 1) advise and assist the President on matters relating to the special needs of older Americans; 2) review and evaluate, on a continuing basis, federal policies regarding the aging, and programs and other activities affecting the aging conducted or assisted by all federal departments and agencies for the purpose of appraising their value and impact on the lives of older Americans; 3) serve as a spokesperson on behalf of older Americans by making recommendations to the President, to the Secretary, to the Commissioner, and to the Congress with respect to federal policies regarding the aging and federally conducted or assisted programs and other activities relating to or affecting them; 4) inform the public about the needs of the aging by collecting and disseminating information, conducting or commissioning studies and publishing the results, and by issuing reports; 5) provide public forums for discussing and publicizing the problems and needs of the aging and obtaining information relating to those needs by holding public hearings, and by conducting or sponsoring conferences, workshops, and other such meetings (Older Americans Act, Section 204, previously Section 205).

The Council was set up to have staff personnel, appointed by the chairperson, to assist it in carrying out its duties (in its last years there was one staff director and one assistant). The heads of other federal agencies and departments are to make available any other information and assistance required to help FCA in carrying out its responsibilities. (A brief summary of FCA's major activities since 1974 and a listing of the membership and budgets of FCA are in Appendices D and E.) The Council is further required to prepare an annual report to be presented to the President by March 31 of the ensuing year. The President is then obligated to transmit each of these reports to the Congress, along with comments and recommendations.

In addition to the identification of highlights of activities of the Council over the years the reader is provided, in the appendix, with a complete listing of the appointed members of the Council, staff directors, operating budget and President at the time of appointment. As the major national advisory group in the field of aging, it should be noted that the value of the Council can be correlated with the names of the appointees and the appointing President. Highly regarded leaders in the field of aging were appointed by Presidents (or leaders of Congress when the appointment procedure changed) who were themselves advocates for debate regarding major national issues in the field of aging. A review of the activities will also demonstrate a more targeted, comprehensive agenda with national significance pursued by Councils having appointees who were closely identified with national concerns and interests in the field of aging.

It should also be noted that funding for the Council had declined steadily from a high of $575,000 in 1976 and 1977 to a 1995 low of approximately $176,000, severely undermining the ability to generate studies that would have impact on national policies.

In the 1996 federal budget no money was allocated for the Council and without fanfare its activities were terminated. There was little evidence of any strong congressional support for the Council, especially with its limited funding and constrained agenda. Although there appears to be a consensus that a citizen's group providing advice to the federal government on aging concerns enables government to be more responsive, a positive attitude toward citizens involvement in government has not been correlated with the perceived value of the Federal Council on the Aging. The aging community generally appeared to feel that the Council had not contributed enough to warrant its continuation, or its budget.

The discontinuance of the Council in 1996 was met with silence, no ceremony, no complaints, and no effort to substitute any alternative structure for citizen involvement.

THE WHITE HOUSE CONFERENCE ON AGING

The 1995 White House Conference on Aging, with its theme "America Now and Into the 21st Century: Generations Aging Together with Independence, Opportunity and Dignity," was the fourth such conference and the last of the twentieth century. It was authorized by the 1992 Amendments to the Older Americans Act and was officially called by President Clinton on February 17, 1994.

White House conferences "are a venerable institution of the American government. The earliest was a White House Conference on conservation called by President Theodore Roosevelt in 1908" (Vinyard, 1979, p. 656). Other conferences have been held over the years on such topics as children, rural education, narcotics and drug abuse, and civil rights. Every conference has the imprimatur of the White House or the presence of the President. "This label heightens its visibility, lends an air of credibility to its deliberation, and cloaks its advice or recommendations with some officiality" (Vinyard, 1979, p. 657). The purpose of such conferences varies with the content area and the timing of the event. Some conferences prepare long wish lists that may serve as a planning agenda for years to come or, conversely, may hinder action by dispersing time and energy. Other conferences may be called to "cool things off" around some sensitive political issue or to put on the heat when focus on some problem is needed. Conferences also can be educational experiences for the participants or staged events designed to attract the attention of national news media.

Unlike the Federal Council on the Aging, which had a standing committee and recurrent appointments, a White House Conference on Aging must be specifically authorized by the Congress. A national conference on the aging in 1951 established a pattern and large national meetings on aging topics have been held in Washington in 1961, 1971 and 1981, and 1995. The reauthorization of the Older Americans Act of 1987 called for a White House Conference on Aging in 1991 and designated a nominal budget to initiate the planning. However, no date was established for the meeting, and it may have been that conflicting national agendas, the recent adverse experience with the Medicare Catastrophic Illness Law and problems with the federal budget deficits discouraged the Bush administration from establishing new goals for national activities that might be recommended by such a conference but which it probably would not support. Congressional reaction to the absence of a specific plan for the conference was slow and, when it came in 1991, it took the form of support for a new National Conference on Aging. In the face of opposition from the Bush administration, Congress established a 1993 conference date, appointing leadership for the conference staff and agreeing to have Congress and the President appoint an advisory committee for the conference. Congress was concerned lest a conference replicate the overpoliticized 1981 event and expressed a hope that the new advisory group would be able to control extremism while permitting and encouraging the expression of views on the issues foremost on the minds of the American public. After repeated postponements, the 1992 Reauthorization of the Older Americans Act called for a new White House Conference on Aging to be held no later than December 31, 1994. In fact, the conference was called by President Clinton in 1994 and held in May 1995.

The legislative authority for each of the successive conferences is presented below.

1951

The first national conference dealing with aging was convened in Washington, D.C. under the sponsorship of the Federal Security Agency. The conference attracted 816 delegates, dealt with eleven broad topics and became the prototype for future decennial conferences. The major outcome of the initial conference was to bring into focus the widespread problems faced by older persons in the United States. Deliberations of the conferees led to the creation of the first federal Committee on Aging and Geriatrics in the Department of Health Education and Welfare (successor in 1953 to the Federal Security Agency) but, unlike the conferences that were to follow, no long list of recommendations was prepared.

"Rather it was suggested that the conference could be judged a success if interest was maintained and if professional organizations developed activities" (Vinyard, 1979, p. 671).

1961

In 1958, Congressman John E. Fogarty (D-R.I.) introduced a bill that resulted in the first White House Conference on Aging in 1961 (National Association of State Units on Aging, 1985). The bill directed the special staff on aging of the Department of Health, Education, and Welfare to implement the conference with the assistance of the other departments and agencies represented on the Federal Council on Aging (the precursor to the Federal Council on the Aging). In addition, it was the intent of this bill to support states in conducting their own special conferences in preparation for the national meeting. This was an important difference from the 1951 meeting. States were to be given adequate time to collect information, organize conferences and agree upon recommendations to be made to the national meeting.

The bill cited the nation's increasing number of older persons as a pressing reason for the conference and noted that in 1900 there were three million persons over sixty-five years of age in the United States; in 1965 there were 14 million such persons; and it was predicted that by 1975 there would be 21 million.

Purposes of the conference included formulating recommendations for action to take advantage of the skills of older people, to improve living conditions and to further research on the problems of aging. A letter from the office of Management and Budget argued against the conference at that time, suggesting that the creation of the Federal Council on Aging and the holding of several conferences on aging had sufficiently increased awareness of the problems of the aging and negated the need for an additional conference. It was further argued that what was needed was research, experimentation and action at the local community and state levels (U.S. Senate Report No. 2363, 1958).

In spite of these objections, the conference was proposed under the administration of President Eisenhower and was implemented in the weeks following the election of John F. Kennedy but prior to the departure of President Eisenhower (Rich and Baum, 1984). Unlike the conference in 1951, this conference resulted from the Congress' having directed the President to call such a meeting.

Under the leadership of Arthur S. Flemming, the Secretary of the Department of Health, Education and Welfare, 2,800 delegates met to discuss 20 subject matter areas and make 947 recommendations. Giving the issue of health care major consideration undoubtedly contributed to achieving support for and the ultimate passage of Medicare in 1965.

The conference also established the importance of popular support for national public policies and provided the impetus for the development of the National Association of State Units on Aging and the National Council of Senior Citizens

(NASUA, 1982). For example, it was estimated that more than 103,000 persons took part in preliminary meetings throughout the country. In addition, "The beginnings of what later was enacted as the Older Americans Act have been traced to the 1961 White House Conference on Aging" (NASUA, 1985, p. 2). Aging issues began to appear on the platform of the major national political parties and activities to monitor success in implementing the recommendations of the conference were initiated.

1971

The call for the 1971 conference, made in 1968, directed the Secretary of Health, Education and Welfare to plan and conduct the conference with the cooperation of other federal agencies. The intent was to bring together representatives of federal, state and local governments as well as professional and lay people working in the field and older people themselves. This call to action enlarged upon the call of the earlier meeting by asking for the participation of a broader-based group of levels of government and older people.

Ensuring broad-based involvement became a central issue in preparing for this conference as the need for greater representation of minority groups in both planning and implementation became increasingly apparent. Dr. Flemming was chairperson of the conference, and under his leadership minority representation was significant and led to the subsequent rise of the National Center on Black Aged, the National Indian Council on Aging and the Association Nacional Por Personas Mayores. In addition, the National Association of Area Agencies on Aging and the Urban Elderly Coalition were initiated after this conference.

It is interesting to note that the report of the Committee on Education and Labor stated that "The committee cannot stress too strongly the importance that this conference be nonpartisan and removed completely from a political climate" (Committee on Education and Labor Report No. 1792, 1969). This statement forecast the increased politicization of the conference, as evidenced by the conflicting views of the Republican President and the Democratic Congress in 1971 and intense pressure for conformance to the administration's point of view at the 1981 conference.

Beginning in the fall of 1970 more than 6,000 forums with over one-half million participants were held in preparation for the 1971 meeting. These were followed by State White House conferences at which more than 38,000 participants were involved in making 663 recommendations. Issues of income maintenance became the primary focus of attention and recommendations dealing with nutrition, transportation, expansion of Medicare, housing and more flexible retirement policies were among the many made.

Following the conference, funding for the Older Americans Act was increased, the Supplemental Security Income Program was established, the House Committee on the Aging and the Federal Council on the Aging were formed, and legislation creating the National Institute on Aging was passed. Although none of these new activities can be called a direct outgrowth of the conference, it was successful in drawing attention to the major issues they addressed. In the words of Bechill, "It can be safely said that the 1971 conference helped set a positive environment for much of the major legislation enacted during the 1970s" (Bechill, 1990, p. 20).

1981

Authority for the 1981 conference was initiated in PL 95-478 when Carter was President but was implemented under the administration of Reagan. In this case a transfer of authority resulted in the mass dismissal of the existing staff which had worked since 1979 to prepare for the conference. Its members were replaced by Reagan and 400 additional delegates selected by the Reagan administration were appointed six months before the conference was to open to ensure that the perspective of the new administration would be visible.

In addition to these 400 newcomers, there were 1,800 delegates, 1,800 observers, 539 congressional appointees, and 150 state coordinators. In advance of the conference over 9,000 community forums, fifty-eight statewide conferences in states, territories and the Navajo Nation and forty-two mini-conferences had been held in 1980 and 1981 to explore specific areas of concern and provide data for the conference. The conference produced 668 recommendations, although some of the delegates complained that they feared being required to vote for all of the recommendations as a package rather than being able to identify their individual responses to each recommendation would obscure the objections many had to some of the recommendations.

The major issue of concern at the conference was Social Security. The charge was made that the Committee on Economic Well-being, which had jurisdiction over the issue, had been stacked with delegates favorable to the administration and its intent to reduce Social Security benefits. Unable to make any progress within that committee, opponents had some of their proposals introduced in other committees. An estimated 800 delegates who were unhappy with the manner in which the conference was being conducted met to air their protests on the evening of the second day of discussion. They were joined by Congressman Claude Pepper of Florida, the chairman of the House Select Committee on Aging who had been barred from the deliberations of the Committee on Economic Well-Being because he had not been assigned to it by the conference planners (Rich and Baum, 1984). This rump session demonstrated the resolve of its participants not to be manipulated on the issue of income maintenance and the mistake the conference leadership had made in denying Pepper access to this important committee. The next day Pepper was invited to participate in a dissidents' workshop and was influential in negotiating the wording of a resolution that urged Congress "to make every possible and fiscally reasonable effort . . . to maintain no less than the real protection which Social Security currently provides to all participants" (Rich and Baum, 1984, p. 34).

The final conference report further alienated many of the delegates by omitting many recommendations and omitting proposals that would have necessitated increased federal expenditures or that dealt with women's issues. Understandably, the desirability of ever having another White House Conference on Aging had become questionable. The admonition to avoid the politicalization of the conference stated in the legislation authorizing the 1971 conference had proved to be prophetic and public policies in the field of aging had become a significant political issue.

Bechill (1990) has said that the 1981 conference was the least satisfactory of the three that had been held and had slight impact on the formation of public policy. Johnson (1982) has commented that the conference demonstrated the capacity of the people to prevail in a democracy in spite of the efforts of the administration to exercise control. In comparing the 1971 with the 1981 conferences, Maddox (1982) found that the earlier one had more of the substance of democratic process, was better focused on key issues and focused on the development of public policy. Each of these commentators found some value in the 1981 conference but their criticisms point to the increasing difficulty of staging a national conference of this magnitude that is not complicated by the political agenda of the presidential leadership.

The history shows that holding of the conference at any time near a change of presidents should be avoided.

1995

Debate regarding the value of the conference continues. PL 100-175, the Older Americans Act of 1987, authorized the President to call a White House Conference in 1991. The conference was to be planned and conducted under the direction of the Secretary of the Department of Health and Human Services in cooperation with the Commissioner on Aging, the Director of the National Institute on Aging and the heads of other appropriate federal departments and agencies. The proposed 1991 conference was twice postponed and it was not until September of 1992 that OAA amendments of that year called for a conference no later than December 31, 1994. Cohen (1990, p. 27) has said that "White House Conferences, as a device for focusing national attention on an issue, are an ineffective, expensive anachronism" that may contribute to the delay of solutions to national problems." Conversely, Thursz (1989) has argued for holding a conference but one that "should serve to review both the successes and the failures of the nation to deal positively with the implications of aging" (pp. 30-31).

The United States should protect an increasing elderly population by providing more home and community based care and shielding existing benefit programs from cuts according to the final report of the 1995 White House Conference on Aging. The report also calls for an intergenerational aging policy that ensures continuing solvency of the Social Security system, endorses a greater investment in aging research, and embodies greater sensitivity to the nation's diversity.

The 590 page report entitled *The Road to an Aging Policy for the 21st Century* represents a composite of the entire White House Conference on Aging process, which involved more than 1,000 regional, state, and local grass roots events and a three-day national conference held in May of 1995. The report also contains comments by forty-six of the nation's governors on the issues raised at the WHCoA. More than 125,000 persons participated in the two-year process including 2,217 delegates at the national event.

The report is based upon the resolutions adopted at the national conference in May. These resolutions were the subject of more than 200 post-conference events, entitled "Turning Resolutions into Results." Participants in these events developed a series of implementation strategies for each of the resolutions.

The following issues were given the highest priority by Conference participants:

Social Security—strong support was registered for full maintenance of current benefits as well as for taking a comprehensive look at how to keep the system solvent now and for the next generation of beneficiaries.

Medicare and Medicaid—strong support was registered for preserving and protecting Medicare and Medicaid, particularly provisions for home and community-based care. Specific opposition was directed at block-grants for Medicaid, as well as the loss of entitlement status for millions of low income children, disabled, and elderly under Medicaid and using savings from Medicare and Medicaid to finance a tax cut.

Older Americans Act—strong support was registered at a number of post-conference forums for a multi-year reauthorization of all existing programs under the Older Americans Act. Especially noted were home-delivered and congregate meals, transportation, senior centers, in-home services, elder abuse prevention, and nursing home ombudsmen. Specific opposition was directed at any block-grants.

Research—strong support was registered for increased expenditures for all forms of aging research, especially that related to Alzheimer's disease as being an investment that will result in substantial long-term cost savings.

Diversity—the report notes that the number of minority elderly will double by the year 2030 and that plans must be made at all levels to ensure services and programs that are more sensitive to this dynamic. The report also notes the rapid growth in the number of *older women* and the special issues confronting them, especially related to health and economic security.

Long-Term Care—throughout the process strong sentiment was registered for making long-term care an essential element in future health care policies. This includes developing home and community based alternatives to institutional care and expanded private long-term care insurance.

Grandparents as Caregivers—the report notes that three million grandchildren are being raised by their grandparents and calls for new and or improved State and Federal laws to help grandparents in this caregiver role.

Senior Volunteers—the report calls for the development of public and private partnerships that provide resources to support senior volunteer efforts in communities across the country. It specifically calls for the Corporation for National Service to recruit and enroll one million senior volunteers by the year 2000.

In addition, the final report directs special attention to issues related to older Veterans; the need for closer policy and service links between the aging and disabled communities; the need for persons to assume greater responsibility for their own health; the strengthening and expanding of public-private partnerships in aging; and improving the media's coverage of aging and the elderly.

It is possible that a long list of recommendations cannot be expected to be sufficiently focused or to be able to follow up and monitor the outcomes of recommendations, even if there is intrinsic value in a large meeting that attracts public attention to issues in an aging society without regard for the recommendations or their implementation. Perhaps a new format might be one in which recommendations of state meetings or mini-conferences could be funneled into a small national working group to establish a priority list of recommendations that would then be reported to the public. Although smaller meetings throughout the country would not have the impact or visibility of a large national meeting, it is arguable that they might equally well call attention to the nation's concern for the elderly.

While it is extremely difficult to evaluate the impact on public policy of such a large conference or to attribute policy changes to one large national event, the absence of any palpable outcome other than an extensive report is significant. The conference was directed by a President affiliated with the Democratic Party during a period when Congress was controlled by Republicans. Resolutions of the conference clearly favored the Democratic agenda. There was no strong opposition from the delegates, but the world outside the halls of the conference hotel did not seem to note the event or the issues. Congress proceeded with its own agenda on issues of Medicare, Medicaid, and the Older Americans Act. The Older Americans Act was not reauthorized, funding for services had declined, funds for new demonstration programs had been reduced, the full protection of Social Security had not been assured for the future, Medicare expenditures had been reduced and the identified spearhead for Congressional leadership on aging issues was missing.

It appears that the format of a decennial presentation of major public policy issues and resolutions no longer is appropriately responsive to the demographic changes in our older population, families, work, health, and leisure time opportunities. A new approach to the involvement of the public's voice in policy formation in aging has to be identified.

ADVISORY GROUP TO THE ADMINISTRATION ON AGING

The Older Americans Act established an advisory Committee on Older Americans in the Department of Health, Education, and Welfare consisting of the Commission on Aging and fifteen persons appointed by the Secretary. Because it was believed that federal-level concern for older persons should not be restricted to this department, the advisory council to the Secretary was replaced by the National Advisory Council on the Aging in 1972. This new group was to be appointed by and report to the President. It was ultimately replaced by the Federal Council on the Aging, which reported to the President and to the Congress and therefore was not directly advisory to the Administration on Aging, which might be more effective if it had a national bipartisan advisory group to review proposed initiatives and build a consensus for the higher priorities for action.

ADVISORY GROUPS TO THE STATE UNITS ON AGING AND AREA AGENCIES ON AGING

Unlike the Federal Council on the Aging or the White House Conference on Aging, state and area agencies are directly related to the implementation of the Older Americans Act and therefore are expected to communicate the needs and interests of older persons as determined through surveys, public hearings, interviews or other outreach methods. It is this information that in turn determines the content of required multi-year work plans and decisions regarding what services are to be provided.

A state agency is to:

> ... provide assurances, satisfactory to the Commissioner, that the state agency will take into account, in connection with matters of general policy arising in the development and administration of the state plan for any fiscal year, the views of recipients of supportive services or nutrition services, or individuals using multipurpose senior centers provided under such plan ... (and) conduct periodic evaluations of, and public hearings on, activities and projects carried out under the State plan, including an evaluation of the effectiveness of the State agency in reaching older individuals with the greatest economic or social needs, with particular attention to low-income minority individuals (Public Law 100-175, 1987).

Regulations regarding the Older Americans Act also require that, "The state must have a mechanism to obtain and must consider the views of older persons in developing and administering its state Plan." In most states this takes the form of an organized state advisory group, about one-third of which report to the governor of the state, one third to the director of an umbrella agency in which the state unit is located and the balance report directly to the state unit.

In contrast to the expectations of a state unit, an area agency is required by the act to have an advisory council

> . . . consisting of older individuals (including minority individuals) who are participants or who are eligible to participate in programs assisted under this Act, representatives of older individuals, local elected officials, providers of veterans' health care (if appropriate), and the general public, to advise continuously the area agency on all matters relating to the development of the area plan, the administration of the plan and operations conducted under the plan (PL 100-175, 1987).

The regulations attached to the statute also call for the advisory group to assist in the development and coordination of community-based systems of services for older persons and require that the advisory group review the area plan before it is submitted to the state. The structure and reporting of these advisory groups differ according to the organizational location of the agency. From a survey conducted of the activities of advisory groups, it was learned that some may be in local government, others in a Council of Governments (COG), still others in a freestanding not-for-profit agency. There are about 730 advisory groups to the state and area agencies with a total of about 14,500 persons involved. This large number of persons represents a formidable group of knowledgeable citizens mostly over age sixty participating in the implementation of Older Americans Act programs (Koff, 1991).

Since only members of advisory groups of state and area agencies were included in the survey from which these data were drawn, advisory groups to RSVP or other aging programs or members of the Silver Haired Legislatures throughout the country are not represented. It is safe to say that there exists a group of volunteers numbering far in excess of 14,000, residing in both rural and metropolitan areas of every state, who are mostly over age sixty and who are all potential participants in a senior advocacy program operated by seniors. There is no evidence either that any such coordinated advocacy program is currently taking place or that there is any reason to expect strong resistance to such an effort. Leaders of state and area agencies certainly would like to find ways to use their advisory groups more effectively to advocate for positive change in the provision of services and resources for older persons in the community.

Recent surveys (Koff, 1991) provide some insights into the sources of problems and suggest directions for improving the value of advisory groups in the aging network. Although there are some exemplary situations where considerable staff efforts are provided, where members are carefully selected and nurtured in their advisory role and where clear expectations are transmitted to the members, they are exceptions to the national experience. For example, over 50 percent of the groups meet less frequently than monthly, with 25 percent meeting quarterly; only

20 percent meet monthly or more frequently. With turnover of membership and the need for education and involvement in many issues, meeting less frequently than monthly cannot be expected to produce strong, well prepared advocacy agents.

All area agencies have written bylaws to direct the activities of the advisory groups, yet many report that they are not uniformly administered. For example, even where terms of office are clearly described they often are not enforced. In some agencies the bylaws have not been reviewed or renewed recently enough to ensure that they are current.

Almost all agencies report that they provide assistance to their advisory groups, ranging from providing a meeting place and sending meeting notices to offering professional staff assistance with agendas for meetings, content of programs, education of members and assistance with advocacy efforts.

While many advisory groups reported the availability of orientation programs for new members, orientation frequently consisted simply of a review of procedures for reimbursement for travel, reading of the bylaws and introduction to the area plan. Ongoing training often was limited to an occasional speaker bringing current information. Specific training for advocacy was rarely mentioned.

Advisory group members have potential political clout, since 41 percent receive appointment from an elected official, but only 16 percent report that they are responsible to a public official.

It appears, then that the requirement for advisory groups is met but that such groups are ineffectively used as advocates on behalf of the elderly. Widespread complaints about the ineffectiveness of advisory groups and their members contribute to self-fulfilling prophesy when minimal effort is given to appointing the most effective community members, minimal effort is provided for education and training, and minimal expectations are communicated regarding the contributions of the participants. Consequently, advisory groups may indeed have been found to be ineffective as advocates in spite of the fact that in terms of their age, identification with services for the elderly, familiarity with problems, political and community associations, they represent a major source of senior advocacy by and for older persons.

Furthermore, there is little interaction among advisory groups nationally and among advisory groups to area agencies and state agencies. Local agenda items do not necessarily become the agenda for state advisory groups and neither the agenda items for the state or area agency advisory groups became the focus of interest of the Federal Council on the Aging. The relationship that exists among the federal, state and local area agencies within the aging network is not replicated in a nationwide structure of advisory groups, even though there exist advisory groups at each of these levels.

There is, moreover, no vertical structure that links these groups or that advances the issues of concern at the local level into the policy process at the national level. An enormous potential has not been tapped. It might be possible, for example, to correlate the activities of the local and state advisory groups and communicate the major issues and recommendations to an advisory group to the Administration on Aging, thereby providing feedback and increased value to a coordinated structure of advisory groups. Such an organizational plan would parallel the federal, state and area agency relationship currently functioning under the Older Americans Act and provide valuable input for a decennial national conference on aging.

INTEREST GROUPS

Interest groups that advocate on behalf of the elderly significantly influence age-related legislation, as has been discussed in an earlier chapter. Although our free society takes for granted that people should be able to pursue their own self-interest and unite with others who agree with them, interest groups can be detrimental if policies that result from their advocacy efforts are detrimental to other groups or to the country as a whole. "In a system such as ours, interest groups constantly push government to enact policies that benefit small constituencies at the expense of the general public" (Berry, 1984). On the other hand, if there were no interest groups, would the needs of any special group, no matter how small or large, be met?

The founders of our society not only assumed that checks and balances would prevent the dominance of power by any single group, they also recognized the presence of interest groups

> . . . as both necessary and dangerous to democracy. James Madison wrote in the Federalist Papers about the "mischiefs of faction," the danger of selfish interest groups working against the good of the community as a whole (Day, 1990, p. 5).

They were, however, unable to predict the size and power of some contemporary interest groups, the persuasiveness of funds generated on behalf of an issue by powerful interest groups or their capacity to generate votes. As has been pointed out by Day (1990, p. 3), "There are more than 1,000 aging-based groups in the United States at the national, state and local levels, not including more than 5,000 local chapters of national organizations." That number represents the potential for powerful advocacy efforts if all were oriented to advocacy efforts and could join in a common agenda.

One of the earliest and most influential age-related interest groups was known as the Townsend Movement, named for its founder, Dr. Francis Townsend. This depression-era, pre-Social Security program had at its peak a membership of over two million, more than 10 percent of Americans then over sixty years of age (Day, 1990). The plan called for a $200 per month pension for persons sixty years of age or older, to be spent with thirty days in order to stimulate the economy. The movement gave impetus to the need for a national social security program, and it declined rapidly following the passage of Social Security.

Day attributes the origin and maintenance of aging-based interest groups to at least four factors: 1) the sense of common needs and interests, 2) the leadership of organizational "entrepreneurs," 3) the variety of incentives offered to members, and 4) patronage by government agencies and private foundations. All of these are characteristic of the interest groups advocating for the elderly that have attracted large membership and survived for a long period of time. Expansion of the aging population and its members' increasing dependency on federally sponsored programs such as Medicare and Social Security have created a bond of special interest. Aging organizations have responded with policy positions in support of these programs and leaders of these groups have become identified as spokespersons and entrepreneurs for their causes. Interest groups have maintained their commitment to the issues most important to older persons while the most successful groups have broadened their agendas to include support of an array of federal and state policies, and have offered additional benefits to their memberships.

The balance of interests in our society is threatened if decisions are influenced more by the amount of money expended to promote an issue than by the merits of arguments on behalf of that issue. This has become of increasing concern because of the persuasiveness of television as a vehicle for communicating to the masses and the high cost of good television presentations. Interest groups are most valuable when they undertake to educate the community and to invite others to join in their cause and participate in the political process. Such groups can bring an important issue to the forefront and place it on the public agenda and can monitor the performance of public officials.

Some criticism has been lodged against the special interest groups advocating on behalf of the elderly, who have been accused of soliciting too large a share of the public resources while neglecting the needs of other segments of the total society. Advocates for older people have won some significant battles, but they have lost others. Advocacy on behalf of aging issues has successfully influenced policies reducing the incidence of poverty among the elderly, assuring the continuity of important programs, and bringing to attention important changes in the make-up of the older population and the need to respond to these changes. It can be argued that advocacy on behalf of the elderly has not resulted in the neglect of other needs in our society but has simply done its job, namely, to promote policy decisions that are important to the elderly population.

Interest groups do not function in a vacuum but merely are one component of the complex political process of interrelating with other advocates. Organized political activity, according to Truman (1971), arises when a group perceives its interests to be threatened or disturbed, as has been the case when Social Security benefit reductions have been threatened and mass political movements were organized by interest groups to circumvent changes.

Fosler (1990) identifies three variables that determine how choices will be made in response to advocacy for the elderly. The first of these is the political strength of those who are most likely to benefit from the programs, older people, their family members who otherwise would bear a greater burden of support, and the general population who want the elderly to be cared for properly.

"The second variable is the political strength of those who have alternative claims on the resources required to support elderly programs" (Fosler, 1990, p. 184). This would include taxpayers who would prefer to have their taxes benefit some other segment of the society. It is in this arena of conflicting requests for limited resources that priorities are established.

The third variable is the political culture in which the conflicting issues must be resolved. Because there is a well established consensus that Social Security, in addition to being good for older persons, is generally good for the society at large, the program finds wide support. This response may be based on the society's acceptance of responsibility to care for its elders. Also implied however, is a widely held belief that old persons are frail and unable to support themselves and that they therefore require community support. This conception inaccurately represents the majority of older persons and also establishes a rationale for support of the elderly that cannot be defended.

It is clear that programs that support the elderly actually are programs that support families. Policies that help the aging also assist family members who otherwise would have to apportion a greater portion of their income and time to older relatives. Aging-related interest groups should clearly enunciate the importance of their efforts in support of families and should openly advocate for policies directed toward just distribution of resources among those who are in need. Social needs of members of the society who are not adequately represented by interest groups should enlist the support of the aging related groups in areas where they have mutual concerns. The call for social justice has to be made for all and by all.

Interest groups may be categorized in two different ways: 1) the recipients of services, and 2) service providers. It is important to note the respective roles of each of these groups and to recognize that legislators and policymakers pay more attention to advocacy efforts made by recipients than those made by providers. Provider advocacy efforts may be suspect because they may be perceived as reflecting self-interest in protecting employment.

While advocacy efforts by older persons on their own behalf are the most persuasive, groups whose membership depends on age alone may not accurately represent all their members' interests. Like members of any other segment of the population, older individuals have a wide range of individual, political and social values. It is highly unlikely that any really large group can speak for all of its members on any one issue. This means that a group may arrive at a consensus regarding members' interests or reflect the concern of the group for a generalized issue, such as the improvement of health care services, without agreeing on how implementation will be delivered or financed.

The large number of existing aging advocacy groups have many diverse points of view and have made possible coalitions focused on issues of shared concerns, thereby strengthening the advocacy effort. Multiplicity of interest groups is to be encouraged in our society, because it ensures representation of the many disparate views and associations that occur in a heterogeneous society. While the presence of many advocacy groups complicates the advocacy process and ensures presentation of diverse points of view, all points of view may not be represented. For example, at the national level, the Congress, because of its heavy workload, welcomes the opportunity to solicit and receive a collective advocacy position that may not be all-encompassing rather than having to solicit individual expressions of interest.

Furthermore, any group acting in its own self interest may not accurately represent the varied points of view of its entire membership, and the larger the group the more difficult it is for it to represent all of its members accurately. Binstock (1972) reinforces this point and cautions that groups which identify themselves as spokespersons for older persons may be perceived as dubious if they seem to be motivated by self-serving issues and organizational maintenance. As middlemen, advocacy groups that have made it easier for the federal bureaucracy to obtain information and support for agenda issues have received financial support for their causes. But dealing with interest groups instead of individuals may have caused federal agencies to narrow their perspectives and ignore large numbers of persons not represented by interest groups.

Of great importance in an advocacy group's ability to represent its members is the clarity of its stated mission and individual members' identification with that mission. For example, a group whose mission is to favor a specific piece of legislation will attract members who share in that interest (i.e., the National Committee to Preserve Social Security). If this group chooses to expand its policy agenda and include issues other than Social Security, it may no longer represent all its members unless the membership confirms its support of the enlarged agenda. Conversely, members in a group attracted by group travel plans may not share a common political philosophy or support a particular piece of legislation, making invalid any claim that the number of its members represents the number of persons who support a certain political issue.

Interest groups played an especially important role in the preparation for the 1971 White House Conference on Aging, when it was reported "that the threat of an interest group boycott of the conference was a major weapon in wringing concessions from a reluctant administration" (Pratt, 1974, p. 106). Interest groups had established themselves as middlemen in the relationship between the elderly and the bureaucracy, and this movement was to continue and be strengthened in successive years. Pratt also attributed the success of aging-related interest groups to increased managerial skills, subsidies from outside sources, focusing of energies through efficient and goal-oriented bureaucracies, and providing members something in addition to advocacy. The last of these sometimes has taken the form of non-policy activities which benefit older persons whether or not they are members.

The conflicting values of advocacy groups are apparent in the composition of the two Congressional advocacy groups, the Senate Special Committee on Aging and the House Select Committee on Aging (discontinued in 1993). Both include members of the major political parties who represent different political agendas but are identified as advocates on behalf of the elderly. In their role as advocates, individual committee members may vote in favor of an age-related issue even if it differs from their own party's platform. Because they are not legislative committees, these two committees can serve as primary advocacy groups within the Congress on behalf of the elderly. They may not always concur as to methods and they are not the only advocates for aging services in the Congress. Others may be found among the general membership of both houses, as well as on their appropriations or authorizing committees.

AGING INTEREST GROUPS

Congressional Committees with Special Interest in Aging Issues

Earlier it was pointed out that the Congress was structured with both standing and select or special committees and that a select or special committee is investigative rather than legislative. In addition to the standing committees that deal with issues related to the elderly, each house of Congress also has a special committee that is specifically focused on the issues of aging.

Senate Special Committee on Aging

First established as the Subcommittee on Problems of the Aged and Aging in 1959, the Senate Special Committee on Aging was created in 1961, mostly through the efforts of Senator Patrick V. McNamara (D-MI), who was concerned that, although a number of committees of the Senate dealt with some issues of concern to the elderly, none of these was able to deal comprehensively with questions that required thorough and systematic consideration of the interrelated nature of problems of aging. According to S 33 establishing the committee, no proposed legislation would be referred to it, nor would it have the power to report bills or otherwise have legislative jurisdiction (U.S. Senate, 1961). The original nine-member committee was increased to twenty-one members in March 1961 and was reauthorized each session of Congress until given permanent status in 1977. It now has nineteen members and no subcommittees.

Pratt (1979) noted that the Senate Special Committee on Aging was atypical among special committees of the Senate in that it was neither short-lived nor lacking in legislative impact, probably because the committee could serve as a vehicle for Senators appointed to it to manifest their sympathies for the elderly and gain national visibility.

The House Select Committee on Aging

On October 2, 1974 the House of Representatives approved the establishment of a special committee, comparable to the Senate Special Committee on Aging but having the status of a permanent committee (Rich and Baum, 1984). A recommendation to establish this committee was made at the 1971 White House Conference on Aging. The committee was initiated with twenty-eight members, had grown to sixty-six members and had six subcommittees: Retirement Income and Employment, Health and Long Term Care, Housing and Consumer Interests, Human Services, a Task Force on Rural Elderly, and a Task Force on Social Security and Women.

While neither the Senate nor the House special committees have legislative authority they do have oversight functions, may conduct investigations and may hold hearings in order to learn about problems and create interest in possible solutions. Through their membership on other standing committees, members of these special committees may be able to introduce legislation and carry the message of the special committee throughout the committees of Congress. Of special importance are the authorizing committees, responsible for developing legislation in specific policy and program areas. The House Select committee on Aging was discontinued in 1993 and was replaced by a caucus on aging issues.

The ability to advocate effectively for an issue depends on being able to identify where (and when) to influence the legislative process. Advocates for aging issues are advised to interact with the committees and subcommittees that have jurisdiction over the various domains affected by aging legislation. This involves developing good working relations with key House and Senate staff members on the committees of interest who work behind the scenes to "develop and shape legislation on issues of concern to older Americans" (Advocates Senior Alert Process, 1987, p. 1). A listing of these Congressional committees and subcommittees is included in Appendix A.

As was noted earlier, the action of Congress is frequently the action of committees. Congress is not a single body but rather an amalgam of multiple committees and subcommittees having specific areas of responsibility as well as competence. Since many of our public policies are generated in the congressional committees it is important that every advocate on behalf of aging policies have access to a listing of the major committees and understand their areas of responsibility. With this knowledge, an advocate for the special interest that a group represents will know where to direct its advocacy efforts with the greatest likelihood of reaching the appropriate responsible committee.

Private Interest Groups

Interest groups differ according to the composition of their membership, their purpose and their size. A mass-membership organization of older persons for which advocacy can be considered a direct expression of the interests of the older population is the National Council of Senior Citizens. Another major mass interest group is the American Association of Retired Persons whose members are interested in a variety of services in addition to their advocacy on behalf of the elderly. Other advocacy groups act as public interest organizations or trade associations representing the providers of services to older persons rather than directly representing the targeted population. The American Association of Homes and Services for the Aged and the American Healthcare Association are such groups. These groups can be considered elitist, in that they speak from the point of view of those who have special knowledge of what is needed by older persons gained through working with them on a regular basis. Service providers can also speak to problems created by constraining regulations or the inadequacy of reimbursement rates.

There also are some groups which, while not specifically representing or primarily serving older persons, advocate for the elderly from a sense of justice. Certain groups may advocate *against* the enhancement of services to the elderly because they are concerned about costs, sources of funds to finance a program, or negative outcomes for their own membership and special interests. As an illustration, the American Medical Association has advocated against some proposed improvements to health care services for the elderly, claiming that such programs would result in a decline in the quality of medical care available to the elderly.

Yet another category of interest groups includes professional associations whose members' interest in aging is related to their research or teaching activities. The Gerontological Society of America and the Association of Gerontology in Higher Education are such groups.

Whether mass membership, service provider or research-oriented, each of these groups has a direct stake in public policies that impinge upon their own areas of concern related to the needs and views of the older population and each is in competition to receive a share of public funds available to implement services, research or teaching.

There is a temptation for federal bureaucrats to simplify their work of negotiating contracts by using national groups as middlemen. This helps senior groups by funding part of their overhead and advancing their organizations' programs. But, in so doing, government officials sacrifice a needed independence of judgment and risk a distortion of the national sense of priorities. Working with certain interest groups also tends to exclude from any benefits the numbers who are not represented by the interest group.

A brief description of thirty-nine of the major interest groups in the field of aging as well as some groups whose public policy positions frequently intersect with policies related to the elderly are included in Appendix F.

With this large number of organizations representing diverse interests it is difficult to find opportunities for coordinated activities among all of the groups. Membership in 1998 had risen to forty-two national organizations.

Leadership Council on Aging

"In the early 1970s the leadership of the national aging organizations began to look to each other for help in responding to some of the more controversial issues coming their way" (NASUA, 1985). Of major concern were the agenda for the 1971 White House Conference on Aging, the proposed elimination of the Senate Special Committee on Aging and the proposed reduction in federal expenditures on behalf of the elderly. At a 1978 meeting held by twenty-two of the groups to develop an Ad Hoc Coalition of Leadership Organizations it was realized that such a coalition "was able to exert a collective influence far beyond that which each member organization could accomplish on its own, and it came to be identified widely by policymakers as a credible and legitimate spokesman for the elderly" (NASUA, 1985).

In 1980 the Ad Hoc Coalition was reconstituted and named the Leadership Council of Aging Organizations (LCAO). The chair of the LCAO is rotated annually among the four members with the largest number of subscribers, American Association of Retired Persons (AARP), National Council on The Aging (NCOA) and National Council of Senior Citizens (NCSC), American Association of Homes and Services for the Aged (AAHSA). While each of the affiliated interest groups has developed its own agenda and strengths, together they acknowledge that their combined strength will be most fully realized in the political process. Coalition building itself will be most effective if it reaches beyond the association of aging-related groups and finds allies among what Day (1990, p. 34) refers to as "shifting coalitions organized temporarily around single issues."

Since aging-based interest groups must compete in the public sector for limited resources, it is not surprising that recent criticism has charged these groups, and older persons, with taking too large a share of public resources, thereby depriving other age groups. While aging-based interest groups must continue to implement their mission of meeting the growing needs of the older population, their accumulated source of power can be effectively used to support the identification of other unmet needs in society and advocacy on their behalf. Evidence of emerging coalition building that represents a wider constituency can be seen in the group called Generation United that includes the National Council on the Aging and the Child Welfare League in addition to a large number of other groups.

Role of the Media

The power of the press, radio and television should not be overlooked in a consideration of advocacy efforts in the public sector. Especially important is the influence of a journalist who has made a specialty of covering issues related to the older population and has advocated on its behalf.

Voting Experience of Older Persons

Interest groups have considerable power when they are able to commit their memberships to vote. Interest groups also have vote-getting capacity from non-members when they advocate for positions favorable to large numbers of older persons. This vote generating capacity gets the attention of legislators, but the effectiveness in directly influencing elections is uncertain. Incumbents seldom are defeated or new legislators selected on the basis of their position on age-related issues (Lammers, 1983). Nevertheless, the fear of sanctions by individual older persons, especially members of prominent advocacy groups, has to be considered by elected officials. "Politicians often are reluctant to vote against the expressed interests of older persons regardless of the extent to which a likely voter sanction can be demonstrated" (Lammers, 1983, p. 56).

Politicians are sensitive to the reality of the voting record of older persons, especially when that record is compared with that of other age groups. For example, in 1988, twenty million of the 102 million who reported voting in the presidential election were sixty-five years of age or older. The percentages for the age groups fifty-five to sixty-four and sixty-five to seventy-four were twice as those of the eighteen to nineteen age group. Voting participation does decline for those over the age seventy-five, but members of this age group are still more likely to vote than those younger than thirty-five (U.S. Senate, 1990). The reported voting record for various age categories in 1994 are displayed in Figure 12.

Cutler (1977) notes that there is no established pattern indicating that older persons withdraw from political activity at any designated age. In fact, voting is one area of political activity that attracts increasing attention as people age. And, as aging individuals recognize the special burdens of aging and their need to rely on federal policies to cope with these burdens, they are more likely to take a group benefit approach to political issues as well as to pay increased attention to their voting.

Summary

Interest group advocacy has emerged as a formidable presence in the field of aging, whether it comes from within the Congress as a function of the special and standing committees, from advisory groups generated by the aging network, from providers of service or from the many private groups representing the interests of the recipients of services—older persons and their families and providers of services. The presence of advocacy activities must continue to be anticipated, especially because policymakers welcome any display of interest that supports their own political philosophy and depend upon the involvement of a variety of groups both to inform them about the views of the electorate and to supply

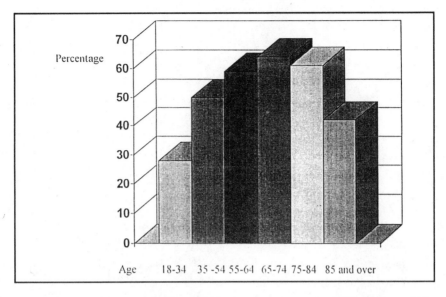

Figure 12. Percentage who reported voting, by age group: 1994. **Source:** U.S. Bureau of the Census, June 4, 1996.

technical assistance that is critical to effective public policy. The role of an advocacy group and its value in the political process depends upon the size of the group, its representativeness of the population, and its level of expertise. Increasingly, the strength of advocacy efforts will be measured by what Day (1990) called shifting coalitions around changing agendas.

If the successes in advancement of aging policy favors older persons over other groups, then we must collectively bear the responsibility for having permitted less than adequate advocacy efforts on behalf of the poor, the homeless, those without health care coverage and those who have been denied access to the benefits of our society.

SUMMARY OF PART TWO

The Older Americans Act and its collateral advisory groups and national conference represents a unique contribution of public involvement in community organizations and advocacy on behalf of a special age group, namely older persons. The Older Americans Act has provided both national and local focal points for greater involvement of additional governmental and private sector agencies by establishing an interrelationship of groups and agencies known as the aging network.

PART THREE

Major Public Policies
on Behalf of the Elderly

CHAPTER
6

Social Security

In 1985, Americans celebrated fifty years of Social Security. Four years earlier Germany had already celebrated the 100th anniversary of its social security program. Why did the United States wait so long to offer income protection to its elderly citizens? Why was Germany seemingly so many years ahead of the United States in providing this security net? An examination of these questions should increase our understanding of this important legislation.

PRECEDENTS TO SOCIAL SECURITY

Germany's early entry into governmentally sponsored social insurance was due in part to Europe's relatively rapid shift from a rural agrarian barter economy to an urban industrial wage-based economy. This economic evolution has been attributed to the maturity of European governmental infrastructures and the need for the technology to accommodate an ever expanding population base dependent on a finite supply of agricultural land (Schottland, 1963). However, the decline in the number of farmers who could feed and support their families directly from the land they tended and the increasing numbers of factory and warehouse employees dependent on money wages paid caused a new and widespread form of hardship. For wage earners, being unable to work due to having been laid off or fired or having become too old or too sick to continue working resulted in immediate economic distress.

The suffering associated with this societal transition gave rise to a large socialist movement in western Europe (Schottland, 1991). In 1881 Chancellor Otto von Bismarck, faced with the challenge of stemming the tide of socialism sweeping his country, saw that the concept of social insurance outlined by Daniel Defoe (author of *Robinson Crusoe*) and others offered a way to encourage loyal support of the national government. The program instituted under Bismarck's leadership required workers and employers to contribute to a fund for disabled workers and later was expanded to cover retired workers as well. France adopted a similar program in 1905, focusing on unemployment assistance, and England followed suit in 1911, implementing the broader German concept of an old age and unemployment insurance program (U.S. Senate, 1990).

These European experiments aroused little interest in the United States in the late 19th century, when the vast western frontier beckoned anyone worth his salt to go and homestead 160 acres. In effect, the vast untamed landscape provided a tangible form of social security, alleviating some of the distress of industrial workers on the industrialized eastern seaboard. A deeply held belief in the value of self-support championed the reliance on individual effort to achieve security and discouraged requesting help from local institutions, state agencies, or the federal government. In fact, it was generally assumed that the federal government should never become involved with the needs or affairs of state or local governments, or their individual citizens.

As a consequence, there were thousands of semiautonomous welfare districts in this country, where localized means-tests (tests to ensure that an applicant has income and/or assets low enough to be eligible for welfare benefits) were adapted to whatever norms local jurisdictions chose to use (Lubove, 1986). The result was a very "capricious system which lacked even the virtue of predictability, [but which] shared one crucial assumption—that an inverse correlation existed between work incentive and the level of security obtainable through public welfare" (Lubove, 1986, p. 184).

However, the industrial revolution in the late 19th and early 20th centuries had begun to moderate the nation's attitude to some extent. As it had in the countries of western Europe, the industrial revolution introduced money (in the form of wages) as the predominant medium of exchange, supplanting a basically rural barter economy and creating a new source of insecurity in the fast-changing American social structure.

On farms in western rural areas the young and the old still had well-established and significant roles, performing chores that were well defined and individualized according to family members' capabilities. In the cities, though, the majority of people worked for others, relying completely on their weekly wage to purchase needed food, shelter and clothing. The unemployed who had no money were unable to obtain even the bare necessities of life. Labor laws now prevented the young from working in many industries, and the physical demands of industrial work often left older men and women as dependents rather than contributors to the family group.

In the early colonial period in America the "poor laws" had benefited needy dependents who were not necessarily "poor." "Legal settlement" and "family responsibility" clauses helped to control the concept of local responsibility. But, as the nation continued to expand, commercial and industrial growth began to attract more immigrants and rural migrants into northern towns and cities, where an influx of so many "strangers" made it very difficult to enforce local responsibility laws. The poor laws of necessity:

... became increasingly rigid, older people in need were auctioned off to the lowest bidder or sent to almshouses. Family responsibility laws also became more difficult to enforce, and when they were implemented, their intent was harsher and more punitive (Quadagno, 1984a, p. 441).

THE SOCIALIST MOVEMENT

The distress experienced by those in the eastern industrial states when jobs and wages were not available began to be felt in other parts of the nation as the 20th century progressed. By the late 1920s, and with the onset of the Great Depression, the impact of huge numbers of unemployed was profound. By 1932 there were fifteen million Americans out of work, in a population of 123 million one-third of the nation's labor force (Winslow, 1976). Even Americans of more comfortable means were upset and confused by these events. Strongly held notions of rugged individualism began to be broken down as many started to understand that poverty might not always be the fault of the victim. Widespread suffering eventually gave rise to a great Socialist movement, perhaps comparable to the one Bismarck had faced in Germany in 1881.

Populist/socialist movements spread like wildfire across the land as people searched for ways to protect themselves against the "three fears" plaguing the work force—unemployment, poverty in old age, and ill health (Achenbaum, 1986). One of the most popular movements focusing on the elderly was headed by a California physician, Dr. Francis Townsend. His plan called for the government to allocate $200 per month to persons sixty years of age and older, and was to be funded by a 2 percent national sales tax. Benefits were to be spent within a thirty-day maximum period, with the rationale that the quick turnaround of these monies would help to invigorate the economy.

Other socialist movements from this era included the National Union for Social Justice founded by the Reverend Charles Coughlin of Detroit, who advocated silver-backed currency and the nationalization of industry; the End Poverty in California plan championed by author Upton Sinclair, which advocated state socialism; and the Share Our Wealth program promoted by Senator Huey P. Long of Louisiana, which would have taxed the very rich and given everyone a $5,000 homestead, car, radio and washing machine. Senator Long boasted that membership in his group exceeded four and one-half million (Gollin, 1981).

Beyond these socialist movements, there was even some concern that the unhappy condition of workers across the country could lead to riot and anarchy. Several major general strikes by workers in Minneapolis and San Francisco, outlined by historian McElvaine (1984) in a chapter ("Thunder on the Left: Rising Unrest 1934-35") of his book on the Depression, were evidence of the general tenor of the labor movement during the Depression era.

The confused state of problems and potential solutions simply underlined the need for *some* sort of national plan to help the increasing number of Americans in distress because of factors beyond their control. It became clear to many that a federal solution would be necessary to provide assistance that state and local communities could not finance.

Social Security works because it speaks to a universal human need. All people throughout human history have faced the uncertainties brought on by death, disability, and old age. Prior to the turn of the twentieth century, the majority of people in the United States lived and worked on farms and economic security was provided by the extended family. However, this arrangement changed as America underwent the Industrial Revolution. The extended family and the family farm as sources of economic security became less common. Then, the Great Depression triggered a crisis in the nation's economic life. It was against this backdrop that the Social Security Act emerged.

THE ROOSEVELT ADMINISTRATION

When Franklin Delano Roosevelt was inaugurated as President in March of 1933 he quickly set the tone for his administration by announcing executive orders and calling on Congress to enact various emergency measures centering on public work and relief projects to support business and employment. Encouraged by the progress that had taken place by the spring of 1934, Roosevelt envisioned a comprehensive, long lasting approach to preventing the recurrence of such dramatic economic ills in the future.

He told Congress on June 8, 1934 that by the following January he would present it with proposals to deal with the economic insecurity that the depression had uncovered. By executive order on June 29, 1934, the Committee on Economic Security was established to help produce constructive proposals for change. The committee was chaired by Frances Perkins, the Secretary of Labor. Other members of the committee included the Secretary of the Treasury, the Secretary of Agriculture, the Attorney General and the Federal Relief Administrator. The major planning of the committee was to be done by a staff of specialists under the guidance of an appointed executive director (Edwin Witte). Each of these specialists was assigned to one of several different social insurance issues which included: old age security, unemployment and health insurance.

Health insurance would later be dropped before the legislation was introduced to Congress because the President felt that time was needed to build public consensus for it. Later, when in 1939 a National Health Conference came out in favor of health insurance, the timing was poor, because Roosevelt was preoccupied with World War II and preventing Hitler from overcoming the British (Schottland, 1991).

While it is widely agreed that the Great Depression brought about federal government involvement in welfare, the route taken to arrive at the specific policies that were created is not as clear. A basic tenet of the Roosevelt administration's philosophy was that social security legislation should not just provide "relief" and "recovery" but should also bring about a "reconstruction"— "rebuilding many of the structures of our economic life and reorganizing it in order to prevent a recurrence of collapse" (Roosevelt, 1934a). Roosevelt (1934b) furthermore insisted that the sweeping social legislation he advocated must be based on beneficiary contributions rather than an increase in taxation:

> We must not allow this type of [unemployment] insurance to become a dole through the mingling of insurance and relief. It is not charity. It must be financed by contributions, not taxes . . . Let us profit by the mistakes of foreign countries and keep out of unemployment insurance every element which is actuarially unsound (Roosevelt, 1938b, pp. 453-454).

There were a variety of rationales for supporting the Social Security Act. Some believed it would give a much needed boost to corporate America. Many saw its old age insurance program as designed to make it easier for older workers to retire in order to provide more work opportunities for the young unemployed:

> There was widespread support for the notion that older workers should make room for the young; it was often stated that employment opportunities for those past 45 would improve if they did not have to compete with their elders for jobs (Achenbaum, 1986, p. 24).

There were those who argued that the act had been "initiated as a means of containing socialism . . . [and] that it was intended to benefit business by expanding purchasing power" (Quadagno, 1984b, pp. 634-635).

Whatever the motivating forces behind the Social Security legislation, it was indeed "a very complex piece of work that harbored three seemingly disparate measures, each operating under a different set of principles" (Quadagno, 1984b, p. 634). To explain conflicts among the unemployment, public assistance and old age insurance articles, Quadagno (1984b) postulates that the Social Security Act was created as "a conservative measure that tied social insurance benefits to labor force participation and left administration of its public assistance programs to the states" (p. 632). She contends that the three different programs covered by the Social Security Act (Old Age Assistance [OAA], Old Age Insurance [OAI] and Unemployment Insurance [UI]) and their different methods of financing (federal supplementation of state payments [OAA], national payroll taxation [OAI], and federal taxation with state control of taxation provisions and coverage [UI]) were the result of states having acted as mediating bodies, weighing the competing demands of various class factions and economic interests, and formulating policies that incorporated "working class demands into legislation on capitalist terms" (p. 632). This was welfare legislation that was based on the contributions of workers in a capitalist system, and not the redistribution of income. Accordingly:

> From the administration's perspective, the stabilization of the economy, not the welfare of workers, was the goal of national welfare programs (Quadagno, 1984b, p. 640).

Skocpol and Ikenberry (1983), on the other hand, did not see these "social-welfare innovations . . . as straightforward products of popular pressures, demands, or political support" (p. 121). Rather, this new legislation was viewed as a politically necessary response to the social distress caused by the Depression, which had by 1932 unraveled "the central ideological tenet of welfare capitalism—the notion that corporate capitalists and managers could adequately look after the economic well-being of the American people" (Skocpol and Ikenberry, 1983, p. 120).

Those charged with the development of the Social Security legislation knew that Congress would seek to protect preexisting state laws and administrative functions that were already in place and packaged the issues they sought to address (unemployment; public assistance for the elderly poor, the disabled and dependent children; and old age insurance) in accordance with preexisting state policies, to which programmatic differences in the legislation can be traced back.

A survey of the existing state legislation in 1934-35 shows that many states were already in the process of preparing legislation concerning unemployment insurance; six states had already passed such bills. In addition, many states already had locally administered public assistance (poor law) programs in place. The one piece that was missing was old age insurance. According to Skocpol and Amenta (1985), "There were no state-level laws or even serious debates [about old age insurance], [so that] the Social Security insurance program as proposed and enacted was purely national" (p. 574).

In 1935, the life expectancy of the average American was not much beyond age sixty-five, so the federal burden represented by the old age assistance and insurance programs actually seemed to be minimal. In fact, Social Security legislation was designed to benefit all generations. It was an omnibus bill that brought together almost all of the existing welfare programs and grants to states for public health and vocational rehabilitation (Berkowitz, 1987). During the legislative deliberations on Social Security, the focus of attention was primarily on unemployment compensation and welfare system proposals, only one aspect of which concerned the elderly—old age assistance (Berkowitz, 1987). Several titles dealing with the immediate concerns of the working-age population included in the act were: unemployment insurance under Titles III and

IX (which gave the states considerable latitude in determining benefits, paid in large part through taxes on employers), aid to dependent children under Title IV, relief to the blind (Title X), and grants to states for maternal and child welfare (Title V).

The transgenerational nature of Social Security can even be perceived in the old age security portions of the act that provided for a system of income transfers which assure that not only would:

> The elderly . . . receive relief and future protection; the middle-aged would [also] be free to devote more of their resources to their own children. By coordinating the old-age insurance program with a system of old-age assistance, the federal government adopted a plan that "amounts to having each generation pay for the support of the people then living who are old." Titles I and II were thus inspired by a genuine (and imaginative) concern for addressing the vicissitudes of old age in the context of the family and the passage of generations (Achenbaum, 1986, pp. 24-25).

The proposal put forth by the Committee on Economic Security would have established a three-point program for alleviating old age dependency. First, a federal-state partnership would be put into place that would require the federal government to partially underwrite old age assistance (or welfare relief) programs. Second, a compulsory old age insurance program would be set up for all manual and nonmanual workers in industrial production earning less than $250 per month. Third, the government would administer a program of voluntary annuities to allow people to put money away for their later years. The third part of the committee's program was quickly dropped by Congress during its deliberations in order to make the act more fiscally responsible (U.S. Committee on Economic Security, 1937).

Although it is not well understood by the general public, the consideration of old age security was essentially a minor issue in the committee's scheme of things. It was greatly overshadowed by the unemployment issue and, in fact, the staff in the old age security section was smaller than those assigned to unemployment and health insurance (Brown, 1969).

Ed Witte, the executive director of the committee, showed little interest in an old age insurance system, and despite Roosevelt's stated intentions to protect the American populace from *all* forms of economic insecurity, the programs to protect the aged were not a priority. This apathy allowed the principals in the old age security section, J. Douglas Brown, a Princeton economist, and Barbara Armstrong, a Berkeley law school professor who had studied the European social insurance models, to be creative in working out plans for a national old age insurance program (Brown, 1969).

The architects of what was to become popularly known as the Social Security program drew extensively from the well-established European programs for social insurance and like them would be national (government sponsored), compulsory, independently financed, and would provide benefits as a matter of right. To convince others on the Committee on Economic Security of the necessity of a national social insurance program required compilation of detailed descriptions of the complex problems that forty-eight separate old age insurance programs would present and provision of a rationale for establishing a standardized national unemployment insurance. Brown (1969) remained convinced long afterward that the many different federal-state systems of unemployment insurance adequately supported his contention that it should have been nationalized as old age insurance had been, given the "slow and spotty progress of unemployment insurance over the years" (p. 9).

Despite the efforts of Brown and Armstrong on behalf of a national old age security program, the differences among the Committee on Economic Security members were reflected in a speech prepared for President Roosevelt by the chairman and executive director for a national conference on economic security on November 14, 1934. This address focused on unemployment and downplayed old age insurance, and in it Roosevelt said, "I do not know whether this is the time for any federal legislation on old age security" (Achenbaum, 1986, p. 20). This slight of the old age insurance component was sharply criticized in the press, in part because the staff of the old age security section utilized some of Barbara Armstrong's influential friends in the press corps (Brown, 1969). A consequence of this outpouring of criticism was that, instead of burying the broad social insurance program, the President's speech only succeeded in bringing it directly to the fore.

In submitting the legislative proposals developed by the Committee on Economic Security to Congress on January 15, 1935, Roosevelt, in an obvious "about face," gave the proposals for alleviating old age dependency top billing as Title I—assistance for needy elderly, and Title II—old age insurance. In order to assure the passage of old age insurance, which was far from a popular program in 1935, Roosevelt pressured Congress to keep intact the complete social welfare legislation package of old age assistance, unemployment compensation, and old age insurance. It is likely that in the absence of any such pressure Congress would have passed only Title I, old age assistance, a program for the needy from which benefits were payable immediately. Old age insurance required contributions to future benefits through additional payroll taxes, a very difficult proposition to make in the middle of a severe depression (Berkowitz, 1989).

As already noted, the coordinated old age benefit proposals presented to Congress that year did not include a plan for compulsory health insurance, because the President and the committee's chairman (Frances Perkins) and executive director

(Ed Witte) feared that the social security measure might fail if such a provision were included. In fact Achenbaum (1986) relates that:

> The Committee on Economic Security opposed the merger of health care programs and income-maintenance programs . . . [their position was that] states were to take the initiative in creating health insurance systems (p. 164).

As finally passed by Congress, the 1935 Social Security Act proposed a combination of old age insurance and assistance. Anyone who met the age, residency and needs requirements established by a state and approved by the federal board would have the right to Title I assistance benefits in that state. After much wrangling with states' rights proponents, states were permitted to establish state-specific benefit levels and eligibility criteria. Old age insurance under Title II was to be funded by a payroll tax which would require an equal contribution to an Old-Age Reserve Account from employer and employee (initially set at 1 percent of an employee's wage, resulting in a 2 percent contribution). Advocates of the Social Security program believed that paying into the system would result in contributors taking ownership of the program and coming to consider its benefits to be a basic right, much like those of any other pension program (Achenbaum, 1986).

However, the complexity of the legislation caused considerable confusion among legislators and continues to permeate the general perception of Social Security. Witte conveyed the frustration of the framers of the act in commenting that, "Despite the numerous articles which have been written, the two parts of the old age security program are confused and many of the essential features have been grossly misrepresented" (Schiltz, 1970, p. 34). While many politicians have finally come to grips with the program's intricacies, most of the general public continues to be unaware of its various offerings. Only in the 1940s and 1950s did old age insurance come to the forefront as the predominant economic security program and become "important enough to monopolize the term 'social security'" (Berkowitz, 1987, p. 6). Nonetheless, when Social Security is considered it should be known that it is not just a pension program for the elderly, but rather a comprehensive and revolutionary law that dramatically altered federal government responsibility.

THE 1935 LAW

The Social Security Act was introduced to the House of Representatives by Robert L. Doughton (D-NC) with assurances that the bill had been given more careful consideration than any since he had been a member of the House. He went on to argue that relating workers' right to benefits to their previous employment put the program out of the realm of charity or welfare, and that would, in fact, do nothing to break down the "sacred American tradition of self-reliance and initiative" (Congressional Record, 74th Congress, 1935, p. 5,467).

The Senate discussed the concept of Social Security in terms of its longevity and its ability to stand the test of time, rather than as a stop-gap measure. Despite some Senators' adamant opposition, calling the bill "Marxist from beginning to end," the most radical, most comprehensive, and most expensive legislative measure in the nation's history passed both chambers of the Congress in August of 1935. The President signed it on August 14, 1935 and the United States finally joined other industrial countries in providing a compulsory social insurance program. The federal government had become involved in areas previously thought to be the concern only of private citizens and/or state and local governments. Furthermore, while:

> Social Security did not try to get at the underlying causes of structural unemployment or old-age pauperism [it had provided the foundation upon which] bolder initiatives [could be built] once the implications of what had already been done became clearer (Achenbaum, 1986, p. 26).

Establishing the system of old age insurance under the auspices of the Social Security Act involved seven underlying principles as fundamental requirements (as adapted from *Research Dialogues*, No. 26, July 1990):

1. *Equity* — Workers earn their benefits and benefits are weighted in favor of those workers who have lower average lifetime earnings. Those who have less, and thus may put less into the system, will get more back due to the progressive payment policy (although since the tax is a fixed percentage on all wage earners, there also tends to be a larger relative burden on the poor, the result of an offsetting regressive contribution system).
2. *Compulsory Participation* — Every working person (ideally) has to pay into the program through the levied tax, otherwise only those who felt they would need it (i.e., the poor) would contribute to the system.
3. *Wage-Related Contributions* — The Social Security system must be related to wages paid in as contributions (i.e., an insurance program, not welfare).
4. *Universal Coverage* — Although it started as an industrial labor program, it was understood that to be fully effective everyone should eventually be covered under Social Security so that the insured risk is spread among the broadest possible group, helping to stabilize the cost of protection for each participant and assuring almost everyone in society a base of economic security.
5. *Concept of Adequacy* — The amount of the benefit should be sufficient for minimal subsistence, providing a financial safety net. It should not, however, be the sole source of income for anyone, but rather should be one part

of a four-tier system made up of savings, pensions, welfare, and social security.

6. *Family Orientation* — Helping one person to be more secure financially also has a positive impact on others in that individual's social network. (This principle was further realized in later years as spouses and surviving children were covered.)

7. *Sound Financing* — The system must be well financed in order to meet its long term demands. This was to be accomplished through setting up trust funds which would be invested in government securities.

The controversy over Social Security did not go away after its passage. Opposition by conservative legislators actually increased during the 1936 elections. Alf Landon, the Republican challenger for the presidency attacked the program as "unjust, unworkable, stupidly drafted and wastefully financed . . . a cruel hoax" (Achenbaum, 1986, p. 29). However, this overzealous attack backfired, probably contributing to an overwhelming defeat of Landon and his party, which represented vindication of Social Security and other New Deal programs.

Several groups brought class action suits questioning the constitutionality of the federal government's insinuating itself into the affairs of the states and private citizens and their employers. Concern also was expressed over whether it was appropriate for the federal government to use its powers of taxation to underwrite a compulsory national insurance program.

In May of 1937 the Supreme Court ruled that the expanded powers of the federal government were not contraindicated by the Constitution. In ruling on two of the most controversial aspects of the Social Security Act: the unemployment excise tax levied on employers and the associated federal-state funding (*Stewart Machine Company* versus *Davis*), and the federal tax for old age insurance and retirement benefits provisions (*Helvering* versus *Davis*) the Supreme Court effectively validated a new era in government responsibility (Achenbaum, 1986). As Justice Benjamin J. Cardoza stated in delivering the majority opinion, "Only a power that is national can serve the interests of all," thereby summarizing the beginning of a change in the general philosophy of the federal government (Schottland, 1991).

In the same month, a twenty-five-member Advisory Council on Social Security was established to deal with problems in the system that had been left unresolved by the Committee on Economic Security. Even advocates of the program had discovered flaws in it and were uncertain about how to proceed. The system started slowly, with a Social Security Board of only three members and their assistants assigned to the task of trying to establish procedures for the newly passed programs. The chairman of that board, Arthur J. Altmeyer, had urged the President to appoint an independent council of experts who could act in an advisory capacity to help "defuse the mounting attacks on Social Security" (Achenbaum, 1986, p. 31).

Such attacks were coming from Townsend Movement adherents and conservative Republicans, and had been instigated by a sharp recession in 1936 which had nearly wiped out all the economic gains of the previous four years. These critics blamed the economic malaise to sudden cuts in government spending and the collection of taxes amounting to almost $2 billion for the new Social Security program (Achenbaum, 1986).

Thus, even before the first benefit was paid, the Advisory Council developed an expanded basic benefit structure for the Social Security system during 1937-38. New benefits included, in addition to basic pensions, a significant change in coverage allowing for the payment of benefits to survivors and dependents of retired workers, as well as approving, in principle, disability benefits. Council members also recommended that the basis for computing the benefit formula be changed from cumulative lifetime earnings to an average of monthly earnings under covered work, which would give workers who were close to retirement age at that time a more adequate retirement benefit (Social Security Administration, 1971).

MAJOR PROVISIONS OF THE ACT

The following material has been adapted from "Social Security—A Brief History," on the World Wide Web, 1998.

The Social Security Act did not quite achieve all the aspirations of its supporters, who had hoped to provide a comprehensive package of protection against the hazards and vicissitudes of life. Certain features of that package, notably disability coverage and medical benefits, would have to await future developments, but a wide range of programs were provided to meet the nation's needs. In addition to the program we now think of as Social Security, the Act included unemployment insurance, old-age assistance, aid to dependent children, and grants to the states to provide various forms of medical care.

The two major provisions relating to the elderly were Title I – Grants to States for Old-Age Assistance, which supported state welfare programs for the aged, and Title II – Federal Old-Age Benefits. It was Title II that was the new social insurance program we now call Social Security. In the original Act benefits were to be paid only to the primary worker at retirement. Benefits were to be based on payroll tax contributions that the worker made while working. Taxes would first be collected in 1937 and monthly benefits would begin in 1942.

The significance of the new social insurance program was that it sought to address the long-range problem of economic security for the aged through a system in which the workers themselves contributed to their own future retirement benefit by making regular payments into a joint fund. It was thus distinct from the welfare benefits provided under Title I of the Act and from various state "old-age pensions." As President Roosevelt conceived the Act, Title I was to be a temporary relief program that would eventually disappear as more people were able to obtain retirement income through the contributory system. The new social insurance system was also a very moderate alternative to the radical calls to action that were so common in the America of the 1930s.

Early Work

The monumental first task was the need to register employers and workers by January 1, 1937, when workers would begin acquiring credits toward old-age insurance benefits. Since the new Social Security Board (SSB) did not have the resources available to accomplish this, they contracted with the U.S. Postal Service to distribute the applications. More than thirty-five million applicants subsequently received Social Security cards from the 151 field offices that had been set up by June 30, 1937.

Trust Funds

After Social Security numbers were assigned, the first Federal Insurance Contributions Act (FICA) taxes were collected, beginning in January 1937. Special Trust Funds were created for these dedicated revenues. Benefits were then paid from the monies in the Social Security Trust Funds. Over the years, more than $4.5 trillion has been paid into the Trust Funds, and more than $4.1 trillion has been paid out in benefits. The remainder is currently on reserve in the Trust Funds and will be used to pay future benefits.

First Payments

From 1937 until 1940, Social Security paid benefits in the form of a single, lump-sum payment. The purpose of these one-time payments was to provide some payback to those people who contributed to the program but would not participate long enough to be vested for monthly benefits. Under the 1935 law (see Figure 13, *The Life and Times of Social Security*) monthly benefits were to begin in 1942, with the period 1937-1942 used both to build up the Trust Funds and to provide a minimum period for participation in order to qualify for monthly benefits.

The earliest reported applicant for a lump-sum benefit was a retired Cleveland motorman named Ernest Ackerman, who retired one day after the Social Security program began. During his one day of participation in the program, a nickel was withheld from Mr. Ackerman's pay for Social Security, and, upon retiring, he received a lump-sum payment of 17 cents. The average lump-sum payment during this period was $58.06. The smallest payment ever made was for 5 cents.

1935	President Roosevelt signs the Social Security Act.
1937	Payroll tax set at one cent on the dollar for a maximum annual deduction of $30 each for employees and employers.
1940	Ida May Fuller receives the first monthly benefit check— for $22.54.
1950	The first tax increase; states get the option to cover employees.
1956	Disability insurance added for workers fifty to sixty-four.
1960	Disability at any age approved.
1961	Early retirement for all workers at age sixty-two (with reduced benefits) approved.
1965	Medicare established.
1969	Social Security moved on budget (included in the federal budget).
1975	Beneficiaries given annual cost-of-living adjustments (COLAs) linked to the Consumer Price Index.
1977	Benefit formula revised; taxes raised to avoid a shortfall.
1980	Disability benefits cut.
1981	President Reagan appoints a bipartisan commission to find a new financial fix.
1983	Social security moved off budget; COLAs delayed; payroll taxes for self-employed pushed up; retirement age to be raised; up to 50 percent of high-income recipients' benefits taxed.
1993	Up to 85 percent of high-income recipients' benefits taxed with the additional revenue channeled to Medicare.
2012	Payouts projected to exceed contributions; interest on Trust Fund tapped.
2019	Payouts projected to exceed contributions and interest; Trust Fund tapped.
2029	Trust Fund depleted. Tax revenues pay only 77 percent of benefits.

Figure 13. The Life and Times of Social Security. **Source:** *Modern Maturity*, January/February, 1997.

MAJOR AMENDMENTS TO THE SOCIAL SECURITY ACT

In 1939, amendments made into law the recommendations from the Advisory Council's December 10, 1938 Final Report, transforming Social Security from an individual insurance program into a bona fide family plan (Bandler, 1989). Policymakers had recognized the need to place a greater emphasis on "social adequacy" through providing protection for the whole family to safeguard it against economic misfortune (Achenbaum, 1987). This family protection (covering elderly wives and husbands, elderly widowers, children from deceased and disabled worker families, and parents caring for children of disabled or deceased workers), although often overlooked as part of the Social Security program, had since grown to cover over 31 percent of its beneficiaries (Bandler, 1989).

The lion's share of advocacy and attention during the 1939 amendments and over the ensuing years, had revolved, however, around elderly beneficiaries (Achenbaum, 1986). The categorical age of eligibility designated by the act (65) had actually come to be recognized as delineating the onset of old age. Policymakers believed that by focusing their attentions on the problems of the elderly other age groups in our aging society would also benefit by becoming more aware of the risks ahead and taking necessary precautions to protect themselves and their children in their later years (Achenbaum, 1987).

The 1939 amendments to Title II had, through including survivors and dependents as beneficiaries, disposed of the simple notion of Social Security as a method of replacing the lost wages of retired workers in the form of an annuity. What had been known as old age insurance or OAI, became old age and survivors insurance or OASI, opening the door for numerous adjustments, exclusions and redistributions which, while accentuating the founding principle of adequacy, also served to introduce an aspect of welfare into the benefit structure of the act (Rich and Baum, 1984).

In an effort to calm concerns about the possible beginnings of a welfare state, the Administration emphasized the insurance features of the Social Security program. As Achenbaum (1986) relates:

> The Old-Age Reserve Account established under Title VIII in 1935 was renamed the Old-Age and Survivors Insurance (OASI) Trust Fund. The original employer and employee taxes were repealed; instead, "insurance contributions" were now imposed under the Federal Insurance Contributions Act (FICA) as part of the Internal Revenue Code. The president and his advisors knew that it would be easier to expand social security if Americans believed that they had earned the right to draw benefits from a system untainted by the stigma of "welfare" (p. 35).

These amendments also clarified certain vague stipulations of the act as originally passed, such as the "Retirement Test" clause in Title II, which stated that to be eligible for benefits one could not be employed in a "gainful occupation" and that "the old age benefit payable to such individual shall be reduced for each calendar month in any part of which regular employment occurred." The 1939 amendments attempted to clarify this passage by replacing the ambiguous term "regular employment" with "covered employment" and placing an earnings ceiling of $15 per month on those in such employ. The imposition of the earnings ceiling had been the response of legislators to the concerns of union officials who believed that older workers who were receiving Social Security benefits might opt for lower pay, with the ultimate result of driving down the wages for younger workers (Cohen, 1957).

Since the "retirement test" applied only to earnings from "covered employment," many older persons realized they could retire and collect Social Security benefits while still employed full time in work not subject to Social Security taxes, such as self-employment. Over the years the "retirement test" has been modified, seeking a compromise balancing the views of those who promote early retirement and those who believe that continuing to work in gainful employment can increase the health and happiness of older adults. One suggested compromise was that those who deferred taking retirement past the age of sixty-five should receive some credit for those years in which they are not collecting Title II benefits. Several recommendations were made for the monthly benefit to be incrementally increased for each month between the ages of sixty-five and seventy-two that a person deferred retirement, but none of these proposals received much attention until the late 1960s and early 1970s (Derthick, 1979).

The next set of major amendments to the Social Security program were made in 1950 when a number of jobs which had been excluded in the original legislation were covered and benefits were substantially increased. Farm and household (domestic) employees, many of the self-employed (other than farmers and professionals), and civilian federal workers not covered by the Civil Service Retirement System were required to enter the Social Security program. Additionally, employees of state and local governments who were not covered by public pension programs, and employees of nonprofit organizations were given the opportunity to join Social Security on a voluntary group basis (Social Security Administration, 1971).

More than twice as many elderly participated in the Title I welfare program as in the old-age insurance program (Title II). Eligibility requirements were changed to make divorced survivors under sixty-five years of age who were caring for a child eligible for support. Dependent husbands and widowers over age sixty-five of insured working women also became eligible to receive benefits.

In an analysis of these amendments Edward Berkowitz (1987) points out that this broadened coverage:

> . . . helped to turn back the threat posed by existing public welfare programs. . . . Because of these amendments, for example, nearly 100,000 people who had been on welfare became eligible for social security, and by the

beginning of 1951 the number of people on social security surpassed the number of people on welfare. . . . No longer was social insurance reserved for urban and industrial America. Now all of America participated (p. 21).

Benefits also were dramatically increased through a revision of the benefit calculation formula. The average benefit was increased by more than 77 percent, though in its historical context this increase only exceeded the inflation in prices since 1937 by 1.5 percent and represented only two-thirds of the increase in wages over this thirteen-year time span (Altmeyer, 1968).

The 1950 amendments also significantly modified the "retirement test," exempting all beneficiaries over the age of seventy-five from being subject to this test and raising the allowed earnings ceiling from $15 per month to $50 per month. Just four years later (in the 1954 amendments) the age at which one could be exempted from the test was lowered again to age seventy-two, and the amount that could be earned was doubled to $100 per month, allowing an annual wage of $1,200 before Social Security pension benefits would be affected.

In 1955 the platform of the Democratic party called for the complete elimination of the "work clause," contending that those contributing to the Social Security Program should be able to draw benefits upon reaching the age of eligibility and still continue to be employed. Arthur J. Altmeyer, the first Commissioner of the Social Security Board (which administered Social Security as set forth in Title VII), strongly disagreed with this statement, arguing that "I have always felt that this proposal (to eliminate the test) ran counter to the basic purpose of social insurance—to compensate in part for loss of income actually sustained" (Altmeyer, 1968, p. 203). Nonetheless, the 1960 amendments created a formula that liberalized the retirement test and effectively "established the logical and equitable basic principle that earnings in excess of the annual exempt amount will always result in more total income" (Myers, 1975, p. 114). According to this formula beneficiaries would simply have their Title II benefits reduced by a given amount for each dollar earned over the earnings limit. As applied to beneficiaries in 1960, benefits were reduced $1 for every $2 earned between $1,201 and $1,500, reverting to $1 for every $1 earned over $1,500.

Reducing the age of eligibility for beneficiaries to age sixty had been first recommended by the members of the 1948 Advisory Council on Social Security and members of Congress as a means of alleviating the problems of working women and widows who were often younger than their husbands but were still constrained by the age sixty-five eligibility requirement. These proposals were not successful, in large part because lawmakers were concerned that providing for those extra years of coverage would prove to be far too costly (Altmeyer, 1968). In 1956, however, the Congress finally saw its way clear to lowering the age of entitlement for women workers and wives of beneficiaries to sixty-two years. Benefits would be actuarially reduced for women workers and wives between the ages of sixty-two and sixty-five years of age, while at age sixty-two widows of beneficiaries would be insured at the same rate that had been originally established under the 1939 amendments for widows over age sixty-five (Bandler, 1989).

The 1956 amendments also broadened the scope of Social Security insurance through the added provision of disability coverage. The Title II old age and survivors insurance (OASI) was now to become known as OASDI or old age, survivors and disability insurance. In order not to penalize unfairly those unable to build a working history of contributions into the Social Security system due to their inability to work, Congress had decided to follow the lead of private sector health insurance and provide disability benefits. So that these amendments would not be abused, however, the legislators decided to put a six-month delay on the awarding of disability benefits to claimants in order to verify their inability to work. Benefits were made available to severely disabled workers between the ages of fifty and sixty-four and to adult children of retired and deceased workers who were disabled before the age of eighteen (Social Security Administration, 1971). It would be 1958 before the act would be further amended to provide benefits for dependents of disabled workers similar to the benefits provided to dependents of retired workers, and in 1960 amendments would eliminate the age fifty limitation, extending coverage of disability benefits to any age below sixty-five (Social Security Administration, 1971).

Business and union leaders increasingly used the age of eligibility for Social Security benefits as the benchmark age around which to build their pension programs and to mandate retirement. Some employers in recent years have even used Social Security benefits as a way to reduce their liability for private retirement pension programs by figuring Social Security benefits into their pension payment formulas, so that pension benefits of a person who became eligible for OASDI benefits could be reduced by the OASDI amount to keep retirement benefits constant.

In a further adjustment to the eligibility age of Social Security, which had started out at age sixty-five for everybody, the amendments of 1961 finally made men eligible for the early retirement benefits to which women had become entitled in 1956. Like women workers and wives, men who claimed their benefits between the ages of sixty-two to sixty-five would have those benefits actuarially reduced to account for the longer period of time over which they would receive benefits. Four years later, under the 1965 amendments, the age of eligibility for widows was lowered even further, to age sixty, although the benefits taken before age sixty-two would be reduced in the same manner as those of early retirement beneficiaries (Achenbaum, 1986).

Amendments of 1965

The year 1965 also saw dramatic Social Security amendments in other areas of coverage. Health Insurance for the elderly became a reality under two new titles,

Title XVIII—Medicare, and Title XIX—Medicaid (which was a consolidation of public health programs for impoverished citizens including the elderly poor). Medicare was put into place to make health care more accessible to those elderly who were eligible for Title II - Old Age Insurance. Medicare was set up with its own trust fund and earnings tax to provide coverage against the costs of hospital care (Part A), and a voluntary supplementary medical insurance plan (Part B) financed through premiums paid by participating elderly and matching funds from the federal government that would cover the cost of physician services and other health care costs not covered by Part A (Social Security Administration, 1971). The total insurance package under Social Security now became OASDHI, with three dedicated trust funds for OASI (Old Age and Survivors Insurance), DI (Disability Insurance) and HI (Hospital Insurance). (See Chapter 7 for discussion of health policies.)

Twenty-one years after the original Social Security Act had eliminated health care insurance as a bad risk that could have doomed its passage, the "Great Society" initiatives of President Lyndon Johnson's administration finally succeeded in getting a national health plan established (Achenbaum, 1986). It may be recalled that in 1944 President Roosevelt had presented an "Economic Bill of Rights" which, while not producing any actual legislated programs, made it known that the administration's desire to have medical care and good health had become a national priority.

From 1966 data it was demonstrated that Social Security had actually done better by the elderly poor in financial assistance (in absolute dollars) than any other government assistance program, including public assistance, unemployment insurance, public housing, veterans' benefits, or health programs offered by the government. And, things were to continue to get better. The 1972 amendments proved to be a watershed for the elderly in terms of benefit increases.

Amendments of 1972

The Congress that year overwhelmingly approved a 20 percent increase in Social Security benefits, the largest increase in real dollars for the elderly since the inception of the Social Security program. To keep pace with inflation and to help retain the value of the benefits, Social Security benefits, beginning in 1975, would be subject to a cost-of-living (COLA) adjustment on an annual basis whenever the Consumer Price Index (CPI) increased at least 3 percent. Medicare benefits were extended to those under age sixty-five who were eligible for disability benefits and those afflicted with acute kidney disease. The retirement test was further liberalized, increasing the earnings ceiling to almost $2,100 per annum, with automatic increase adjustments built in by means of the 1973 amendments.

Supplemental Security Income (SSI) also was created in 1972. Scheduled to take effect in 1974, SSI dramatically changed the formula of Title I old age assistance by providing a guaranteed basic income. SSI was supposed to guarantee a set amount of funds to those eligible due to very low income and set the stage for the concept of "universal income-maintenance programs that may come in the future" (Achenbaum, 1986, p. 58). SSI, under Title XX of the Social Security Act, replaced Title I (Old Age Assistance), Title X (Assistance to the Blind), and Title XIV (Aid to the Permanently and Totally Disabled) and provided assistance to more of the nation's neediest citizens than had been the case under the former programs administered at the state level.

Unfortunately, the level of adequacy that had been set by SSI was well below the government's official poverty level, so that recipients of the program did not receive enough assistance to bring them up to within 80 percent of that stated level (SOS Education Fund, 1984). Although it may initially have been perceived as an entitlement, the underlying welfare attributes of this federal program significantly diminished its impact. The strict earnings limit under SSI discouraged participants from finding employment, and the adequacy of benefits was seriously undermined when the states did not increase their component of the SSI benefit, leaving elderly beneficiaries worse off in times of inflation. SSI therefore has not succeeded in its stated mission of reducing the differences among the various "adequate" base levels of income support across the country.

As mounting economic problems throughout the 1970s uncovered some potentially fatal flaws in the fabric of its system, additional questions about Social Security were raised. The newly passed cost-of-living increases caused benefits to soar with out-of-control inflation. Unemployment rose precipitously during the 1974 recession, reducing contributions through FICA payroll tax revenues. A serious technical error in the 1972 amendments had over-indexed the adjustment for inflation in the initial benefit amount and was wreaking havoc with the trust fund reserves. Policymakers had woefully mis-predicted the economic experience of the 1970s, and subsequent amendments were required to repair the financial damage that resulted from the 1972 legislation.

Amendments of 1977

In 1977 Congress enacted a new set of amendments to the Social Security Act which were intended to rectify the program's ills. Their solution involved a reallocation of some of the Medicare (Hospital Insurance) payroll tax to the OASI and DI trust funds, the correction of the technical flaw in the inflation adjustment for initial benefits, and an increase in the payroll tax to be put into effect in 1979 (Special Committee on Aging, 1990).

Despite these efforts, difficulties persisted. In the 1972 amendments, the policymakers had indexed benefits to adjust to inflationary changes in the economy according to the Consumer Price Index (CPI), which historically rose more slowly than wage indexes (Achenbaum, 1986). This pattern was somehow reversed in the 1970s and from 1977 through 1980 prices increased much more rapidly than wages. In fact, wages even declined somewhat during this period. While the CPI continued to rise out of control with inflation (over 10 percent after 1979), changes in real wages had stayed around zero or become negative. To make matters even worse, unemployment rose. As unemployment rates began to exceed 7 percent, inflation caused a continued increase in Social Security benefits, and income to the OASDI trust funds failed to cover expenditures. There was fear that the combination of high unemployment and high inflation would bankrupt the trust funds by 1984 or 1985 (Schottland, 1991). "Lower trust fund balances, combined with rapidly increasing expenditures, brought reserves down to less than three months' benefit payments by 1980" (Special Committee on Aging, 1990).

Into the middle of this delicate situation came a new president, Ronald Reagan, who took office in 1980 prepared to do battle with what he and his colleagues considered an unwieldy federal bureaucracy. Reagan's attitude toward Social Security was particularly antagonistic. As governor of California, he had recommended that Social Security be made voluntary, a move that would effectively have destroyed the program. Eliminating one of the seven mainstay principles underlying Social Security, that social insurance be compulsory, could cause the program to fall short of universal coverage and attract participation only by those in dire need (the poor), whose contributions would be inadequate to assure financial viability.

Reagan's attitude seemed to change somewhat when he discovered the very strong support Social Security enjoyed on Capitol Hill, although he remained determined to cut a program that was quickly going broke. The Reagan administration chipped away at Social Security benefits by first cutting the death benefit and then the survivors' benefits of dependents eighteen to twenty-one years of age. The latter had helped many children to complete their education after a family had lost its primary wage earner. It next was proposed that the minimum benefit be eliminated. This raised a large outcry among those most affected, women, who quickly demonstrated their political power. Congress was deluged with expressions of their concern and this benefit cut was handily defeated, as was a subsequent 25 percent proposed cut in benefits (Schottland, 1991).

It had become obvious that these piecemeal attacks on the Social Security system were not solving the financial problems that were plaguing it. Unfortunately, President Reagan had effectively tied his own hands on this matter by proclaiming that he would under no conditions allow the Federal Treasury to loan money to Social Security to shore up its funds, nor would he ever approve raising FICA taxes. Without these steps it was unclear how Social Security was going to make it through the next few years.

Then the President seemed to have a change of heart. After some closed door politicking, the administration recommended that a commission be appointed to resolve the Social Security financial crisis. Fifteen members were to be selected as follows: five Representatives to be recommended by the liberal Speaker of the House, Tip O'Neill (D-MA); five to be chosen by Howard Baker (R-TN), the conservative majority leader of the Senate; and five to be appointed by the President. The result was a diverse group of experts on Social Security from the public and private sectors. Allan Greenspan, a respected conservative economist, was named chairman by the President.

This National Commission on Social Security Reform (NCSSR) was given one year to solve the financial problems of Social Security and was able to reach a surprisingly effective consensus agreement. It can safely be said that not one of the members of the bipartisan commission agreed with all of the twenty-four recommendations that resulted, but all of the members did agree to vote for the changes and help to push them through Congress.

Amendments of 1983

The major changes recommended by the NCSSR (and passed in the Social Security Amendments of 1983) were in the areas of coverage, beneficiary taxation, payroll taxation, and annual adjustments of benefits.

> Once the National Commission on Social Security Reform reached agreement on its recommendations, Congress moved quickly to enact legislation to restore financial solvency to the OASDI trust funds. This comprehensive package improved financing by $166 billion between 1983 and 1989, and eliminated [slightly more than two-thirds of] a deficit which had been expected to average 2.1 percent of payroll over 75 years (U.S. Senate, 1990, p. 7).

A major portion ($40 billion) of the $166 billion savings was made possible by two provisions which were prime examples of the creative solutions devised by the commission. First, COLA increases were delayed six months by moving them from the federal government's fiscal year to a calendar year basis. A stipulation was added that if the trust fund reserves did not equal 15 percent of the outgo (until December 1988, 20 percent thereafter) the COLA would be calculated on the lesser of the wage or consumer price index increases (U.S. Senate, 1990).

Second, the tax rate schedule was revised so that the tax rate increase that was to go into effect in 1990 would be moved forward to 1984 in stages, accelerating the increase over those six years. The third largest source of revenue to come out of these amendments was generated from a tax on the benefits of beneficiaries who had incomes of over $25,000 per year for an individual, $32,000 for a couple. One half of the benefits received by these taxpayers would be subject to income taxes, with the revenue going back into the trust funds.

Other significant changes in the 1983 amendments that increased the earning potential of Social Security included: FICA tax rates of the self-employed were increased; the retirement age would be gradually increased from sixty-five to sixty- seven, to be phased in between 2000 and 2022; state and local governments would no longer be able to terminate Social Security coverage; all federal employees hired after January 1, 1984 would be covered under Social Security; the current and future employees of private nonprofit, tax-exempt organizations would now be covered as well; the amounts of uncashed Social Security benefit checks of a deceased beneficiary would now be earmarked for the trust funds rather than the federal general revenue fund; and, larger reductions in the Social Security benefits of those who take early retirement at age sixty-two would commence in 2005 (increasing from the current 20 percent reduction to 25 percent in 2005, and 30 percent in 2022).

> House and Senate leaders emphasized that there were two reasons for keeping to the commission's final set of recommendations. First, it was doubtful that 435 representatives and 100 senators could develop a better set of proposals than those already endorsed by the President, the Speaker, and powerful members of Congress. Second, the Social Security system could not meet its expenses by midsummer without prompt legislative action (Achenbaum, 1986, p. 87).

Many special interest groups expressed their opinions on these recommendations, but the bottom line was that those lined up *against* the commission's recommendations were outmatched by those in favor of them. All of the commission members who had promised to stand up in favor of the proposals did so, and were extremely effective in lining up both Republicans and Democrats behind the compromise legislation. In Achenbaum's (1986) description of the events of the time:

> Critics had ample time to express their views. The American Association of Retired Persons spent thousands of dollars on a mail campaign protesting the COLA delay and taxation of Social Security benefits; the National Alliance of Senior Citizens, which claimed to be the nation's second largest old-age interest group of individual members, rejected the compromise; Maggie Kuhn of the Gray Panthers praised some items but declared the package as a whole unacceptable. The U.S. Chamber of Commerce and the National Federation of Independent Business denounced the new taxes imposed on older people and self-employed workers . . . Several public employee unions protested the mandatory coverage of new federal workers (p. 88).

The amendments of 1983 were so effective, though, that the trust funds which had been running dry began to develop large surpluses. The concern that people had raised over the years about the ability of the Social Security program to survive as a "pay-as-you-go" system had been answered. The surpluses would help to offset expenditures in the early 21st century when the numbers of working persons contributing funds is forecast to decrease in proportion to the number of retirees drawing benefits. The Social Security program had been made fundamentally sound. The huge surpluses that were developing would cover all but 5 percent of projected expenditures, so that only slight payroll tax increases or slight benefit reductions would be necessary for thirty to forty years (Kingson, 1989).

The successes of the Social Security system since the landmark 1983 amendments have, however, recently stirred up a quite different concern. In 1969 President Johnson had brought the Social Security trust funds into the accounting of the federal government's general revenues to offset large military expenditures during the Vietnam war. Ever since that time there have been calls to take the trust funds off the budget, most recently because it has been claimed that they are hiding the true magnitude of the federal deficit.

In fact, the 1983 amendments had tried to address this issue by requiring that Social Security be removed from the budget process by fiscal year 1993. The Gramm-Rudman-Hollings deficit reduction law (1985) tried to accelerate this removal to fiscal year 1986 and, to further protect the trust funds, Social Security was excluded from any budget documents, budget resolutions, or reconciliation, and it was barred from any across-the-board cuts that may be caused by Gramm-Rudman-Hollings budget reduction mandates (Special Committee on Aging, 1990).

Nevertheless, the trust fund surpluses were still factored into the calculation which determine how much of a deficit the government was running, disguising how deep a budget cut Gramm-Rudman-Hollings will require to meet reduction targets.

Future of Social Security

Several proposals have been put forth since 1989 that would remove the trust funds from the calculations for deficit reduction. A bipartisan approach to taking Social Security off-budget was at the top of the Congressional legislative agenda in 1990, but debate on it became contentious and partisan in the wake of proposals to reduce Social Security payroll taxes. At the forefront of the ongoing debate was a tax cut proposal by Senator Daniel Moynihan (D-NY), one of the principals of the NCSSR who had helped to create the trust fund surpluses. He now felt that the surpluses were much too tempting to a deficit-ridden federal government. Moynihan had charged the federal government with "extortion" by hiding the true size of the budget deficit behind the bloated trust fund. His Social Security Tax Cut Act of 1991, although not approved, sought to curtail the government's spending of the surplus, estimated as $74 billion in 1991 and to have grown to $225 billion by the year 2000. Moynihan contended that the Social Security tax is one of the country's most regressive levies, putting a greater burden on middle- and low-level earners than does the income tax (Prud'Homme, 1991).

Moynihan had proposed that the federal government reduce payroll taxes and return the Social Security program to a pay-as-you-go system in which current contributions are used for current benefits. The plan would have cut the tax to

5.7 percent in 1991, to 5.5 percent in 1994, and 5.2 percent in 1996 (Prud'Homme, 1991). Critics of this proposal warned that cutting taxes when the federal deficit loomed so large might be foolish. Others suggested that the cap on wages subject to the Social Security payroll tax be raised to offset any loss in revenues.

In 1992 the issue of modifying or completely removing the earnings test became a focus of discussion. Some argued that the need for persons over age sixty-five to remain in the work force negated the need to discourage continued employment after receiving Social Security benefits. Others argued that maintaining the earnings test preserved the intention of the Social Security program to serve as a replacement of income. The validity of applying an earnings test up to age seventy and removing it thereafter at an age when few remain in the work force also was questioned. Demographic and economic changes make this an area of Social Security policy that deserves a comprehensive review and updating.

The Social Security Amendments of the 1980s made many changes in the disability program. Most of these focused on various work incentive provisions for both Social Security and Supplementary Security Income (SSI) disability benefits. These amendments also required the Social Security Administration (SSA) to conduct periodic reviews of current disability beneficiaries to certify their continuing eligibility. This was to become a massive workload for the SSA and one that was highly controversial. SSA was chosen to administer the new program because of its reputation for successful administration of the existing social insurance programs. SSA's nationwide network of field offices and large-scale data processing and recordkeeping operations also made it the logical choice to perform the major task of converting over three million people from State welfare programs to SSI.

Throughout the 1980s and 1990s there was growing bipartisan support for removing SSA from under its departmental umbrella and establishing it as an independent agency. Finally, in 1994 the Social Security Independence and Program Improvements Act of 1994 (PL 103-296) was passed unanimously by Congress. In a ceremony in the Rose Garden of the White House, on August 14, 1994, President Bill Clinton signed the act into law.

Interest in the future security of the Social Security System is increasing as the large number of persons become eligible for Social Security retirement benefits. Citizens born in the post World Was II period—the much discussed baby-boom generation—is heading toward retirement, and the generation that will take its place in the workforce is far smaller, raising fears about the sustainability of the program.

The following list of important current characteristics of the Social Security System is taken from Social Security Reform 1996, A Twentieth Century Fund Guide to the Issues:

• The average monthly Social Security check of retirees (in 1995) was $860.

- The Social Security benefits of an average wage earner retiring in 1996 will be about 42 percent of his or her average earnings, while comparable figures for low and high wage earners are 78 percent and 28 percent, respectively.
- About 95 percent of American workers are required to contribute to the Social Security program.
- All who work the required ten years are eligible for benefits when they reach retirement age. Benefits are based on average covered earnings over thirty-five years.
- Administrative costs for Social Security are about 1 percent of benefits (administrative costs for private insurance are between 12 and 14 percent of annual benefit amounts).
- The Social Security Trust Fund is invested in U.S. Government Securities.
- Social Security is not responsible for any growth in the federal deficit.

In addition to this list of positive attributes of the system, the same publication raises questions about current problems Social Security must confront in order to maintain its viability. These issues are summarized as follows:

- It may be impossible to maintain the current level of benefits because of the aging of the baby-boom generation scheduled to become eligible for full Social Security benefits in 2010.
- Recipients up to now receive far more in benefits than they contributed in payroll tax.
- In 2030, there will be slightly fewer than three persons between the ages of twenty and sixty-four for each person sixty-five and older. This compares to a ratio of five to one in 1996.
- Many younger workers believe that they will receive few if any Social Security benefits when they retire because there will not be enough workers to pay for their benefits.
- The Trust Fund had about $459 billion in reserves in 1996. Under existing conditions, interest from the Trust Fund would be needed to meet current obligations in 2012. In 2019, it would be necessary to use Trust Fund principal along with accruing tax revenues to meet expenses.
- Many proposals have been advanced to reform the Social Security system. As yet there is no consensus about how to adjust the program's operations to avoid the anticipated depletion of the Trust Fund.

It is apparent that some revisions in the Social Security system need to be implemented in order to assure its continuity and to maintain its broad public support. Obviously, a highly productive society with low inflation and ample opportunities for continuing employment—either full or part time—will contribute to the soundness of the program. The Trustees of Social Security use conservative scenarios to project the future of the system. Any enhancement of the economy would improve its financial status. But, because economic growth has been cyclical it is prudent for conservative financial projections to be used to protect the economic interests of a large portion of our population.

Many proposals to close the gap of the shortfall projected for 2029 have been made. Proposals that maintain existing principles of the system include the following:

- Raise the eligibility age for full retirement, currently at age sixty-seven.
- Increase the annual wage income on which Social Security taxes are computed.
- Permit a portion of the Trust Fund to be invested at a higher rate of interest than currently provided in U.S. Government Securities.

In addition, there are a series of proposals that depart from the current principles of Social Security. These include:

- Privatization of investment to assure each beneficiary a basic benefit along with a secondary benefit derived from the investment of a portion of the Trust Fund.
- Means testing that would reduce or eliminate Social Security benefits for retirees who have other sources of income.

Chen (1996) notes that "privatizing Social Security means that the primary responsibility for retirement income will shift from the tax payer and government to workers who are required to save and to invest the savings in the private sector." What would the costs be for administering the investments and what are the risks of investment in the private market? Chen adds that "the privatization debate essentially revolves around the comparative advantages and disadvantages of defined benefit plans with pay-as-you-go financing and defined contribution plans. In general, Social Security is a defined benefit plan; it guarantees a benefit based on a predetermined formula. Privatized plans are defined contribution plans; they do *not* guarantee a specific level of retirement income" (1996).

Advocates for privatizing Social Security assume that interest rates on investments will be high. This may not be the case consistently. Also, Social Security provides a combination of retirement, survivorship, and disability benefits in a single package. Private insurers do not offer this total package. In addition, the Social Security program favors a redistribution of income to the lowest wage earners, a feature that would be lost in privatization proposals.

While we cannot always accurately forecast the soundness of our economy we should not be rushed into major changes in the Social Security system. However, prudent management of this major program requires careful analysis of funds and changes to assure the continuity of the program.

In 1995, about forty-three million Americans received benefits under the old-age survivors and disability programs. This group included some twenty-six million elderly retirees, six million spouses and children, seven million survivors of deceased workers, and four million disabled workers. Social Security in combination with Medicare distributes among all working families the burdens of caring for the elderly and the disabled, so that no one family has to bear the huge costs of caring for elderly relatives who are sicker than average or who outlive their savings. Without Social Security, approximately half of the older population in this country would fall below the poverty level.

More than seven million survivors of deceased workers (including 1.4 million children) receive benefits under Old-Age Survivors and Disability Insurance (OASDI). Some 5.5 million workers (and their spouses and children) receive monthly cash benefits as a result of severe and prolonged disability. Similar retirement and disability insurance policies in the marketplace would be very expensive. The disability policy provided by Social Security is equivalent to a $203,000 policy in the private sector. A similar dependent and survivor policy for a twenty-seven-year old, average-wage worker with two children would be equivalent to a $295,000 policy.

Contract with America Advancement Act of 1996 (PL 104-121)

This bill, signed by the President on March 29, 1996, made a change in the basic philosophy of the disability program. Beginning on that date, new applicants for Social Security or SSI disability benefits can no longer be eligible for benefits if drug addiction or alcoholism is a material factor to their disability. Unless they can qualify on some other medical basis, they cannot receive disability benefits. Individuals in this category already receiving benefits had their benefits terminated as of January 1, 1997. Previous policy had been that a person who had a medical condition that prevented working was disabled for Social Security and SSI purposes—regardless of the cause of the disability. Another significant provision of this law doubled the earnings limit exemption amount for retired Social Security beneficiaries on a gradual schedule from 1996 to 2002. In 2002, the exempt amount will be $30,000 per year in earnings, compared with $14,760 under previous law.

The Personal Responsibility and Work Opportunity Reconciliation Act of 1996 (PL 104-193)

This "welfare reform" legislation signed by the President on August 22, 1996, terminated SSI eligibility for most non-citizens. Previously, lawfully admitted aliens could receive SSI if they met the other conditions of entitlement. As of the date of enactment, no new non-citizens could be added to the benefit rolls and all existing non-citizen beneficiaries were eventually to be removed from the rolls (unless they met one of the exceptions in the law). Also effective upon enactment were provisions eliminating the "comparable severity standard" and reference to "maladaptive behavior" in the determination of disability for children to receive SSI. Also, children currently receiving benefits under the old standards were to be reviewed and removed from the rolls if they could not qualify under the new standards.

TAX ABATEMENT AND RELIEF PROGRAMS FOR THE ELDERLY

The issues surrounding Social Security and Medicare are so widely publicized in our society that we seldom consider some of the other benefits accruing to our elderly population—all along the income spectrum—from the very wealthy to the very poor. As Hendricks and Hendricks (1986) note:

> Because the debate has concentrated on direct expenditures, such as Social Security and Medicare, the impact of tax preference and relief programs has been neglected (p. 471).

The provisions in our tax code that preferentially recognize older men and women include the income tax credit for the elderly, the one-time-only exclusion of capital gains of up to $125,000 from the sale of a house for those fifty-five years or older, an increased standard deduction, and the exclusion of benefits under Social Security (and Railroad Retirement Tier I) for low and moderate income beneficiaries.

Taxation of Social Security Benefits

However, concerns over the solvency of Social Security in the early 1980s raised questions about the tax-exempt status of Social Security benefits. It became clear that Congress had not specifically excluded such benefits from taxation but that the Bureau of Internal Revenue had ruled in 1938 and 1941 that, because Congress had never provided the legislative authority to tax them, Social Security benefits were not subject to taxation.

The National Commission on Social Security Reform, recommended in 1983 that the benefits of higher income recipients be taxed and that the resulting revenue be added to the Social Security trust funds. The Social Security Act Amendments of 1983 incorporated this recommendation for individuals having annual incomes over $25,000 and for joint-filing couples with incomes over $32,000. These thresholds are determined by the total of all other taxable income and tax-exempt interest income. Because beneficiaries have already been taxed in the amount of their half of Social Security contributions during their term of employment, only one-half of the benefits over the designated threshold levels were considered taxable (as constituting the employer's share of contributions to Social Security).

The intent of the income thresholds was to avoid lower-income elderly being affected by the taxation of benefits. However, the income thresholds were not indexed, and it probably will not be many years before Social Security beneficiaries of more moderate income will be affected.

Capital Gains

Home ownership provides a potential asset for retired elderly persons. In order to protect against the impact of inflationary gains to the value of a home, the Internal Revenue Act of 1964 established a one-time exclusion of capital gains on the sale of a home by a person aged sixty-five years or older. This protection from tax liability encourages the elderly to sell their homes, reduce their expenses and realize a windfall. Although initially only capital gains of $20,000 for persons sixty-five or older were excluded, the maximum excludable gain has been increased by Congress over the years to $125,000 of the adjusted sale price of a home, and the age at which the capital gain exclusion can be taken has been lowered to fifty-five years.

Tax Credit for the Elderly

In 1954 Congress passed the Tax Credit for the Elderly. This provision of the Internal Revenue Code qualifies single retirees, aged sixty-five or older, to take a tax credit equal to 15 percent of the first $5,000 or, for qualified joint filers, the first $7,500 of total retirement income. This credit had initially been instituted to correct the inequity between most retirement income, which was fully taxable, and the tax-free status of Social Security and Railroad Retirement Tier I benefits. The Social Security Act of 1983 extended this benefit to the totally and permanently disabled and increased the initial amount which qualifies for the credit.

Tax Reform Act of 1986

A sweeping change of the Internal Revenue Code, the Tax Reform Act of 1986, provided the elderly with an increase in the amount of their standard deduction, allowed those sixty-five and older to forgo filing a return if their income is below $5,650 for an individual, $9,400 for joint married filers with one spouse sixty-five or older, or $10,000 if both spouses are sixty-five or older. Offsetting this increased standard deduction in this Act was the repeal of the extra personal exemption for the elderly that had been enacted in 1948 and provided some post-war economic relief to elderly taxpayers. As of 1987 this exemption was no longer available, and the 1986 Act also raised the deductible amount of medical and dental expenses from 5 percent of a taxpayer's adjusted gross income to

7.5 percent. The latter move had a potentially negative impact on the elderly, who consume a large proportion of health care.

While tax incentives may have quite a bit of appeal to persons who have above-average incomes and are subject to high marginal tax rates, those with lower incomes realize very little benefit. In fact, because tax incentives have not contributed significantly to personal savings among the young or lower income taxpayers, Congress has started to question the wisdom of providing them. On the whole, income from assets provides a much higher and more important portion of total retirement income than savings or pension annuities. Less than one in three elderly retirees have pension benefits, very few low-income earners utilize Individual Retirement Accounts (IRAs) and the personal savings rate for Americans tends to range from one-third to one-half lower than the savings rate in Europe at 5 percent to 8 percent of total disposable income.

The Food Stamp Program

A major relief program started by Executive Order in 1961 under the auspices of an experimental eight-county hunger project, the Food Stamp Program now serves an estimated thirty million people in the United States who receive monthly food stamp allotments to buy food in the marketplace. The program was conceived as a way to increase income security and to help alleviate malnutrition and hunger by increasing food purchasing power while reducing surplus food stocks by increasing farm and retail food sales. The rules for elderly persons' participation in the Food Stamp Program differ from those for the general population; assets, medical costs and shelter expenses are treated much more liberally for the elderly due to their high medical costs and fixed income status. Ninety percent of all the elderly participants in the Food Stamp Program live alone, and 80 percent of these participants are single elderly women.

Special assistance in applying for Food Stamp benefits is available to the elderly who are eligible for or recipients of Social Security or Supplement Security Income (SSI) benefits through local Social Security offices. Run by the United States Department of Agriculture (USDA), the Food Stamp Program expects each participating household to contribute 15-20 percent of its gross income toward the purchase of food. Approximately one-fourth of elderly household participants receive only the minimum $10 per month benefit. The average monthly benefit for elderly recipients in 1990 was about $40. In rural areas, where many poor elderly reside, only 31 percent receive Food Stamp benefits.

The nonparticipation of many low-income households, as reported by the Government Accounting Office in 1985 (based on reports from private organizations, the USDA and the President's Task Force on Food Assistance), concluded that: 1) a majority of households were unaware of their eligibility to participate, 2) low benefits provided little incentive for elderly to apply, 3) the complexity of the applications required documentation and administrative requirements were intimidating, 4) the difficulty of physically getting to offices to make application posed a seemingly insurmountable obstacle for many, and 5) the social stigma of receiving government assistance discouraged many who were eligible from participation in the program.

A 1988 study by the Congressional Budget Office indicated that households with elderly members had participation rates of 34 percent to 44 percent. Two studies released by the USDA's Food and Nutrition Service in 1989 also found that participation rates for the elderly were quite low, with only 33 percent of all eligible elderly individuals participating. Under the weight of the huge budget deficit facing the federal government it is doubtful whether any new initiatives to increase participation levels for entitlement programs such as Food Stamps will be forthcoming, however.

Summary

What the future brings in the way of meeting the economic security needs of the elderly in our population will depend on how we adapt to a changing world in which technologies may alter dramatically our perception of the trajectory of an individual's productive working years. One important question is whether programs providing income security at a certain chronological age stand in the way of market flexibility, or whether we have created a social environment that stifles innovation and experimentation in our social roles and expectations (Myles, 1991). In an examination of the "short history of retirement," Myles found that:

> There are already signs that many European and North American countries may be experiencing what one authority calls the "dechronologizing" of the life-course . . . New technologies and the transition to service-based economies have reduced the importance of a labor pool constituted by muscular young people with quick reflexes.

> Indeed, in some scenarios the new technologies in goods production require a return to a craft-based model of production, in which the knowledge and skills of older workers are at a premium.

> It is possible to imagine a future in which periodic labor-force exits for retraining and child-rearing—and even leisure—extend over the whole of the life course rather than being confined to the beginning and end of the economic life cycle (Myles, 1991, p. 8).

CHAPTER
7

Health Care Policies

Conflicts in policy formation in the area of health care result from basic differences regarding the role of government, federal or the state, in providing or supporting health care services. Arguments about whether health care is a right or an accommodation to an important human need continue and proponents of each side of the debate staunchly defend the correctness of their views. Opponents of government health programs say they are not guaranteed in the Constitution and proponents say they are implied by the general welfare clause. The issue is complicated by considerations such as whether the provision of health is the primary responsibility of employers, the private sector through insurance, the individual through savings or the public sector. The debate also invites discussion of how much care should be provided, whether all people should have the same access to care irrespective of their financial status, and whether there are some areas of the care delivery system that are more appropriate for public sector rather than private sector involvement.

While some of these arguments have been applied to a variety of other policy issues, they are particularly heated in the area of health care services because of the critical nature of health care, because illness arouses compassion, especially toward those who are in great pain or in life-threatening situations. Despite obvious humanitarian impulses, there is, however, a strong anti-public-sector lobby that is supported by skepticism about the ability of the public sector to manage a large public program and an overriding concern about payment for care, with its inevitable impact on federal or state budgets and taxes.

Thus far, society has been unable to reconcile these differences or to present viable alternatives to government programs. In the last decade of the 20th century, "one of the major issues confronting the nation is the crisis in health care and its effects on the American people and our economy" (Lee, 1991, p. vii). Lee has elaborated on his perception of the current crisis by saying that the current system is structurally flawed, that health care costs are out of control, that access is difficult for tens of millions, and that serious problems continue to diminish the quality and efficiency of care.

> ... although the nation spends $2 billion a day on health care, there are 30-40 million Americans without any health insurance and at least as many with health care coverage that is inadequate to meet their needs (Lee, 1991, p. vii).

It is in the context of a crisis in health care that we look back to review the evolution of health care policies, noting that some aspects of national health care coverage for specific segments of our society currently exist and could ultimately be incorporated into a comprehensive national health care system. For example, people who serve in the military, their dependents and veterans of military service all have access to a separate medical care program that essentially is fully paid for by the federal government out of general revenues from tax dollars on the total society. Native Americans are eligible for health care services provided by agencies of the federal government and paid for by general revenue taxes. The President, Vice President and members of Congress all have access to a specialized health care system fully paid for by general revenue taxes.

Each of these systems could be called socialized medicine in that the providers of the services are employees of the federal government, operating under the aegis of the federal government and following rules promulgated by the federal government and experiencing no, or very limited, competition from the private sector. Grouping of these programs does not suggest that they are all of the same quality, but an evolving national health care policy should consider whether or not it is desirable to maintain them as separate special programs, to build incrementally on all or some of these precedents or to design an entirely new program.

A REVIEW OF HEALTH CARE POLICY IN THE UNITED STATES

Hill-Burton

An early involvement of the federal government in health care policies was seen in an amendment to the Public Health Services Act, the Hospital Survey and Construction Act of 1946 (PL 79-725; August 13, 1946), which authorized grants to the states for surveying their hospitals and public health centers and for planning construction of additional facilities, as well as authorizing grants to assist in such construction. The act clearly established the need for a designated single state agency to carry out the purposes of the law and introduced a methodology for determining need for additional facilities. It established standards for construction of health care facilities, specified that facilities built under this program would provide the care without discrimination on account of race, creed or color (although separate but equal facilities were allowed), and designated that there should be a reasonable volume of services to persons unable to pay for their care.

This legislation established planning principles that were to be used for the next forty to fifty years and were based on a methodology that correlated demographic changes in the targeted population with the need for additional construction of health service beds. Also of importance was the required commitment of institutions receiving a grant from the federal government to provide services to those who were unable to pay. This law stimulated rapid growth of health care services to correct the decline in health care construction that had occurred during the Second World War.

Valuable as it was in establishing a planning principle for health care construction, this law initially was limited to planning for the construction of hospital beds and did not incorporate planning for a comprehensive health care service system. In 1949, the program was extended and appropriations were increased (PL 81-380). The Medical Facilities Survey and Construction Act of 1954 (PL 83-482; June 30, 1954) continued the grants for hospital construction and also made them available for diagnostic treatment centers, chronic disease hospitals, nursing homes and rehabilitation facilities. In 1964 the law was amended and continued. At this time, chronic disease hospitals and nursing homes were combined into a new category of long term care facilities (PL 88-443, August 1964). (This may have been the first formal designation of nursing homes as long term care facilities, a much narrower definition than the current usage of long term care as referring to the continuum of chronic care services.) The Medical Facilities Construction and Modernization Amendments of 1970 (PL 91-296), passed by Congress in an override of a presidential veto, provided grants and loans and loan guarantees for construction and modernization of health facilities.

Thus, over a period of twenty-five years, the Hill-Burton program clearly defined a role for the federal government in the stimulation and support of health care. Of special importance to the later development of health care policies, it also established a relationship between the federal and state governments in the implementation of the law. The program initiated federal participation in planning for the availability and distribution of health services at the community level. "Until the Hill-Burton Act was passed in 1946, the federal government's role in the delivery of health services was confined largely to specific disease control activities primarily focused on infectious disease" (U.S. Senate, 1973). The act also established the Federal Hospital Council, an eight-person advisory group to the Surgeon General that was to assist in implementation.

Meanwhile, in 1963, President Johnson formed a Commission on Heart Disease, Cancer and Stroke to explore ways to reduce the incidence of these diseases. The recommendations of this commission had been enacted into law as the Heart Disease, Cancer and Stroke Amendments of 1965 (PL 89-239), which created the Regional Medical Programs (RMP) for the purpose of establishing a comprehensive approach to bringing the latest and best knowledge related to these diseases to practicing clinicians and the public. Important characteristics of this act were the delegation of responsibility to local communities rather than to the federal government and a change in the direction of health planning from an emphasis on facilities of the Hill-Burton approach to one on comprehensive delivery of services.

The Allied Health Professions Personnel Training Act was passed in 1966 "to meet the growing need for supervisors of paraprofessional workers, for teachers in allied health professions, highly skilled technical specialists, and allied health professionals in new areas of medicine" (Hyman, 1975, p. 19). Two years later the Health Manpower Act of 1968 (PL 90-490) represented a more comprehensive approach to planning for health services manpower.

Comprehensive Health Planning

The Comprehensive Health Planning and Public Health Services Amendments of 1966 (PL 89-749; November 3, 1966) established a federal grants program to states, with state contributions based upon a predetermined formula, to assist states in comprehensive and continuing planning for their current and future health needs. This act amended prior Public Health Service Acts to provide a more effective use of federal funds for health services planning. In order for states to participate they were required to establish a single state agency for administering or supervising the administration of the state's health planning functions under the act. Furthermore, additional grants were made available for comprehensive regional or metropolitan planning activities as well as for special studies, training or demonstration programs.

The rapid growth of health services spurred by federal legislation, especially the Medicare and Medicaid programs combined with the growth of the population to so greatly increase health care costs that they required a larger percentage of the gross national product. The Social Security Amendments of 1972 (PL 92-603; October 30, 1972) therefore was passed in an effort to install some mechanism to control costs while assuring both an equitable distribution of resources and the availability of personnel to provide services. Certificate-of-need programs were introduced to limit the construction of new health care facilities in a rational way that would respond to demonstrated needs in the population to be served. The expectation was that limiting construction costs and maintaining high occupancy of existing facilities would reduce costs of providing services.

Section 1122 of this law gave states that had not already passed certificate-of-need (CON) laws the authority to review and approve requests for health facilities and programs that involved federal funds. The law also was intended to spur states that had not yet done so to pass CON legislation, which requires a health institution to obtain a CON from the state to show its need before venturing into a new building program or new service. Although only four states had passed CON legislation prior to 1971, 19 additional states did so within the next three years. During the Reagan administration, withdrawal of funds to administer the program led to the expiration of the Comprehensive Health Planning legislation. While this did not eliminate state-authorized CON requirements, it did stimulate the withdrawal of state controls in many states.

While many western countries, including many much poorer than our own, offer national health care insurance plans, the idea of such a plan in the United States has been the subject of much debate for most of this century. Nevertheless, public opinion polls over many years have shown that a majority of all adult age groups favor a national health care plan (Riley and Froner, 1968). Recent national public opinion polls have shown that approximately 90 percent of Americans favor a federally sponsored universal plan that would cover all age groups (Kligman, 1990).

However, despite the support of many leading proponents over the years (including Presidents Theodore Roosevelt, Franklin D. Roosevelt and Harry S Truman), it finally came to be accepted that Congress simply would not pass such legislation and that a compromise was in order. Medicare and Medicaid were born out of such a compromise in 1965, which showcased an incremental approach to public policy. Medicare did indeed offer national health care coverage, in the form of universal health care insurance for acute and rehabilitative care, but only for the elderly, defined as those sixty-five years of age and older. Medicaid provides health benefits to all age groups, but only after a screening process known as "means-testing" has determined that a beneficiary is sufficiently impoverished to be eligible for coverage. Medicaid has proven to be especially helpful for elderly persons needing long term health care in nursing homes, because Medicare will cover only a very limited period of "rehabilitative care" in a long term care setting. However, Medicaid requires personal impoverishment.

Even though these two federal health care programs provide important support for the elderly, a recent speaker at a health care issue forum at the 1990 Governor's Conference on Aging in Arizona noted that:

> In regard to our way of delivering health care and implementing rational health policy, we are about as sophisticated as chicken soup. A comforter is needed for all Americans, including the elderly. We have only a tattered patchwork quilt (Kligman, 1990, p. 1).

A patchwork is generally the result of piecing together readily available materials, and the evolution of major health care legislation through incremental policy-making in our country makes this analogy quite appropriate.

How did we end up with an essentially "tattered" patchwork? How have we remained so far behind other western industrialized countries in the provision of comprehensive national health care? The following discussion of the major health care policies in force in the United States, Medicare and Medicaid, may help answer these and other questions.

Precedents to Medicare and Medicaid

One of the greatest impediments to our country's developing a consistent and universal health care policy has been the strong influence of interest groups. A proposal for compulsory health insurance was advocated as early as 1912 by President Theodore Roosevelt and the Progressive Party and was initially endorsed in 1916-1917 by such important interests as the American Medical Association (AMA). The AMA reversed its position in 1920 and has since opposed any suggestion for implementing a national health care plan (Rich and Baum, 1984). It has been suggested that this reversal occurred because of an overwhelmingly unfavorable response from rural physicians and the political climate of noninterference that prevailed during the 1920s (Blumenthal, 1988). The AMA has since become known as the nation's most vigorous opponent of governmentally sponsored health insurance in any form.

The idea of a national health policy disappeared in the midst of a conservative political climate and the seeming prosperity of the 1920s even though "reform leaders in the 1920s predicted that health insurance would be among the first items of progressive legislation to be part of the Social Security Act" (David, 1985, in the introduction).

President Franklin D. Roosevelt wanted to include a health care plan in the Social Security Act of 1935, but fear that the powerful AMA could effectively block the entire legislation through intensive lobbying (including protesting telegrams from hundreds of physicians) led to its elimination from the initial Social Security package. Debate over national health insurance for the next two decades was dominated by this initial political show of strength by the American Medical Association.

The AMA further solidified its place as a formidable interest group when in 1939 it helped defeat a bill introduced by Senator Robert Wagner, Sr. (D-NY) proposing matching federal grants to support state public health systems. With re-election looming in 1940, President Roosevelt withdrew the support he initially had offered. The Wagner bill died in committee and the AMA's success in opposing federal health care policies had acquired an aura of invincibility.

By 1943, though, another proposal for national health insurance came to the floor of Congress, again under the auspices of Senator Wagner but this time jointly with Senator James E. Murray (D-MT) and Representative John Dingell (D-MI). Drafted by Social Security Administration Officials Wilbur Cohen and I. S. Falk, the Wagner-Murray-Dingell bill was said to have had President Roosevelt's support after the 1944 election, but his death in 1945 effectively muted the call for national health insurance for the next several years.

National health insurance was brought back to the center stage of political action in 1948 when President Harry S Truman strongly supported the Wagner-Murray-Dingell bill in his State of the Union address. The motivation behind Truman's support, however, was suspect. It was suggested that he was simply using Congress's inaction on this national health care bill as an example of the "do-nothing Congress" he had cited in his successful, but narrowly won bid for re-election in 1948. Political animosity generated between the President and Congress meant that national health insurance under Truman's supportive guidance was doomed to defeat.

AMA opposition to national health insurance in the ensuing years showed an intensity that would become legendary. During 1948-1951, a nationwide lobbying campaign costing over $4,000,000 was conducted by the medical association in an attempt to kill the concept of national health insurance once and for all. In 1950, defeat of several members of Congress who had been actively opposed by the AMA was interpreted widely as a sign of the popular rejection of national health insurance (Derthick, 1979). The record shows that no progress toward national health insurance was made during Truman's presidency. Whether this was a result of AMA lobbying or the political climate under Truman is open to debate.

The AMA declared victory, but other forces also were at work. Political conservatives had always been, as they still remain, adamantly opposed to any policy promoting an increase in the size and scope of the federal government's responsibilities or redistribution of resources among social groups. This ingrained opposition allowed the AMA to recruit hundreds of other conservative lobbying groups, from the Daughters of the American Revolution (DAR) to the U.S. Chamber of Commerce, to join the fight against national health insurance (Corning, 1969; Harris, 1969). The conservative domination of key committees in Congress by Southern Democrats and Northern Republicans during the postwar era, and the slow-changing composition of congressional committees, also benefited opponents (Blumenthal, 1988).

Always looking ahead at the "big picture," however, was Wilbur J. Cohen, a member of the original Social Security Board. As early as 1949, Cohen proposed that the Social Security Administration should gain experience with a limited or experimental public health plan in order to determine problems that might be encountered. Legislative steps he helped to initiate provide insight into the logical incremental political progression that has led the country toward "the health care mainstream." Beginning in 1950, he:

> Drew up a strategy that involved congressional authorization for "vendor payments" for medical assistance to the aged, blind, and disabled (enacted in the Social Security Amendments of 1950, 1956, and 1960); medical determination for a disability "freeze" [eliminating the interrupted earnings period of disability from the computation of social security old age or death benefits] (1952 and 1954), disability insurance benefits (1956), and [finally] Medicare and Medicaid (1965). This sequence of events brought the Federal Government into the mainstream of health policy administration. I felt we had to get our feet wet in working with hospitals and physicians to discover ways and means of resolving problems, rather than debating ideology in a vacuum (Cohen, 1985, p. 4).

The AMA originally opposed early versions of medical public assistance proposals such as the direct vendor payment suggested by Cohen. On April 24, 1956 the AMA informed Congress that:

> The American Medical Association is vigorously opposed to the proposed changes in the medical care provisions for the public assistance sections of the Social Security Act. We are opposed to those changes because they are needless, wasteful, dangerous, and contrary to the established policy of gradual Federal withdrawal from local public assistance programs (U.S. Congress: House Committee on Ways and Means. Public Assistance Titles of the Social Security Act, Hearings on HR 9120, 84th Congress, 2nd Session, 1956).

The AMA obviously had gained considerable clout in the health care arena. The health insurance debate had been fundamentally altered by the AMA and its conservative cohorts to the extent that proponents of such legislation were now weighing political factors as heavily as substantive ones (Blumenthal, 1988). As noted by Marmor in *The Politics of Medicare* (1970, p. 23), legislators had started to identify the least disputed problems and to advocate modest solutions which they felt would obtain the most wide-ranging support. In this environment,

> From a political standpoint, the decision to focus on health insurance for the elderly was inspired. The elderly go to the polls, and even in the 1950s, demographic trends made clear that they were growing rapidly in numbers. As a defined group with certain common interests (not the least of which was their need for health insurance), they were also easier to organize and mobilize than the electorate as a whole. If politicians opposed health care for the elderly, they ran the risk of seeming to be against aged Americans (Blumenthal, 1988, pp. 6-7).

Focusing on health care for the elderly also represented a rational approach, since there was increasing evidence that the elderly required more medical care and were less financially able to pay for it (Achenbaum, 1986). Three additional specific reasons made building an incremental plan for a national health program for the elderly onto the existing Social Security framework a logical choice: 1) because medical costs tended to vary so much from time to time and from person to person, the cost of medical care in retirement could not be budgeted; 2) the premiums for adequate health insurance were too costly for most people in retirement to pay out of retirement income or savings; and 3) adequate and affordable private-sector health insurance was generally available only through group coverage, and retired persons usually could not be brought together for this purpose (Schulz, 1988).

As early as 1944 the Social Security Board had discussed the idea of providing up to sixty days of free hospital care to Social Security beneficiaries (Achenbaum, 1986). In 1950, as a fall-back position after the defeat of the Truman national health care proposal, Wilbur Cohen suggested to Oscar Ewing, chief of the Federal Security Agency (FSA), a Medicare-type proposal (Cohen, 1985). Ewing subsequently publicly proposed in June 1951 that pensioners, as part of their Social Security benefits, should receive sixty free days of hospital care (Blumenthal, 1988).

Their frequently needy status as a group made the aged a far more politically acceptable recipient of federal assistance than other sectors of the American population. Tying health care for the elderly to Social Security had the added advantage of associating the health care benefit with a popular public program that countered conservative arguments that governmental aid programs destroy the incentive of recipients to provide for themselves, since no one can receive benefits under Social Security without having paid into the program during his or her working years.

Still, many conservatives felt that any new health insurance for the elderly should be means-tested, to ensure that benefits would be restricted to those in need. To avoid any appearance of creating a welfare program, advocates of health insurance carefully tried to design a program that would be very difficult to oppose, and Oscar Ewing's initial proposal offered a bare minimum of benefits, covering only 60 days of hospital care.

From 1950 to 1957, support for health care proposals tended to be overshadowed by the push for disability insurance, the passage of which was perhaps a necessary prelude to national health insurance for the elderly (Derthick, 1979). Then in 1957, a national health insurance program was introduced by Representative Aime Forand (D-RI) to the House Ways and Means Committee, calling for a package of benefits somewhat expanded from that suggested by Ewing's proposal. The bill probably had been prepared by a coalition of former and current Social Security Administration officials and Nelson Cruikshank, the social security director for the AFL-CIO. Forand may have been the only member of the Ways and Means Committee willing to sponsor the bill; the Committee's chairman and most powerful member, Wilbur Mills (D-AK) adamantly opposed it. Mills' opposition to the bill was perhaps the "biggest single obstacle to their success" (Derthick, 1979, p. 321), and his opposition to health care amendments to the Social Security Act would continue for almost eight years.

After it was rejected in 1958, Forand reintroduced the bill to the committee in 1959, only to have it turned down again. In hearings concerning the bill in July 1959, Arthur S. Flemming, then Secretary of the Department of Health, Education and Welfare, stated the Eisenhower Administration's view that adequate medical care could be achieved through public assistance or voluntary plans. Voluntary versus compulsory health insurance continued to be a major issue in the long-standing debate about government's role in health care.

Despite the administration's stated position, a newly established Senate Subcommittee on Problems of the Aged and Aging in 1960 recommended that health benefits should indeed be added to the Social Security system. The subcommittee had been founded in 1959, was headed by Senator Patrick V. McNamara (D-MI), and held many public hearings that received extensive publicity.

During the presidential campaign of 1960, John F. Kennedy increasingly made health insurance for the elderly an issue. In the spring of that year, Richard M. Nixon, who had been pleading with Republican leaders to endorse some sort of health insurance for the elderly program as a response to Kennedy's proposal, finally prevailed on the Eisenhower administration to introduce a measure. The administration program, introduced by Flemming, was called "Medicare" (but was radically different from the Medicare plan later introduced during the Johnson administration (Pearman and Starr, 1988). The 1960 proposal would have set up a state-sponsored, means-tested health program that would offer protection against long-term (catastrophic) illness for the low-income elderly (David, 1985).

Another bill, introduced by Senator Jacob Javits (R-NY) and other liberal Republicans was, however, more to Nixon's liking. It offered matching grants to states subsidizing state programs to help low-income persons over age sixty-five purchase limited private health insurance plans (David, 1985).

Because both the Nixon and Kennedy campaigns were calling for some new form of medical assistance for the aged, Congress in 1960 finally increased the federal grants-in-aid to states that were disbursing medical payments to beneficiaries of Title I old-age assistance (Achenbaum, 1986).

Neither the Forand bill or the Republican proposals received much support in the powerful House Ways and Means Committee, where even Chairman Mills "could recognize a preelection political stampede when he stood in its path" (Blumenthal, 1988, p. 9). Although Mills remained as strongly opposed as ever to attaching health care insurance to Social Security:

> He rapidly introduced and shepherded through his committee and the House of Representatives a health care program that he could live with—an expansion of the existing Old Age Assistance program that, since 1956, had provided limited funds to States to cover the health care costs of the very poor elderly. Comparable legislation quickly passed the Senate under the sponsorship of a powerful conservative member of the Senate Finance Committee, Robert Kerr (D-OK) of Oklahoma (Blumenthal, 1988, p. 9).

This bill, which was to become known as Kerr-Mills for the two men who had shepherded it through Congress, created a new category of federal grants to address the problem of elderly persons being impoverished as a result of medical costs. Both Mills and Kerr had been leading proponents of disability insurance and had greatly increased their political capital through their successes in that arena during the 1950s. Kerr-Mills provided for the health care of the needy elderly through unlimited federal support, but only so long as the states provided matching funds:

As a means-tested welfare program administered at the State level, it was far more acceptable to conservatives than a universal health insurance program for the aged funded through Social Security and administered by the Federal Government (Blumenthal, 1988, p. 9).

Mills had no objections to increased federal involvement in social problems provided the funding source was sound, and financing the Kerr-Mills program through joint state and federal general revenues insured against depleting the Social Security trust fund.

The passage of the Kerr-Mills Bill under the Social Security Amendments of 1960, signed into law by President Eisenhower on September 13 (PL 86-778), seemed to answer the concern in Congress for providing for the elderly ill (David, 1985). Known as Medical Assistance for the Aged (MAA) under the new Title XVI, it expanded the existing welfare structure by increasing the money available for vendor payments for persons in the Old Age Assistance program (the non-contributory welfare assistance plan for elderly persons not entitled to Social Security pensions).

The precedent for this sort of aid had already been set three decades earlier when federal funds were made available to the states to cover the medical expenses of the needy unemployed (Rich and Baum, 1984). Now with the advent of MAA, the category of need was broadened to include a new category—the "medically needy," who were by definition elderly persons whose income minus medical expenditures was below a predetermined eligibility level (Rich and Baum, 1984).

Initially, the medical community opposed the Kerr-Mills bill as an unwelcome extension of government into the health care field (David, 1985). Eventually though, the AMA began to see the bill's advantages, foremost of which was that it would serve to quiet further discussion of health insurance if Kennedy should win the election.

However, at least one group of doctors, known as the Physicians Forum (an organization of 1,000 doctors connected with the large teaching universities of the east) dissented from the AMA's position (David, 1985). Their chairman, Dr. Allen M. Butler, stated in a letter to the *New York Times* that Kerr-Mills was simply "an unsound extension of charity medicine—and is no solution to the health needs of the aged. . . . Quality of care can be protected only if benefits are in the form of services, not cash indemnities" (October 15, 1960, p. 1).

Similarly, at the annual meeting of the National Conference on Social Welfare in July of 1960, keynote speaker Charles Schottland pointed out that Title XVI "would merely set up another group on relief . . . the wealthier States would be obliged to add a new category to public assistance while the poorer States could continue their negligence" (Myers, 1970). The consensus at this national conference was that:

> Kerr-Mills was a disappointing new law that added further confusion to the welfare situation. Its benefits were too few to make up for the complications in application (David, 1985, p. 43).

However, Wilbur Cohen saw the benefits of Title XVI (Kerr-Mills) in preparing the way for a Social Security-based compulsory health insurance program. He had helped formulate the final version of the Kerr-Mills bill for Senator Kerr in a spirit of compromise that may have cost him some liberal support. He had suggested that:

> All during 1960-65 I took the position that both Medicare-type and Medicaid-type programs were necessary and desirable and were not in conflict with each other. Mr. Mills readily accepted this view. The only other strong Medicare supporters I was able to persuade to take this view were my long-term friend, Senator Paul Douglas (D-IL), and Senator Albert Gore (D-TN). The leading opponent was Senator Pat McNamara (D-MI), the Senator from my home State (Cohen, 1985, p. 9).

Senator McNamara apparently believed that any alternative or compromises, no matter how appealing, would severely dilute the potential chances for the passage of compulsory national health insurance for the elderly (David, 1985).

Such a compulsory Social Security-based health insurance program for the elderly had been embodied in a 1960 bill introduced by Senators John Kennedy (D-MA) and Clinton Anderson (D-NM). To counter that proposal, the AMA had taken out a full page ad supporting Kerr-Mills in major papers around the country, proclaiming Title XVI to be the answer for needy elderly who required help with their medical expenses.

Kennedy-Anderson bill provisions were carried forward in 1961 under Senators Cecil King (D-CA) and Anderson. Their bill (which represented official administration policy during the Kennedy and Johnson administrations), covered ninety days of hospital care, 180 days of nursing home care, outpatient diagnostic services, and 240 home visits by a nurse. In an attempt to deflect AMA and provider group opposition, the King-Anderson bill provided no coverage for physician services and assured provider groups that there was nothing in the legislation that would "give federal agencies any authority to alter the practice of medicine, the provision of hospital or nursing home care, or the management of hospital or nursing home personnel" (Blumenthal, 1988, p. 8).

The battle lines were drawn. Title XVI (Kerr-Mills), which was now providing national health care for the indigent elderly population, had taken a needs-based approach that required participation and partial financing by state governments. Many states had refused to participate, and five states having just 32 percent of the elderly population were receiving almost 90 percent of the funds (Rich and Baum, 1984). Kennedy, as noted above, supported the King-Anderson proposal to finance hospital insurance through Social Security.

The alliances pitted against the latter policy were formidable and included the AMA, all insurance carriers, most Republicans from the south, the American Nursing Home Association and the American Hospital Association. Although the latter two organizations would potentially benefit from this proposal, they appeared unwilling to oppose the powerful AMA publicly.

Alliances that championed a compulsory health care plan for the elderly through Social Security included Democrats from the north (the old Civil War issue of states' rights may have deterred many Southern Democrats), nurses, social workers, labor unions, the National Council of Senior Citizen Organizations, and other groups of the elderly.

On February 21, 1963, Kennedy delivered the first presidential message to deal solely with the problems of the elderly. It was entitled "Special Message on Aiding Our Senior Citizens" and its key proposal was a national health insurance plan for the elderly which Kennedy had named the "Hospital Insurance Act of 1963." He called for expanding the scope of the King-Anderson bill and creating a Federal Health Insurance Trust Fund that would separate health insurance funds from the Social Security Trust Fund in order to allay fears among the more conservative members of Congress (such as Wilbur Mills) that the proposed compulsory health insurance program would bankrupt the whole Social Security system (David, 1985).

Kennedy, however, was unable to muster the support needed to get the King-Anderson legislation through Congress. When pushed to a vote in the Senate in July 1962, King-Anderson lost by a very narrow margin of 52 to 48 and it would not be until after Kennedy's death that the proposal would finally be passed by Congress.

During the national elections of 1964, Lyndon Johnson continued to support most of Kennedy's unfinished legislative agenda, showing his commitment to King-Anderson by campaigning vigorously for improvement in health care for the elderly. His subsequent landslide victory paved the way for the passage of the Social Security-based national health insurance program that was to become known as "Medicare" and its relatively unheralded companion legislation for the poor—"Medicaid" (an expanded version of Kerr-Mills).

The increased number of liberals and Democrats elected to the Congress on the coattails of Johnson's victory greatly increased the chances for passage of this health care legislation. Several aspects of the country's demographic picture also presaged success for such a proposal. The number of Americans aged fifty and older had increased significantly in the late 1950s and early 1960s, and the increasing politicization of the elderly (22% of the vote in the 1964 election was cast by citizens aged 60 and over), had led to the development of many self-interest and advocacy groups, such as the National Council of Senior Citizens (Pearman and Starr, 1988).

Even Wilbur Mills realized that he should now support some kind of measure along the lines of the Johnson administration Medicare proposal. Mills had dramatically changed his stance in order to assume a leadership position with regard to the administration proposals that symbolically had been given the highest Congressional priority by making them S 1 and HR 1, the first bills to come before the 89th Congress. Johnson, on his part, realized the need to give Mills time and room to operate and did not try to influence Mills as to how he should report the Medicare bill out of the House Ways and Means Committee.

The AMA, feeling threatened, offered a substitute proposal to Medicare, as did some of the Republicans on the House Ways and Means Committee. The common element between these two proposals was that both went beyond hospital care and provided for coverage of physician services. The AMA sought to counter the King-Anderson-based Medicare proposal by saying its benefits were too limited. An AMA endorsed Eldercare proposal was an expanded version of the Kerr-Mills bill that would have funded state programs subsidizing more comprehensive private health insurance programs for the elderly and covered payment of physicians' services (Blumenthal 1988). The Republicans criticized the Administration bill as being compulsory and proposed a voluntary program of comprehensive health and physicians' insurance. A bill introduced by the ranking Republican on the House Ways and Means Committee, John Byrnes (R-WI) was derived from private policies of the Aetna Insurance Company and would be financed in part by beneficiary premiums and in part by general federal revenues.

In January of 1965, Chairman Mills took the House Ways and Means Committee into executive session for six weeks of intensive bargaining and discussion. In early March Mills asked Wilbur Cohen (present at the executive session proceedings to provide technical assistance) why the two proposals could not be united. Mills suggested that a voluntary program of hospital and physicians' insurance as put forth by the Republicans be included in the King-Anderson Medicare hospital plan, along with a third component borrowed from the AMA's Eldercare proposal that would cover the health care of indigent elderly.

> Mills did not spell out any specifics to me. Rather, he urged prompt action on a draft of such a proposal. I asked for a little more time to complete such a major undertaking. Mills said no, he wanted it the next day. I felt he sensed he had caught his critics off guard, and he did not want them to have time to regroup. He was like a general who saw he could rout his opposition and follow them as they retreated. Mills recessed the Committee in his eagerness to forge ahead under the momentum that had been created. It was a brilliant tour de force (Cohen, 1985, p. 6).

Medicare and Medicaid

A three-tiered legislative package within the Social Security Amendments of 1965 was thus created by the House Ways and Means Committee and was approved by the House of Representatives on April 9, 1965. The keystone legislation, the King-Anderson compulsory hospital insurance had become Part A of the

Medicare bill. Voluntary insurance with premiums costing initially only $36 per year ($3 per month), to be matched by the federal government out of general revenue funds, had become Supplementary Medical Insurance (or Part B) and would cover physician and a range of other medical/provider services. An expanded version of the state-operated, income-based Kerr-Mills program, much like the Eldercare proposal from the AMA, was included as a separate health insurance program, Medicaid, that would allow states to provide coverage to all individuals, regardless of age, who were either medically indigent or welfare recipients (Hughes, 1986). All of the interests appeared to have been accommodated: legislators, bureaucrats, the health insurance and drug industries, the physicians and the hospitals (Pearman and Starr, 1988).

A last ditch effort to block these amendments to Social Security was to come in the Senate Finance Committee from Senator Russell Long (D-LA), who complained that the bill did not provide significant protection against the costs of catastrophic illness. To correct a legitimate coverage lapse in the legislation that would come back to haunt the legislators in later years, Long offered a solution of unlimited hospital and physician benefits that would be financed through deductibles and a co-insurance payment based on ability to pay (Blumenthal, 1988). However, President Johnson prevailed over the Senate Finance Committee, and the Senate passed the Social Security Amendments of 1965 on July 9 without Long's amendment, although with 513 changes from the House version.

Six meetings were required to work out the differences between the bills, and it is testimony to Mill's influence that the final version of the Medicare legislation was essentially that passed by the House. The conference report was then quickly accepted by both houses of Congress in late July and signed into law by President Johnson on July 30, 1965 at Independence, Missouri in the presence of former President Truman.

The bill was quite a bit more comprehensive in scope than anyone had previously imagined possible because Mills had orchestrated an ambitious combination of three very different programs. A new Title XVIII of the Social Security Act created Medicare, a hospital, nursing home, and home health insurance plan financed by a new trust fund; Part B of the package was a voluntary major medical plan; and Medicaid, the new title XIX, was a total health package for the poor.

> Title XIX removed certain restrictions that had hampered the effectiveness of Kerr-Mills. First, States could no longer hold adult children responsible for medical expenses of parents . . . Second, States had to remove all residence requirements for applicants . . . an advantage for those elderly who moved from one State to another for retirement. Third, States had to provide reimbursement for comprehensive services: hospital care, nursing home care, home health visits, doctor's fees, drugs, and diagnostic work. In 1965 only five States offered those services under Kerr-Mills (David, 1985, p. 148).

The patchwork health care package that prevails to this day was thus formed through compromise among those in favor of compulsory health insurance, those in favor of voluntary insurance, and those who felt that eligibility for government-sponsored health insurance should be income-based. The charity/social insurance dilemma had not been resolved, however. It had only been postponed temporarily.

While the final product was a victory of sorts for elderly interest groups, the AMA had managed to quash enactment of a truly comprehensive health care program. The resulting structure of Medicare was a hybrid including the federal government, fiscal intermediaries (insurance companies), and service providers. It has been suggested that Medicare was able to be passed because insurance companies were bought off by assuring them a piece of the action as fiscal intermediaries. Instead of providers dealing directly with the federal government, they must deal with a local insurance company acting as the fiscal intermediary. Hospitals-providers in each state are allowed jointly to select their fiscal intermediary.

Hospital associations were pleased that Part A of the Medicare package provided for hospital insurance. Physicians were placated by the legislation's Part B, which assured them of a method of payment. Finally, the southern contingent (including Wilbur Mills) were happy because the Kerr-Mills Bill had been retained in an expanded version (Medicaid). Physicians liked Medicaid because it provided them with a direct source of payment and eliminated their need to do volunteer work for the poor.

Major Amendments to the Original Medicare and Medicaid Legislation

The result of all these negotiations contained a potential for unforeseen future problems that could not be easily rectified because they were rooted in the history of the legislative political process (Blumenthal, 1988). Medicare's most glaring problem was the way rapidly increasing costs of health care were stimulated by its payment policies, such as payment to hospitals on the basis of reasonable costs and reimbursement physicians on the basis of usual and customary fees. Mills had pushed the legislation through the House so quickly that a complete estimate of its costs had not been possible. Perhaps more importantly, resistance by health care providers had effectively convinced legislators that unless providers were paid the way they wanted to be paid, they would refuse to serve Medicare patients (Blumenthal, 1988).

Many of the problems that continue to haunt Medicaid are also the product of its legislative past.

> While Medicaid's roots were in America's welfare tradition, the law itself was poorly conceived. Hospital Insurance, or Medicare Part A, had been discussed over a seven-year period, debated in thousands of pages of hearings, and written about in numerous special reports and investigations.

. . . Medicaid, Title XIX was casually added as an afterthought in March 1965. It was Mills' attempt to include the opposition. Medicaid was an application of the AMA's own Eldercare Bill, which was in turn an elaboration of the 1960 Kerr-Mills program. The Kerr-Mills program, itself a hastily passed law without benefit of much Congressional discussion, was not working well, and Mills was happy to find a way to dispose of it (David, 1985, pp. 148-149).

In 1971, Congress started to try to deal with escalating costs and other problems that emerged in the Medicare and Medicaid programs. The Senate Finance Committee in that year mandated the creation of Professional Standard Review Organizations (PSROs) that would supersede all state and fiscal intermediary review policies. Under the 1972 Social Security Amendments, the country was divided into 203 regions, each with its own PSRO made up of local doctors who would review the medical profession's service to Medicare and Medicaid patients.

From the start the PSROs were criticized as soft, inaccurate, and weak in terms of teeth to check providers. The Carter Administration of 1976-1980 kept pressure on the PSROs to prove their worth through tough reviews (Pearman and Starr, 1988, p. 17).

Another step taken to try to control costs was the authorization under Medicare of HMOs, which would provide services on a capitation basis (Achenbaum, 1986).

Congress also tried dealing with payment mechanisms and regulations within the Medicare system. An economic index was introduced into the Medicare payment formula to allow charges for services to rise only as much as inflation in general (Pearman and Starr, 1988). Other provisions in the amendments of 1972 "perpetuated this pattern of extending health care and broadening the scope of governmental responsibility" (Achenbaum, 1986, p. 169). Kidney transplants and dialysis treatments were covered, Part B now authorized chiropractic services, as well as podiatry and speech pathology. Coverage for nursing home care was detailed in nineteen separate provisions under Medicare and Medicaid.

In 1974, the National Health Planning and Resources Development Act was passed to avoid costly duplication and waste in the construction of health facilities, and a National Health Planning Board was created and charged with coordinating health services in 200 designated sectors.

By 1982, important new directions in the financing of Medicare were established in PL 97-248, the Tax Equity and Fiscal Responsibility Act (TEFRA). Automatic increases in Part B deductibles were initiated, Part B premiums were set at a constant percentage of costs, employers were required to offer to workers aged sixty-five to sixty-nine and their dependents the same benefits offered to younger workers, and Medicare was downgraded from the first to the second payer of health costs for workers, shifting more responsibility to the private-insurance sector (Pearman and Starr, 1988).

TEFRA of 1982 also added benefits for the terminally ill (hospice care), including such services as medical social services, counseling, nursing and physician services, home health aid, therapies and medical supplies, and short-term hospital care. A 5 percent co-payment was required for hospice services and drugs.

Federal employees were for the first time required to buy into the Medicare program for hospital insurance, increasing the pool of revenues available.

The TEFRA legislation also incorporated reimbursement controls by setting hospital budget targets for expenditures, denying duplicate payment for outpatient services, eliminating private room subsidies, refusing reimbursement for ineffective medicines, placing limits on Medicare payment for ancillary operating costs, and instituting a cap of 9.7 percent per case on overall hospital rate increases. The Secretary of Health and Human Services was directed to develop methods to pay providers on a prospective basis. Finally, the PSRO program was repealed and the Secretary of HHS was required to enter into contracts with professional peer review organizations to promote effective, efficient, and economical delivery of health care under Medicare.

By 1983, the prospective payment system introduced for study under TEFRA was put into practice in the Social Security Amendments of 1983 (PL 98-21). In order to try to control costs of medical service that had increased 18 percent per year between 1972 and 1982 (David, 1985), hospitals would now be paid a specific reimbursement based on previously established flat fees per illness.

> Illnesses were broken down to 467 diagnostically related groups [DRGs]. Illnesses within the same group are reimbursed at the same fixed amount of money, no matter how long a patient remains in a hospital (David, 1985, p. 153).

Critics of this provision charge that DRGs do not allow for individual differences in disease state, leading to the possibility of premature hospital discharge they designate as "quicker and sicker."

Other measures passed by Congress in 1983 to ease the financial burdens on the Medicare Hospital Insurance Trust Fund included the doubling of the medical insurance withholdings of self-employed individuals, increasing the first day deductible for hospital services, and increasing monthly premiums for Part B. A measure (PL 98-90) that did not change any cost estimates was the technical correction of raising the stated cap for hospice services under Medicare that had resulted from a Congressional Budget Office error in calculation.

In 1984 the reimbursement rate for hospice care was increased and in April of 1986 the Medicare and Medicaid Budget Reconciliation Amendments of 1985 enacted numerous adjustments. This act amended the TEFRA of 1982 to make the hospice benefit permanent and to increase its Medicare reimbursement. The Age Discrimination in Employment Act was amended to extend Medicare coverage to workers seventy and older. (See Chapter 9). Medicare coverage was made mandatory for state and local government employees hired after April 1, 1986 and voluntary for workers hired before that date. This legislation also expanded Medicaid coverage to provide optional Medicaid hospice benefits and required HHS demonstration projects on home and community services for Medicaid recipients, concentrating on the needs of those with mental retardation and Alzheimer's disease. Finally, this budget reconciliation measure limited the ability of persons who have placed their assets in a trust to qualify for Medicaid benefits and revised various Medicaid provisions pertaining to nursing home reimbursement.

The Medicare and Medicaid Patient and Program Protection Act of 1987 (PL 100-93), attempted to stem the tide of corruption that was threatening to overwhelm the federal health care system (especially in Medicaid) by issuing clear standards that medical practitioners must meet to participate in these federal programs. This law focused on providers.

> Ironically, it is *not* the recipients of Medicaid who are misusing funds, but the purveyors of services. Instead of evidence that the poor are receiving quality care, headlines after Congressional investigation describe Medicaid services in derogatory terms such as "Medicaid mills" (David, 1985, p. 152).

The provisions of PL 100-93 amending Titles XI, XVIII, and XIX of the Social Security Act were directed toward protecting beneficiaries from unethical health care providers and improving anti-fraud provisions. The law expanded and recodified HHS authority to prohibit participation in federal and state health care programs by medical practitioners convicted of: 1) fraud and abuse; 2) criminal offenses related to health care delivery under Medicare, Medicaid and other federal and state health programs; and 3) non-program related offenses. It also authorized criminal penalties for claims submitted by unlicensed or fraudulently licensed practitioners, required states to provide HHS with information on physician license revocations or suspensions, and limited Medicare beneficiary liability for costs of health care provided by excluded practitioners.

Resource-Based Relative-Value Scale

Although Part B of Medicare has been an important source of payment of physicians' fees for the elderly, it has not adequately supported the services of geriatricians, medical specialists in the field of geriatrics. Because these physicians need to spend time with their patients in order to understand the complexity of the problems presented, which rarely constitute a single diagnosis, they often must serve as case managers who coordinate other services. This frequently involves working with family members on issues related to medical decisions. However, the time needed to perform this role for older persons has not received adequate reimbursement from the Medicare program. The Omnibus Budget

Reconciliation Act of 1989 addressed the disparity between payments for procedures and payment for cognitive care—taking a patient's history, giving advice, or developing a treatment plan. In this law, Congress authorized the development of a resource-based relative-value scale (RBRVS) on which an appropriate fee schedule would be constructed. Since January 1, 1992, physicians' services are to be ranked according to the resource costs involved in providing them. It was recognized that primary care had been substantially undervalued and Medicare payments to different kinds of physicians were changed. Payments for internal medicine and family practice were increased and those for radiology and for some areas of surgery were reduced. This change was intended to improve the primary care given to older persons and make possible more appropriate payments to physicians who care for the elderly (Iglehart, 1990).

However, the regulations prepared in 1991 may have thwarted the intention of the law. Although the OBRA 1987 regulations called for physicians to be more involved in resident assessment and care planning, the new rate schedule does not include the cost of meeting these requirements for residents in nursing homes unless the resident is transported to the physician's office, when there is additional reimbursement for the physician as well as for the transportation. Under old rules physicians had been paid at a lower rate for each resident treated after the first one during a nursing home visit. As of 1992, physicians are to be paid the same amount for visiting each resident, regardless of how many are seen and may be paid for more than one visit per month to the same patient. Prior regulations limited payments to no more than one visit per month (AAHA, February 1992).

Catastrophic Care Coverage

In 1988, an important new bill was passed, calling for coverage of care of catastrophic illness under the Medicare legislation. Such coverage had been favored as far back as 1964 when Senator Russell Long (D-LA) had tried to amend Medicare to extend its benefits (David, 1985) and in 1974, when President Gerald Ford's administration had backed an effort to add catastrophic illness coverage to Medicare.

Otis Bowen, Secretary of HHS, in December of 1986 had presented a number of programs designed to protect elderly Americans against the costs of catastrophic illness. Bowen proposed expanding Medicare so that no beneficiary would have to pay over $2,000 a year for acute care, making the cost of additional coverage an extra $4.92 per month in Medicare Part B premiums. Another part of Bowen's plan would have encouraged individuals to save and private companies to provide coverage for long-term care in nursing homes through tax incentives. The Reagan administration embraced all aspects of Bowen's plan except for the crucial long-term care nursing home incentives. Through ruling out this key element of Bowen's catastrophic care plan, the Reagan administration effectively doomed this legislation.

Passed into law on July 1, 1988 as PL 100-360 the Medicare Catastrophic Coverage Act (MCCA) was hailed by its framers as a landmark bill protecting the elderly against ruinous health costs, protecting older Americans who could be devastated by the potentially catastrophic costs of acute illnesses. This was the largest single expansion of the Medicare program in its history to that date and was to represent a major step forward in achieving comprehensive coverage of health care costs for older persons.

The act met with almost instantaneous disapproval from many of the elderly who perceived that this new law offered only a minimum of new coverage for chronic care while taxing them to pay for the benefits through supplemental premiums and income tax surcharges. Their violently negative reaction to the law resulted in its being repealed on December 13, 1989 by PL 101-234, the Medicare Catastrophic Coverage Repeal Act of 1989.

The short-lived law would have included unlimited hospital coverage after an annual deductible, increased skilled care coverage in nursing homes from 100 days per episode of illness to 150 days per year with no prior hospitalization required, payment for 50 percent of outpatient prescription drug expenses exceeding $600 per year (with the share of coverage increasing in subsequent years), and increasing home health care coverage to include eighty hours of respite care for relatives attending patients at home. In addition, spouses of Medicaid nursing home residents would have been able to keep approximately 50 percent of a couple's resources in order to avoid spousal impoverishment and Medicaid was to have paid Medicare deductibles, premiums and coinsurance for those below the poverty level. The biggest gap in the new coverage was its failure to cover the catastrophic costs for the older person of having to spend prolonged periods in a nursing home, whether for skilled or nonskilled care or requiring home-delivered services not covered by existing programs. The financing plan involved a two-tier payment system. All beneficiaries were to have paid a flat premium and those with higher incomes were to have paid a surcharge on their income taxes (Coleman, 1990).

Major objections to the new law were two-fold. One was to the inadequate provision of nursing home care and other was to the cost and financing arrangements. Prior Medicare funding was from basic deductions from wages of all employees covered by Social Security, whether they used the service or not. Under the new law, wealthier older persons were to pay a larger share of the cost of all of the program rather than spreading the cost among all Social Security participants irrespective of income. This was seen as "the imposition of an apparently progressive Medicare surtax to pay for benefits that masked a major retreat from social insurance financing of Medicare" (Thursz, 1989, p. 30).

Although the law was repealed, several benefits expanding coverage through Medicaid were retained. These include: the requirements that states pay all Medicare premiums, deductibles and copayments for Medicare beneficiaries who have incomes less than 100 percent of the federal poverty threshold but do not qualify for Medicaid coverage; that states increase the amount of income and assets that may be kept by a person whose spouse's nursing home costs are being paid by Medicaid (the spousal impoverishment provision); and continuation of the activities of the Pepper Commission, a bipartisan group charged with making recommendations for legislation to cover costs of long term care for the elderly and ensuring adequate health coverage for the estimated 31 million Americans who lack health insurance.

Although the rejection by older persons of the unusual financing method that placed the bulk of the responsibility on the users gave rise to characterization of older persons as "greedy geezers" unwilling to assume the full responsibility for the financing of the new law, it actually was a combination of disappointment in the content of the law and protest against a change in a long established principle of funding public programs that fostered the rebellion and ultimate repeal of the law.

The Pepper Commission, under the leadership of Senator John D. Rockefeller (D-WV), on March 2, 1990 made the following two major recommendations:

1. To assure universal health care coverage for all Americans through a job-based/public system.
   - Businesses with 100 or fewer employees are encouraged to provide health insurance for their employees and nonworking dependents.
   - All business with more than 100 employees must provide private health insurance or contribute to the public plan for all employees and non-working dependents.
   - The public plan will cover employees and dependents who contribute and nonworking individuals who buy in or are subsidized.
   - The minimum benefit package must include primary and preventive care, physician and hospital care and other services.
   - At full implementation, all Americans will be required to have health insurance through their employer or the public plan.
2. To provide home and community-based long term care services and protection against impoverishment for people in nursing homes.
   - Severely disabled persons of all ages should be eligible for social insurance for home and community-based care.
   - The plan should establish a Nursing Home Program (NHP) for nursing home care to provide an ample floor of financial protection, ensuring that no one faces impoverishment.
   - In addition, all nursing home users should be entitled to social insurance for the first three months of nursing home care. This "front-end" insurance would allow people who have short stays to return home with resources intact.

However, neither of these recommendations was implemented.

Unlike many proposals for changes in health care policies that Congress has seen, this was a bipartisan effort to find both a way to provide health care insurance for millions who do not have coverage and a way to minimize the risk of impoverishment for those who require nursing home institutionalization.

The severe national budget deficit and state budget crises loom as the greatest obstacle to the development of a new comprehensive health care policy. However, many earlier objections to a universal health care program have subsided because the business sector wants to reduce the high cost of providing health care benefits for employees. A change in the political orientation of Europe and disintegration of Communism and the Soviet Union have reduced some of the need for massive defense budgets and Congress may find it easier to allocate funds for incremental changes rather than comprehensive revisions.

Seidman (1991) has identified eight goals essential for consideration in the evolution of health care policies. These are: universal coverage; comprehensive benefits; built-in cost controls; improved quality of care; a broad range of long term care services; affordable, adequate and equitable financing; a favorable impact on U.S. competitiveness; and compatibility with American traditions, principles and institutions. The issue of compatibility with American traditions and institutions argues for incremental changes of existing and historical approaches rather than the introduction of totally new approaches.

Also of considerable interest in the debate about national health care coverage will be whether any new program will be more responsive to the needs of chronically ill persons, especially extended chronic care service that would include institutional as well as home-delivered services. Because Medicare focuses on acute care requirements, hospitalizations and physicians care, it inadequately addresses older persons' needs arising from increased disability and dependency. Medicare coverage in a nursing home is limited to skilled care and that for only a defined period of rehabilitation. When progress toward some specific goal no longer is evident, the care required is reclassified as custodial and no longer is supported by Medicare. Payment for nursing home care has caused impoverishment of so many older persons that Medicaid rather than Medicare has become the primary payor for nursing home care. Not only the Pepper Commission's recognition of the critical importance of long term care funding but also a National Planning Association study titled "Curing U.S. Health Care Ills" (Seidman, 1991) have emphasized the need to include long term care in a national health program. Many proposals that have been offered in Congress have included long-term care, but usually as a separate provision because of concern regarding its high cost. Nevertheless, nursing home care, the provision of its services, ready access, its relationship to noninstitutional services, the quality of the services, and sources of payments for the care must be considered an important part of health care policies.

Although long term care or chronic care should be viewed in its entirety, which includes institutional and noninstitutional care, much of the policy focus historically has been on improving the quality and reducing the cost of institutional care, which now constitutes from 23 percent to 50 percent of the cost of Medicaid (Holahan and Cohen, 1990). Medicaid has become one of the major state expenditures. Although most people in need of supportive services express a desire to receive these services while continuing to live at home, both the Medicare and Medicaid programs encourage the use of institutional settings through the greater availability of funding for nursing home care rather than home care. "Medicare payments of home health care comprise a relatively small 2.7 percent of total program outlays" (U.S. Senate, 1990). "For every person age sixty-five and older residing in a nursing home, there are nearly two times as many living in the community requiring some form of long term care . . . About 70 percent of the noninstitutionalized disabled elderly relied exclusively on unpaid sources of home- and community-based health care in 1989" (U.S. Senate, 1990). This means that support of coordinated systems that integrate multiple service programs with multiple sources of payments is critical to the development of chronic care policies.

The On Lok model in San Francisco illustrates how a consolidation of funding resources and a comprehensive program has been able to provide care at home, keep quality high while controlling costs. "By preserving or enhancing participants' health and independence, the care team minimizes the use of hospital and nursing home care" (Ansak, 1990, p. 73). The Chelsea-Village program in New York City, sponsored by the Sisters of Charity of Saint Vincent de Paul, provides another successful illustration of how to bring together programs and funding to "help older people stay in their own homes and out of institutions" (Brickner, 1978, p. 23). Any modification of the long term care policies should place emphasis on correcting the institutional bias currently practiced while searching for additional ways to enable people to receive care required while remaining at home.

Balanced Budget Act of 1997

The Balanced Budget Act of 1997 resulted in some major budget cuts. The budget agreement called for roughly $110 billion in Medicare savings over five years. This would come from slowing the growth of payments to hospitals, doctors, HMOs, nursing homes, laboratories, and home health agencies.

For the most part, these providers are financially strong enough to absorb such cuts without lowering the quality or availability of care. The cuts, however necessary, will do almost nothing to address the crisis the program will face when the first baby boomers start receiving benefits. This is because in many markets, payments by Medicare to hospitals are more generous than private insurance plans. Even where payments by Medicare to doctors are well below those of private payers, the Federal system remains attractive to doctors because it generally places far fewer restrictions on their decisions and treatments than private insurers now do.

Under the new agreement, recipients will have to contribute about $15 billion more in premiums over the next five years, a sacrifice smaller than it may seem. Almost two-thirds of the money will come from canceling a provision which allows the percentage of the cost of Medicare supported by premiums to fall after 1998.

The remaining $6 billion will be raised through a gradual increase in premiums, $4.50 a month per recipient by 2002. This small rise will be more than offset by about $10 billion of new benefits such as colorectal screening, annual mammography, diabetes management programs, and lower coinsurance payments for outpatient treatment. These benefits should cut participants' out-of-pocket expenses and their premiums for supplemental Medigap insurance.

Cutting the payments to doctors and hospitals will slow the growth of Medicare spending over the next few years, but it will do little to slow the program's spending over the long run because it does nothing to encourage efficiency (Reischauer, 1997).

Managed Care Issues and Themes

Managed care is a term that refers to capitated, prepaid services delivered by Managed Care Organizations (MCOs). Some general definitions used in a discussin of managed care are:

Managed Care refers, in general, to efforts to coordinate, rationalize, and channel the use of services to achieve desired access to services and outcomes while controlling costs. Such a definition can apply to health care services, social services, or a combination of the two.

Risk-based Managed Care describes care delivered by Managed Care Organizations (MCOs) that provide or contract to provide health care in broad but specified areas for a defined population and for a fixed prepaid price. The MCO is at financial risk to provide the services for the price and it uses various cost-controlling strategies to achieve that goal. An MCO is responsible for the health care of a population; benefits are specified (e.g., whether long-term care or mental health is included) but also are comprehensive within the established parameters; and the organization is at financial risk to provide the care within its resources.

Medicare Managed Care

Medicare Health Maintenance Organizations (HMOs) come in a variety of forms, with different internal incentives for participating providers. However organized, all Medicare HMOs are responsible for providing all services that Medicare fee-for-service covers, but the amount of capitation the Medicare HMO receives varies enormously within and between states. Medicare HMO capitation reflects 95 percent of the average fee-for-service Medicare billings in the county where the Medicare beneficiary lives. Thus, managed care revenues are directly linked to fee-for-service billings. Medicare HMOs (also known as TEFRA HMOs, because they were authorized by the Tax Equity and Fiscal Responsibility Act of

1982) allow seniors to direct their Medicare benefits to an HMO, which in turn is responsible for providing all covered Medicare services.

Variation in Medicare's Average Adjusted Per Capita Costs (AAPCC) is extreme, and it is AAPCC figures that determine the rates that Medicare pays to MCOs. These rates are also adjusted by specific factors including age and whether the beneficiary lives in a nursing home. Medicare HMOs receive 95 percent of a county's AAPCC for each enrollee; if the HMO enrolls Medicare beneficiaries whose care needs fall well below that average, the tax-payer does not save 5 percent, but rather pays something in excess of 100 percent of the fee-for-service costs. Ironically, if this leaves a sicker group in fee-for-service and results in even higher average fee-for-service costs, the Medicare HMOs are assigned a higher AAPCC the next year.

Medicaid MCOs for the Dually Eligible

To cap their financial liabilities, states have moved vigorously into capitation of Medicaid programs, particularly for care of women and children in the AFDC programs and, to some extent, for mental health and disability programs. States also have heavy liabilities for Medicaid for the elderly, falling into two general headings (payment of Medicare copayments, deductibles, and premiums so elderly Medicaid clients can access Medicare; and LTC expenditures, drug costs, and other costs not covered by Medicare). States have a keen interest in using managed care and capitation to manage their Medicaid programs for those people who are dually eligible for Medicare and Medicaid, but many practical problems arise.

Managed care is neither a panacea nor a disaster for older people. It has great potential for improved care, much of it unrealized. Each MCO plan and program must be evaluated individually on its merits. There are incentives for MCOs to save money by limiting access to all forms of care. Aging network personnel have already identified some of these problems, especially in localities where penetration rates of Medicare HMOs are high. The aging network needs to refine its ability to evaluate the strengths and weaknesses of individual MCOs, particularly in the light of their ability to serve the most vulnerable of seniors and avoid sweeping generalizations about all managed care.

HEALTH RESEARCH ON AGING IN
THE FEDERAL GOVERNMENT

With the increasing demands that the growing older population will place on the availability of a network of health and social services, considerable attention must also be directed toward preventing or reducing disabilities experienced as people age. In a recent report, the Institute of Medicine (1990) identified four areas of high-priority research where success would minimize disabilities associated with old age while reducing the financial burdens of chronic illness. These research priorities include: Alzheimer's disease and related dementias, incontinence, strokes, and the demineralization of bones and osteoporosis.

The major source of support for biomedical research under public auspices is allocations to the National Institutes of Health, founded in 1887 as the Laboratory of Hygiene to conduct research on cholera and other infectious diseases. In 1930, Congress passed the Ransdell Act renaming the laboratory the National Institute of Health. In 1937 the National Cancer Institute was established and in 1948 the National Heart Institute was established and the name of the overall organization was changed to the National Institutes of Health. At least 11 National Institutes of Health currently are investigating areas of particular importance to the elderly (U.S. Senate, 1990). A listing of these, as well as all of the institutes, is included in Appendix I. Of special importance is the National Institute on Aging, whose history is described below.

National Institute on Aging

The need for a National Institute on Aging that could serve as a focal point for conducting research studies into the medical, social, and behavioral aspects of the aging process was initially recommended by the 1961 White House Conference on Aging. After repeated administration resistance to this proposal over the years, one was finally created in 1974.

The major problem for the elderly had been identified by the House Committee on Interstate and Foreign Commerce to be:

> ... the maintenance of functional capabilities, both mental and physical, to the maximum extent so as to make life worth living as long as possible . . . The Committee feels that the importance of this goal is such that an institute should be created with the function of concentrating its efforts in this area, rather than continuing the existing situation (*U.S. Code Congressional and Administrative News,* 1974, p. 3,245).

The response to the recommendation of the 1961 White House Conference on Aging had been to give responsibility for aging research to the newly created (1962) National Institute of Child Health and Human Development (NICHHD), but only about 11 percent of the NICHHD's budget was allocated to aging research from 1964 to 1972.

Accordingly, at the White House Conference on Aging in 1971, delegates again called for the establishment of a dedicated National Institute on Aging that could respond to the need for research into the aging process, confront the problems inherent in an ever-growing aging population, and not have to compete with other program needs within the NICHHD.

There was extensive opposition from the Nixon administration. At the hearings held by the Public Health and Environment Subcommittee of the House Interstate and Foreign Commerce Committee on March 14, 15, and 16, 1972, administration witnesses expressed concern that creating an institute dedicated to aging research would only duplicate work already being done in other institutes. Dr. Merlin K. Duval, assistant secretary for health and scientific affairs in the Department of HEW, stated:

> ... There is little basis for separating this activity from research on the same disease when it afflicts the young or the middle aged. To do so would cause the almost inevitable result of duplicative work at two or more institutes, merely because a disease, such as cancer, can affect persons at many levels (*CQ Almanac*, 1972, p. 425).

Nonetheless, identical versions of a bill creating a National Institute on Aging passed the Senate and the House without going to conference in October 1972. Differences had been reconciled through amendments. As sent to the president, the final bill (HR 14424) included provisions for establishing community mental health programs for the elderly and for directing the secretary of HEW to prepare a comprehensive plan for aging research within one year.

President Richard M. Nixon promptly pocket vetoed the bill, contending that the creation of such an institute constituted an unnecessary administrative move that would simply duplicate current research efforts. In explaining his action Nixon remarked:

> In my Special Message to the Congress on Older Americans last March, I also emphasized the need to develop a comprehensive, coordinated program of aging research—one which includes disciplines ranging from biomedical research to transportation systems analysis, from psychology and sociology to management science and economics. The Secretary of Health, Education and Welfare has since appointed a new Technical Advisory Committee for Aging Research to develop a plan for bringing together all the resources available to the Federal Government in the aging research field (*CQ Weekly Report*, Vol. XXXI, 1973, p. 1,909).

> HR 14424, however, would set up an entirely separate aging research institute that would duplicate these activities . . . it could even fragment existing research efforts . . . I feel that both research and mental health programs for the aging should be carried out in the broader context of research on life-span processes and comprehensive mental health treatment programs now under-way (*CQ Almanac*, 1972, p. 82-A).

The following year Congress again sent bills to committee to create a National Institute on Aging. In the House, the Subcommittee on Public Health and Environment held hearings on HR 65 in March 1973 at which Under Secretary Frank Carlucci outlined the Department of HEW's objections to a National Institute on Aging. Similar arguments were sent to the chairman of the House Committee on Interstate and Foreign Commerce by Caspar Weinberger, Secretary of HEW, who pointed out that:

... the President did not sign a similar bill, HR 14424, in the 92nd Congress because it would have needlessly created another institute and would have unnecessarily duplicated authorities for activities already have (sic) carried on by the National Institute of Child Health and Human Development. We do not believe HR 65 would improve the quality or progress of aging research. It would simply create a new administrative structure with attendant overhead costs and administrative jobs to do what is already being done by the NICHHD and the disease-oriented institutes at the National Institutes of Health. Moreover, it would adversely affect ongoing aging research by fragmenting existing, well-integrated research efforts (*U.S. Code Congressional and Administrative News,* 1974, pp. 3,248-3,249).

Not long thereafter, and despite continuing administration opposition, on July 9, 1973, the Senate easily approved a similar bill (S 775) to establish a National Institute on Aging within the National Institutes of Health. One of Nixon's criticisms was addressed in this new bill, from which a provision for a community mental health program for the aged had been removed. Nixon's criticism concerning the overlapping of responsibilities was satisfied by a provision giving the Secretary of HEW the authority to coordinate overlapping areas of research and training and to assign responsibility to one institute or another when both had functions relating to the same subject (*U.S. Code Congressional and Administrative News,* 1974, p. 3,245).

In stating its reasons for calling once again for an Institute on Aging, the Senate Labor and Public Welfare Committee remarked that, in contrast to Nixon's veto statement and the statements of administration officials, aging research was fragmented throughout various agencies of the federal government and was being funded at very low levels. Specific reference was made to the National Institute of Child Health and Human Development's allocation of only an average of 10 percent of its budget for aging research (*CQ Weekly Report,* Vol. XXXI, 1973, p. 1,909).

The House on May 2, 1974 passed a virtually identical bill (HR 6175) with widespread bipartisan support. Reported out of the Subcommittee on Public Health and Environment by unanimous voice vote, the bill was co-sponsored by all members of the subcommittee and was subsequently reported from the full committee (Interstate and Foreign Commerce) by unanimous voice vote on March 7, 1974. The Research on Aging Act of 1974 (HR 6175) was signed into law (PL 93-296) by President Nixon on May 31, 1974.

As testament to the need for a dedicated institute responsible for research and training in the biomedical, social and behavioral aspects of aging, the National Institute on Aging has actively addressed many diverse issues over the years. In a report by a committee looking into the organizational structure of the National Institutes of Health (1984), the National Institute of Aging was singled out as having the longest sustained growth for a new institute relative to the remainder of

NIH, as measured from 1976 (the year funds were first appropriated) to 1984 (Institute of Medicine, 1984, p. 12).

As one of the thirteen institutes of the National Institutes of Health, NIA has often engaged in collaborative operations with federal agencies and the other NIH institutes. Current priorities for NIA include research and training in: 1) Alzheimer's Disease and Related Disorders—Research into the causes, diagnostic methods, treatment, management of symptoms, epidemiological studies, and the psychosocial factors associated with caregivers; 2) understanding the genetic and environmental bases for differences in the aging process; 3) studies that lead to improvement of the health and functional status of frail older persons; 4) research into the possible connections between dietary deficiencies and/or exercise and its impact on the health and effective functioning of older people; 5) preventing the need for long term care or institutionalization, easing the burden of family care, and forecasting the supply of long term care and related demand; 6) research into ways to improve the health and longevity of ethnic and racial minority populations; 7) training and career development to prepare individuals for careers in research and teaching in geriatric medicine and the social sciences; and, 8) cross-cultural and cross- national comparative studies concerning diverse populations.

National Institute of Mental Health

Also in 1974, a Center for Aging was created by administrative action within the National Institute of Mental Health (NIMH), perhaps in response to prior Congressional interest in addressing the mental health needs of older Americans. Mental health provisions had been eliminated from the 1974 Research on Aging Act to facilitate its passage.

The National Institute of Mental Health, originally one of the National Institutes of Health under the Public Health Service, had been made a separate entity under the 1966 reorganization of the PHS. A strong, well organized and well connected mental health lobby helped it achieve this status, which many officials within the Public Health Service supported because of the innovative approach of NIMH to coordinating its research programs with programs providing direct services (CQ Weekly Report, Vol. XXVII, 1969, p. 170). The move away from the primary mission of NIH, research, and toward direct service response efforts (or applied social problems research) had been a critical deciding factor in the removal of NIMH from NIH in 1967 (Institute of Medicine, 1984, p. 21).

Even before the 1966 reorganization of PHS had gone into effect, another reorganization was planned for implementation in 1968. Under it, PHS was divided into three administrations, each reporting to the Under Secretary for Health: 1) health services—Health Services and Mental Health Administration (HSMHA); 2) research and education—National Institutes of Health; 3) consumer and environmental health activities—Consumer Protection and Environmental

Health Service. With a goal of bringing together all public health efforts dealing with health services and individual health, the National Institute of Mental Health was absorbed into the newly created Health Services and Mental Health Administration. That entity was disbanded in 1973 and NIMH was subsequently housed within another new health agency—the Alcohol, Drug Abuse, and Mental Health Administration.

This move back into an administration which had parallel status with the National Institutes of Health with PHS was strongly opposed by then director of NIMH, Dr. Stanley R. Yolles, who did not want the institute to give up its newfound independence (*CQ Weekly Report*, Vol. XXVII, 1969, p. 172). The NIMH has since continued its emphasis on "social problems research," an approach that continues to be controversial (Nelson, 1984, p. 7).

As important as it is to have a Center for Aging in the National Institute of Mental Health, the most pervasive mental health policies for the elderly do not emanate from this research oriented center but rather evolve from the sources of payment for care, i.e., Medicare and Medicaid. Not unlike the manner in which mental health services are regarded for all age groups, the mental health policies for the elderly are generally separate from the other health care policies and are less generous and more complicated to understand than the general scope of health care policies. Yet the prevalence of mental health problems among the elderly affects about 15-20 percent of the population (Biegel et al., 1989; Durenberger, 1989; Grau, 1989; McGuire, 1989; Roybal, 1988) in contrast to approximately 10 percent for the total population (Grau, 1989). While the elderly represent about 12 percent of the total population only 6 percent of the users of community mental health facilities and 2 percent of clients receiving services from private therapists are older persons (Biegel et al., 1989; Grau, 1989; Roybal, 1988). Older persons may not have been socialized to seeking help for mental illnesses because of the social stigma associated with being "crazy" as well as the fear of commitment to a state hospital stemming from the diagnosis of mental illness. While these cohort effects will change with time and mental illness will be recognized as an illness requiring appropriate treatment, the appropriate utilization of mental health services for the elderly will not vary until there is greater acceptance that mental illnesses of the elderly require specialized mental health treatment services and that older persons can benefit from appropriate intervention.

The mental health policy and the systems that follow should provide greater access for the older person to preventive and remedial care primarily in the community setting away from institutionalization. When institutionalization is the preferred site for treatment, care should be provided by professionals appropriately prepared to treat the older person and the specific illness.

Depression is one of the most prevalent of mental illness among the elderly, with estimates of incidence ranging from 10 to 60 percent (Grau, 1989; Roybal, 1988). Depression often masks other illnesses or is itself masked by somatic complaints. However, depression can be successfully treated and sometimes can be prevented by appropriate intervention. It is unfortunate that such intervention may not be viewed as mental health care. Yet counseling in a social worker's office, group meetings in a senior center or participation in activities available through senior centers, schools or other recreational organizations may be appropriate mental health intervention. Because these valuable services are not reimbursed as mental health services, they may not be available to persons who need them.

The other major mental illness confronting older persons is dementia, the older you grow, the greater your risk. From ages sixty-five to seventy-four, about 3 percent of people have Alzheimer's; from ages seventy-five to eighty-four, the figure rises to 19 percent; and for those eighty-five and older, Alzheimer's afflicts 47 percent (Evans, et al., 1990). Yet this disease is rarely treated as a mental health problem. It is most often viewed as a custodial problem, for which the solution is removing the individual in need to an institutional setting, rather than providing supportive policies such as offering financial assistance to the patients living at home and to their family caregivers.

Mental health issues that are more difficult to quantify are those problems relating to homeless older persons, who may in fact be homeless because of mental illness, alcoholism or multiple problems caused by the misuse of medications (Roybal, 1988; Toufexis, 1990; Brickner et al., 1990). Also of great concern are the needs of older persons living in rural communities where there is limited availability of mental health services as well as a limited supply of health services in general (Durenberger, 1989; Roybal, 1988). Predominantly minority communities also generally have fewer resources available and fewer trained personnel who are members of the minority group (Roybal, 1988).

Typically, funding for mental health services has been focused on inpatient care, with more than 70 percent of mental health money spent on hospitalization (Bickman and Dokecki, 1989; Durenberger, 1989; Toufexis, 1990). Only about 40 percent of mental health inpatient episodes are paid for under DRG-based prospective payment system. Expenditures for outpatient mental health care is less than one-tenth of 1 percent of total Medicare expenditures (McGuire, 1989). Any mental health policy, and the systems that follow to implement it, should provide older persons with greater access to preventive and remedial care and should emphasize community settings rather than institutionalization. When an institution is the preferred site for treatment, care should be provided by professionals who have been appropriately prepared to treat the elderly and the specific illness.

These goals are consistent with the Omnibus Budget Reconciliation Act of 1987 (OBRA 87) mandate that a nursing home may not be used as the site for the treatment of mental illness unless it qualifies as meeting the needs of the individual under treatment. However, our uncoordinated public policies have attempted to discourage the availability of the nursing home as a treatment center for mental illness without having provided any significant alternatives for providing residential care for older persons with mental illness who need it. The Medicare benefit structure needs to be redesigned to provide appropriate levels of payments for both institutional and noninstitutional services.

In 1983, the benefits of hospice care were included in the extension of the Medicare program. Everyone covered by Part A became eligible for hospice care contingent on the presence of all three of the following condtions: the patient's physician and hospice medical director certify that the person is terminally ill or has a life expectancy of no more than six months; the person forgoes standard Medicare benefits; and finally, care is provided by a Medicare certified hospice program. Medicare coverage includes two ninety-day periods, one additional thirty-day period, and an open extension allotment if the person is reassessed as terminally ill. The individual has the option to return to standard care at any time. The mission of hospice programs is to provide holistic and palliative care by an interdisciplinary team to terminally ill persons on a twenty-four-hour basis in a comfortable setting, either the individual's home or a hospice in-patient unit. Supportive services for the dying person's family are also available. Medicaid followed the lead of Medicare and many states now provide hospice benefits in the Medicaid program.

Summary

The American tragedy represented by 30-40 million residents who have no health care coverage has elevated the issue of health care policy to a new priority. Many proposals are being considered by advocacy groups and the Congress, as their members seek a way to provide health care benefits to all, but there are persistent differences in expectations of what is the proper public role in providing health care coverage and in views of how programs should be financed.

The Federal Government continues to have a forceful influence on the national health care system, even though Clinton's reform proposals were never enacted. With the Federal Government controlling approximately 10 percent of U.S. health care expenditures, its influence on the health care system will continue. This is felt most directly for Medicare and Medicaid where funding has been reduced or has failed to keep up with growing demand. Reduced government funding diverts pressure to private funding, prompting momentum toward managed care systems. Governmental action continues to change the health care system (Katzoff, et al., 1996, pp. 35-44).

Medicare funding is being reduced. The question now is by what amount. The Medicare budget in 1995 represented nearly 15 percent of the federal budget, a sum of about a quarter of a trillion dollars. Clinton proposes to cut Medicare expenditures by $124 billion over the next five years; the Republican Congress proposes to cut $226 billion from Medicare (Katzoff, et al., 1996, pp. 35-44).

The loss of Medicare dollars has already put pressure on hospitals (particularly rural and non-profit hospitals), physicians, and providers. Managed care providers in 1996 enrolled 14 percent of Medicare's beneficiaries, on the assumption that they can provide similar benefits to Medicare recipients at a lower cost. Even though the government has contracted Medicare privately since the late 1970s, the shift has been slow. Currently, the government is championing the "choices" available in addition to traditional Medicare, and the trend is toward managed care programs for the elderly.

While recipients of Medicare have access to basic health care coverage—unlike the large numbers who lack this coverage—they are seriously limited in their access to chronic care services, especially home care, nursing home care and pharmaceuticals. Current practices also do not adequately support mental health programs or the special needs of rural communities.

The practice of developing health care policies incrementally has advanced coverage and programs but this type of process has neglected major segments of the population and omitted major services. What is needed at this time is a major overhaul of our national health care policies to ensure access for all residents to health care that includes chronic care services provided at home or in institutions and funded by a progressive income tax equitably administered on all income.

CHAPTER
8

Coordinated System of
Chronic Care

For many years, and for many people in health care today, long-term care has meant nursing home care. That definition is no longer valid. Although we may not yet be able to boast of a coordinated system of chronic care in most communities, we have advanced considerably since 1965, when the Older Americans Act, Medicare and Medicaid laws were passed, providing the stimulus for development of a coordinated system of chronic care.

Not just nursing homes but home health agencies, assisted living, retirement communities, congregate housing, senior centers, care coordination, and even hospitals are part of long-term care. Obviously, long-term care services must include members of the family as well as the recipient of direct services.

Chronic care consists of those services designed to provide diagnostic, preventive, therapeutic, rehabilitative, supportive and maintenance services for individuals who have chronic physical and/or mental impairments. Such services may be provided in a variety of institutional and non-institutional health settings (including the home) with the goal of promoting optimal physical, social, and psychological functioning (Koff, 1982).

This definition emphasizes several important characteristics of chronic care.

- First, it refers to *chronicity*, which characterizes most of the ailments of older people. Because these impairments cannot be "cured," *services must be sustained*, not simply provided for a limited time and then withdrawn.
- Second, it refers to *physical, social*, and *psychological functioning*. These three areas are interlocked and interact; therefore, they cannot be treated in isolation from each other.
- Third, the word *functioning* reflects the view that the way in which the individual functions, rather than the diagnosis alone, determines the nature of the services required.

Elaine Brody added the elements of compassion and entitlement to care in her definition. In her view, chronic care is "one or more services provided on a sustained basis to enable individuals whose functional capacities are chronically impaired to be maintained at their maximum level of health and well-being. The underlying values are that all people share certain basic human needs, that they have a right to services designed to meet those needs and to be furnished services when needs cannot be met through their own resources (social, emotional, physical, financial)" (1977, pp. 14-15).

An examination of these definitions makes clear how far-reaching and encompassing chronic care actually is.

- It incorporates multiple services, because the needs of a person with a chronic illness generally affect several areas of personal functioning.
- Care must be provided on a sustained basis, because neither the duration of a chronic condition nor the regularity with which intervention may be required can be known in advance. Some services may be needed for only a short time. Because how long care will be required can be determined only by the individual's needs and functional capacities, it cannot be stated as a specific period (Koff, 1982).

Agreement on standard terminology is likely to be a problem in any emerging field. Because the language of chronic health care reflects the growth of ideas, it is evolving and therefore sometimes confusing.

There is an inherent danger in any new field: that of creating new names for existing functions for the sole purpose of demonstrating creativity or uniqueness. The transfer of ideas and concepts—communication—depends upon using *consistent* terminology. Especially when a complex program involving a number of disciplines is in its developmental phase, it is critical that professional personnel, whatever their specialty, agree to a consistent and mutually acceptable taxonomy. Such a taxonomy is still to be developed for chronic care.

The critical need for a widely accepted taxonomy is typified by problems associated with the very phrase *long term care*, which suggests that its governing characteristic is the length of time service will be required. Much more significant factors in defining the need for delivery of health care services to an individual who does not require acute care are existence of a chronic condition and the level of individual impairment (Koff, 1982).

Appropriate intervention at the appropriate time can result in a reduction, sometimes to a relatively brief period, in the length of time services are required. What is needed is a way to designate the nature of care, based on the patient's needs, without regard to how long care may have to be provided. Just as *acute care* is the term used to describe care required by an acute episode of impaired health, health care responsive to chronic illness should most appropriately be called *chronic care.* Although chronic care and long term care are used interchangeably, our preference is for the use of chronic care to describe services required by the chronically ill.

There is a similar need to establish one term, consistently used, to describe what is now generally referred to as *case management.* While the concept is widely accepted, some practitioners and clients find the term objectionable; they dislike its implication that the "case" (in reality an individual and family) is "managed" by some service agency. They feel that this language is contrary to the inherent goal of the proposed system which is to enable the client and family to maintain self-sufficiency and competence by retaining responsibility and managing their own affairs. Preferable alternative terms may be *care coordination* performed by *care coordinators.*

Services that can and cannot be provided in a licensed nursing home are defined by statute. Such is not the case for emerging new levels of care called assisted living, congregate living, retirement facilities or any of a number of other names. Potential users of services should be able to know what name refers to what specific service or services.

The Complexity of Chronic Illness and Chronic Care

There is a complex service system necessary to respond to a patient and his or her caregivers, to illness or multiple illnesses, and to the impact of illness on the individual over some extended period of time. No single or simple approach can adequately respond to the multiplicity of needs. The complicated presentation of chronic health problems requires effective coordination of diverse services as dictated by the needs of patient and caregivers (Koff, 1982).

A plan for serving persons who have chronic problems therefore must take into consideration that:

1. *Chronic illnesses are long-term by nature.* Services must be so organized that they provide for repeated interaction over a long time period and are responsive to the complex problems that grow out of a long-term illness.
2. *Chronic illnesses have uncertain prognoses,* resulting in considerable stress for the patient and care providers, and the general course of the illness may be interrupted by episodes requiring acute care. Provision must be made for the patient to move readily from one care level to another.
3. *Chronic diseases require proportionately great efforts at palliation.* Every effort must be made to control pain and discomfort without interfering with the functional capacities of the individual..
4. *Chronic diseases are multiple diseases.* Long-term illnesses tend to multiply, with a single chronic condition often leading to additional problems, making management of the patient's total condition more difficult.

5. *Chronic diseases are disproportionately intrusive on the lives of patients,* causing limitations in activities of daily living and sometimes resulting in social isolation from friends and community activities.

6. *Chronic diseases require a wide variety of services* if they are to be properly addressed by a variety of care providers. The coordination of services becomes an intrinsic responsibility of chronic care.

7. *Chronic illnesses are expensive,* because multiple services must be provided for so long, because institutionalization, when necessary, costs so much, and because of "opportunity costs" to family and friends (Strauss, 1984, pp. 11-15).

Chronic care represents an intervention on behalf of a person who has chronic illness in order to offset functional losses resulting from illness or injury. The intervention may be introduced to prevent an impairment, to avoid a disability, or to offset the consequences of a handicap. There are multiple options for intervention in terms of timing (at which particular point in the trajectory of the illness does one intervene?) and intensity. Some intervention activities may be advocated even prior to the onset of an anticipated chronic condition in an effort to maintain wellness; such intervention should be considered an appropriate part of chronic care.

COORDINATING SERVICES INTO A CONTINUUM OF CARE: A RESPONSE TO THE COMPLEXITY OF CHRONIC ILLNESS

A continuum of chronic care services is the purposeful association of health and social services, each having varying elements responsive to the multiple and diverse needs of a chronically ill person and members of that person's family. This clearly differs from a single, free-standing organization that provides services that respond only to a single component of the total array of potential services. For the following reasons a continuum of chronic care is the best structure for organizing the delivery of services to persons who must live with chronic conditions:

• A change in health or competence associated with a particular time of life may not portend a progressive decline. Rather, there may be periods of improvement as well as periods of decline. Any potential for enhanced functioning must be recognized and supported. The availability of a coordinated continuum permits the quick reorientation of services to a more appropriate level of care in response to changing needs.

• The erratic and uncertain nature of the trajectory of chronic illness requires flexibility and resourcefulness on the part of the system. This can best be provided through the coordinated continuum.

- Because chronic illness is a problem for the family and friends of the patient, chronic care services must be available and responsive to changing family involvement in the provision of care. This includes providing family caregivers with support, care, and respite. A complex package of services may be needed and may need to be modified frequently. This flexibility is possible with a continuum.
- Depending upon the changing needs of the patient and the extent of intervention that will be required to maintain or restore function, prevent impairment, or treat illness, there are many chronic care services that could be introduced, and the continuum permits a display of all services and opportunities for choices based on the best fit.
- Funding of chronic care services from public and private resources is complicated by confusing requirements that sometimes result in denial or disruption of needed services. The disruption can be avoided through coordination of the resources of the continuum.

Establishing the Continuum of Chronic Care

Over the last thirty years, the chronic care system of the United States has dramatically evolved from a disjointed smattering of services to one that more closely resembles a coordinated network. However, the transformation is incomplete. Obstacles such as inadequate financing, fragmentation, unequal availability and access, poor care quality and low staffing expertise must be overcome in order to create a comprehensive and integrated chronic care system that will meet the ongoing and fluctuating needs of the client. Chronic care is most frequently provided on an unpaid, informal basis by family and friends, even though a coordinated system of paid and informal care would be desirable.

Other data indicate that informal sources furnish up to 90 percent of chronic care services. Furthermore, when individuals do utilize formal chronic care services, the experience can be a lengthy and confusing one. "The existing system of providing care to persons with long-term, complex problems is both complicated and inadequate" (Torrens and Williams, 1993). The current system is problem ridden. Regulation procedures are one example. Numerous individual regulatory programs that have evolved as responses to specific problems have led to serious fragmentation and unnecessary cost burdens. Those in need of chronic care must subject themselves to repeated intake assessments and enrollment procedures for each service they use and then receive services in a haphazard, uncoordinated way (Evashwick, 1996). Performing the "Medicare dance" to obtain funding is often frustrating and unfruitful. In order to receive complete care for all aspects of one's often complex health problems, one must often deal with an underfinanced disarray of fragmented services (Torrens and Williams, 1993). This may present a sizable challenge for the average older person.

To avoid this dilemma and establish a continuum of chronic care, reform of four essential mechanisms must be employed: *professional collaboration, care coordination,* an *integrated information arrangement, and comprehensive financing.* Evashwick (1996) suggests, "the ideal system is thus one that provides comprehensive, integrated care on an ongoing basis and offers various levels of service intensity that change as a client's needs change." The objective is to furnish the medical and affiliated support services that empower a person to maximize his or her functional independence. The cardinal mission of a chronic care system is to provide optimal care to the client. "Each management function and patient care activity should be thought of not from the perspective of the organization, but from the perspective of the full continuum of care, and also from the patient's perspective because they will be part of the continuum not only on the first day of their illness, but on an ongoing basis through periods of both wellness and illness" (Evashwick, 1996).

Professional collaboration requires an organized set of operating policies among different health service organizations. Participants should encompass the entire range of health care providers, from home care to assisted living facilities to nursing homes to hospitals. Criteria for referral as well as protocol on financial trade-offs must be established through formal arrangements to avoid later disagreements. Mandatory administrative obligations include establishing clear lines of authority, accountability, and responsibility for patient care services (Torrens and Williams, 1993). Though this may entail the loss of some management independence in decision-making, it greatly facilitates coordinated care. Communication is also imperative. "Regular communication among those responsible for planning each service of the continuum is essential to avoid duplication and to maximize the market and resource advantages of a continuum" (Evashwick, 1996). Inter-organizational discussion and interaction promote the smooth transfer of clients to the necessary specialists. Such an establishment also avoids replication of services.

Care coordination involves a multidisciplinary team of experts who assess the patient's needs and develop a comprehensive plan of action. "The plan outlines the problems, type and level of assistance needed, the roles of patient/client and family who will provide the services and desired outcomes" (Evashwick, 1996). Team members designing the plan may include a dietitian, social worker, nurse, physical therapist, physician, or relevant consultant. One or more of the team members should follow the individual throughout the program in order to supply service continuity and support. The plan should include consideration of the individual's biological, psychosociological, and environmental situation. An assessment by the multidisciplinary team is "broader in scope than a medical or psychiatric examination; questions regarding physical and mental health, functional ability, family and social supports, home environment, and financial resources are included to determine the full range of capability and needs" (Evashwick, 1996).

A single local public access point greatly simplifies entry into the system. It also eases the uninformed client's worry, and most people in need of long-term care are unaware of the range of services that are available (Evashwick, 1996). By easing access into the system, both client and agency profit. In the United States, local area networks (LANs) are being formed to preserve integration, especially in linking physicians with hospitals and guiding the client and family through the maze of services (Torrens and Williams, 1996).

Quality of care is monitored by the care coordinator. Knowledge of service opportunities, local resources, delivery systems, quality providers, financial alternatives, available benefits, and eligibility requirements for assistance are critical (Evashwick, 1996). Service coordination is a complicated job entailing the implementation of care plans by arranging the delivery of various services. Care coordinators must possess intimate knowledge of the health care system.

An *integrated information arrangement* that allows a comprehensive client file to follow the individual should encompass medical as well as other pertinent information that could affect care. "The ideal system of long-term care is a continuum of care . . . a client-oriented system composed of both services and integrating mechanisms that guides and tracks patients over time through a comprehensive array of health, mental health and social services spanning all levels of intensity of care" (Torrens and Williams, 1993). This aim is achieved by creating an all inclusive patient file.

The Integrated Information System (IIS) is an example of an entity that "eliminates the need for duplication of data collection since one entry serves all" (Evashwick, 1996).

Comprehensive financing ensures payment continuity. The current mechanisms of financing inhibit the operation of a continuum of care (Torrens and Williams, 1993). Neither a national policy nor a program that funds chronic care exists. Consequently, the streams of payment for chronic care are seriously fragmented and will remain so as long as the funding streams are separate. To achieve pooling of funding streams in order to provide the specific services required by an individual (Torrens and Williams, 1993) is one of the most difficult challenges to an integrated chronic care system.

Family and Medical Leave Act of 1993 (FMLA)

After eight years of frequently bitter debate, Congress passed the Family and Medical Leave Act of 1993 on February 4, 1993, and President Clinton signed the measure into law the following day. The act became effective on August 5, 1993, and requires employers with fifty or more employees within a seventy-five mile radius to offer eligible workers up to twelve weeks of unpaid leave during a twelve-month period for birth or adoption, to care for a seriously ill parent, spouse, or child, or to undergo medical treatment for their own serious illness. State and local governments are covered by the act under the same conditions as private employers. It is estimated the act will affect 5 percent of America's employers and 40 percent of all employees.

To be eligible to take family leave, a worker must have been employed for at least twelve months and have worked a minimum of 1,250 hours (this is an average of 25 hours per week). While the year of service to the employer does not have to be performed consecutively, the 1,250 hours of work must have been performed during the twelve calendar months immediately prior to the beginning of the leave. The act does not cover seasonal or part-time employees working fewer than 1,250 hours per year; however, they must be included when calculating the number of employees stationed at a particular work site.

Eligible employees may take up to twelve weeks of unpaid leave during a one-year period to care for a son, daughter, spouse, or parent if that individual has a serious health condition, which is defined as an "illness, injury, impairment, or any physical or mental condition that requires inpatient medical care or continuing treatment by a health care provider." The Senate Report on the act cites as examples of such serious health conditions: emphysema, appendicitis, severe respiratory distress conditions, heart conditions requiring bypass or valve operations, back conditions requiring surgery or extensive therapy, and severe nervous disorders. The report also makes it clear this is not to be considered an exhaustive list of serious health conditions.

When an employee returns to work after taking leave, an employer must guarantee the employee can return to the job he or she held before the leave or an equivalent position. While there is certain to be debate regarding the interpretation of these terms, the Senate Report indicates the job reinstatement requirement is to be strictly construed a "similar" or "comparable" position is probably not an "equivalent" position. To be an equivalent position, all privileges, duties, terms, and conditions of the worker's previous job must arguably correspond.

Those in favor of a national standard for family leave have argued for years that employers who have adopted family and medical leave policies have already experienced cost savings through reduced employee turnover and decreased hiring and training expenses. Such policies are viewed as a way to protect a company's investment of time and money in its most valuable commodity: its workers. Supporters have also argued the act will be cost effective from a public policy standpoint and the benefits outweigh the problems because society as a whole often pays the price for failed, fragmented family units. On the other hand, many smaller employers see the law as just the latest in a series of expensive, bureaucratic nightmares that will disrupt the workplace and result in lost productivity.

NURSING HOME POLICIES

The term nursing home has been applied to many types of facilities, but under federal law, refers specifically to an institution that provides skilled nursing care or rehabilitation services for injured, disabled or sick persons (Frolik, 1995). This definition could be disregarded had not federal funding been made contingent upon adhering to it, and the definition is present in both Medicare and Medicaid laws, which supply a major portion of nursing home coverage payment. The more stringent Medicare provision allows reimbursement only for care provided in a "skilled nursing facility," one primarily involved in offering skilled nursing care. Medicaid is more liberal, funding care in facilities offering services ranging from supervisory care to skilled professional nursing. Since licensing of health care facilities is provided by the states, which also share financial participation in the Medicaid program, states are jointly responsible with the federal government for nursing home care provided through Medicare and Medicaid.

Dunlop (1979) has described three precursors of the nursing home. The local almshouse or county poor farm evolved from the belief that impoverished persons were undesirables who should be removed from the mainstream of society by placing them in an institution. A second approach was the founding of charitable private homes created to help persons with limited income or without family. Such homes often were affiliated immigrant self-help organizations and various religious groups and essentially cared for the well elderly (Johnson and Grant, 1985). The third alternative was the private proprietary boarding home, catering to those able to pay for the care provided.

In response to increased health care needs of the residents of the homes for older persons or boarding homes, many of these facilities added nursing care and in time evolved into nursing homes, especially after Social Security gave many older persons a small but consistent source of income. This provided the elderly with a degree of independence in the selection of a place to live and meant they no longer needed to depend solely upon the largesse of either local government or a private charity. Because there was, until 1950, a prohibition against the use of income from Social Security programs for payments to publicly sponsored homes, many of these went through a metamorphosis that often included a stage as a chronic disease hospital. Shortages of acute care hospital beds, partially created by the advent of health care insurance like Blue Cross and Blue Shield, created a need for increased availability of nursing home care for persons having chronic diseases. The Hill-Burton construction program, Old Age Assistance, Aid to the Aged Blind and Disabled, Medical Assistance for the Aged and then Medicare and Medicaid all contributed to the rapid proliferation of nursing homes, and since the early 60s nursing homes clearly have emerged as the specialized setting for the delivery of long term care for older persons in this country (Dunlop, 1979, p. 101).

For the most part, contemporary nursing homes have been skilled care facilities, adhering to what is referred to as the "medical model," in which service delivery focuses primarily on the illness rather than on the total functioning person. Recognizing that many who need institutional care do not require skilled care but something less medically oriented, the intermediate care facility (ICF) was defined and made eligible to receive funding under one of the 1967 Amendments to the Social Security Act (Title XI). ICFs were brought under Medicaid coverage in 1972 and in 1987 OBRA regulations defined a new category of nursing facility (NF), authorized to offer a range of services that depend upon the assessed need of the resident, and merged the roles of skilled and intermediate care facilities.

Dunlop (1979) also provides some additional understanding of the major expansion in nursing homes observed in the 1970s, attributing it to four major causes: biomedical advances prolonging life for many older persons; demographic and social changes resulting in decreased availability of continuing family support; absence of alternative forms of care in the community, and diminished public resistance to use of nursing home care.

Johnson and Grant (1985) added to this list by pointing out that the deinstitutionalization of patients in mental hospitals, especially the state mental hospitals, introduced another and a very difficult population to be cared for in nursing homes. It was believed that these discharged patients would receive more responsive and personal care in their home communities. Unfortunately, many of them were referred to nursing homes that all too often were not equipped to provide appropriate care. Experience has also shown that many individuals discharged from mental hospitals have been unable to adjust to independent living and become a significant part of the homeless population. In addition, from the inception of Medicare and Medicaid, payment for institutional care has been made more readily available than support for the provision of home health care services. This bias has encouraged high occupancy rates for nursing homes and been an obstacle to the development of a comprehensive continuum of chronic care services.

Nursing homes are subject to multiple public policies that deal with: human resources management (Occupational Safety and Health Act, Workers Compensation, Wage and Hour Laws), the Life Safety Code for building safety, sanitary and infection control, food service management and professional health care practices. For example, the Omnibus Budget Reconciliation Act of 1987, PL 100-201 (OBRA), provides:

> *Definition of a Nursing Facility (NF)*—The distinction between Skilled Nursing Facility (NSF) and Intermediate Care Facilities (ICF) was eliminated and a requirement that states pay less for ICF services than for SNF services repealed. All nursing homes participating in either Medicare or Medicaid must meet the same requirements for provision of services, the rights of residents, staffing and training, and other administrative matters.

> *Requirements for Care*—Facilities must, at least once a year, conduct a comprehensive assessment of each patient's ability to perform such everyday activities as bathing, dressing, eating, and walking. Results of such assessments will be used in a written plan of care, describing how a person's medical, psychological, and social needs will be met. Nursing homes are prohibited from admitting residents who are mentally ill or mentally retarded

unless they also require the level of care provided in the facility. Applicants with Alzheimer's disease are exempt from this process. Preadmission screening must be completed on all prospective residents, whether the costs of care are covered by private or public sources.

Residents' Rights—Residents are to be informed both orally and in writing of their legal rights, including the rights to: choose a personal physician and be informed in advance of treatment; be free from physical and chemical restraints; have privacy in accommodations, medical treatment, written and telephone communications, confidentiality of personal and clinical records, and have immediate access to a state or chronic care ombudsman.

Staffing Requirements—All participating nursing homes must have at least one registered nurse on duty 8 hours per day, 7 days per week, and at least one licensed nurse on duty 24 hours per day, 7 days per week. All facilities with more than 120 beds must employ at least one full-time social worker.

Training for Nurse Aides—Nurse aides must complete an approved training course of 75 hours that includes instruction in basic nursing and personal care skills; cognitive, behavioral, and social care; and residents' rights. The state must approve a competence testing program and maintain a registry of individuals who have successfully completed such a course.

Survey and Certification Process—States are responsible for ensuring compliance with the new requirements except for federal facilities.

Enforcement Process—If a facility is out of compliance and the deficiencies immediately jeopardize the health or safety of the residents, the state or the Department of Health and Human Services must take immediate action to correct the deficiencies through the appointment of temporary management or terminate the facility's participation in the Medicare or Medicaid program. Other intermediate sanctions may be imposed for lesser deficiencies (U.S. Senate, 1990).

Over 1.5 million Americans currently live in nursing homes and about 15,000 nursing homes are currently operating in the United States. Because of a history of less than adequate care and treatment in nursing homes, over the past two decades there has been creation of both federal and state protections for nursing home residents. One of the most important developments in the law occurred with the introduction of the OBRA 1987 amendments which included the first federal resident rights provisions. These provisions outline the minimum standards of health, safety, patient autonomy, notice requirements, and fiduciary duties of facilities. Though federal regulations had previously supported residents' rights, the enumeration of explicit statutory protections was an historic event. These rights were now documented in what represented a solid and moral victory for all nursing home residents. Residents no longer needed to rely on the goodwill of the government; they were now entitled to protection. With management by the

Department of Health and Human Services, standards were placed high. The regulations required that nursing homes not merely maintain, but enhance their residents' quality of life. This was a tall order, but one backed by a strong policing force. The act provides explicit protections for nursing home residents, and mandatory annual reviews of nursing home compliance with these protections (Frolik, 1995). Careful and comprehensive inspections ensure enforcement.

Failure to comply with any federal provisions can result in a loss of Medicare or Medicaid certification for the facility. Such a loss could be financially devastating to a long-term care facility as a large part of their revenue is supported by some type of federal reimbursement. Before losing either certification, a nursing facility is entitled to a hearing and usually the opportunity to correct existing violations. In addition to the withdrawal of federal certification, both federal and state surveyors may impose sanctions on facilities not in compliance with statutory mandates.

Nursing Home Residents Rights from OBRA 1987

1. Freedom of Choice
   A resident shall have the right:
   - to choose a personal attending physician;
   - to be informed in advance about care and treatment;
   - to be informed in advance about any changes in care and treatment which could affect resident well being;
   - to participate in changes in care and treatment or planning care and treatment.

2. Freedom from Abuse and Restraints
   Residents should expect to be free from physical or mental abuse, corporal punishment, involuntary seclusion, and any physical or chemical restraints imposed for purposes of discipline or convenience and not necessary to treat a medical symptom.

3. Privacy
   A resident should have a right to privacy regarding accommodations, medical treatment, written and telephonic communications, visits, and meetings of family and resident groups.

4. Confidentiality
   A resident has a right to confidentiality regarding medical and personal records.

5. Grievances
   - The resident shall have the right to voice complaints about care without fear of discrimination or reprisal for voicing concerns.

- The resident shall have the right to prompt action by the facility to resolve grievances, including those about the behavior of other residents.

6. Accommodation of Needs
   The resident shall receive services with reasonable accommodation of individual needs and preferences, except where granting such accommodation would endanger the health and safety of others.

7. Participation in Resident and Family Groups
   - The residential facility must promote and protect the right of residents to organize and participate in resident groups in the facility and the right of the resident's family to meet in the facility with the families of other residents of the facility.
   - The resident has the right to participate in social, religious, and community activities that do not interfere with the rights of other residents.

8. Access and Visitation Rights
   A nursing facility must:
   - permit immediate access to a resident by any representative of the Secretary of HHS, by any representative of the state, by an Ombudsman or an advocate for the mentally or developmentally disabled, or by the resident's individual physician;
   - permit immediate access to a resident, subject to reasonable restrictions and the resident's right to deny or withdraw consent at any time, by immediate family or other relatives of the resident;
   - permit reasonable access to a resident by any entity or individual that provides health, social, legal or other services to the resident, subject to the resident's right to deny or withdraw consent at any time;
   - permit representatives of the state Ombudsman, with the permission of the resident or the resident's legal representative and consistent with state law, to examine a resident's clinical record.

9. Equal Access to Quality Care
   A nursing home must establish and maintain identical policies and practices regarding transfer, discharge, and the provision of services required under the state plan for all individuals regardless of the source of payment.

10. Rights of Incompetent Resident
    In the case of a resident adjudged incompetent under the laws of a state, the rights of the resident under this title shall devolve upon, and to the extent judged necessary by a court of competent jurisdiction, be exercised by, the person appointed under state law to act on the resident's behalf.

11. Admissions Policy

A nursing facility must, in respect to admission policy:

- not require individuals applying to reside or residing in the facility to waive their rights to benefits under the Medicare or Medicaid program;
- not require oral or written assurance that such individuals are not eligible for, or will not apply for, benefits under Medicare and Medicaid;
- prominently display in the facility written information, and provide oral and written information, about how to apply for and use such benefits and how to receive funds for previous payments not covered by such benefits;
- not require a third-party guarantee of payment to the facility as a condition of admission to, or expedited admission to, or continued stay in, the facility; and
- in the case of a Medicaid recipient, not charge, solicit, accept, or receive, in addition to any amount otherwise required to be paid under the state plan, any gift, money, donation, or other consideration as a precondition of admitting, or expediting the admission of, the individual to the facility or as a requirement for the individual's continued stay in the facility.

12. Transfer and Discharge

A resident has the right to remain in a facility and must not be transferred or discharged unless:

- the transfer or discharge is necessary to meet the resident's welfare and the resident's welfare cannot be met in the facility;
- the transfer or discharge is appropriate because of the resident's health has improved enough that the resident no longer requires the services provided by the facility;
- the health and safety of individuals in the facility are otherwise endangered;
- the resident has failed, after reasonable notice, to pay an allowable charge imposed by the facility for an item or service which the resident requested and for which the resident may be charged above the basic rate;
- the facility ceases to operate.

13. Preparation and Orientation

A facility must provide sufficient preparation and orientation to a facility to ensure sage and orderly transfer or discharge.

14. Notice of Bed-Hold Period

- Before a resident is transferred for hospitalization or therapeutic leave, a facility must provide written information to the resident and a family member or legal representative concerning the period during which the resident will be permitted to return and resume residence in the facility under the state plan, and the policies of the facility, regarding such bed hold period.

- At the time of transfer of a resident to a hospital or for therapeutic leave, a nursing facility must provide written notice to the resident and a family member or legal representative of the bed hold period.

15. Priority Readmission

A nursing facility must establish and follow a written policy under which a resident:

- who is eligible for medical assistance for nursing facility services under a state plan,
- who is transferred from the facility for hospitalization or therapeutic leave, and
- whose hospitalization or therapeutic leave exceeds a period paid for under the state plan for the holding of a bed in the facility for a resident, will be permitted to be readmitted to the facility immediately upon the first availability of a bed in a semi-private room in the facility if, at the time of readmission, the resident requires the services provided by the facility.

16. Relocation

A resident is entitled to receive notice before the room or roommate of the resident is changed in the facility.

17. Information Regarding Payment Obligations

A nursing facility must inform each resident who is entitled to medical assistance at the time of admission to the facility or, if later, at the time the resident becomes eligible for such assistance:

- of the items and services that are included in nursing facility services under the state plan and for which the resident may not be charged; and
- of those other items and services that the facility offers and for which the resident may be charged and the amount of the charges for such items and services; and
- of changes in the items and services or in charges imposed for items and services included in the state plan; and
- inform each other resident, in writing before or at the time of admission and periodically during the resident's stay, of services available in the facility and of related charges for such services, including any charges for services not covered under Title 18 or by the facility's basic per diem charge.

18. Inspection of Survey Results

Upon reasonable request, the facility must provide the results of the most recent survey of the facility conducted by the Secretary of HHS or a state licensing department with respect to the facility and any plan of correction in effect with respect to the facility. The facility must also protect and promote this right to examine survey results.

19. Personal Funds

- A facility may not require residents to deposit their personal funds with the facility.
- Once a facility has accepted written authorization from the resident for the safekeeping of a resident's account, the facility must hold, safeguard, and account for such personal funds under a system established and maintained in accordance with the following:

1. The facility must deposit any resident's funds in excess of $50 in an interest bearing account (or accounts separate from any of the facility's operating accounts and credits all interest earned to the account). With respect to other funds, the facility must maintain such funds in a noninterest-bearing account or petty cash funds.

2. The facility must assure a full and complete separate accounting of each resident's personal funds, maintain a written record of all financial transactions involving a resident's personal funds, and afford the resident or their legal representative reasonable access to such record.

3. The facility must notify each resident receiving Medicaid when the amount in the resident's account reaches $200 less than the applicable resource limit, and that if the amount in the account (in addition with the resident's other resources) reaches above the allowable resource limit, the resident may lose income eligibility for Medicaid or SSI.

4. Upon the death of a resident with an account, the facility must promptly convey the resident's personal funds and an accounting to the estate.

20. Information About Rights

A nursing facility must:

- inform each resident, orally and in writing at the time of admission to the facility, of the resident's legal rights during the stay at the facility;
- make available to each resident, upon reasonable request, a written statement of such rights, which shall include a description of the requirements for protection of personal funds and a statement that a resident may file a complaint with a state survey and certification agency respecting resident abuse and neglect and misappropriation of resident property in the

facility. Written statements of rights must be updated when changes are made in rights provided by state or federal law.

The most influential role of the federal government in nursing home practice is in overseeing nursing home policy. The federal government imposes operation requirements and sets state responsibilities. The Federal Nursing Home Reform Act (NHRA), a sub-provision of OBRA 1987, is the most significant federal protection measure and represented a major change in nursing home laws as significant and pervasive as the emergence of Medicare and Medicaid in the 1960s (Frolik, 1995).

The Nursing Home Reform Act (NHRA) made significant changes in how nursing homes are evaluated, changing the survey process from one that focused on physical and task criteria to one that focuses on the caring process, resident feelings, and patient care outcomes (Torrens and Williams, 1993). Qualitative measures gained importance. Because a facility had to meet or exceed NHRA requirements to receive federal reimbursement under Medicare or Medicaid, financial necessity forced facilities to comply with these regulations. Since almost half of nursing home residents receive Medicaid coverage, nursing homes had to take patients' quality of life seriously.

In addition to satisfying federal government requirements, facilities must meet state mandates. The predominant source of public regulation of nursing homes flows from state licensing requirements, since a facility is not allowed to operate without a license. Under various laws, regulations, and licensing requirements, states thus have the power to mold the policies and behavior of nursing homes.

Medicaid certified nursing facilities must operate a Pre-admission Screening and Annual Resident Review (PASARR) program for both entering and continuing residents. The goal of this review is to determine the mental status of the present or potential resident. If an individual is deemed mentally ill (other than having a dementia) or retarded according to a prescribed definition, the facility is then evaluated on its ability to care for the individual to ensure that the individual is receiving proper care in the most appropriate setting. No regulation requires that a nursing home admit a mentally ill or retarded individual, however. Individuals who were residents prior to the 1987 enforcement of NHRA are annually reviewed concerning mental status. Those found to be mentally ill or retarded and not requiring nursing services will be discharged to a suitable facility, provided they have not lived in the facility for longer than two and one-half years. Those individuals who exceed this time limitation retain the option to remain in the facility.

The federal government also regulates nursing home admittance. It prohibits nursing homes that receive Medicaid reimbursement from forcing residents to forego applying for, or receiving, Medicaid benefits. Neither Medicaid- nor Medicare-covered residents can be required to pay advance deposits as a prerequisite for admission. In order to prevent nursing homes from circumventing the intent of the law, requiring third party payment guarantees in order for an applicant to be eligible for admission is also forbidden. Despite federal law, some facilities require a responsible party to agree to be personally liable if a patient is unable to provide payment from his or her own income or resources (Frolik, 1995).

The basic thrust of the NHRA is to assure quality of life for nursing home residents. As a result, nursing homes must have a quality assessment and assurance committee that meets at least quarterly to define and carry out plans which assure the highest achievable psychosocial, physical, and mental well-being of their residents. A detailed file for each individual, including information on abilities and limitations, must be compiled in the form of a care plan. Time restrictions concerning care management are strict. A facility has two weeks following a resident's admission to formulate a plan and thereafter must amend the plan yearly or in response to any significant change in the resident's mental or physical status. It is the facility's responsibility to perform the services deemed necessary to implement the resident's plan.

Regulations also apply to persons who implement the care plan. Foremost, the provision of direct medical care must adhere to certain rules. All patients must be under the supervision of a physician unless the state permits the substitution of another professional, such as a nurse practitioner (Frolik, 1995). Licensed nursing services are to be offered twenty-four hours a day and, unless waived by the state, the nursing facility is required to provide a registered professional nurse for a minimum of seven days a week, eight hours a day. Candidates for aide positions are to be screened for competence and any evidence of a background of patient abuse. Though the federal government sets the broad guidelines, it is up to states to fill in the details. In order to meet the residents' more personal needs, facilities with more than 120 beds must also employ a minimum of one full-time social worker.

Providers of nursing home care had many problems in implementing OBRA 1987. Regulations were not established in a timely manner, surveyors were not adequately prepared to implement the provisions of the new surveys and there was an inadequate increase in funding to cover the cost of the changes. Uncertainty and indecision prevented an orderly transition to a new set of standards for care of the elderly.

All of the OBRA 1987 regulations dealing with nursing home care stem from Congressional concern that nursing homes might not provide quality care in the absence of strong federal regulations and sanctions but despite these good intentions, many problems persist. These include declining health as residents age, with attendant issues of frailty, incontinence and dementia; the limited supply of specifically trained and competent personnel to meet demands for the care required; limited reimbursement, especially from the Medicaid program; the absence of integration of nursing homes into a coordinated continuum of care; and lack of local community involvement in the oversight of quality of care issues.

Licensing of Administrators of Nursing Homes

Nursing home administrators must have a diverse background that includes health care and human services management, care of the elderly, family care, community involvement, and the ability to manage a budget. It is equally important that they be able to make a positive contribution to the life style of residents and members of their families.

The implementation of Title 19, the Medicaid program, included a requirement for licensing of nursing home administrators as a measure to ensure appropriate quality of care. No requirement for the licensing of hospital administrators had ever existed and none was specified in the Medicaid law, apparently because it was assumed that such personnel would be appropriately educated. Nursing home administrators were not so highly regarded. Although many qualified individuals were managing institutional settings for the elderly, many totally unprepared individuals also had been put in charge of nursing homes, so the Social Security Act was amended to include a provision that "no nursing home within (a) state may operate except under the supervision of an administrator licensed in the manner provided in this section" (United States Statutes at Large, 1967).

Licensing was to be carried out by a board consisting of professional providers of care of the chronically ill who would determine standards for licensing, develop examinations or other techniques to demonstrate that candidates had met those standards, issue licenses, ensure that license requirements were maintained, respond to any complaints against a licensed administrator and study ways to improve the quality of nursing home care. A National Advisory Council on Nursing Home Administration was created to advise the Secretary of Health and Human Services and states on implementation. It functioned until 1973, when it was determined that it had fulfilled its mission and that a voluntary group of representatives of state boards of nursing home administrators was believed adequate to oversee licensure.

PAYMENTS FOR NURSING HOME CARE

Figure 14 and the discussion that follows delineate the major sources of funding nursing home care.

A lengthy stay in a nursing home can spell financial ruin for all but the wealthiest persons. With the cost of a one-year stay often exceeding $50,000, savings accumulated over a lifetime can evaporate in a matter of months. After a resident's own money is gone, some families cover the costs of care, but sooner or later many will come to rely on government help.

Medicare and Medicaid, the two main government programs that pay for chronic care, already cover about 60 percent of all nursing home expenses. The two programs spent some $42 billion on nursing home bills for 1.4 million elderly Americans in 1993.

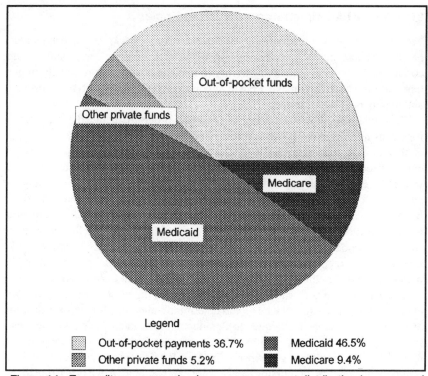

Figure 14. Expenditures on nursing home care: percent distribution by source of funds. **Source**: Office of National Health Statistics, Office of the Actuary, National Health Expenditures, 1995.

How Medicare Pays

Medicare, the national health insurance system for the elderly, covers hospital and physicians' services for acute illnesses. Contrary to what many beneficiaries believe, it pays only for relatively short nursing home stays directly related to an illness or injury that requires hospitalization. Medicare pays for a maximum of 100 days of skilled nursing care during each benefit period. Skilled care includes specific medical services. Medicare does not pay for custodial care that involves help with bathing, dressing, eating and toileting and is the only kind of care many infirm people require.

For a patient who enters a nursing home directly from a hospital and who needs skilled nursing care, Medicare covers costs for the first twenty days. After that, it pays an amount that changes annually, currently $89.50 per day. That can leave a big financial gap since many nursing homes charge between $100 and $200 a day. A patient must be admitted to a Medicare-certified facility, usually within thirty days of a hospital stay that lasts for at least three days. A physician must order that daily nursing care is required for the same condition that caused the hospitalization.

If these conditions are met, Medicare covers not only the daily rate, meals, drugs, and supplies, but also such skilled nursing services as intravenous and tube feedings; injection of insulin; insertion of catheters; tracheotomy aspiration; training in self-injections and diet for diabetics; and speech, occupational, and physical therapy rehabilitation services if they are required at least five days a week, if they are restorative, and not simply repetitive to maintain functioning, and if the person continues to improve. Medicare stops paying for rehabilitation services once there is no further improvement in function. Many other services, such as routine preventive skin care, routine care for incontinence, and assistance with activities of daily living, do not qualify a patient for a skilled nursing stay. But if that person otherwise qualifies based on a need for skilled care, those services are covered as well.

Nursing homes seek to have all beds occupied. When openings arise, as they do daily in many facilities, admissions personnel try to fill them as quickly as possible with residents who will contribute most to the bottom line. That usually means Medicare patients get preference. In the scheme of nursing home finance, Medicare pays a lot, Medicaid pays a little, and patients ineligible for either program pay what the market will bear or go without.

Nursing homes designate some of their beds as "Medicare certified" and try to increase the number of covered services the residents in them receive. (Medicare allows nursing homes to allocate to those beds as many other costs as can be justified, on the theory that patients occupying them require the heaviest care).

Many nursing homes have begun to focus on offering almost exclusively Medicare-covered services. Other homes are marketing units for "sub-acute" care, special wings or floors that provide hospital-level care. Even hospitals are setting aside skilled nursing wings as a way to continue receiving Medicare money once patients move out of acute-care beds.

Eventually, Medicare stops paying, either because qualifications for benefits are no longer met or 100 days have passed. For many families, coverage ends sooner than expected. On average, beneficiaries use about fifty-seven days of skilled nursing care in any calendar year. When benefits end, residents may have to move if the private pay rate cannot be paid or if the facility is not certified for Medicaid, the fallback government program. According to Torrens and Williams (1993), Medicare is exploring and considering payment of nursing homes and home health agencies not by fee for service but by bundling of specific services.

Figure 15 shows the growth in Medicare enrollment since 1966, projected to 1998.

How Medicaid Pays

As the health insurance system for the poor, including people made poor by nursing home bills, Medicaid is the payer of last resort and the largest financier of nursing home care, paying some $38 billion in 1993.

Many homes try to avoid Medicaid as a source of payment because others are more lucrative. Medicaid is funded jointly by the federal and state governments; the federal treasury contributes between 50 and 80 percent of every dollar spent on Medicaid benefits, with the greatest share going to states with the lowest per capita incomes and the states pay the rest. States also set the reimbursement rates, which according to federal law must be reasonable and adequate to meet the costs incurred by efficiently and economically operated facilities.

To qualify for Medicaid, a patient must meet an income and asset test, which varies from state to state. In most states, however, if income is less than the private pay rate, the patient can be eligible for Medicaid. Each month most of that income

July	Total Persons	Aged Persons	Disabled Persons
	(In Millions)		
1966	19.1	19.1	—
1970	20.5	20.5	—
1975	25.0	22.8	2.2
1980	28.5	25.5	3.0
1985	31.1	28.2	2.9
1990	34.2	30.9	3.3
1991	34.9	31.5	3.4
1992	35.6	32.0	3.6
1993	36.3	32.4	3.8
1994	36.9	32.8	4.1
1995	37.3	33.0	4.3
1996[1]	38.1	33.4	4.7
1997[1]	38.6	33.6	5.0
1998[1]	39.1	33.8	5.3

Data for 1966-1995 are as of July. [1]Data for 1996-1998 represent enrolled estimates.

Figure 15. Medicare enrollment/trends. **Source:** Health Care Financing Administration, Bureau of Data Management and Strategy, 1996.

including Social Security payments, Supplemental Security Income, and pension benefits—goes directly to the nursing home. Medicaid pays the difference between income and the Medicaid rates. (States allow each resident to keep a small monthly personal-needs allowance of at least $30).

All assets other than a home, household furnishings, a car, a burial plot and burial fund, and $2,000 must be spent on nursing care before Medicaid will pay. Using up those assets is called a "spend-down." Many nursing home residents spend themselves into poverty, as defined by Medicaid, in less than twelve months.

Federal rules offer some protection for spouses who remain at home. In 1995, they were able to keep a minimum of $15,000 and a maximum of $75,000 in assets. Those numbers change annually. States can increase the minimum amount. Spouses who have no income of their own can keep between $1,254 and $1,871 a month.

Some people use trusts and other financial devices to give what they have to their children before the health-care system takes it all, but under federal law such transfers must usually be made at least thirty-six months (60 months in the case of trusts) before a person applies for Medicaid. If they occur sooner, Medicaid may not pay for a certain period, and the transferred assets may go to the nursing home anyway.

Financial eligibility is only the first hurdle. Medical requirements, which are set by federal law, are the second. States have discretion to decide what level of disability qualifies a patient for a Medicaid-supported nursing home stay; and the medical requirements, like the financial requirements, vary from state to state. To thin the ranks of people eligible for benefits, some states are tightening the medical criteria in ways that disqualify many people who suffer from Alzheimer's disease and other kinds of dementia, but who are otherwise in good physical condition.

The Balanced Budget Act of 1997 gave states new freedom to reduce Medicaid payments to nursing homes and made the states responsible for making up the difference, although nursing homes claim that the losses will be felt directly by the residents of the homes who rely on Medicaid to pay the bills. Prior law had required states to pay nursing homes "reasonable and adequate" prices to meet government quality and safety standards. States now need only to ensure that their rate-setting process is clearly defined and provides a chance for public comment. The outcome of these changes is not yet clear. Will the states make up the difference and maintain the same level of funding for Medicaid residents? Will there be additional federal intervention, or will the level of care be reduced substantially to make up for lost income?

It is estimated that although 2.4 million people who require chronic care reside in institutions, the majority, over four times this number, or 10.4 million, live at home or in some supervised home setting (GAO, 1995). Though it has been repeatedly reported that people prefer living at home our government continues to grant the major share of financial support to chronic care institutions. In 1993, total public and private expenditures were an estimated $75.2 billion for institutional care and $32.6 billion for home and community-based care (GAO, 1995).

Since 1981, states have had the option of applying for Medicaid waivers to fund home and community based services to people who meet Medicaid eligibility requirements and would otherwise require institutional care (GAO, 1995), based on the assumption that the provision of a significant number of home delivered services could delay or prevent institutionalization.

Strategies for Controlling Growth of Medicaid Expenditures for the Elderly:

- *Bring more private resources into the long term care system.* This could be accomplished by encouraging people to purchase long term care insurance, enforcing prohibitions against the elderly transferring their assets to meet eligibility requirements, or more aggressively recovering money from the estates of deceased nursing home residents. These strategies have several shortcomings: long-term care insurance is unaffordable for most elderly people, transferring assets is not as common as was previously thought, and estate recovery programs have historically recouped only small proportions of nursing home expenditures.
- *Integrate acute and long term care services through managed care.* A number of demonstration projects are underway, including Social HMOs, On Lok and its Program of All Inclusive Care for the Elderly (PACE), and the Arizona Long-term Care System. Some of the preliminary data are encouraging, especially in the sense that acute care use can be lowered in capitated care settings, but it is unclear whether integration of services generates long term savings.
- *Reduce eligibility, reimbursement services, and quality standards.* If the methods above should prove to be ineffective, states are likely to return to traditional cost cutting methods (The Commonwealth Fund, 1996).

Figure 16 summarizes trends in payments from both Medicare and Medicaid payments from 1980 through 1996.

OTHER INSTITUTIONAL SETTINGS

Board and Care Homes

Examination of institutional care policies must include consideration of facilities that are not licensed to provide nursing services yet care for a large number of persons. These facilities are referred to by a variety of names and are treated differently by states in their regulations.

A 1993 national study by the American Association of Retired Persons (AARP) estimated that there are between 30,000 and 40,000 board and care facilities, with a million residents. The number is increasing each year. The study found such facilities to be not uniformly well-regulated, well monitored or well-run (Nicholas and Harker, 1997). Some of them are licensed in some states, but there is no national standard that incorporates all of these "non-skilled" programs that meet a variety of special care needs of persons unable to pay for nursing home or other skilled care, some of the mentally ill, some retarded persons and some of the increasing numbers of older persons suffering from a dementia. These facilities, which are regulated by the states with few federal protections, have responded to demand as the frail older population grows and the need for care increases. They are attractive to many because of their small size and "home-like" atmosphere and because the monthly costs are less than those of the more conventional care facilities.

Concerned about problems in board and care homes, Congress enacted the Keyes Amendment to the Social Security Act in 1976, requiring all facilities in which a large number of residents receive Supplementary Security Income (SSI) to meet appropriate standards. Lack of direct funding from the federal government to these facilities means that no sanctions for non-conformance are available for failure to meet local building and safety codes.

Licensure requirements as well as the monitoring of the performance, have been questioned as being inadequate to meet the requirements for care of a frail population where perhaps 50 percent are institutionalized because of dementia. However, in one state alone, of an estimated 2,000 to 4,000 facilities only about 1,200 have the required state license. The remainder operate as a lucrative underground industry unseen by any state inspector (Nichols and Harker, 1997).

	Program Outlays/Trends		
	Total	Medicare[1]	Medicaid[2]
Fiscal Year	In Billions		
1980	57.9	33.9	24.0
1990	175.9	107.2	68.7
1995	326.7	176.9	149.8
1996[3]	354.0	193.9	160.1

[1]Medicare amounts are gross outlays for benefits and administration.
[2]Medicaid amounts include both federal and state shares of benefit payments and administrative costs.
[3]Estimated
Source: Health Care Financing Administration, Office of Financial and Human Resources: Data from the Division of Budget,1997.

Figure 16. Trends in payments from Medicare and Medicaid.

Nothing remotely similar to the federal "bill of rights" for nursing home residents exists for their board and care counterparts. It is evident that the entire institutional environment defined as board and care homes is in need of a thorough review to determine what public policies are necessary to assure the protection of the residents and the presence of suitable levels of care.

Assisted Living

Assisted living, the largest growing type of supportive housing, provides a special combination of residential housing, personalized services and health care designed to meet the individual needs of persons who require help with activities of daily living but do not need the skilled medical care provided in a nursing home (Senior Living Alternatives, 1997). Most assisted living communities help with dressing, grooming, bathing, and other daily activities. Assistance with medications depends upon state regulations. Meals, laundry, and housekeeping are usually provided within private and semi-private rooms in a residential setting. Most assisted living communities accept only private pay, although some states offer public assistance payment.

Assisted living communities can be free standing; part of a continuing care community that provides independent, assisted and nursing care services; affiliated with a nursing home, or represent specialized services brought within an independent retirement community.

Assisted living quarters frequently have a sitting room, a bedroom, and a small service kitchen in an environment that responds to the needs of a population prepared to give up some independence in return for meal service, transportation, housekeeping, recreation, and, most importantly, twenty-four-hour monitoring or response to emergencies.

The assisted living setting usually does not provide much medical care. Kaplan says, the true model is to provide part time assistance and high-level luxury housing with assistance (Wagner and Vickery, 1997). In some cases, the operator will arrange for home delivered health care services through a local home health agency or physician. However, aging-in-place makes its residents subject to frequent changes in their health care requirements and expectations of the assisted living environment.

As assisted living operators add more health care to the service mix, they face the challenge of retaining a residential environment, which is the industry's hallmark (Wagner and Vickery, 1997). By adding or enhancing additional services the assisted living program could meet a broader range of resident's medical needs and mitigate the need for transfer. How much care can, or should, an assisted living environment provide without being redesignated as a nursing home with an entirely different set of regulations? State regulatory agencies have sometimes intervened to evict assisted living residents whose care needs have increased. Some regulatory agencies have required the transfer of a resident from the assisted living setting, even when the consumer, provider, physician, and family all agree the resident is receiving appropriate care in a reasonably safe environment (Elkins, 1997). Some states are allowing assisted living facilities to offer nursing services, but higher levels of care have brought higher levels of state regulation and scrutiny. In some states, an assisted living administrator must be licensed and comply with annual educational requirements.

Assisted living facilities are seeking to broaden their repertoire in the chronic care realm by keeping their clientele as they age in place. A recent survey conducted by the American Health Care Association found that a majority of residents left their assisted living residences, usually to a nursing facility, because they needed a higher level of care (Elkins, 1997).

Some states specify which services can and cannot be delivered in the assisted living setting, and some specifically prohibit admission or retention of individuals with certain health conditions (Elkins, 1997). Assisted living facilities are seeking to modify the limits on providing higher levels of care by supporting increased state staffing regulations. As more states allow higher levels of care in assisted living settings, having a licensed nurse on staff allows the provision of more services and accommodates the stepped-up documentation and accountability. It has been reported that about 75 percent of these facilities now provide some level of nursing care.

However, with higher levels of care have come higher levels of state regulation and scrutiny, including more rigorous required training programs. Physical design may be a problem associated with more intensive care. Apartments originally designed for privacy may not be suitable for an individual requiring increasing surveillance and assistance. Delivering various levels of care to individuals scattered throughout a facility may present staffing challenges. Notwithstanding more assisted living facilities are looking in the direction of expansion, and a growing number of states are allowing assisted living facilities to offer nursing services (Wagner, 1997).

Figure 17 provides a summary of national data on experiences with the level of assisted living services.

Social Health Maintenance Organizations (S/HMOs) Programs of All-inclusive Care for the Elderly (PACE) Models

Valuable lessons can be learned from S/HMOs and PACE (the On Lok replications). These are very different *federal* demonstration projects. S/HMOs offer little nursing home care and, at least to date, have little to do with Medicaid.

PACE is a program that has grown out of the highly regarded On Lok program, an early demonstration program of integrated acute and chronic care for nursing home-level, low-income clients in San Francisco's Chinatown. PACE offers a model for capitating an entity to provide acute and chronic care for low-income populations.

Resident Profile

The average assisted living resident:

Is eighty-two years old, female and ambulatory:

- Needs help with one or two activities of daily living, and:
- Likely moved to the assisted living residence from home and will move to a nursing facility or hospital when her medical needs become too serious for an assisted living environment.

Special Assistance Needs

Twenty-five percent of residents need help with early-stage dementia, while 6 percent need assistance with late-stage dementia:

- Seventeen percent need help dealing with incontinence, and ;
- Only 1 percent need special care due to pressure ulcers.

Moving In and Out

The average length of stay in assisted living facilities is 3.3 years:

- The average stay is shorter—2.8 years—in assisted living residences that are part of a nursing facility;
- Forty-five percent of residents who leave an assisted living setting move to nursing facilities; 11 percent move to hospitals, and
- Sixteen percent of residents die in their assisted living residence.

Figure 17. Highlights from assisted living facts and trends. **Source:** National Center for Assisted Living Facts and Trends: The Assisted Living Sourcebook, 1997.

PACE projects are small, completely at-risk organizations that serve only those who would qualify for nursing home admission and are almost exclusively Medicaid recipients. PACE programs receive a combined Medicare and Medicaid capitation; the Medicare reimbursement is at the nursing home Medicare Average Adjusted Per Capita Costs (MPCC) rate even when the clients are not in nursing homes. A scholarly debate is raging about whether the levels of payment are appropriate or too high compared to fee-for-service under Medicare and Medicaid.

The essential elements of the program include: capitation of both Medicare and Medicaid; assumption of financial risk by the program for all acute and chronic care; a staff-model medical program, where staff physicians are responsible for primary and preventive care; mandatory attendance at adult day health centers (also the site for primary health care); and a multidisciplinary model care management team. Enrollees tend to be highly positive about PACE, but in many communities enrollment has lagged because of the requirement of using PACE physicians and of attendance at adult day care, even on a minimal schedule.

Four S/HMOs were funded in the 1980s; these were Medicare HMOs that received 100 percent rather than 95 percent of the MPCC and were at risk to provide all Medicare services and a limited amount of institutional services. These S/HMOs involved partnerships of health care providers and Long Term Care organizations. A second-generation S/HMO demonstration is now in the planning stage with a different way of setting the MPCC; it will give greater attention to forging true integration of acute and chronic care, and applying the best principles of geriatrics into managed care. As with S/HMO1, S/HMO2 will have limited nursing home benefits.

The National Chronic Care Consortium

The National Chronic Care Consortium (NCCC), is a national, mission-driven organization of twenty health networks dedicated to transforming the delivery of chronic care services. The NCCCs mission is: *To serve as an operational laboratory for enabling innovative health networks to establish prototype systems for better serving persons with serious and persistent chronic conditions.* It is funded by General Mills, The John A. Hartford Foundation, The Retirement Research Foundation, and member fees.

Each NCCC member is a health care provider or strategically-aligned group of providers that holds a national reputation for leadership in health care delivery and reform. NCCC members provide exemplary leadership in health care reform. sharing a commitment to excellence and the NCCC vision of integrated chronic care. NCCC members have been directly involved in virtually every major national demonstration in long term care over the last ten years, including On Lok replications, Social HMOs and the Channeling Project. Each NCCC site has a complete continuum of hospital, nursing home, physician, and community based long term care programs.

Long-Term Care Insurance

Limited Medicare payments for nursing home care and the requirements of Medicaid that applicants meet their state's income and asset eligibility level to receive payments for nursing home care have heightened interest in the availability of long term care insurance. A generally poor market for such insurance stems primarily from a misconception that Medicare will provide for the cost of nursing home care. In addition, by the time most people investigate its purchase, it is too late to buy the insurance or it is too expensive. Furthermore, the issue of long term care and long term care insurance is so confusing that prospective purchasers find it difficult to make rational choices about coverage or company reliability. Lack of adequate federally subsidized coverage for chronic care illnesses stimulated Congressional interest in the marketing of private insurance and both houses of the 102nd Congress considered several bills that dealt with establishing standards for long term care insurance and providing incentives for individuals to purchase private insurance. None of these proposals was enacted.

Currently, policies pay a daily benefit, usually between $50 and $200, that helps defray nursing home expenses. That benefit can be paid for as short a time as one year, or it can last until the policyholder dies.

Policies can begin paying as soon as a person enters a nursing home or after a waiting period of thirty, sixty, ninety, or even 100 days. (The longer the waiting period, the lower the premium.) An inflation rider, which can double the premium, increases the value of the benefit, usually by 5 percent a year. Despite its cost, the rider is essential; otherwise, the insurance benefit may be meaningless after twenty or thirty years when it may be needed. Many policies also pay benefits for home care—an amount that is usually equal to 100 percent of the nursing home benefit if medical or skilled care is needed and half of the benefit if non-skilled or personal care services are required.

State insurance regulators, acting through the National Association of Insurance Commissioners, adopted model laws that require inflation protection as an option, caps on rates, prohibitions on certain underwriting practices, and non-forfeiture benefits, which return some value to policyholders who lapse their coverage. Some states have adopted some of these model laws, others have adopted parts of them, and a few companies have incorporated some of the improvements on their own.

Nevertheless, there is still no uniformity in the quality of coverage across states. Policy comparisons remain virtually impossible, and new, troublesome, issues are emerging. For example, some companies are refusing to pay benefits if care is provided in assisted living facilities, and regulators have yet to grapple with the question of whether a policy purchased today will indeed pay benefits twenty years from now when new types and places of care will undoubtedly have surfaced.

Long-term care insurance may be an option for people who can qualify medically (many policies are stringently underwritten to weed out those likely to need nursing home care) and who can afford the premiums before they become prohibitively expensive. Long term care insurance is not suitable for people with few assets who can expect Medicaid to cover a nursing home stay or for elderly individuals who might have to sacrifice more pressing needs to pay thousands of dollars each year in premiums.

Protection of Resident's Rights

To collect federal funds for benefits to the vulnerable elderly, each state is required to establish and operate a Long-Term Care Ombudsman Office, which has many, demanding responsibilities (Frolik, 1995). He or she is sworn to address and resolve complaints issued by nursing home residents, to uphold resident rights, and to protect their safety, health, and welfare. The Ombudsman must also promote the development and implementation of policies and regulations compatible with needs and wishes of the elderly.

Common law tort and contract solutions are also relevant to nursing home regulation. Nursing homes are liable for both unintentional (i.e., neglect) and intentional (e.g., assault) torts, though unintentional torts are more frequent. Of course, a nursing home is not automatically responsible for a resident's suffering an injury. "Unless guilty of an intentional tort, the nursing home must be shown to have acted in a negligent manner" (Frolik, 1995). Suing a nursing home demands the same burden of proof as a traditional case. The standard of care by which a facility is measured takes into consideration "community" standards or those of neighboring facilities, as well as the resident's particular needs and habits. Nursing home residents may also sue under contract law. "Breach of contract, misrepresentation, fraud, and breach of implied warranties are all legitimate grounds for a lawsuit" (Frolik, 1995). In general, however, these cases are rarely decided in the resident's favor, since contracts are usually written by and for the facility. The important point is that the legal rights of the residents are protected.

Occupational Safety and Health Administration (OSHA)

OSHA has recently announced a Cooperative Compliance Program (CCP) to replace the agency's 1996 seven-state Nursing Home Employee Safety and Health Initiatives, which OSHA officials dismissed as ineffective.

This program offers employers a choice, partnership or traditional enforcement. Employers are not forced or required to join the CCP. Those that do join are placed on a secondary or tertiary inspection scheduling list. Those that elect not to join will remain on OSHA's primary inspection list.

One of the most persistent conceptual criticisms of the current CCP is that its cooperative component is not based on a true voluntary relationship between OSHA and the employer, but instead arises out of a threat of enforcement activity. This criticism may be well supported by the fact that employers on OSHA's target list receive a letter from their local or regional OSHA office inviting them to participate in the CCP on the one hand, but on the other informing them that declining to cooperate is likely to result in a wall-to-wall facility inspection.

Facilities that agree to participate must sign an agreement to identify and correct work-place hazards, work toward significant reductions in employee injuries and illnesses, implement or improve a safety and health program, and fully involve their employees in the facilities' safety and health programs. In return facilities would be removed from the primary inspection list. Larger employers would be placed on a secondary inspection list with a 30 percent chance of inspection, while work sites with fewer than 100 employees would be placed on a tertiary list with only a 10 percent chance of inspection. OSHA also suggested that inspections of facilities that participate in the program are likely to be shorter and result in lower penalties.

In other words, CCP would require employers to go beyond the minimum requirements of OSHA standards and to identify and correct other hazards such as ergonomics, violence, tuberculosis, and latex allergies in the absence of specific regulations. OSHA has not said how it will judge the effectiveness of the CCP and does not include results-oriented criteria or concrete goals to be achieved within its description of the program. OSHA has been considering using such criteria as a reduction in lost work days due to injury or illness or the number of workers' compensation claims as possible benchmarks.

The CCP program was based on OSHA's Maine 2000 program, a statewide voluntary compliance demonstration that won the Innovation in American Government Award from the Ford Foundation and the Hammer Award from Vice President Al Gore's National Performance Review.

Regulatory Issues

Private organizations also participate in the regulation of chronic care facilities. Professional organizations and consumer groups are also active in establishing criteria and programs to enhance the quality of long-term care (Torrens and Williams, 1993). One organization, originally named The Joint Committee on the Accreditation of Hospitals, changed its name in the 1980s to The Joint Commission on the Accreditation of Healthcare Organizations in order to expand its authority to other facilities such as nursing homes and home health agencies. Market demand has allowed this organization to expand its services. The Community Health Accreditation Program, a subsidiary of the National League for Nursing is another agency growing in popularity. With the growing number of health care services in the United States straining the government's regulatory resources, the importance of private agencies will undoubtedly increase.

In 1987, investigators for the General Accounting Office (GAO) told Congress that the rampant home health care fraud found by Medicare in four states probably is prevalent throughout the country.

Forty percent of all home health visits to senior citizens in California, Illinois, New York, and Texas should not have been paid for by Medicare, according to a report by the GAO assessing the result of recent Health and Human Services (HHS) investigations. One fourth of the companies that provide such care in the four states, plus Florida, have abused or defrauded Medicare or misused taxpayer money, the report found.

The Clinton administration and many in Congress also are trying to craft a long-term solution, including a system that would set standardized payments in advance for each type of home care. In 1990, there were 5,656 home health agencies participating in Medicare; by 1996 there were more than 9,800. Meanwhile, the government screens very few claims before paying bills and does virtually no on-site visits to check work, the GAO study found.

Federal, state, and private regulatory agencies have an immense job in ensuring that chronic care facilities adhere to the strict mandates of quality care. The last few decades have shown progress in curbing abuse and ensuring quality care for all residents. Similar measures will be initiated for assisted living facilities and they will also have to bear the weight of increased regulation.

SUMMARY

Federal, state, and private regulatory agencies have an immense job in ensuring that chronic care facilities adhere to the strict mandates of quality care. The last few decades have shown incredible progress in curbing abuse and ensuring quality care for all elderly citizens. OBRA 1987 warrants special mention for its profound impact in this field. Perhaps similar measures could be initiated for board and care homes. Assisted living facilities have responded to the aging-in-place of their residents by expanding their role in chronic care. It will be interesting to see the way in which licensing requirements shape their course, and how they in turn will influence these requirements. However, assisted living facilities will also have to bear the weight of increased regulation. With the growing number of states regulating such things as staffing ratios, many operators are becoming wary of this trend and caution that we will see assisted living regulated like nursing facilities. Though the basis of these organizations is somewhat different, the message rings true for all chronic care facilities—regulation is necessary and beneficial in protecting the elderly individual, so long as it does not become excessive.

CHAPTER
9

Employment and Retirement

In our society, and especially in the non-agrarian sector, work and jobs often determine how we perceive our social role and how we define our status. Much of the daily schedule of the worker, and indeed much of the worker's lifetime, is spent in work related activities. Having a work schedule establishes a routine, involves one in the community and is especially important in providing opportunities for socialization and broadening nonworking-hours social contacts. People who work together go to the movies or to lunch or to parties together and the working environment provides access to a wider social network of friends. All these are in addition to a salary, health insurance, and work-related accomplishments. However, to older workers living on a marginal income the continued availability of work may be necessary to meet the basic needs of food, shelter and health care.

It is important for employers to recognize that some older people want to work because they need income, desire the socialization a job provides or need to maintain the schedule around which their lives have been structured. For whatever reason elderly persons want to work, an employer should welcome their contribution to a changing employee market. Older workers represent a still untapped resource of job-related skills and experiences. Kelly reports that significant numbers of retirees would prefer to work and that their desire to stay on the job increases as they approach retirement. "Older workers offer many advantages beyond experience, skill and availability. Employers report that most workers in this age group are efficient, productive and committed to the work ethic . . . have good work habits, low turnover, few accidents on the job, good people skills and can be retrained successfully" (Kelly, 1990, p. 44).

No longer working, even for those who voluntarily retire, may represent a decline in income, absence of social contacts and a loss of the sense of usefulness. Although many retirees report that they have never felt more productive or useful, many others feel an extreme sense of loss that is correlated with the meaning and value of the work experience and reduced economic status. Over the years the policies dealing with retirement and opportunities for retirement with sufficient funds to maintain a reasonable lifestyle have been developed. The increased interest of employees in their personal retirement funds has resulted in their gaining greater autonomy over the investment and use of retirement benefits. The great success of the Medicare program has protected retirement benefits from the ravages of major medical expenses. All of these changes have represented great advances in retirement policies. What remains to be accomplished is the acceptance of the older worker in the work force, recognition of the potential contributions that can be made by the older worker and development of flex-time scheduling so that capable older workers can find a way to withdraw from the full time active work role to a more leisurely paced transition to retirement.

For lower income older persons, whose retirement benefits are not sufficient to meet their basic requirements, a major program providing subsidized employment in the public sector and preparation of new job skills is the Senior Community Service Employment Program (SCSEP). This program is funded in the Older Americans Act and administered by the Department of Labor. While funding for this program has been substantial, it has not been sufficient to meet the needs of the growing older population in need of employment or redevelopment of employable skills.

In this chapter we examine policy issues related to work and retirement, and opportunities for older persons with limited income to continue to work. This chapter also discusses several opportunities for volunteer assignments which provide rewards for work, enhance the individual's lifestyle, and provide structure and schedule in a person's daily routine.

AGE DISCRIMINATION IN EMPLOYMENT

The problem of age discrimination in the workplace is not new but has existed for over a century. Age limits for hiring and restrictive physical examinations emerged in the United States as early as the late 1800s. Negative attitudes toward the capacities and productivity of the elderly were already common, and an emerging perception of a period of decline in function and retirement as normal in an individual's life helped legitimize employment discrimination due to age. This was true despite already emerging evidence that older employees were conscientious, capable, and productive workers.

Prior to 1920, modern technology was used as the justification for age discrimination in employment, on the grounds that substantial physical strength, agility, and endurance were required for efficient execution of industrial technology. Publication of industrial studies in the 1930s that supported older workers' abilities in terms of productivity, reliability, and physical capacities failed to convince personnel managers and other corporate officials of these stated advantages.

Rigid age limits for hiring became the subject of early studies of age discrimination, many of which concluded that age discrimination was largely based more on factors such as pensions, group insurance and workers' compensation, than on the demands of the technological environment, implying a greater financial burden in employing an older worker.

The passage of the Social Security Act in 1935 exacerbated the employment problems of older workers by encouraging retirement so that employers could hire younger workers. Discriminatory practices based on age were reinforced by the gradual institution of early retirement policies (offering incentives for older workers to leave the work force before reaching the mandatory retirement age). Together, these factors constituted a significant social pattern that resulted in substantially reduced participation in the labor force by older workers.

In response to the growing concerns and frustrations of older workers across the nation, President Lyndon B. Johnson issued Executive Order No. 11141 on February 12, 1964 declaring a public policy against age discrimination in employment. An extended debate over how to balance the rights of older workers with the prerogatives of the employer to control managerial decisions had continued over the years.

Age protections had been contemplated but were not included during consideration of Title VII of the Civil Rights Act of 1964, which prohibited job discrimination on the basis of race, color, sex or national origin and mandated the hiring and placement of workers solely on the basis of merit. However, Title VII called for the Secretary of Labor to conduct a study on the prevalence and seriousness of age discrimination in employment. A report submitted to Congress in 1965 stated that:

> There is a persistent and widespread use of age limits in hiring that in a great many cases can be attributed to arbitrary discrimination against older workers on the basis of age and regardless of ability. The use of these age limits continues despite years of effort to reduce this type of discrimination through studies, information, and general education by the Government. The possibility of new non-statutory means of dealing with arbitrary discrimination has been explored. That area is barren (U.S. Senate, Developments in Aging, 1981, p. 271).

While it was increasingly evident that employment discrimination solely based on age was not defensible, no major policies were initiated to protect the older worker until 1967.

Chronology of Age Discrimination Legislation

1967

Congress was prompted to hold a number of hearings which, along with the President's 1964 executive order, led to the eventual enactment of the Age Discrimination in Employment Act of 1967 (ADEA). Signed into law as Public

Law 90-202 on December 12, the ADEA's purpose was to "promote employment of older persons based on their ability rather than age; to prohibit arbitrary age discrimination in employment; and to help employers and workers find ways of meeting problems arising from the impact of age on employment." As originally enacted, the ADEA prohibited age discrimination in employment against persons aged forty to sixty-five. These age limits were chosen in order to focus statutory coverage on those persons most likely to experience discrimination due to age. The sixty-five upper age limit was based on the common retirement age in the nation's industry and the normal eligibility age for full benefits under Social Security.

The act permitted the following mitigating considerations:

1. Where age is a "bona fide occupational qualification" (BFOQ) deemed reasonably necessary to the normal operation of a particular business.
2. Where differentiation (in fitness for a job) is based on "reasonable factors other than age" (RFOA); such as the use of physical examinations that require minimum standards for specific job tasks.
3. Where the terms of a bona fide seniority system (or bona fide employee benefit plan such as a retirement, pension, or insurance plan)—given the qualification that no seniority system or benefit plan may require or permit the involuntary retirement of any individual who is covered by the ADEA—must be observed.
4. Where an employee is discharged or otherwise disciplined for good cause.

A provision known as the "executive exemption" was designed to effect turn-over at the top levels of organizations and was strongly supported by business leaders. It allowed for the mandatory retirement of high-ranking executives or policymakers in the private sector provided they were entitled to annual retirement benefits in excess of $27,000.

These exceptions have been the basis for much litigation. The BFOQ exception, based on the assumption that aging affects an individual's ability to perform certain job functions, has remained unchanged since the ADEA went into effect in 1968, but it has yet to have been determined whether or not age is a factor on which employers may base employment decisions.

The second exception, based on reasonable factors other than age (RFOA), is similarly ambiguous. To apply this exception an employer must show objective evidence that age was coincidental to the personnel procedure that adversely impacted an older worker. Such evidence is very difficult to demonstrate.

The third exception allowed employers and labor unions to bargain collectively for a mandatory retirement age lower than sixty-five. This interpretation was challenged in the courts and eventually abolished through the 1978 ADEA amend-ments. This exception also permitted a stipulation for early retirement as part of a bona fide pension plan (instituted prior to the ADEA), as long as it was not used as subterfuge to undermine the protections of the act.

The final exception dealing with dismissal on grounds of good cause is perhaps the least controversial, as insubordination and related matters to show good cause can be demonstrated.

1974

The Fair Labor Standards Amendment of 1974 (PL 93-259) extended the provisions of the ADEA of 1967 to include federal, state, and local government employers as well as expanding coverage under the ADEA to include employers with twenty or more employees, rather than twenty-five or more.

1978

The Age Discrimination in Employment Amendments of 1978 extended protections beyond age sixty-five to age seventy for private sector, state, and local government employment and removed any age limit for federal government employees. Regulations implementing the 1978 amendments, however, stipulated that employers were not bound to credit years of service worked beyond age sixty-five to final pension benefit levels, thereby creating a disincentive to continue work beyond age sixty-five.

The major provisions of the 1978 amendments were:

> *Compulsory Retirement* — This provision allowed for compulsory retirement of bona fide executives and high-ranking policy-making employees at age 65 in the private sector. It further stipulated that these workers had to be entitled to annual pension benefits of at least $27,000.

> *Tenured Employees* — This section permitted colleges and universities to retire tenured faculty members at age 65 until July 1, 1982.

> *Charges of Age Discrimination* — This section allowed an aggrieved party to file a charge of age discrimination against an employer rather than a notice of intent to sue and authorized the utilization of a jury trial to determine "issues of fact" under any ADEA action.

> *Statute of Limitations* — This provision placed a hold on the running of the statute of limitations for up to one year while conciliation procedures are in effect.

Exceptions to the elimination of the mandatory retirement age for federal workers were made for prison guards, air traffic controllers, foreign service officers, and some other special groups.

In addition to the statutory changes made in the 1978 amendments, the legislation also required the Secretary of Labor to conduct an extensive study of the consequences of new provisions of the law, including: 1) examination of the effects of raising the age limit to seventy; 2) examination of the feasibility of further raising the age limit, or eliminating the age limit altogether; and

3) examination of the effects of the exemptions related to the mandatory retirement of tenured faculty members at institutions of higher learning and certain business executives.

A May 1979 Department of Labor interpretive bulletin regarding the 1978 amendments to the ADEA stipulated that employers with pension plans regulated under ERISA could cease pension contributions and pension credits for employees who worked beyond such a plan's normal retirement age.

Initially the responsibility of the Department of Labor and the Civil Service Commission, enforcement of the ADEA was shifted to the Equal Employment Opportunity Commission (EEOC) by President Jimmy Carter's Executive Order 12144, effective July 1, 1979. This change was implemented to consolidate within one agency the enforcement of all laws prohibiting discrimination in the workplace. Currently, the EEOC is responsible for: 1) Title VII of the Civil Rights Act of 1964; 2) The Age Discrimination in Employment Act of 1967; 3) The Equal Pay Act of 1963; and 4) Sections 501 and 505 of the Rehabilitation Act of 1973. Responsibility for the research function of the ADEA remains with the Department of Labor.

1982

The Tax Equity and Fiscal Responsibility Act of 1982 (TEFRA), passed into law as PL 97-248 on September 3, amended the ADEA to include a "working aged" clause requiring employers to retain their over-sixty-five workers on the company health plan rather than automatically shifting them to Medicare after their sixty-fifth birthday. TEFRA made Medicare the payor of last resort, whereas it previously had been the primary payor. Designed as a cost saver for Medicare, this legislation increased the cost of employing older workers. Not only did insurance plans increase their premium costs for those over sixty-five years of age, this legislation also raised costs to employers by making them responsible for primary payment of benefits for workers age sixty-five to sixty-nine and requiring coverage of employees aged sixty-five to sixty-nine if the employer offered a plan to any of its employees.

1984

Two major provisions of the Deficit Reduction Act of 1984 (DEFRA), or PL 98-369, signed into law on July 18, also had some effect on the costs of employment of older workers. Section 2301 of DEFRA modified the working aged clause in TEFRA to require employers to offer employees under age sixty-five the same family group health coverage, including that for spouses aged sixty-five to sixty-nine. Section 2338 of DEFRA provided an incentive for older workers to remain on the employer's health plan by waiving Medicare's Part B premium for workers (and their spouses) aged sixty-five through sixty-nine who elected private coverage. Previously, workers who did not enroll in Part B of Medicare after their sixty-fifth birthday were charged an additional 10 percent annual premium for each twelve months delay of enrollment after reaching age sixty-five.

The 1984 reauthorization of the Older Americans Act (PL 98-459) contained amendments that extended ADEA provisions to U.S. citizens employed by U.S. employers in foreign countries and stipulated that the annual retirement benefit eligible for the executive exemption be increased from $27,000 to $44,000.

A study by the Secretary of Labor of the 1978 ADEA amendments was submitted to Congress in 1982. This report stated not only that raising the mandatory retirement age from sixty-five to seventy would have only a very small effect on the availability of jobs for younger, female, and minority workers but also that total elimination of mandatory retirement would have a similar minimal impact.

In 1986, a survey by Louis Harris and Associates carried out for the National Council on the Aging, Inc. showed that almost 90 percent of the general population agreed with the statement, "Nobody should be forced to retire because of age if he wants to continue working and is still able to do a good job." Only 37 percent agreed that "Older people should retire when they can to give younger people more of a chance on the job." Similarly, a survey released in January 1985 by *USA Today* indicated that 70 percent of the American public disapproved of mandatory retirement.

1986

By the time the Age Discrimination in Employment Amendments (PL 99-592) were passed (October 31, 1986), most states had passed their own laws meeting or exceeding federal age discrimination laws. Until then, thirteen states had enacted statutes specifically banning mandatory retirement for public and private employees, while nineteen others had enacted laws protecting employees' right to work until age seventy. The 1986 amendments eliminated mandatory retirement in both the public and the private sectors, effective January 1, 1987. The intent of Congress in removing the upper age limit was to protect workers forty years of age and older from discrimination in all types of employment action, including forced retirement, hiring, promotions, and terms and conditions of employment.

However, it was not deemed unlawful to continue to fail or refuse to hire or to discharge any individual as a firefighter or law enforcement officer because of age if such action is taken in relation to the work. Four years after the enactment of this law, the Secretary of Labor and the Equal Employment Opportunity Commission were to have conducted a study "to determine whether physical and mental fitness tests are valid measurements of the ability and competency of police officers and firefighters to perform the requirements of their jobs" (PL 99-592, Oct. 31, 1986). If such tests were found to be valid, a change was to be made in the age discrimination clause protecting these positions.

The amendments to the Age Discrimination in Employment Act of 1967 (which terminated in 1993) permitted "mandatory retirement of any employee who is serving under a contract of unlimited tenure at an institution of higher education and who has attained seventy years of age" (Hammond and Morgan, 1991, p. 7). Unlike exemptions made for airline pilots based on concerns regarding reaction time and stamina of older workers and the high risk of piloting a large plane with many lives at stake, this exemption was based on fears "that postponed faculty retirements would prevent colleges and universities from hiring new faculty, who are traditionally a source of new ideas" (Hammond and Morgan, 1991, p. 7).

Data on the average age of faculty and the numbers who work past age seventy failed to indicate any evidence of a decline in faculty performance caused by age. Since tenured faculty can still be dismissed if an institution can prove that the individual no longer performs at the expected level, the study, completed in 1991, recommended that the "ADEA exemption permitting the mandatory retirement of tenured faculty be allowed to expire at the end of 1993."

The temporary exemption for state and local public safety officers has prompted objections to applying one standard to federal public safety personnel and another to state and local public safety personnel. Opponents also contend that job performance does not invariably decline with age, that age affects each individual differently, and that there are accurate and economical ways to test physical fitness and predict levels of performance for public safety occupations. The 1986 amendments required the Secretary of Labor and the Equal Employment Opportunity Commission to study the feasibility of utilizing physical and mental fitness tests to determine the competency of police officers and firefighters and to develop recommendations on standards for such tests. The police and firefighter exception was first enacted in 1978; it was extended by the 1986 amendments through 1993.

Further amendment of the ADEA resulted from the Omnibus Reconciliation Act of 1986 (PL 99-272), signed into law on April 7, 1986. Its provisions expanded employers' health care insurance obligations by requiring employers to offer employees and their spouses aged sixty-nine and over the same group health insurance coverage as that provided to younger workers.

1988

In 1987 an investigation carried out by the staff of the Senate Special Committee on Aging revealed that EEOC inaction resulted in the statute of limitations on many age discrimination cases having been allowed to run out. Under provisions in the ADEA a person filing an age discrimination complaint has up to two years to file a civil action in federal court. If the EEOC fails to process such a complaint within that time frame the complainant loses the chance to pursue the case in court. To correct this problem, S 2117, the Age Discrimination Claims Assistance Act of 1988, was introduced. It provided that person whose complaint had been filed with the EEOC on or after January 1, 1984, but whose claim had not been processed in time to meet the applicable statute of limitations be given an additional eighteen months to file suit in federal court. This legislation was enacted as Public Law 100-283.

Recognizing the difficulty of reentry into the work force by older workers, Congress was prompted on December 22, 1987 to pass a law (Public Law 100-202) requiring a study of this problem by the Department of Labor. A January 1989 report entitled "Labor Market Problems of Older Workers" subsequently stated that many older workers are pressured into early retirement and that "pension rules and job market realities severely limit their options and opportunities." Low pay of part-time work and the Social Security earnings limitation were also cited as financial obstacles to reentering the workplace. The report concluded that, in the final analysis, it will be the state of the U.S. economy that will determine the future value of older workers to the job market.

1990-1999

In response to Ohio versus Betts, in which the Supreme Court held that the Age Discrimination in Employment Act does not protect older workers from discrimination in the area of employee benefits, Congress passed the Older Workers Benefit Protection Act (OWBPA). This law, enacted in 1990, ensures that older workers are not compelled or pressured into waiving their rights under the ADEA. Specifically, OWBPA states that employees who are eligible for early retirement incentive plans must be provided with complete and accurate information concerning what benefits are available under the plan. An employee may be offered a severance package as part of his termination which includes language stating that in order to get severance pay the employee must sign an agreement that he waives all rights to sue the employer because of age discrimination.

However, an employee cannot waive his right to sue his employer for age discrimination under the ADEA unless several conditions are met. If the employer does not meet these conditions when obtaining the employee's written agreement not to sue (sometimes called a "Release"), the agreement may be unenforceable and the employee may still be able to bring a claim for age discrimination. The U.S. Supreme Court recently put the question to rest and decided in Oubre v. Energy, Inc., [118 S.Ct.838 (January 26, 1998)], that if the written termination agreement does not comply with the conditions set forth in OWBPA, then the employee maintains the right to sue for age discrimination under the ADEA, whether or not they accepted severance pay, and that return of any severance pay is not required before an age discrimination case can be brought.

Waivers or releases must be in writing and must contain the following:

- Must refer to waiver of claims specifically arising under ADEA;
- Must state that rights or claims that may arise after the date on which the waiver is executed are not covered;
- Must advise the employee to consult with an attorney before signing;
- Must give the employee at least twenty-one days within which to decide whether or not to sign;

- Must give the employee seven days from the date of execution to revoke the waiver.

FEDERAL PROGRAMS FOR EMPLOYMENT
OF THE ELDERLY

There is little doubt that older persons who want or need to work may face age discrimination in the work place, whether because of a preference for younger workers, or an inclination to separate older workers in times of retrenchment of the work force, or higher health care costs to the employer. Opportunities for employment of a person who is technologically unprepared to meet the expectations of the modern work force are particularly limited.

Title V of the Older Americans Act

Some older persons may lack the skills for substantive employment but need an income from work although they are unable to compete in the employment market. For them, Operation Mainstream of the Economic Opportunity Act of 1965 was established as a pilot program to assist poor and chronically unemployed adults find employment, primarily in rural areas. This program was transferred to the Department of Labor in 1967 and in 1973 was again transferred, this time to Title IX of the Older Americans Comprehensive Services Amendments.

The 1978 amendments to the Older Americans Act redesignated the program as Title V, The Older Americans Community Service Employment Program. The program is authorized and funded under the Older Americans Act but is administered by the Department of Labor as the Senior Community Service Employment Program (SCSEP). As the only federally sponsored job creation program for adults, it was established to foster and promote useful part-time opportunities in community service activities for persons with low incomes who are fifty-five years old or older.

The Employment and Training Administration (ETA) of the Department of Labor operates the program through grants, contracts and other agreements with eligible organizations, such as governmental entities, and certain public and private nonprofit agencies and organizations (Federal Register, 1985, p. 29,606). In addition to providing job opportunities, this program "contributes to the general welfare of communities by providing a source of labor for various community service activities, such as schools, hospitals and social service agencies" (U.S. House of Representatives, 1989, p. 1). Its focus recently has been modified to prepare participants in the program for unsubsidized employment. It is anticipated that about 100,000 persons will have participated in the program at the 1985 funding level.

While eligibility can be established at age fifty-five, priority is given to those who are over the age of sixty years and whose income does not exceed 125 percent of the poverty level announced by the Department of Health and Human Services and established by the Office of Management and Budget. A survey in 1988 reported that about 37 percent of jobs were in services to the elderly and about 63 percent were in services to the general community. Most persons enrolled in the program were women (69%), about 25 percent were over the age of seventy years, and about one-third were members of minority groups (U.S. House of Representatives, 1989).

Corporation for National Service

The Domestic Volunteer Service Act of 1973 authorized the federal agency ACTION that in turn sponsors the Older Volunteer Programs. This program is now identified as the National Senior Service Corps, as part of the Corporation for National Service, and includes the *Senior Companion Program*, the *Foster Grandparent Program*, and the *Retired Senior Volunteer Program*.

Senior Companion Program

Efforts to develop this program were initiated by Congress in 1968 in order to evolve a program targeted to service by and for older persons. Efforts to legislate for the program were aided by the development of two model programs and finally were successful when Title II of the Domestic Volunteer Service Act of 1973 was passed into law. In 1984, amendments to the act authorized the program to assist the homebound elderly to remain in their homes. The program's dual purpose is to create part-time stipendiary volunteer community service opportunities for low-income persons age sixty and older and to provide supportive person-to-person services to assist adults having exceptional needs, developmental disabilities, or other special needs for companionship. Eligibility for becoming a Senior Companion is restricted to those who are fifty-five years of age or older, are no longer in the regular work force, are physically capable of working in the program and have an annual income not exceeding the ACTION income eligibility guidelines for the state in which the program is offered.

Senior Companions serve twenty hours per week and receive a yearly stipend based on 1,044 hours of service annually. Senior Companions whose income exceeds the eligibility requirements but who otherwise would be eligible to participate may be assigned to a twenty-hour work week without stipend. Work assignments seek to fulfill the following objectives: to assist in preventing or delaying institutionalization of the clients, to assist in the discharge of adults from residential health care facilities, and to provide care to terminally ill patients.

Foster Grandparent Program (FGP)

This program was initiated in 1965 in the Office of Economic Opportunity (OEO) to demonstrate the value of having low-income persons aged sixty and older use their experience and maturity to establish a personal relationship with children having special needs. Funding authority was transferred to AoA in 1969 under Title VI of the Older Americans Act, as amended. At this time FGP became a stipendiary volunteer program in which low-income elderly, ages sixty and older, continued to serve children up through seventeen years of age. In 1971 the program was transferred to ACTION and in 1976 the maximum age for a child was redefined as twenty-one years.

Foster Grandparents are fifty-five years of age or older, no longer in the regular work force and free from any physical limitations that would impair their ability to work with children. They cannot have an annual income that exceeds the ACTION eligibility guidelines for the state in which the program is held. Foster Grandparents serve twenty hours per week and receive a stipend based on 1,044 hours of service annually. An individual who exceeds these income requirements may serve twenty hours per week without stipend.

Under professional supervision, Foster Grandparents assist with institutionalized children, children in public or private schools, adolescents and youths in correctional facilities, status offenders and delinquent youth offenders, abused or neglected children, and are involved in the prevention of juvenile delinquency.

Retired Senior Volunteer Program (RSVP)

Initiated under the Older Americans Act in 1969 as its Title VI and transferred to ACTION in 1971, the purpose of RSVP is to help retired persons avail themselves of opportunities for voluntary service in their communities. This program gives retired persons the chance to continue using their professional experience by working with local service organizations doing such things as conducting employment workshops and acting as consultants to nonprofit organizations. Participants must be fifty-five years of age or older, retired and willing to serve on a regular basis. They receive no stipend, but to enable them to afford to become volunteers, participants may be reimbursed for the expenses of transportation and meals. RSVP volunteers are placed in volunteer stations that are either a public agency or a private nonprofit organization.

Senior Corps Facts

- 80,000 children, teenagers, and their families are supported by the services of Foster Grandparents.
- Nearly 24,000 Foster Grandparents contribute 21.6 million hours of service annually. The value of this service is estimated at $262 million.

- The Foster Grandparents 1994 federal budget of $66.1 million was matched with $30.7 million in cash and donations from states and the local communities in which Foster Grandparents serve.
- Over 12,000 Senior Companions provide 12 million hours of service annually to help more than 32,000 frail elderly individuals live independently. The estimated value in terms of saved nursing home costs and services is $150 million.
- The Senior Companions 1994 federal budget of $29.8 million was supplemented by $17.8 million in cash and in-kind donations from states and the local communities in which Senior Companions serve.
- Retired and Senior Volunteer Program (RSVP) participants provide over 80 million hours of service annually to communities across the country. The value of this service is about $1 billion.
- Nearly 450,000 RSVP participants serve through more than 60,000 public and nonprofit community organizations.
- The RSVP 1994 federal budget of $34.4 million is matched with $36.7 million contributed by states, local governments, and the private sector, demonstration broad support for RSVP across the country. (Senior Corps, http://www.cns.gov).

HISTORICAL DEVELOPMENT OF PENSION PLANS

Toward the end of the 19th century, policymakers began to feel a need to improve the stability and productivity of labor forces and saw pensions as a way to encourage loyalty and longevity. Pensions also provided employers with a viable, humane adjunct to mandatory retirement. Federal tax laws and trade unions supported the creation of pension plans by exempting contributions to such plans from corporate income tax liability. Unions took the position that it was the "moral obligation of the employer to compensate workers for depreciation over a career of employment" (U.S. Senate, 1988).

In the United States, the Social Security program was not designed to provide entire retirement income but was intended to ensure a minimal level of income as an entitlement for citizens in their retirement years, unlike private pensions, which provide retirement income as a reward for years of service to an employer.

Since the objective of any retirement plan is to replace the worker's preretirement income with sufficient income and benefits to maintain an established standard of living (U.S. Senate, *Development in Aging*: 1989, 1990), such a plan ideally includes at least three sources of income and benefits: Social Security, a private pension, and personal savings. Depending on their employment and personal histories, retirees may have access to Social Security, private employer-sponsored pensions, state and local public pensions, the Federal Employees

Retirement System (FERS), the Railroad Retirement System, military pensions, Individual Retirement Accounts (IRAs), or other forms of personal savings, investments and intergenerational transfers. For some employees with low retirement income, Social Security may be augmented by Supplemental Security Income (SSI) (see Chapter 6).

Three factors contributed to a sudden escalation during the 1940s and 1950s. First, corporate and personal tax rates were steeply raised in 1940, making tax sheltering an important concern. Then the Revenue Act of 1941, (PL 753) regulated tax incentives by tightening requirements for the qualification of plans and improving the tax advantages for qualified plans. Second, wage freezes during World War II and the Korean War forced firms to provide some form of compensation (other than cash) to workers, and many firms accomplished this by offering benefits such as pension plans. Third, during the 1940s, having recognized that Social Security benefits would not be adequate as the sole source of retirement income, unions became increasingly interested in including pension benefits in compensation negotiations.

Subsequent to the Revenue Act of 1942, which required that plans not discriminate in coverage, benefits, or financing in favor of supervisors, highly paid employees, officers, or shareholders, the IRS strengthened regulations over the following twelve years. Requirements intended to protect general employee interests and prevent the misuse of pension plans as tax shelters were added.

However, no regulations were put in place to govern the administration of plans and the management of plan assets or to provide for the adequate funding of pension plans, guaranteed pension benefits, or the enforcement of participants' rights to benefits.

From 1940 to 1960, the largest employers dominated pension plan expansion. Over the same period, as the number of qualified profit-sharing pensions and stock bonus plans rose from 700 to 64,000, the proportion of workers covered increased from 12 percent to 33 percent. During the 1950s, after an economic slump, complaints surfaced about losses of employee pension benefits. For loyal employees who had voluntarily or involuntarily retired before reaching eligibility age, the requirements for age and service had become barriers to their receiving pension benefits.

These problems were exacerbated by growing evidence of fraud, embezzlement, and mismanagement in the investment of pension funds, and in 1958 Congress responded to them by enacting the Welfare and Pension Plans Disclosure Act of 1958 (PL 85-836). A major weakness of this legislation was that primary responsibility for monitoring pension plan activity was placed in the hands of plan participants, who were expected to spot fraud or criminal activity through the annual reports made available to them by plan administrators. The Welfare and Pension Plans Disclosure Act Amendments of 1962 (PL 87-420) shifted the burden of investigation and enforcement from plan participants to the

Departments of Justice and Labor, but still provided inadequate protection for the rights of individual participants.

After 1960, the growth of private pensions experienced a considerable slow-down. But while the proportion of workers covered by private pensions during this time only increased from 33 percent to 40 percent, the number of plans rose dramatically from 64,000 to almost 425,000. And, despite three major legislative efforts, major problems still were associated with private pensions.

Employer-sponsored pension plans may be one of two types: a defined benefit plan or a defined contribution plan.

Defined Benefit Plans

Defined benefit plans delineate the specific benefit(s) to be received in retirement and are usually based on years of service under the plan or a combination of years of service and pay. Today, beneficiaries of these plans, which pay out a fixed dollar amount, account for less than one-third of all participants in large or medium sized private plans (ERISA: Selected Legislative History, 1988). In general, defined benefit plans are collectively bargained between a union and an employer and cover union members or hourly employees. Commonly found in such industries as public utilities, manufacturing and mining, defined benefit plans are usually funded entirely by employers, some of whom supplement them with one or more defined contribution plans. Plans such as these base benefits on the employee's final three or five years' pay or on a fixed percentage of pay averaged over the worker's career.

Defined Contribution Plans

Today, the majority of pension plan participants are in salary-related plans known as defined contribution plans and are jointly funded by both employer and employee contributions made to each individual's account at a predetermined rate. The resulting benefits are an unspecified function of the account balance, including interest, at the time of retirement.

Defined contribution plans, while not pension plans in the strictest sense because not all of them are intended for retirement income, qualify under Internal Revenue Code definition of plans that are subject to tax qualifications and fiduciary requirements. This is because they permit tax-free accumulation of trust interest and benefits received under them are subject to a generally low tax rate.

THE EMPLOYEE RETIREMENT
INCOME SECURITY ACT OF 1974 (ERISA)

In March of 1962, President John F. Kennedy established the President's Committee on Corporate Pension Funds. This committee's preliminary report in November of 1962 prompted Congress to appropriate funding for a more intensive study. In January 1965, the committee's final report, "Public Policy and Private Pension Programs," recommended the imposition of federal standards on private pension plans. Specifically, the committee recommended that mandatory minimum vesting and funding standards be developed and that a pension plan termination program and a mechanism for portability of pension benefits be studied.

Although the report prompted the introduction of the Pension Benefit Security Act to Congress in 1968, this bill and others introduced in successive sessions of Congress failed to pass until the Employee Retirement Income Security Act (ERISA) was finally enacted in 1974.

Problems ERISA was designed to address included the collapse of a number of private pension funds in the 1960s and early 1970s, the elimination of individual workers from their pension programs as they neared retirement, and the need to ensure the future stability of the nation's retirement systems. Enactment of the law marked the beginning of a broadened federal interest in liberalizing and expanding private pension plans.

The average older American will rely on pension savings for eighteen years after retirement. ERISA was designed to establish minimum standards so that pension funding would be adequate to provide benefits for those years during retirement. ERISA does not require an employer to devise a pension plan, nor does it define a dollar benefit for the employee.

ERISA does provide the following:

1. Requires the plan to regularly inform participants regarding the pension plan features and funding.
2. Sets minimum standards for participation, vesting, benefit accrual and funding.
3. Requires accountability of pension plan fiduciaries and exercises sanctions against mismanagement.
4. Provides participants the right to sue for benefits.
5. Establishes the Pension Benefit Guaranty Corporation (PBGC) to guarantee payment of certain designated benefits if a defined benefit plan is terminated.

The Department of Labor is responsible for the enforcement of ERISA, Title I. It does so through the Pension and Welfare Benefits Administration (PWBA) and its regional offices. The Treasury Department, through the Internal Revenue Service, establishes the rules and exacts compliance for tax-qualified pension loans. The PBGC guarantees certain pension benefits.

Provisions of ERISA

The complexity of ERISA suggests that a review of the major policy characteristics of the law and some significant amendments to it will assist in understanding the policy issues involved.

Coverage

Employers are not obliged to offer pensions, but those who do are obliged to offer a pension program that is consistent with the requirements set forth in ERISA, its amendments, the Tax Reform Act of 1986, and various other laws.

For years, employers offering pensions were required to prove their pension coverage was nondiscriminatory by meeting either a *percentage test* or a *classification test*. The *percentage test* required an employer to offer the pension plan to at least 70 percent of its workforce (excluding part-time, newly hired and/or employees under age 25), or, for a defined-contribution plan, 56 percent of the total work force.

Many employers unable to meet the percentage test utilized a less stringent *classification test* that was intended to show that benefits of the plan were provided to a broad cross-section of employees and did not discriminate in favor of highly paid workers. Until 1986, however, vague interpretation by the IRS of the classification test permitted employers to discriminate and provide coverage almost entirely to higher-paid workers.

Participation

These provisions apply federal rules to pension plans so that all employees aged twenty-one or older must be given the opportunity to enroll in an employer's pension plan (the only exceptions are for part-time employees and new hires).

Benefit Accruals

Benefit accruals are earnings accumulated to an employee's account in a particular pension at a particular time (date). ERISA regulates neither benefit levels nor how they accumulate. The Pension Plan document regulates and explains these benefits. The provisions also require employers to credit employees for all service with the same employer both before and after a break-in-service and to establish a uniform standard for the rates of benefit accrual, thus preventing plans from having lower accrual rates in early years of employment or for younger employees. Finally, portability of pension benefit credits from one employer to another before vesting is not included.

Benefit Adequacy

Retirement income and benefits sufficient to allow a retiree to maintain his or her preretirement standard of living, must be calculated on the basis of their replacement ratio or coverage. This is a comparison of the specific benefit paid at some future date with the previous earnings. For example, Social Security pays a relatively high return (or approximately 25% of preretirement earnings) for average to low income earners whereas private pensions often provide a higher replacement ratio to higher income earners since the latter receive proportionately less from Social Security.

Three-fourths of the elderly poor are women. Almost 15 percent of women aged sixty-five and over live below the poverty level, a figure nearly twice that for elderly men. Women face a particularly high risk of poverty after retirement due to minimal payouts from Social Security and pensions. Because Social Security benefits are wage based, women's lower earnings and time away from the paid labor force to care for family members results in Social Security benefits that are 73 percent lower than those for men. Women's retirement payments are also decreased because of short average job tenure, high rate of part time employment, lower rate of union membership, and employment in areas that offer few pensions —predominately small businesses, retail trade and service industries.

Pension Funding

ERISA provisions are designed to ensure that plans would have the money to pay benefit obligations in the future by setting standards for funding. While previous plans were allowed forty years to develop full funding of their benefit obligations, those created after ERISA's enactment are required to be fully funded in thirty years. ERISA sets minimum funding rules and regulations. Detailed rules protect the employee from inadequate employer funding. The rule effective after December 8, 1994, requires pension plan participants to be notified each year regarding the fund status and the PBCG guarantees, if a defined benefit plan is less than 90% funded.

Two potential problems of pension funding are termination of underfunded plans and reversion of assets from termination of overfunded plans. An underfunded plan termination occurs when an employer discontinues a plan when faced with probable financial ruin. A pension reversion occurs when an employer seeks to gain access to plan funds that exceed the amount necessary to fulfill obligations by terminating a current plan and instituting a new one in order to gain access to a plan balance that has been enriched by substantial increases in stock market and other asset values. Plan reversions have been used to finance or fight corporate takeovers, improve corporate cash-flow, and modify corporate pension benefit plans.

Vesting

Vesting is defined as the length of time an employee is required to work before earning a nonforfeitable right to accrued benefits. When fully vested, the accrued benefit will belong to the worker, even upon leaving the company before reaching retirement age. Generally, if employed when reaching the plan's "normal" retirement age (usually 65), the worker will be fully vested. Employees must also be permitted to earn a vested right to accrued benefits through service. The worker is always entitled to 100 percent vesting in his or her own contributions and their investment earnings. However, if the employer contributes to the accrued benefit (as most do) the worker may be required to complete a certain number of years of service with the employer before the employer portion of the accrued benefit becomes vested. Thus, if employment is terminated without having worked for a long enough period, all or part of the accrued benefit provided by the employer may be forfeited. (What You Should Know About Your Pension Rights, 1995, page 23).

Benefit Distribution

Distribution may be by lump sum or annuity and is, for the most part a function of an employee's wages just prior to retirement. Lump sum distributions, commonly found in defined contribution plans, are generally the most portable. They are paid to an employee upon separation and can easily be converted to another tax-sheltered retirement plan. Defined benefit plans generally distribute benefits in the form of an annuity and only upon retirement.

Joint and Survivor

ERISA provisions improve benefits for spouses by stipulating that plans provide for joint and survivor benefits if requested by an employee within a specified time in exchange for an overall lower pension amount. If an employee is married at the time of retirement, Joint and Survivor is the automatic benefit provided. However, distribution may be in some other form of annuity, specifically authorized with the notarized signatures of both the employee and spouse.

Portability

An employee's nonforfeitable earned right to receive a pension originated as a function of a worker's length of service, reserving benefits for long-term workers and providing an incentive for them to remain on the job. However because relatively few workers remain within a single organization over time, the concept of portability, or the ability to transfer pension benefits upon separation from an organization, has been introduced.

Most pensions are now portable. When a vested worker in a defined contribution plan leaves the labor market to assume family obligations or changes jobs because of family concerns, the worker can take the pension and convert it to a Rollover IRA which was established for this purpose. This action allows the worker to avoid the tax burden at the time of transition, and the funds can be returned to another defined contribution plan on reentry into the workforce. When a vested worker leaves a defined benefit pension plan, the benefit can remain in that plan and be taken as a monthly pension when retirement age is reached.

Fiduciary

ERISA also requires standards for the management of pension plan funds by requiring diversification of plan assets and disallowing the diversion of plan assets for any other use other than the payment of benefits for reasonable plan administration expenses. Mismanagement is subject to legal action.

Reporting and Disclosure

These provisions mandate various standards and reporting procedures for the administration of plan funds. Trustees are required to inform employees and beneficiaries of their rights and obligations by providing each of them with copies of the summary plan description and annual reports, as well as any other statements required when firms merge or transfer assets of a qualified plan, terminate a qualified plan, or when an employee with vested benefits leaves a plan.

Plan Termination Insurance

ERISA also established a federally-run pension plan termination insurance corporation, the Pension Benefit Guaranty Corporation (PBGC). Funded through annual premiums paid by employers, this nonprofit corporation guarantees that persons with vested benefits would still receive pensions in the event of corporate bankruptcy. Initially, single-employer and multi-employer plans were treated differently, with plan termination insurance extended only to a single-employer plans. PBGC guarantees that pension benefits for defined benefit plans will be paid up to the limits of the law and not to exceed PBGC's limits. ERISA provides other benefits in the event of a plan termination. If a plan terminates before the employee is vested, the accrued benefit is 100 percent vested to the extent funded upon termination of the plan. Also, if the pension plan merges with another plan, the benefit to the employee after the merger must be at least equal to the benefit before the merger.

Individual Retirement Accounts

This innovative provision allows a worker not covered by an employer-sponsored pension to open an Individual Retirement Account (IRA), thus qualifying a portion of gross income for a special tax exemption.

Keogh Plans

Keogh Plans are intended for self-employed individuals and their employees. Self-employed means being a sole proprietor or a partner in a partnership. If the self-employed individual has a Keogh Plan and has employees, the employees must be covered under the plan if they work 1,000 hours or more each year and have worked for the company more than three years. Twenty-five percent of "self-employment income" or $30,000 is the maximum amount an employer may contribute to his or her own account annually. Self-employment income may not include dividends, interest, or capital gains from investments. Whatever percentage contribution the employer makes to his or her own account must also be made to each employee's account. Any person taking a distribution from a Keogh Plan before age fifty-nine and one-half is subject to all taxes due and a 10 percent early distribution fee.

At retirement, there are two options for distribution: lump sum payout, in which case the IRS allows income averaging, or reporting 20 percent of the amount each year for five years, or monthly payouts, which are regarded as ordinary income for income tax purposes.

AMENDMENTS TO ERISA

1977

By 1977 it had become clear that the premiums set by the PBGC to cover terminated pensions for single employer plans would need to be increased. ERISA set the initial annual premium per participant at $1.00. After December 31, 1977, premiums were increased to $2.60 by PL 95-214.

1982

The Tax Equity and Fiscal Responsibility Act (TEFRA), Public Law 97-248, passed on September 3, 1982 was intended to prevent discrimination among pension plans of small corporations. TEFRA required small corporations, generally known for offering greater benefits to key, usually top-level employees, to accelerate vesting and offer a minimum benefit to short-service workers.

Ten years after the enactment of ERISA, 67.1 percent of all U.S. wage and salary workers (52.7 million) were covered by employer-sponsored pension plans. The majority, or more than 70 percent, were employed in professional and related services, public utilities, and the manufacturing and mining industries. Persons in business and repair services, retail trade, agricultural and personal services were less likely to be covered (U.S. Senate, Developments in Aging, 1988). Further modifications to ERISA were still necessary.

1984

The Retirement Equity Act (REA), or PL 98-397, passed on August 23, 1984, was intended to improve the distribution of pension benefits by providing survivor benefits to spouses of vested workers, clarifying the division of benefits under circumstance of divorce, and lowering the minimum ages for participation in pension plans from twenty-five to twenty-one years of age.

In the same year, both the Department of Labor and the Treasury Department clarified provisions for terminations of plans and successor plans by means of Implementation Guidelines for Asset Reversions. These provisions allowed an employer to terminate a pension plan provided a similar successor plan, which covered vested participants, was established. Unfortunately, plan terminations that conformed to this interpretation often left plan participants covered under similar but less secure successor plans. Additionally, much of the money recovered by employers through these plan terminations (which amounted to nearly $16 billion in recovered assets since 1980), went for mergers, takeovers, and other purposes that were not in the best interests of the workers.

1985-1988

Title XI of the Tax Reform Act of 1986 (PL 99-514), established: 1) limitations on the employer's ability to integrate pension benefits; 2) reform of coverage, vesting, and nondiscrimination rules; 3) changes in the rules governing the distribution of benefits; and 4) modifications of limits on the maximum amount of benefits and contributions in tax-favored plans.

The Tax Reform Act of 1986 established substantial disincentives to use pension or deferred compensation plan accruals for any purpose other than providing a stream of retirement income. It imposes on an employee an excise tax of 10 percent on distributions from a qualified plan before age fifty-nine and one-half, other than those that are taken as a life annuity, taken upon the death of the employee, upon early retirement at or after age fifty-five, or used to pay medical expenses (U.S. Senate, 1990).

ERISA was enacted to protect employees' interests in the provision, operation, and administration of employee benefit plans. ERISA applies to both pension plans and welfare benefit plans, of which a health plan is one, according to section 302(C) of the Labor Management Relations Act. The U.S. General Accounting Office in July 1995 established that 114 million people (approximately 44% of the population of the United States) were covered by ERISA health care plans.

ERISA requires that a fiduciary govern the health care plan in the sole interest of the beneficiaries, exercising responsible financial prudence. The assets of the plan are placed in a trust for safekeeping.

COBRA

One of the problems with employee health care plans is the termination of coverage when changes occur in an employee's status. To counter the problem, Congress enacted the Consolidated Omnibus Budget Reconciliation Act (COBRA) of 1985 (Public Law 99-272). COBRA required that coverage remain available to employees, spouses and dependents who are covered on the day before certain life events, as follows:

1. Termination (unless for gross misconduct) or reduction of hours;
2. Death of the covered employee;

3. Divorce or legal separation;
4. Medicare entitlement;
5. Loss of dependent child status.

The law generally covers group health plans maintained by employers with twenty or more employees in the prior year. It applies to plans in the private sector and those sponsored by state and local governments. The law does not, however, apply to plans sponsored by the Federal government and certain church-related organizations.

OBRA

The Omnibus Budget Reconciliation Act of 1986 (OBRA), or PL 99-509, required employers to continue to accrue benefits for working employees even past their normal retirement age. The IRS, Equal Employment Opportunity Commission (EEOC) and the Department of Labor were mandated to create these provisions before 1988.

The financing problems in the PBGC continued to escalate despite the significant changes made in 1986. The termination of several of LTV Corporation's pension plans in late 1986 caused the PBGC's deficit to double from $2 billion to $4 billion.

A remedy intended to alleviate this financial dilemma was provided in the Omnibus Budget Reconciliation Act of 1987 (OBRA 87) or PL 100-203, which was passed on December 22. A provision in this act called for an additional increase in premiums paid to PBGC. This new "variable rate premium," which ranged from $16 to $50 per employee, was instituted in 1989 to penalize companies that had large unfunded liabilities. Companies sponsoring pension plans that were adequately funded (which totaled 82% of the number of plans insured by the PBGC), paid only $16 per employee, while those companies responsible for the remaining 17 percent of the debt were charged a variable rate depending on their level of underfunding. The PBGC maintained that only 4 percent of the underfunded plans would be forced to pay the full $50 per employee maximum rate. Additionally, premium payments to PBGC were required to be made quarterly instead of annually, as had been the case.

OBRA 86 also attempted to reduce substantial overfunding of pension programs by providing that employers no longer would be allowed to make tax-free contributions to a plan that was overfunded to 150 percent of current obligations. This meant that employers whose plans had only a small asset cushion were less attractive to buy-out companies looking for some quick cash and therefore less subject to hostile takeovers.

The 100th Congress (in 1987 and 1988) struggled with the complex issues surrounding pension plan reversions but was unable to tighten the loophole that allowed companies with overfunded pension plans to terminate those plans in order to secure the surplus assets for other purposes. Opponents of these "cash-outs" suggested that excess assets be used to fund plan improvements, such as cost-of-living adjustments. As Senator Howard M. Metzenbaum (D-OH) declared during debate over reversions, "Companies have turned their pension plans into corporate piggy banks" (*Almanac*, 100th Congress 2nd Session, 1988, p. 271), and, as with most piggy banks, the only way to get the money out is to destroy them.

Instead of a temporary 60 percent excise tax on surplus funds collected from terminated plans that was intended to give Congress time to find a permanent way to discourage pension fund reversions, Congressional conferees instituted a permanent increase in the excise tax from 10 percent to 15 percent. An aide to Representative William L. Clay (D-MO), noted that this meager increase would not be a disincentive for employers and that it definitely would not help the workers.

Despite intense debate, no resolution to the problem was forthcoming through 1988. It was still the prerogative of a company to terminate plans without regard to the future benefit security of its employees, and without sharing the benefits.

The debate over excess pension assets continued through 1989. Although the Treasury Department agreed in October 1988 to place a temporary moratorium on approvals of reversions, efforts to reach compromises between lawmakers and employers interests faltered.

Representative William Clay (D-MO) and Senator Howard Metzenbaum (D-OH), who introduced HR 1661 and S 685 respectively, encountered major political opposition. A reconciliation measure, approved by the House Ways and Means Committee (and expected to find similar favor in the Senate Finance Committee), would have permitted firms to make limited transfers of assets to pay for their share of the health benefits of retired workers. This plan did not, however, provide any benefit increases for workers and retirees and once again served only the needs of employers (by allowing the use of overfunded assets for premium payments).

Although the AARP and other interest groups representing organized labor and retired workers regarded this issue as a top priority, their foes were formidable. The Bush administration and Republican lawmakers argued that tight restrictions on employers' use of excess pension funds would backfire by discouraging employers from establishing pension plans. Top industry lobbyists promised to take a "hard line" against the Clay and Metzenbaum legislation, promising "full-scale engagement" against the AARP and other backers of these proposals. Even the U.S. Treasury would have suffered a potential loss of revenue from a plan that limited pension reversions. (Current law forces employers to pay a 15% excise tax on assets that revert to them upon termination of a plan.) If additional restrictions were placed on reversions, this income to the treasury would be lost.

The potential loss of an estimated $200 million in fiscal 1990, and $1.2 billion over the next five years was a major obstacle to the approval of reversion restrictions (particularly in light of the country's severe deficit problems).

Minimal adjustments were made in 1987 to strengthen "the requirement governing employer contributions to defined-benefit plans, in order to assure adequate levels of assets for employee pension benefits." Premiums for employers in the Pension Benefit Guarantee Corporation were increased to $19 per participant (U.S. Senate, 1990).

1990

The Older Workers Benefit Protection Act (PL 101-433) was passed on October 16, 1990 and was designed to overturn Public Employees Retirement System of Ohio versus Betts, in which the Supreme Court held that the ADEA does not protect older workers from discrimination in the area of employee benefits. June Betts was a public employee in Ohio who at age sixty-one retired because of a serious disability. Disability retirement was limited to those under the age of sixty, therefore denying her disability benefits which would have been substantially higher than her retirement benefits. The Supreme Court Decision immunized virtually all employee benefit programs from liability under the age Discrimination in Employment Act (U.S. Senate, 1990). This Older Workers Benefit Protection Act prohibits discrimination against older workers in all employee benefits.

Additionally, premiums for employers in the Pension Benefit Guarantee Corporation were increased to $19 per participant (U.S. Senate, 1990).

1994

Section 404(c) of ERISA, effective January 1, 1994, allows an employer to shift responsibility for retirement plan investments to the plan participants. Employer sponsored 401(k) plans could be designed to incorporate investment alternatives in order to shift liability for performance (risk/reward) of investments to the plan participant (the employee). The final regulations became effective January 1, 1996.

1997

The Health Insurance Portability and Accountability Act of 1996 (HIPAA) was signed into law on August 21, 1996. This law includes protections for millions of working Americans and their families who have preexisting medical conditions or might suffer discrimination in health coverage based on a factor that relates to an individual's health. HIPAA's provisions amend Title I of ERISA of 1974 and place requirements on employer-sponsored group health plans, insurance companies, and health maintenance organizations including: limiting exclusions for preexisting conditions; prohibiting discrimination against employees and dependents based on their health status; guaranteeing renewability and availability of health coverage to certain employers and individuals; and protecting many workers who lose health coverage by providing better access to individual health insurance coverage.

AMERICANS WITH DISABILITY ACT (ADA)

More than 40 million Americans have disabilities that significantly influence their independence, and because the prevalence and severity of functional limitations increase with age, it is estimated that more than 37 percent of adults age seventy or older have functional limitations. It is therefore imperative that effective policies and programs be implemented to avert the problems associated with disabilities. The Americans with Disabilities Act established policy provisions that are important for older persons in our society. Implementation of the law should be carefully scrutinized to assure that it displays no age bias and additional efforts should be mounted to investigate the causes and prevention of disabilities among older persons, especially those that interfere with the ability to remain employable.

This culmination of a two-decade effort to secure for disabled persons the same protection against discrimination enjoyed by women, minorities and the elderly was a major step toward realization of that goal. "For twenty-five years our handicapped citizens have been outside the umbrella of basic civil rights," said Senator Tom Harkin (D-IA), chairman of the Labor Subcommittee on the Handicapped and sponsor of S 933. "Today we bring them in" (CQ, August 5, 1989, p. 2,044).

Individuals whose disabilities impair their mobility or access to employment, public services, and public accommodations were the designated beneficiaries of The Americans with Disabilities Act (PL 101-336) passed July 26, 1990, the first provisions of which became effective in 1990. Provision of sidewalk curb cuts, now commonplace throughout this country, illustrates an important accommodation to individuals using wheel chairs or other mobility aids as well as how access by the handicapped can be achieved over a reasonable period of time and without encumbering those not constrained in their mobility. If anything, the curb cuts have made the streets safer for everyone. The Americans with Disabilities Act greatly expands the number of environments accessible to the handicapped.

The Act's four titles had different dates for implementation. Title 1 dealt with employment and provided that no covered entity shall discriminate against a qualified individual because of disability in job-application procedures, hiring, advancement, employee compensation, job training or other privileges of employment. Title 1 took effect July 26, 1992 for employers with twenty-five or more employees and was to be implemented on July 26, 1994, for employees with fifteen or more employees. Employers with fewer than fifteen workers were exempted. Complaints may be filed with the Equal Employment Opportunity Commission. Available remedies include back pay and court orders to stop discrimination.

Title 2 provides that no qualified individual with a disability shall be excluded from participation in or be denied the benefits of the services, programs or activities of public entities, including transportation facilities. This section was initiated on August 26, 1990, when all new public buses and light and rapid rail vehicles ordered were to be accessible. By July 26, 1995 one car per train must be accessible and key commuter stations were to have been retrofitted by July 26, 1993. All existing Amtrak stations are to be retrofitted by July 26, 2010. Individuals may bring private lawsuits to obtain court orders to stop discrimination and can also file complaints with the Attorney General, who may file lawsuits to stop discrimination.

Title 3 provides that people with disabilities must have access to existing private businesses that serve the public whenever accommodation is "readily achievable." Facilities include hotels, restaurants, theaters, self-serve laundries, museums, zoos, private schools and offices of health care providers. This public accommodation section took effect on January 26, 1992. Individuals may file complaints with the Attorney General or bring private lawsuits under the public accommodations procedure.

Title 4 deals with telecommunications and requires that interstate and intrastate telecommunications relay services were to have been made available to hearing-impaired and speech-impaired individuals by July 26, 1993. Individuals may file complaints with the Federal Communications Commission (FCC).

While the benefits of the Americans with Disabilities Act are not specifically directed to the elderly in our society it is obvious that their employability or use of public services or accommodations are enhanced by this law.

SUMMARY

Because it is so complex, ERISA has generated a large number of regulations and placed substantial administrative costs on private pension systems. The many changes it has undergone in the years since its enactment have also served to make it even more complex. And, as has been noted, upon its enactment in 1974, some very important issues ERISA did not address would need to be resolved in subsequent years, such as faster vesting, better coverage, the indexing of benefits against inflation, and a system that would allow for greater portability of benefits.

There have been dramatic improvements in the average economic well-being of older Americans over the last two decades, but many still subsist near or below the poverty line. Nearly one-half of all men aged sixty-five and over worked in 1950, as did 87 percent of men aged fifty-five to sixty-four. By 1985, these figures had dropped to 16 percent and 68 percent respectively, and they have remained steady since then. Older women's labor force participation has been about 9 percent, while that of women aged fifty-five to sixty-four rose from 27 percent in 1950 to 46 percent in 1992 (Quinn and Smeeding, 1993, p. 5).

Social Security payments represent the most important source of income for all groups of retirees. More than one-half of all groups except white men and their wives relied on Social Security for more than 50 percent or more of their income. Indicative of the importance of progressive Social Security benefits to unmarried men and women, 33 percent of black and 42 percent of Hispanic retirees received more that 50 percent of their income from Social Security.

Very large differences exist in the financial status of retired workers across white, black, and Hispanic groups. The three-legged stool of retirement—Social Security, pensions, and individual savings—provides a sturdy retirement seat for many newly retired workers. Hispanic retirees have, on average, a less stable retirement with fewer assest than their white counterparts. Black retirees most often have a very unstable retirement, their assets are almost entirely missing (Snyder, 1993).

The aging of the work force will apply pressure on many employers to retain their older workers, and as this occurs there may be less and less need for any sort of federal intervention to assure that age discrimination does not occur. The availability of job-related training will extend the productive work life. Meanwhile, the workers' rights provided under the ADEA will need continued protection by the EEOC in a timely manner (U.S. Senate, *Developments in Aging*: 1988, 1989, 1990).

Future discussions in pension reform will surely encompass the controversial subject of pension reversions as well as the question of whether or not employees should directly benefit from them. Likewise, although Congress previously has tried to deal with the issue of portability, there is still a great need for a plan that provides for an equitable system.

As noted throughout this volume, policy formation occurs at different levels of government, which sometimes are supportive of each other and other times display conflicts. Initially, policy opposing discrimination in employment was introduced by executive order of the president, and therefore was limited to federal employees. It had to be replaced and especially reinforced by the action of Congress resulting in the ADEA Law and all of its subsequent amendments. In 1989, the Supreme Court reinterpreted the ADEA law in a manner that was inconsistent with the intent of Congress, requiring that the Congress pass the Older Workers Benefit Protection Act of 1990 in order to clarify its intent in the law and to reverse a decision of the Supreme Court.

CHAPTER
10

Housing and Social Services

It is reasonable to question why in this volume about public policies for the elderly we have chosen to put issues of housing and social services in the same chapter. Traditional differences between the two subjects are immediately apparent. Many housing programs are supported by the Department of Housing and Urban Development (HUD); many social service programs are provided through the Administration on Aging (AoA). Housing represents bricks and mortar, and social services include food programs, activities, senior centers, counseling and education. However, there is today a growing realization that if housing programs for the elderly are to succeed, especially in meeting the changing needs of those who age in place, they must be accompanied by a responsive social service program. The issue of sponsorship or in whose domain a program lies is of less concern than ensuring the availability of services for older persons. In addition to the relationship among all public policies (i.e., income, health, employment, housing and social services), there is a particularly symbiotic relationship between housing and social services policies, a point that will be elaborated upon in this chapter.

Housing specifically designed for occupancy by the elderly could extend their ability to live independently as contributing members of their communities while delaying or avoiding the need for costly and more restrictive institutionalization. Housing for the elderly should be designed to compensate for the effects of declining physical capacity and psychological and emotional changes as well as for the loss of spouse, relatives, and older friends by offering opportunities to find new friends and neighbors of similar capacities, experiences and interests (National Council On The Aging, 1991). We discuss housing and social services in the same chapter because housing should respond to different personal needs and also should meet changing individual needs as people age in place. Housing policies involve far more than construction of new dwellings; they also must integrate issues of lifestyle and opportunities for personal growth. We therefore include some ideas related to the importance of lifestyle in this chapter on housing.

HOUSING

Where we live and how we live can be major contributors to quality of life. The place of residence can represent security and comfort for some, while for others in less adequate facilities it may represent constraints on life style and threats to personal freedom. The ability of housing and the environment to adapt to changing requirements of the occupant contributes to the appropriateness of the housing. Problems of access by reason of stairs, or inability to reach cabinets or fully use bathing or toileting facilities could impair the utility of the housing. A neighborhood perceived to be hostile to the older resident may result in an imposed constraint on mobility by the individual into the community. Residents may age in place and neighborhoods may change, upsetting the balance of person to housing and community for which that housing was initially selected. Large homes, once the sanctuary for family units may be too big for a single aged person. The fit of the older individual to housing is contingent upon many factors, including the health of the occupant, physical condition of the housing and neighborhood, preference of the individual and the financial status of the individual.

Housing is much more than shelter. It is also "the symbol of one's status in the community and an articulation of what one feels is significant in life" (Fahey and Tilson, 1990, p. xv). Therefore, "a principal value guiding the developing of housing for the future . . . [should be] the creation of environments which stimulate persons to live life to the fullest until its very end" (Fahey, 1989, p. 5). Housing is thus "not only a functional place in meeting narrowly defined human needs, but also a place in which family and other significant relationships are experienced . . . It is a place of identity. It is manifestation of one's power to choose, to exercise autonomy" (Fahey and Tilson, p. xv).

The ability to experience this autonomy through the selection of housing may not be available for older persons with limited income for whom the choice of housing may be restricted to the public housing or other low income housing available on the market at the time of need. Others with limited income may find themselves on long waiting lists for the few resources available to them. Even for those individuals with limited income who may be fortunate to have subsidized housing available to them there is a very limited likelihood that the housing will be accompanied by a range of social services critical to the maintenance of independence for the tenant. Many of our public policies in housing have been directly related to assisting people who cannot afford to pay market rates to obtain suitable housing.

Too few federal housing policies for the elderly have considered the quality of life in the housing but instead have mainly focused on providing "maintenance" environments that are only just adequate as shelter. The insufficiency of this policy direction is made clear in Lawton's (1989) explication of the three functions that should obtain in residential settings. He asserts that "all people require stimulation, maintenance, and support from their residential environments" (p. 36). And, while certain residences serve some functions better than others, older persons, regardless of their level of competence, can actively determine how these functions are distributed and potentially achieve an acceptable balance of these three functions that will provide them with a sense of personal satisfaction and well-being. This sort of active, creative interaction with the environment provides a sense of control over their lives that needs to be encouraged.

The interaction of an environmental situation of a given level of demand (demanding a certain response) with a person of a given level of competence was theorized by Lawton and Nahemow (1973) to result in a particular behavior and effect. The higher the level of personal competence, the greater the amount of environmental demand one would be able to deal with in a positive manner. Accordingly,

> . . . too great an excess of demand over competence results in anxiety, stress, or maladaptive behavior . . . Clearly if a person in an unchanging maintenance environment declines in competence, the formerly maintaining environment will become a dysfunctional environment unless personal competence can be reinforced or the now-too-demanding environment can be moderated [made more supportive] (Lawton, 1989, p. 40).

The ability of older persons to adjust to an environment and achieve an easy familiarity with it is an important characteristic of a residence that aspires to cater to the elderly. An environment in which maintenance is the dominant function is characterized by stability and predictability. The components of this environment are so familiar that we do not even have to think about them. The context is so well known that there are, in effect, "no surprises." Everything has its place and can be so relegated into the background of consciousness that the individual is free to concentrate on issues and activities other than the immediate environment.

The two other functions of the residential environment, stimulation and support, can be conceptualized as being on either side of the maintenance function on an environmental continuum. Stimulation, in Lawton's terms, "represents . . . a departure from the usual, [providing] a novel array of stimuli, a problem to solve" (p. 37). A stimulating environment calls upon the resident to respond in ways that may be unfamiliar, causing a more active and autonomous relationship with the surroundings. A more stimulating environment may be created simply by redecoration, rearrangement of furniture, keeping busy doing chores around the home, or moving to a community specifically designed for the active elderly.

A supporting environment differs from the state of maintenance to whatever extent the environmental demands are reduced. When an elderly resident's competence declines, a need for increased support is indicated. Lawton has lamented that, "there has been gross neglect of the potentials for enhancing the supportive functions of ordinary dwelling units" (1989, p. 43). A supportive environment therefore can be characterized as one that simultaneously lacks variation while making available the resources necessary to maintain life (Lawton, 1989). Supportive services might include increased nursing care, meals served in a common dining room, grab bars in hallways and bathrooms, and/or the provision of waist-high electrical outlets (Lawton, 1989).

The presence of "stimulation," "maintenance" and "support" in the housing environment becomes especially important in understanding the issue of "aging-in-place" for older persons whose competence declines as they age. The supportive environment will be capable of modifying its level of services in order to meet the changing needs of the individual. The housing program without social services cannot be responsive to the changing needs of tenants.

Federal policy should take into account these functions of the residential environment if it is to be responsive and flexible in meeting the special needs of the elderly and achieve the national goals for housing for the elderly clearly stated in Title I of the Older Americans Act:

> . . . obtaining and maintaining suitable housing, independently selected, designed and located with reference to special needs and available at costs which older citizens can afford.

> Full restorative services for those who require institutional care, and a comprehensive array of community-based long term care services adequate to appropriately sustain older people in their communities and their homes.

> Efficient community services, including access to transportation, which provides a choice in supported living arrangements and social assistance in a coordinated manner and which are readily available when needed, with emphasis on maintaining a continuum of care for the vulnerable elderly (United States Congress, March 2, 1989).

Housing policies for the elderly should address the importance of enabling individuals to remain at home by making available home-delivered social and health services, home repair or modification, tax benefits or assistance with refinancing or the provision of alternate living arrangements in public or private housing designed to meet the special needs of this population.

Each of the above-mentioned three functions identified by Lawton and reinforced in the goals of the Older Americans Act responds to a specific purpose that is interrelated with the other two. Accordingly, a residence should be stimulating and provide active enjoyment by "being different, enriching, and plastic to the touch of the older person who wishes to introduce change" at the same time it provides stability through being familiar and predictable, giving "the strength to deal with the unusual" (Lawton, 1989, pp. 48-49). And finally, as physical or mental deficits become more likely with increasing age, a residence should be designed to "solve some of our problems, and reduce the complexity of external demands . . . and thus [help to] maintain a sense of security or allay anxiety about being able to cope" (Lawton, 1989, p. 49). Appropriate residential environments can balance the elements of a person's psychological existence, and may prove to be a central factor in determining the individual's psychological health (Lawton, 1989, p. 47). These nobly articulated goals, while difficult to fulfill in large metropolitan areas, are considerably harder to attain in rural communities.

FOCUSING ON HUMAN NEEDS

Pynoos (1987) has identified several objectives as being applicable to housing for the elderly. These include promoting housing choice, providing appropriate neighborhood and service supports, maximizing independence, ensuring housing fit, providing adaptable or accommodating housing, and enhancing residential satisfaction and control. In combination, these factors direct housing policies away from a primary focus on the financing and construction of new facilities toward providing an environment that enhances the life satisfaction of residents.

Public policies regarding housing for the elderly should recognize changing family patterns, dismiss the mistaken notion (perpetuated by public policy) that frailty begins at age sixty-five, and respond to the growing numbers of single, impoverished elderly females. Special attention should be given to the problems of ethnic minorities, rural residents and the poor because these are among the most pressing problems to which housing must be responsive.

Since the turn of the century there has been a shift in the composition of the American family away from multigenerational units to the "nuclear" family composed only of parents and children. This change in familial housing composition has been accompanied by a change in relationships between older persons and their adult children (Lowy, 1980, p. 131). Our elders have become more independent and their children have shown a diminished sense of day-to-day responsibility for older parents. Continued economic and social changes, however, are encouraging a revival of multigenerational units, often with adult children coming back to their parents' home as a result of financial difficulties or divorce. The problems associated with generations living together are sometimes difficult, however, particularly when it is an involuntary arrangement or when a third generation is involved.

Age itself is not a determinant of frailty yet increasing age is accompanied by increasing incidence of frailty. We cannot expect that a single model of housing and services will be appropriately responsive to the varied needs of persons whose age may range from sixty to 100 years.

For example, the issue of aging in place has been identified as being important for the development of supportive services. In recent years thousands of healthy, vigorous persons in their sixties and seventies have elected to move to retirement communities that feature an active leisure life style. Many of these affluent or relatively well-to-do elderly individuals, now approaching their eighties and nineties, are discovering a need for supportive services as they reach old age.

The issue of the age of entry into the system is equally important in assuring the ability of the housing environment to respond to the needs of the tenants. Housing programs should be capable of offering entry at different levels of needs with different programs and services available on admission. This goal can best be accomplished in an environment that offers a campus of services with multiple levels of points of entry and continuity of services.

Figures 18-21 illustrate the increasing incidence of singleness among older women, who often survive a spouse for whom they may have provided a significant measure of personal care during a period of declining health. This can be assumed from the pattern of women marrying men older than they are as well as women's longer life expectancy. This singleness is frequently accompanied by a high level of poverty caused by the loss of income of the supporting male (Figures 22 through 24). Reduction in the size of the family and the mobility of families limits options of older women to reside with siblings.

Serving those who are female, alone and poor presents major challenges to the creation of housing policies and should be considered in neighborhood selection, services and admissions standards. These issues are complicated even further

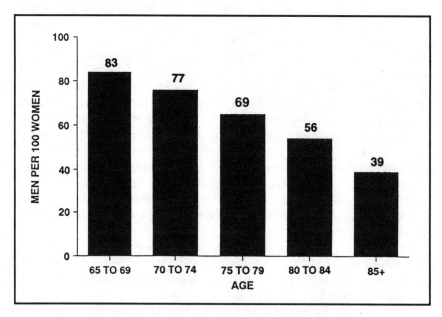

Figure 18. Numbers of men per 100 women by age group. **Source:** U.S. Bureau of the Census, "U.S. Population Estimates" (July 1995).

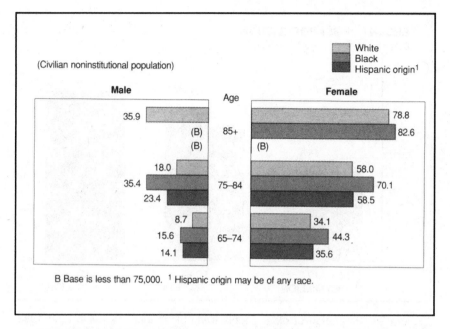

Figure 19. Percent of persons sixty-five years and over living alone by age, sex, race, and Hispanic origin (1993). **Source:** U.S. Bureau of the Census, "Marital Status and Living Arrangements: March 1993." *Current Population Reports,* P20-478, U.S. Government Printing Office, Washington, DC, 1994, table 7.

where the housing is to be built in a rural community with more limited resources than might be available in a metropolitan community.

Another important consideration for policy makers is the fact that, although "approximately 80 percent of people over sixty own their own homes, [which] is their major asset" (Streib, 1990, p. 93), federal programs generally have offered aid to elderly renters rather than elderly homeowners. Current housing policy in the United States principally supports living arrangements only "at two ends of the spectrum: middle- to large-sized housing projects for the well, active elderly; and nursing homes for those who need medical attention and personal care services" (Pynoos, 1987, p. 30).

There are many gaps in our public policies regarding housing for the elderly. First, there is insufficient housing offered in an intermediate range between independent housing and an institutional setting . . . Second, federal housing policy has been primarily that of construction of rental housing . . . It is clear that this cannot possibly be sufficient to address fully the housing needs of older persons (Sherman, 1990, p. 503).

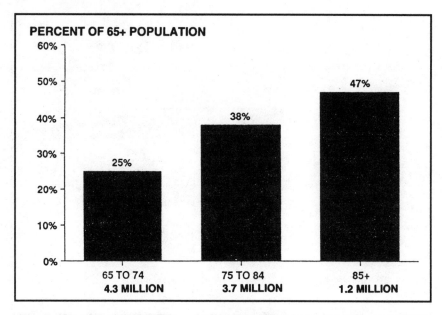

Figure 20. Proportion of older people living alone increases with age: 1993. **Source:** U.S. Bureau of the Census, "Marital Status and Living Arrangements: March 1993." *Current Population Reports,* Series P-20, No. 445 (1993).

MAJOR HOUSING POLICIES FOR THE ELDERLY

The titles in federal law with the most impact on housing the elderly are: Section 202—low interest direct loans to sponsors of rental projects for the construction or rehabilitation of residential projects (resulting in substantially lower than market monthly rents); Section 8—rental subsidies paid to the owners of existing housing, which make up the difference between the amount required of the tenant (30% of their adjusted income) and the fair market rent for an adequate housing unit; and housing vouchers—instituted during the Reagan administration as an alternative to the Section 8 subsidies, as assistance payments made directly to the renter to provide the same subsidy rate as Section 8, and give individuals the option of finding rental housing below the fair market rate in the area and retaining the difference.

In order to address the housing needs of the elderly effectively, and enable them to live alone successfully, a set of public policies is needed to "incorporate the necessary linkages among housing, social service, income maintenance, health, welfare, tax, and zoning policies to foster aging in place" (Fahey and Tilson, 1990, p. xvii). Although many housing policies have been promulgated since 1956 to deal with the housing needs of the elderly, none has come close to providing a sufficient number of services to satisfy existing need. Despite the "impressive

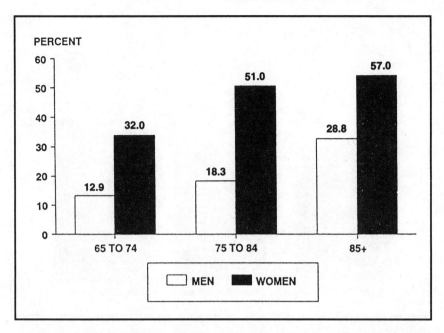

Figure 21. Older people living alone by age and sex: 1993. **Source:** U.S. Bureau of the Census, "Marital Status and Living Arrangements: March 1989," *Current Population Reports,* Series P-20, No. 445 (1993).

amount of construction . . . [and the fact that] HUD has rehoused approximately 1.5 million older people" (Gelfand, 1988, p. 165), federal programs have had limited impact and the number of persons affected has been relatively small (Rich and Baum, 1984).

Housing policies have had a checkered past, with many notable successes as well as failures. Many persons of all ages have been provided with safe and sanitary shelter that would have been unaffordable without public support. Yet there never have been sufficient numbers of housing units to meet the needs of the large number of people in this country unable to afford the market rate for safe and sanitary housing. A focus on housing policies that subsidize rental costs raises the important question about our public policies regarding income maintenance. Generally our policies have provided a subsidy for the use of a public service (such as housing, food, transportation, etc.), which has the effect of increasing the finances available rather than increasing the level of the minimum income to enable the poor to afford the market rate rent for housing and not have to depend on the availability of subsidized housing units or other categorical assistance.

Supplementary Security Income (SSI), a primary public policy designed to assure that some specific groups in our society are provided a minimum income

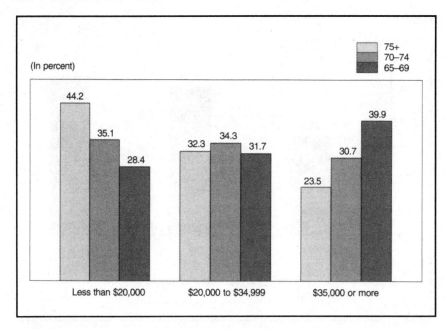

Figure 22. Income of married-couple households by age of householder: 1992.
Source: U.S. Bureau of the Census, *Money Income of Households, Families and Persons in the United States: 1992*, Current Population Reports, P60-184, U.S. Government Printing Office, Washington, DC, 1993, table 8.

has been discussed in Chapter 6. It represents one alternative to the subsidies that currently provide access to essential services, although the SSI income is too low for many persons to meet their basic needs adequately and not enough of our population is covered by it.

In order to provide housing for large numbers of people in need, especially in large metropolitan areas, public housing policies have supported the development of large apartment projects that housed thousands of persons in one development. The concept of a homogeneous environment of poor persons was an attractive notion because it enabled the masses of the poor to be segregated from the remainder of the society and not intrude in the environment of the middle and upper classes. Sites selected for the public housing were obviously not in the most desirable locations in the community, thereby creating problems for the tenants. But the most serious of the problems encountered in this mass housing of the poor is that society expected that having the housing would solve the social problems of the tenants.

What actually was experienced was the massing of large numbers of persons with significant social problems, resulting in the heightened presence of difficult and frequently unmanageable situations. Problems of destructive behavior, crimes

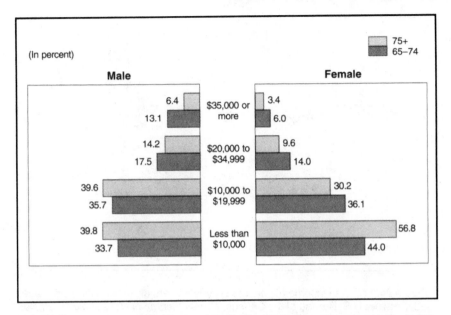

Figure 23. Income of elderly householders living alone by age and sex: 1992. **Source:** U.S. Bureau of the Census, *Money Income of Households, Families and Persons in the United States: 1992*, Current Population Reports, P60-184, U.S. Government Printing Office, Washington, DC, 1993, table 8.

against neighbors, drug use, and nonpayment of rent collectively caused a deterioration of the quality of the neighborhood and the housing. Those who were able to relocate did so. Apartments were burned and destroyed by tenants or visitors, resulting in boarded up sections that were closed but unofficially housed homeless people. Public services were curtailed as employees were reluctant to enter the projects and encounter a threatening environment. Instead of becoming a supportive environment, in the sense described by Lawton, public housing in these situations became a battleground among tenants and between tenants and the society.

In some communities the only option was to vacate a project and destroy the entire building. In other situations self-help groups evolved from within the tenant population who, through their own determination and hard work, undertook to rid the environment of crime and maintain a decent living environment.

Among the many illustrations of the failures in public housing was a major disaster that occurred in St. Louis. From the mid-1950s till the mid-1970s a project known as Pruitt-Igoe that combined two public housing programs was operated as a conventional public housing program (i.e., housing developed, owned and operated by a public housing authority). Meehan (1979) says that the project was doomed to disaster by "a set of public policies programmed for failure, impossible

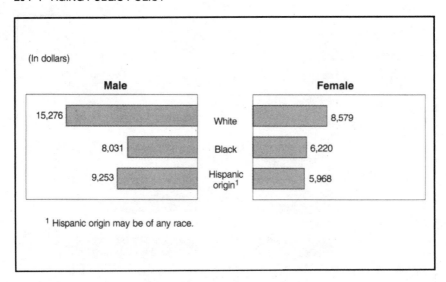

Figure 24. Median income of persons sixty-five years and over by sex and race: 1992. **Source:** U.S. Bureau of the Census, *Money Income of Households, Families and Persons in the United States: 1992*, Current Population Reports, P60-184, U.S. Government Printing Office, Washington, DC, 1993, table 26.

to implement successfully in the long run, and a set of institutions unable to correct or improve them."

One initial problem was the inability of the public housing agency to control development costs and construction quality. The St. Louis Housing Authority, which had paid for its projects at costs equal to or greater than the cost of luxury housing in the suburbs but received little value from the housing industry. In addition, the large public housing programs were unable to deal with the 1960s disintegration of existing codes of behavior. As such institutions as law, police, courts, schools, churches and families that traditionally maintain stability and order were challenged blindly and persistently, public housing and all public property were subjected to abuse. Declining income resulted in a decline in the number of public employees and an increase in the number of families wholly or partially dependent on public assistance. Declining revenues forced deferred maintenance which led to increased deterioration and vandalism.

> Public housing became the prime repository for the very poor: the black, the elderly, the female head of household and her brood of children, the unemployed and the unemployable . . . The end result was too often a ghastly landscape of mutilated buildings, broken glass, empty apartments, abandoned automobiles, litter, and garbage; a wasteland hostage to the criminal, vagrant, truant, and street gang; a hazard to the passerby; and a nightmare to the resident (Meehan, 1979).

Many other large-scale public housing projects experienced similar declines in the 1960s and 1970s. Pruitt-Igoe, which when developed received laudatory notices in architectural magazines for its thirty-three eleven-story buildings with 2,870 living units, ended up as the first experimental site to use dynamite to raze large buildings. The concentration of living units had a population density of as many as fifty-five units per acre, permitting little recreational space for all of the peak-occupancy 12,000 tenants, perhaps half of whom were minors, in a community having one day care center that served thirty-five children. With the demolition of the buildings in 1972 the era of high rise concentrated public housing had come to a sad end.

The adverse experience of mass public housing resulted in a major modification of the HUD policy regarding segregated housing for the poor and evolved into a scattered housing plan that would locate small units of public housing throughout the community thereby integrating the population through school attendance, community social and religious functions. While this new approach obviously minimized the congregating of masses of people who together magnified the effects of social ills, the policy encountered other objections, particularly the reluctance of middle-class communities to accept public housing in their neighborhoods, known as the "not in my back yard" (NIMBY) syndrome. Where there was consensus that it would not be wise to repeat the disasters of mass public housing, it became extremely difficult to develop even small-scale public housing in middle-class neighborhoods.

A basic question remains. What is society's responsibility to provide housing for those without the income to purchase market-rate housing and can this responsibility be accomplished best through an appropriate adjustment in minimal income or through housing assistance programs?

While much of this discussion has been related to the broad issues of public housing for family units, and while low-income public housing was not intended initially to provide special assistance for the elderly, the number of public housing units occupied by the elderly in 1988 was 45 percent (U.S. Senate, 1990). In 1992, HUD continued to search for ways to meet the housing needs of low-income elderly persons and responded with a variety of programs that included vouchers for rental assistance, public housing, Section 202 projects, and conversion of existing housing into special housing for the elderly. Each of these programs will be discussed.

But before proceeding to that discussion, it is important to identify another HUD policy that has significance for older persons. HUD policies for the elderly have not been restricted to the elderly but have been designated for "the elderly and handicapped." The handicapped have not been defined by age but rather by their need for safe and affordable housing. In combining the aged and disabled, who have different interests and needs, services for the elderly have been compromised. This has been especially evident where being housed along with tenants having severe mental illnesses has resulted in flagrant abuse of the rights of elderly residents and intrusion in their privacy and safety. The National Affordable Housing Act of 1990 assures that housing developed under the Section 202 program will fully separate programs for persons with disabilities from the elderly. This obviously important change in policy favoring the older person may not have any impact on the policies of public housing, however.

In addition, the severe measures undertaken to contain the costs for construction in the Section 202 program resulted in design features that omitted common recreational spaces and facilities to respond to the aging in place of the resident population. This was shortsighted because it has forced many tenants to relocate to programs designed to meet their changing needs. The National Affordable Housing Act of 1990 provides for the development of congregate housing services programs that will enable tenants to remain in their housing for longer periods of time, but these programmatic changes, although highly significant, will not be able to change space allocations in existing buildings but apply only to the design and construction of new facilities.

FEDERAL HOUSING PROGRAMS

The primary focus of federal housing programs has been to provide housing for moderate- and low-income renters (Gelfand, 1988). To achieve this goal federal housing policies have been developed under four general headings: public housing, mortgage and construction assistance, rent supplements, and program development (Lammers, 1983). While the major federal housing agency, the Department of Housing and Urban Development, was established by Congress in 1965 (P.L. 89-174), federal housing policies go back to the National Housing Act of 1934 (P.L. 73-479) when the first home mortgage program was initiated (Gelfand, 1988). This was followed by the U.S. Housing Act of 1937 (P.L. 75-412), conceived during the Great Depression to aid the housing industry and to provide decent housing for unemployed workers. Under this policy, which introduced subsidized housing for low-income American families, federal assistance was provided to communities that established authorities to operate public housing.

Critics say that the Housing Act of 1937 and the act that followed in 1949 were not primarily focused on the provision of housing for the poor but rather were primarily concerned with unemployment and slum clearance. The emphasis was on the development and construction of buildings rather than on the provision of housing services (Meehan, 1979).

Approximately 541,000 of the nation's more than 1.2 million public housing units were occupied by older persons (U.S. Senate, 1989). This program was not initially intended to serve the elderly, but it has become a significant resource for older persons, although long waits for access to subsidized housing attest to its limited ability to respond to a pressing need.

"Heightened concern with elderly related housing issues had its origins in 1950 when the first National Conference on Aging recommended greater federal emphasis on the housing needs of older persons" (U.S. Senate, 1989). Prior to the Housing Act of 1956 older single persons were not eligible for public housing and the death of an elderly individual meant that a surviving spouse had to find other living arrangements (Rich and Baum, 1984).

The Nursing Home Mortgage Insurance was introduced as an amendment to the National Housing Act of 1959 and promoted the construction of nursing homes by providing mortgage insurance for both proprietary and nonprofit corporations (Rich and Baum, 1984). Mortgage and construction assistance was initiated in 1959 in the direct loan program for the elderly as Title II: Section 202 of P.L. 86-372. This program provided low-cost loans to developers of private housing and was the forerunner of later mortgage subsidy programs.

Congregate Housing Services

In 1990, HUD initiated a grants program for eligible housing projects for the elderly and handicapped. HUD makes direct five-year renewable grants to eligible applicants for a meals program, seven days a week, and other supportive services needed by eligible residents to prevent premature and unnessary institutionalization. An independent professional assessment committee, appointed by the grantee, screens residents who apply for the program, determines individual eligibility for services, and recommends a service package to management. Applicants may be states, Indian tribes, units of general local government, or nonprofit corporations (which includes public housing agencies [PHAs]). Applicants may apply to fund one or more eligible housing projects for elderly or non-elderly handicapped persons funded under Section 202, conventional public housing and Indian housing or Farmers Home Administration Sections 514, 515, and 516 (http://www.hud.gov).

Section 8

In 1974, the Housing and Community Development Act was passed, introducing the Section 8 rent subsidy program. This program, unlike earlier ones, did not provide funding to the developer but instead subsidized rent payments to encourage the private development of housing. Under the Section 8 program the rent paid is not related to the rental charge but is determined as 30 percent of a tenant's adjusted monthly income. The difference between what the tenant pays and the fair market rent for an apartment is provided as a government subsidy, thereby assuring that the housing developer will receive the full market rate for the apartment. Fair Market Rate (FMR) is determined by HUD on the basis of comparable rents in a market area and is reviewed annually.

The Section 8 *Rental Certificate Program* helps very low income families lease privately owned, decent, safe, and sanitary rental housing. HUD enters into contracts with local public housing agencies (PHAs) and Indian housing agencies (IHAs) that administer the program. The PHA issues rental certificates to eligible families who are then free to locate suitable rental units that meet their needs. The PHA makes assistance payments to the private owners who lease their rental units to assisted families. The assistance payment makes up the difference between what a very low income family can afford and the approved rent for the dwelling unit. Assisted families must pay the highest of 30 percent of adjusted income, 10 percent of gross income, or the portion of welfare assistance designated for housing toward rent. Rental units leased under this program must meet HUD housing quality standards. Rents must be reasonable in relation to rents charged for comparable unassisted rental units in the market area and at or below the fair market rent for the area as determined by HUD (http://www.hud.gov).

The Rental Voucher Program assists very low income families in finding decent, safe, and sanitary rental housing. HUD enters into contracts with local PHAs and IHAs that administer the program. The PHA issues rental vouchers to eligible families and the families are free to locate suitable rental units that meet their needs. The PHA makes assistance payments to the private owners who lease their rental units to assisted families. There are no rent limits in the rental voucher program, but the assistance payment on behalf of the family is fixed so as to make up the difference between what a very low income family can afford and the PHA established payment standard for the area. The amount the family can afford is the higher of 30 percent of adjusted income or 10 percent of gross income. A rental voucher holder may choose housing that rents for more or less than the payment standard and therefore may pay more or less than 30 percent of adjusted income for rent. Rental units leased under this program must meet HUD housing quality standards. Very low income families whose incomes do not exceed 50 percent of the median income for the area are eligible (http://www.hud.gov).

The Moderate Rehabilitation Single Room Occupancy Program (SRO), assists very low income single homeless individuals in obtaining decent, safe, and sanitary housing in privately owned, rehabilitated buildings. Under the SRO program, HUD enters into annual contributions contracts with PHAs in connection with the moderate rehabilitation of residential properties in which some or all of dwelling units may not contain either food preparation or sanitary facilities. These PHAs make Section 8 rental assistance payments to participating landlords on behalf of homeless individuals who rent the rehabilitated dwellings. The rental assistance payments cover the difference between 30 percent of the tenant's income and the unit's rent, which must be within the fair market limit established by HUD. Rental assistance for SRO units is provided by HUD for a period of ten years. Owners are compensated for the cost of rehabilitaion (as well as other costs of owning and maintaining the property) through housing assistance payments. The amount to be compensated cannot exceed $15,500 per SRO unit. At the same time, each unit must need a minimum of $3,000 of eligible rehabilitation to qualify for the program (http://www.hud.gov).

Multifamily Management Reform Act

Over the next few years, Section 8 rental assistance contracts with thousands of landlords will expire. These contracts assist over 850,000 persons living in half a million apartments nationwide. The contracts for these projects subsidize rents that far exceed market rents for comparable housing. Congress must ensure that any approach to the issue of renewal of subsidy contracts takes into account the need to protect low income tenants and reflects the Administration's commitment to balancing the budget. However, compounding the problem is the fact that HUD not only subsidizes the rents but also insures the mortgage through the Federal Housing Administration (FHA). If the rents are lowered to market levels to eliminate the wasteful subsidies, many of the owners would be unable to pay their federally insured mortgages and would be forced into default. These defaults would create a multi-billion dollar liability for the federal government that could jeopardize the physical condition and financial stability of these apartment buildings. The result of lowering rents without addressing the mortgage problem would be the potential loss of a significant portion of the stock of affordable housing.

HUD has proposed a comprehensive solution (called a multifamily restructuring approach) to protect low income families, elderly, and disabled residents who receive Section 8 rental assistance and at the same time reduce the long-term costs to the federal government. The multifamily restructuring approach will allow the administration and Congress to accomplish four critical goals:

- preserve and extend a commitment to affordable housing for 850,000 people
- ensure that these projects are put on a financially sound footing well into the twenty-first century
- protect low income tenants
- reduce HUD's long-term costs for Section 8 contracts.

Under HUD's proposal, responsible landlords would have their FHA insured mortgages reduced to a level that can be supported by market rents. Writing down the mortgage and reducing the rental assistance payments would reduce the contingent liability of the federal government and also the excessive subsidy costs to U.S. taxpayers. In addition to mortgage write-down, or debt restructuring, rehabilitation of properties can be undertaken where necessary. Rehabilitation may be financed by using accumulated project reserves, new equity provided by the owner, and further debt write-downs. In addition, rehabilitation funds from the insurance fund may be available to restructured projects to accomplish repairs and rehabilitation.

HUD proposes to renew expiring housing contracts with tenant based and project-based assistance. In about half the projects, HUD will renew the contracts with project-based subsidies. This would occur in housing markets where market indicators demonstrate that it would be difficult to use tenant based subsidies (for example, in areas with less than a 6% vacancy rate) and for projects which are predominantly (90% and higher occupancy) for elderly and/or disabled households. In the case of tenant based assistance, the assistance will be calculated to provide the tenant with an option to remain in the project at a reasonable market rent or to search for an apartment in the private market.

Finally, the legislation calls for the use of third parties (designees) to assit HUD in administering the multifamily restructuring initiative. This reflects the existing constraints upon HUD resources and is designed to make the best use of public and private managerial and housing expertise. State and local government agencies will have a priority choice to be designees (http://www.hud.gov).

Section 202

The Housing and Community Development Act of 1974 also reinstated Section 202 and linked it with Section 8 rent subsidies. Approval of Section 202 loans is based on the feasibility of getting Section 8 financing so that if the number of Section 8 units for a section of a state has been committed, Section 202 construction financing cannot be granted (Gelfand, 1988). Combining Sections 202 and 8 brought together the HUD insurance program and reduced interest rates for construction and development financing with the rent subsidy program. That did just about everything necessary to assure a high occupancy at the fair market rate and therefore the promise of a successful project. The new combined program resulted in major developments of private, subsidized housing for the elderly and has been considered the most successful of all assisted housing programs.

The Direct Loans for Housing for the Elderly or Handicapped Program provides housing and related facilities for the elderly or handicapped through long term direct loans to eligible private nonprofit sponsors to finance rental or cooperative housing facilities for occupancy by elderly or handicapped persons. The interest rate is determined annually. Section 8 funds are made available for 100 percent of Section 202 units. Beginning in 1989, rental assistance rather than Section 8 funds were provided for 100 percent of the units for handicapped persons. Private nonprofit sponsors may qualify for loans. Households of one or more persons, the head of which is at least sixty-two years old, or is a qualified non-elderly handicapped person between the ages of eighteen and sixty-two, are eligible to live in the structures (http://www.hud.gov).

The Supportive Housing for the Elderly Program provides assistance to expand the supply of housing with supportive services for the elderly. Capital advances, rather than direct loans, are made to eligible private, nonprofit sponsors to finance the development of rental housing with supportive services for the elderly. The advance is interest free and does not have to be repaid so long as the housing remains available for very low income elderly persons for at least forty years. Project rental assistance covers the difference between the HUD approved operating cost per unit and the amount the resident pays. Private, non profit organizations and consumer cooperatives may qualify for assistance. Occupancy is open to very low income households which include at least one person sixty-two years of age or older (http://www.hud.gov).

However, all of the assisted housing programs face an increasing problem of the aging in place of the population and the need to respond to changing tenant needs with services that would support continuing residence in a unit. The Congregate Housing Services Program was introduced in 1978 to enable housing for the elderly to provide meals and other supportive services. This program, along with many others, has been under review to determine what new policies should be put in place to deal with the increasing needs of the elderly in subsidized housing. Unfortunately, the budget reductions of the 1980s severely curtailed the construction of new units and reduced the number of amenities new units could offer.

Vouchers

In the Housing Act of 1983, the Section 8 new construction program was repealed except for that portion attached to the Section 202 program (U.S. Senate, 1990). The modified Section 8 introduced a demonstration program to provide vouchers subsidizing the difference between 30 percent of a family's income and the fair market rent of a suitable living unit. This program differs from the former Section 8 program in that the tenant may negotiate a rent different from the fair market rent while retaining a subsidy based on 30 percent of his or her income.

Philosophy of Housing Legislation

The Housing and Urban-Rural Recovery Act of 1983 was designed to increase the supply of low-income rental housing through subsidies that would stimulate investment in the rehabilitation of existing housing. Housing vouchers were to be made available to accompany this program.

The Housing and Community Development Act of 1987 reauthorized most housing and community development programs. It was especially important for older persons that the law made the Congregate Housing Services Program permanent and also established the home equity conversion demonstration, a program that enables a home owner to use equity in a home to meet current obligations, especially for health care.

HUD scandals in the late 1980s resulted in a moratorium on the development of many programs and a slowdown in the processing of continuing programs. While HUD and the Congress were investigating the misuse of public funds, the need for low cost housing continued to grow and "federal housing efforts have fallen far short of meeting elderly housing needs" (U.S. Senate, 1990). In addition, prepayment of mortgages, expiration of Federal Section 8 subsidies and defaults on mortgages threaten to reduce even further the availability of affordable housing to low income older persons.

The National Affordable Housing Act (NAHA, 1990; PL 101-625) recognized the need for special living arrangements and supportive services for the older persons who without them would be forced to leave their homes. Included in this legislation was the HOME Investment Partnership Act providing block grants to states and local communities that were primarily to be used to rehabilitate existing housing projects. Also included were Homeownership and Opportunity for People Everywhere (HOPE) programs "to promote the sale of public and other federally assisted housing to its tenants" (U.S. Senate, 1990). The HOPE for Elderly Independence program was designed to test the effectiveness of combining supportive services with housing programs. This law for the first time addressed a lingering problem for the elderly that resulted from combining housing for the elderly with housing for the disabled. Subsequent new Section 202 development programs for persons with disabilities were to be fully separated from those for the elderly.

HUD's concept of aging has not until recently been willing to accommodate any significant change in health status. Residents "in the HUD-subsidized projects . . . were required to be independent, and if they were no longer able to perform activities of daily living (ADLs) without assistance they were expected to transfer out of the facility, usually to a nursing home" (Fahey and Tilson, 1990, p. xxii).

> Public policy has tended to provide incentives for older persons to move out of their residences to more supportive environments when they become frail. However, serious problems have often been associated with relocation, and it has been found that most older persons prefer to stay in their own homes for as long as possible (Pynoos, 1987, p. 32).

Part of the problem has been the notion that offering too many services through federal housing policy would only serve to "encourage passivity and lead to health declines. [Therefore,] more traditional housing aimed at these elderly should be associated with challenge and continued independent behavior" (Pynoos, 1987, p. 31). The validity of this notion is based on the theory that the "maintenance of independent function is facilitated by an environment that demands active behavior from its inhabitants, and conversely, the presence of too easily accessible services will erode independence among those who are still relatively competent" (Lawton, 1976, p. 240 [Gelfand]). However, Lawton's most recent analysis revises this earlier view by pointing out that rather than being harmful, "the residence that is habitually more supportive, or that can be turned toward supportive functions when needed, represents protection against negative effect" (1989, p. 48).

As a case in point, Section 202, perhaps the primary program to provide housing for low- and moderate-income elderly, has been so hampered by HUD's space and design restrictions that the provision of any ancillary services to tenants has been practically impossible. Supportive service amenities needed by elderly residents, such as personal care services, have been circumscribed by space constraints (Fahey and Tilson, 1990, p. xxiii).

The Housing Act of 1990 represents a major departure for HUD away from strict cost containment to the opening of new opportunities to serve the frail elderly and to respond to the issues of aging in place. A new dimension has been added to HUD's earlier focus on the development of housing units. HUD also has retreated from the development of mass projects of housing for the poor, having recognized that the concentration of large numbers of persons with critical social problems cannot be resolved by housing alone. New emphasis on fewer units dispersed throughout the community, support for a variety of alternative housing arrangements and commitment to a network of supportive services give promise that housing policies that are more responsive to older persons will emerge.

Housing for Rural Communities

The development of specialized housing with services for the elderly in rural areas, especially those who are poor, requires confrontation with an array of problems that are common both to metropolitan and nonmetropolitan areas. Growing numbers of people in need of affordable housing, limited public funds for new construction, constrained budgets for services and an inadequate pool of experienced administrators all are formidable obstacles to attempting to meet the housing needs of an expanding elderly population.

The problems were exacerbated in the 1980s when there was decline, after inflation, in federal outlays for low-income families. Hardest hit were rural housing programs for the elderly and handicapped, for which funding declined more than 64 percent (National Council on the Aging, March/April 1990).

Among the major uncontrollable events confronting rural communities are farm failures, out-migration of young people, hospital closures, shortage of health services and personnel, an eroding housing stock, a shrinking tax base, escalating numbers of employees and retirees who lack health insurance, few and over-burdened transportation systems and declining land values (National Council on the Aging, March/April 1990). All of these ultimately affect lifestyle opportunities for older people.

Rural communities are perceived as having a special culture that is based on strong community ties, long history and ethnic and cultural attachments. Yet these positive attributes may not be present where there are predominant migratory patterns or severe economic decline.

Residents of some rural communities may represent great wealth while those in others, especially those who are old and frail, live in poverty. Invariably this means an emphasis on older women, because singleness and longevity of women are of special concern. Women live longer than men, spend longer periods in adulthood alone, are poorer than men and generally are vulnerable to the problems of aging in rural settings (Fahey, 1988, pp. 3-4).

What are some of the problems encountered in the development of housing for the rural elderly?

- Small scale of projects, which increases cost per unit.
- Reluctance of residents to leave long-established family homes.
- Distances between homes and community services and the absence of adequate transportation systems.
- Concentrations of poverty in rural areas, limiting options for new housing or converted facilities.
- Limited personnel resources to develop programs, prepare funding applications and administer programs.

Yet rural communities, because of their strong cultural attachments and "rootedness," demonstrate strengths and resources that provide resiliency and capability of overcoming many problems if resources are provided.

HUD programs that provide some services to urban areas are not positioned to provide comparable resources to rural communities. Instead, the Farmers Home Administration of the U.S. Department of Agriculture was authorized in Section 502 of the Housing Act of 1949 to lend money to poor farm families unable to obtain loans from any other source to construct homes on farms. In 1961 the Farmers Home Administration was authorized to assist in the development of housing for the elderly in communities of not more than 2,500 persons, a limit later to be increased to 20,000. The Housing and Community Development Act of 1974 authorized the payment of rent supplements for low-income families in rural rental housing (Rich and Baum, 1984). The Administration on Aging joined with the Farmers Home Administration in 1979 under the authority of the 515 Rural Housing Program to construct and provide services in housing for the elderly, initiating a new cooperative program of bringing together bricks and mortar and services.

The following is a summary of Rural Housing Services programs:

- Community Facilities Loans are made to construct, enlarge, extend, or otherwise improve community facilites providing essential services in rural areas and towns with a population of 50,000 or less. The funds are available to public entities such as municipalities, counties, special purpose districts, Indian tribes, and corporations not operated for profit. Rural Housing Services also guarantees community facility loans made by banks or other eligible lenders.

- Home Ownership Loans are made to help low income and moderate income rural residents purchase, construct, repair, or relocate a dwelling and related facilities.
- Rural Rental Housing Loans are made to allow individuals or organizations to build or rehabilitate rental units for low income and moderate income residents in rural areas.
- Rental Assistance is used to reduce the amount of out-of-pocket cash that very low income families must pay for rent, including utilities.
- Home Improvement and Repair Loans and Grants are made to enable very low income rural homeowners to remove health and safety hazards in their homes and to make homes accessible for persons with disabilities. Grants are available for people sixty-two years of age and older who cannot afford to repay a loan.
- Congregate Housing and Group Homes provide living units for persons with low and moderate incomes and for those age sixty-two or older.
- Housing Preservation Grants are made to provide qualified public nonprofit organizations and public agencies with grant funds for effective programs to assist very low and low income homeowners repair and rehabilitate their homes in rural areas and to assist rental property owners and co-ops to repair and rehabilitate their units if they agree to make such units available to low and very low income persons (http://www.hud.gov).

Nursing Homes, Intermediate Care Facilities and Board & Care Homes (Section 232)

Federal mortgage insurance to finance or rehabilitate nursing, intermediate care, or board and care facilities is available. HUD insures mortgages made by private lending institutions to finance construction or renovation of facilities to accommodate twenty or more patients requiring skilled nursing care and related medical services, or those in need of minimum but continuous care provided by licensed or trained personnel. Board and care facilities may contain no fewer than five one-bedroom or efficiency units. Nursing home, intermediate care, and board and care services may be combined in the same facility covered by an insured mortgage or may be in separate facilities. Major equipment needed to operate the facility may be included in the mortgage. Facilities for day care may be included. Legislation establishing this program was enacted in 1969. Investors, builders, developers, and private nonprofit corporations or associations, and public agencies (nursing homes only), or public entities that are licensed or regulated by the state to accommodate convalescents and persons requiring skilled nursing care or intermediate care, may qualify for mortgage insurance. Patients requiring skilled nursing, intermediate care, and/or board and care are eligible to live in these facilities (http://www.hud.gov).

Congregate Housing

The development of congregate housing for the elderly is the newest and most rapidly growing segment of services for older persons in our society. It has evolved because of the increase in the numbers of older persons, the aging of the older population, and the absence of services in a continuum between independent housing and nursing home care.

There are many reasons for people to select congregate housing as their preferred lifestyle. For example, very sophisticated health care has made it possible for some older persons to avoid the hazards of some illnesses, retaining a degree of wellness even with some frailties. Others, because of limited vision and mobility, have restricted their use of an automobile or given up driving. Some older individuals are widowed and others have found fewer social opportunities as they have aged. Still others come to congregate housing in search of a more leisurely lifestyle, freeing them from home ownership, house maintenance and meal preparation. Some come for fun and socialization, some for security, some because of dependency. Whatever the reason, determining to move to congregate housing is a very significant decision on the part of older persons and their relatives.

It should be apparent that all the varied needs suggested cannot be met to the same extent at any one facility, so it is essential to define the target market for any proposed project. For this reason, we provide a basic definition of congregate housing.

Congregate housing is a facility providing for its residents a sheltered environment that includes such services as meals, social activities, housekeeping, protective oversight, transportation, assistance with personal care activities, and intervention in crisis situations.

It is important to note that congregate housing provides living quarters for persons who can live independently but would benefit from the array of services offered, the increased socialization provided by the presence of a large group of people of similar age and interests, as well as the security provided. The congregate housing program is not a licensed health care facility and therefore its management cannot permit continued residence by persons who require ongoing health care services (unless provided in a licensed unit on a campus).

There are different ways in which the congregate housing market is stratified. One major method is by charges for services, but it is important to define the various types of programs because they serve different markets.

Subsidized housing is provided under private or public sponsorship to persons who meet certain qualifications, usually limited income. Included are public housing and units subsidized by the U.S. Department of Housing and Urban Development through such programs as the one known as Section 202/8.

Market-rate housing refers to programs that are without subsidy and charge a monthly rent that is competitive with the private market of the community, based on the accommodations and services provided.

Life care is congregate housing in which a contractual agreement is made for the provision of a continuum of health care services in exchange for an entrance fee and monthly payments. These programs also are known as continuing care retirement communities.

There are no licensing requirements for congregate housing programs unless formal health care services are provided. Many states have developed insurance laws to protect consumers' investments in life care or continuing care programs.

Licensing by the State Department of Health Services is required when nursing care services are provided. These programs must conform to statutes regarding building design, staffing and programs. (Nursing home policies are discussed in Chapter 7, Health Care Policies.)

Another vaguely defined area of services is referred to as *assisted living*. This is frequently provided within a congregate housing environment and offers assistance with aspects of personal care to residents whose capacity for self-care has become limited (see Chapter 8).

Title VIII of the Housing Act of 1990 has a Subtitle A dealing with supportive housing for the elderly and holds promise of continuing support for incorporating services in a housing program. Specifically, the purpose of this section "is to enable elderly persons to live with dignity and independence by expanding the supply of supportive housing that: 1) is designed to accommodate the special needs of elderly persons; and 2) provides a range of services that are tailored to the needs of elderly persons occupying such housing" (U.S. Congress, Housing Act of 1990, p. 229).

Services to be included are meals, housekeeping, personal assistance, transportation, health related services, and such other services deemed by the Secretary to be essential to maintain independence. In addition, program managers are to have the ability to assess the service needs of the residents, and coordinate the services that are provided. These expectations of housing for the elderly heretofore had not been included in any previous law except the Older Americans Act.

It also is important to note that for purposes of these benefits the law defines the elderly "as a household composed of one or more persons at least one of whom is sixty-two years of age or more at the time of occupancy . . . frail elderly means an elderly person who is unable to perform at least three activities of daily living . . ." (U.S. Congress Housing Act of 1990, p. 234). Acknowledging the increasing burden of advancing age, the law provides for support of assisted living and an array of services to minimize the need to transfer to a setting that provides a more intensive level of services. Many services that respond to increased frailty obviously can be provided in an assisted living setting. Support for such services previously have not been made available in the amount necessary to encourage development of programs specific to this type of setting. Nor were such services expected of the housing programs or their managers. The 1990 Housing Act also acknowledges the importance of retrofitting living spaces and providing congregate spaces to accommodate to the changing needs of the elderly population.

Contracts for congregate service programs are to be made through the Department of Housing and Urban Development and the Farmers Home Administration of the Department of Agriculture so that both urban and rural areas may benefit. Beyond the provision of meals, the range of services that can be included in a service package are transportation, personal care, housekeeping, chore assistance, nonmedical counseling, group and socialization activities, assistance with medications (in accordance with any applicable state law), case management, personal emergency response, and other services to prevent premature and unnecessary institutionalization. In essence this law commits assisted housing to providing its residents a comprehensive chronic care system.

This far-reaching policy may duplicate some community developments sponsored by the Older Americans Act but goes beyond the ability of the Older Americans Act to fund such an array of services.

There are some who believe a program of this magnitude, with accompanying funds, would more appropriately have been assigned to the Administration on Aging to add to its existing network. Would this have provided greater assurance of continuity as HUD funding declines? Does assigning this new activity to HUD assure that residents living in assisted housing will receive a service priority they would not have enjoyed in a community-wide program? This new arrangement deserves careful observation and evaluation to determine if it is the most effective way of developing a community-wide chronic care system.

Home Equity Conversion

A major financial asset of many older persons is the value of the equity in a home, a resource that may not always be readily available to meet the costs of daily living, especially the cost of health care. Often, although the home may be without any mortgage, it may also be old and require substantial maintenance. The older resident may have sufficient income to meet the anticipated expenses of living but not have sufficient resources to meet the unplanned costs of major illness or major home improvements. "Homes are older Americans' most commonly held and most valuable assets" (U.S. Senate, 1990). Yet the equity resource of the funds may only be available to the homeowner if the house is sold and the resident relocates. A forced sale of a home and relocation is a major traumatic event that may not be in the best interest of the homeowner.

Recently, with the emergence of the Home Equity Conversion Plan, also known as the Reverse Annuity Mortgage (RAM), equity in a home can be converted to cash without having to sell the home or to leave the dwelling. The ability to use this program depends upon the amount of home equity and the availability of a bank to process the loan. In 1989, under the authority of the Housing and Community Development Act of 1987, HUD created a demonstration program to provide mortgage insurance for home equity conversion mortgages for the elderly.

Home Equity Conversion Mortgage (HECM) Insurance (Section 255)

This is Federal mortgage insurance to allow borrowers who are sixty-two years of age and older to convert the equity in their homes into a monthly stream of income or a line of credit.

Under the HECM, the FHA insures reverse mortgages that allow older homeowners to convert their home equity into spendable dollars. Reverse mortgages provide a valuable financing alternative for older homeowners who wish to remain in their homes but have become "house rich and cash poor." Any lender authorized to make HUD insured loans may originate reverse mortgages. Borrowers may choose from among five payment options:

- *Tenure.* The borrower receives monthly payments from the lender for as long as the borrower lives and continues to occupy the home as a principal residence.
- *Term.* The borrower receives monthly payments for a fixed period selected by the borrower.
- *Line of Credit.* The borrower can make withdrawals up to a maximum amount, at times and in amounts of the borrower's choosing.
- *Modified Tenure.* The tenure option is combined with a line of credit.
- *Modified Term.* The term option is combined with a line of credit.

The borrower retains ownership of the property and may sell the home and move at any time, keeping the sales proceeds in excess of the mortgage balance. A borrower cannot be forced to sell the home to pay off the mortgage, even if the mortgage balance grows to exceed the value of the property. An FHA insured reverse mortgage need not be repaid until the borrower moves, sells, or dies. When the loan is due and payable, if the loan exceeds the value of the property, the borrower (or the heirs) will owe no more than the value of the property. FHA insurance will cover any balance due the lender. All borrowers must be at least sixty-two years of age. Any existing lien on the property must be small enough to be paid off at settlement of the reverse mortgage (http://www.hud.gov).

The Homeless Older Persons

One of the most serious housing problems in this country is homelessness. Having no place to live may be a problem itself or may be a manifestation of other personal and social problems that have alienated a person from society. The homeless older person may be without family or disconnected from supportive relationships or traditional helping systems. For some, being homeless may represent the final stage of a lifelong series of problems (Damrosch and Strasser, 1988). Many factors may have contributed to an individual's homelessness and these may include unstable family relationships, social deviance in various forms, under- and unemployment, poverty, physical or mental disability, and drug and alcohol abuse. One or more of these may have contributed to an individual's problem.

In addition, some serious societal issues related to the availability of housing may also have contributed to homelessness for some. There appears to be a hierarchy in the homeless society that results in the pushing out of older persons from shelters and the best places in the streets, making them invisible and difficult to count (Dobkin, 1989). There has been a decline in rooming house and single room occupancy facilities, which have been replaced through urban renewal and gentrification of downtown areas in many communities. An increasingly inadequate supply of low cost housing, new rules for nursing homes intended to deny admission to people who are mentally ill or developmentally disabled, and difficulties encountered by the homeless who seek to gain access to entitlements to state and federal programs also contribute to homelessness.

In 1987 the Congress passed the Stewart B. McKinney Homeless Assistance Act to provide housing and other services for the homeless. The first program initiated under the act was the redirection of the Federal Emergency Management Agency, established in 1978 as an independent agency to provide emergency food and shelter programs. Several programs were begun in the Department of Housing and Urban Development to encourage the states to develop shelters and housing programs that demonstrate approaches to reducing the problem of homelessness. Among the HUD activities are provision of assistance for the rehabilitation of single-room occupancy units and converting surplus or underutilized federal properties to housing for the homeless. Additional services offered through other federal agencies include health services, adult education, job training and access to food. The law also removed permanent address requirements and other barriers that prevented participation of the homeless in federal programs such as Supplementary Security Income (SSI), Aid to Families with Dependent Children (AFDC), Veterans benefits, food stamps, and Medicaid.

Being elderly and homeless represents multiple jeopardies with regard to access to health services, nutrition, personal sanitation and social supports. The availability of emergency shelters is critical for those who have no home and need protection from the dangers of bad weather, illness or crime in the streets. "A 1989 study conducted by Eastern Michigan University found that more than half the elderly homeless in Detroit had been beaten, robbed or raped in the preceding year" (Dobkin, 1989). There are no available records to determine the extent of such problems nationally.

Temporary residence in what have been known as welfare hotels is an important emergency measure but not a solution to the problem. Many older persons who have been long-term street survivors will continue living in the street, using shelters when available and benefiting from community services that provide food and health care when available. Brickner and Scanlan (1990) suggest that the increased risks of living in the street probably shorten the homeless person's life span by twenty years.

Society can only deal more effectively with the issues of poverty, access to health care, and the availability of housing for the poor by actively addressing the problem of homelessness. More specifically, attention has to be given to the use of Section 8 rent subsidies for single room occupancies (SROs), development of new housing opportunities. Especially important is understanding the issues of homeless persons and appreciation of the "inherent dignity of each (person) as an individual human being" (Brickner and Scanlan, 1990). The reality of homelessness continues. The size of the homeless population is continuing to grow and the population is continually changing. The McKinney Act may have become a "crutch for the government, allowing it to ignore the need for new, preventive legislation by reauthorizing already existing programs. The programs that were inaugurated through the McKinney Act were supposed to be experimental. Instead, they have become permanent programs that inefficiently assist the homeless. Emergency relief does not address the causes of homelessness but instead ameliorates the symptoms (Foscarinis, 1996). Congress has not passed new legislation that addresses the underlying causes of homelessness since McKinney. The Act's programs have become heavily bureaucratized and direct delivery of services to homeless individuals has diminished.

The Housing Enforcement Act of 1997 contains a number of initiatives to strengthen HUD and FHA enforcement authority in order to minimize the incidence of fraud and abuse in FHA and assisted housing programs. Key provisions of the bill expand the ability of the Mortgage Review Board to impose sanctions on lenders; expand equity skimming prohibitions to all National Housing Act programs and to the Section 202 elderly housing and Section 542 multifamily risk-sharing programs; broaden HUD's authority to impose civil monetary penalties; and clarify the Department's authority to terminate a mortgagee's approval to originate FHA-insured single family mortgages because of a high level of early serious defaults and claims.

SOCIAL SERVICES

In an earlier chapter the Older Americans Act was described in detail, as were many of the social services it supports. In addition to OAA programs, a variety of social services are supported by different funding resources. A social service should not be defined by its source of funding but by its contribution to the quality of life of the person served. Although appropriately delivered social services may contribute to the health of an individual or may become part of a health treatment plan, health and social services are viewed separately and dealt with through separate policies, funding resources and administration of programs. Most health care programs for the elderly emanate from Medicare and Medicaid policies and most social service programs evolve from provisions of the Older Americans Act. On the other hand, a significant number of social service programs evolve from Social Services Block Grants (SSBG), Community Service Block Grants (CSBG), legal services, Action programs, and activities of agencies that provide transportation and education. Many of these, although not specifically designed to assist the elderly, require strong local advocacy as they compete with other groups in order to achieve a share of available funding. Sustaining programs that benefit the elderly pits their advocates against others seeking a share of limited dollars. When limited funding causes divisiveness in community planning, cooperative efforts to address the unmet needs of a community are seriously hampered. This problem is exacerbated if limited local funding for programs is combined with the federal government's abrogating its responsibility toward those in need. The federal government should be strong enough to provide the resources necessary for adequate social services and should take responsibility for setting priorities for funding. Unlike the categorical grants made to states for services to the elderly, the block grants that replaced them were in broad areas and required little federal regulation and reporting (Gelfand, 1988).

Social Services Block Grants came about as a result of the Title 20 Amendments to the Social Security Act of 1935 (Social Service Amendments of 1974, PL 93-647). Between 1956 and the Social Security Act Amendments of 1962, matching funds for provision of social services had been made available to the states within the public assistance categories of the Social Security Act. The services, which were to meet the goals of self-care and self-support, were financed as administrative costs at a federal matching rate of 50 percent.

The Public Welfare Amendments of 1962 (PL 87-543) for the first time required states to provide social services to recipients of public assistance and authorized up to 75 percent federal participation in the costs incurred by the state in so doing. The new law did not define services, it merely stated their purpose as being to enhance self-support, self-care and strengthening family life and to prevent and reduce dependency. Earlier it had been the policy of the federal government to specify what social services would be eligible for reimbursement. In its new position, the federal government was concerned with the goals to be accomplished rather than with specific programs, but at the same time it retained final review of programs.

The Social Security Amendments of 1967 contained provisions that had significant impact on the delivery of social services by the states under the Social Security Act. For the first time, states were enabled to purchase social services from nonpublic agencies using moneys available under the Social Security Act. This significant change in policy marked the beginning of a period in which private nonprofit organizations would play a major role in the provision of social services. These amendments also introduced the concept of group eligibility whereby residents of low-income neighborhoods and other groups such as those in institutional settings became eligible for services.

The Social Security Amendments of 1972 (PL 92-603) removed a prior requirement that social services had to be provided statewide, thereby permitting greater flexibility in the planning and delivery of services. The State and Local Fiscal Assistance Act of 1972 removed the open-ended nature of the social service provisions and established a ceiling on the amount of federal moneys that could be used to reimburse states for social services provided under the Social Security Act.

When, on January 4, 1975, President Ford signed into law the Social Services Amendments of 1974 (PL 93-647), the planning, coordinating and provision of social services finally were brought together as Title 20. This gave states the flexibility to determine within limits which social services they needed rather than prescribing which social services could receive federal support. National goals established under Title 20 were:

1. Achieving or maintaining economic self-support to prevent, reduce or eliminate dependency.
2. Achieving or maintaining self-sufficiency, including reduction or prevention of dependency.
3. Preventing or remedying neglect, abuse or exploitation of children and adults unable to protect their own interests, or preserving, rehabilitating or reuniting families.
4. Preventing or reducing inappropriate institutional care by providing for community-based care, home-based care or other forms of less intensive care.
5. Securing referral or admission for institutional care when other forms of care are not appropriate, or providing services to individuals in institutions (PL 93-647).

While eligibility under Title 20 was primarily dependent upon family income adjusted for family size, the law did narrowly define three services which states could provide to all people in need without regard to income. These were basic information and referral, protective services and family planning services. At least 50 percent of the Title 20 money was required to be spent on services to members of the following groups: Aid to Families with Dependent Children (AFDC), Medicaid and Supplementary Security Income (SSI).

During the early 1960s social services had been viewed primarily as designed to eliminate poverty through intensive casework services that presumably would rehabilitate poor people, changing their behavior in ways that would help them to become economically independent. Beginning about 1962, however, there was a move away from services which are intangible and limited in scope to services which are concrete and more diversified. More attention began to be given to enhancing human development and general quality of life, since it had become apparent that to deal with the deficiencies of an individual without dealing with the deficiencies of the person's environment was to not deal with the real problem.

In the evolution of the Title 20 program, decision-making authority has been transferred from the federal government to the state level, with the federal government assuming a monitoring and technical assistance role while providing the states with a mechanism for planning, developing and implementing social services which address the needs they have individually determined. In 1981 the Title 20 program was converted to the Social Service Block Grant (SSBG) program as part of that year's Omnibus Budget Reconciliation Act. States were no longer required to provide minimum funding for designated programs and were now allowed to design their own mix of services and to establish their own eligibility requirements. Greater autonomy was accompanied by a reduced allocation of federal dollars and the absence of requirements to provide services to older persons, however.

The Community Services Block Grant (CSBG) program, an outgrowth of the community action poverty programs of the 1960s, was initially known as the Office of Economic Opportunity. In 1975, the Office of Economic Opportunity was renamed the Community Services Administration (CSA) and in 1981 became the Community Services Block Grant program, administered by the Office of Community Services under the Department of Health and Human Services. States requesting funds under this program must agree to use block grants to promote self-sufficiency for low-income persons, to provide emergency food and nutrition services, to coordinate public and private social service programs, and to encourage the use of private-sector entities in antipoverty activities. In a 1989 survey it was reported that the CSBG funds had been used for the following programs: emergency services (20%), nutrition programs (14%), employment programs (13%), education initiatives (8%), neighborhood and economic development (8%), income management programs (8%), and housing initiatives (6%). The Community Services Block Grant was scheduled to expire in 1986, was then extended through 1990 and then again extended to 1994. It is clear that despite administration efforts to close down this program beginning in 1981, the Congress has prevailed in retaining the program, even with increased funding (U.S. Senate, 1990). For an additional discussion of the new "welfare reform" law (see Chapter 6).

EDUCATION

Many retirees today and in the future are expected to spend as many years in retirement as in the work force. How the retirement years will be spent will determine the quality of life available to each individual. Some may prefer leisure and withdrawal from daily responsibilities. Others may seek opportunities for volunteerism that allows them to contribute their time and talents to enhancing opportunities for others and improving the community where they live. For some, volunteerism may take the form of teaching and sharing with others the accumulated knowledge of many years of living and working. There is a special opportunity in taking part in intergenerational activities through which elders help youngsters learn. Many will seek to complete educational goals that may have been interrupted earlier in life or choose to pursue new areas of knowledge. Some universities and community colleges now are making older persons feel welcome in an environment that was previously dedicated primarily to the young. Recognition of lifetime experiences as providing eligibility for advanced standing, offering courses for audit rather than degree, and the reduction of fees have helped make schools of higher education accessible to older persons.

As aging and the role of the older person in our society are redefined and updated, the expectation that education is a lifelong experience takes on additional importance. Continuous learning is essential to retaining good health, to adapting to a changing environment, to knowing how to use leisure time and to remaining a productive member of the work force or a participant in public service. Rather than exemplifying a linear model of school-work-retirement, lifelong education at various phases of life has different purposes. Most federal statutes that support adult lifelong learning provide resources to appropriate state agencies to implement programs. A few policies directly support education for elderly persons who meet certain eligibility requirements. Some of these federal statutes are:

Adult Education Act — Provides for basic education through grants to the states (November 3, 1966, PL 89-750; May 11, 1989, PL 100-26).

Bilingual Education Act — Adults with limited English proficiency may be trained to become literate in the English language (January 2, 1968, PL 90-247; November 1, 1978, PL 95-561).

Carl D. Perkins Vocational and Applied Technology Education Act of 1990 — Provides resources to improve educational programs leading to academic and occupational skill competencies needed to work in a technologically advanced society (September 25, 1990, PL 101-392).

Displaced Homemakers Self-Sufficiency Assistance Act of 1990 — Provides grants to state agencies and nonprofit organizations to support the provision of education, employment training, and supportive services to displaced homemakers (November 15, 1990, PL 101-554).

Higher Education Act of 1965 — Establishes a comprehensive program of financial assistance to students to help defray the costs of acquiring a postsecondary education through grants, insured loans, work-study, fellowships, and scholarships (November 8, 1965, PL 89-329).

Job Training Partnership Act — Provides federal assistance to the states to develop programs to prepare youth and unskilled adults for entry into the labor force (October 13, 1982, PL 97-300).

National Community Service Act of 1990 — Created the Commission on National Community Service to create full and part-time community service programs including a Special Senior Service program for which eligibility is limited to persons 60 years and older (November 16, 1990, PL 101-610).

National Environmental Education Act of 1990 — Establishes and supports a program of education on the environment through activities in schools, institutions of higher education and other educational activities (November 16, 1990, PL 101-619).

National Literacy Act of 1991 — Creates programs to provide for basic literacy skills for adults (July 25, 1991, PL 102-73).

Rehabilitation Act of 1973 — Authorizes vocational rehabilitation and training programs designed to maximize the employability, independence, and integration into the work place and the community of disabled persons (September 26, 1973, PL 93-112).

Veteran's Educational Assistance Act of 1991 — Assists in the readjustment of members of the armed forces to civilian life after their separation from military service (October 10, 1991, PL 102-127).

Women's Educational Equity Act of 1978 — Increases opportunities for adult women, including continuing education programs and programs for under-employed and unemployed women (November 1, 1978, PL 95-561).

In addition to the statutes of the federal government, state governments have established separate policies regarding education for adults. For example, twenty-eight states have established guidelines which would allow or require a waiver or reduction of tuition fees for elderly persons who attend courses at state-supported institutions of higher education. Nine additional states have created a state policy to waive or reduce such fees on a space-available basis (U.S. Senate, 1991).

LEGAL SERVICES

Equal justice under the law is a goal for all persons in our society. This holds true for the elderly and is of special concern for the elderly poor who may be without access to legal representation and susceptible to receiving unequal justice. Older persons may need appropriate representation in issues related to eligibility for public benefits, especially Social Security, Medicare, Medicaid, Supplementary Security Income and housing. In addition older persons' legal problems often involve consumer fraud, property tax exemptions, special property tax assessments, guardianships, involuntary commitment to institutions, nursing homes and probate matters (U.S. Senate, 1990). Assuring that an older person has access to the services to which he or she is entitled is the essence of fair legal representation. In recent years the scope of legal services has been enlarged to include representation by an ombudsman to assure that the individuals human rights have not been violated and may be accomplished through negotiations rather than legal processes. Issues of fraud, abuse and neglect have become concerns of the Congress, whose members have noted an increase in the frailty of the older population. Expanding the role of the ombudsman will be critical if all these increasing needs are to be met.

"The first federally sponsored programs providing legal services for the poor were initiated in 1965. Under the authority of the Economic Opportunity Act, neighborhood legal-service offices were established in many communities" (Rich and Baum, 1984, p. 123). In 1972 the National Senior Citizens Law Center was established, providing the forerunner of continuing legal services for poor older persons. In 1974 the Legal Services Corporation Act created the Legal Services Corporation, whose responsibility it was to distribute funds appropriated by the Congress to more than three hundred legal service offices around the country. The corporation is independent, with its members appointed by the President with the approval of the Senate.

There was no specific reference to legal services in the initial Older Americans Act but the 1973 regulations developed by the Administration On Aging made legal services eligible for funding under the Act. The 1975 amendments to the Older Americans Act identified legal services as one of the services to receive funds under Title III and by 1982 the Legal Services Corporation was the principle delivery mechanism for legal services funded by the OAA (Rich and Baum, 1984). Subsequent reauthorizations of the act in 1978, 1981, 1984, 1987 and 1992 continued the inclusion of legal services in the program. In addition to legal services, the Older Americans Act requires every state agency to develop an ombudsman program for long-term care facilities in order to investigate and resolve complaints of the residents in these facilities.

CAREGIVER SUPPORT

No discussion of social services would be complete without some reference to families and their role in caregiving. Members of middle-aged working families, especially women, are often referred to as belonging to the sandwich generation because they are faced with caring for both their children and aging parents. In an economy where women are often required to work outside the home to support or contribute to the support of their households, the burdens of work and family care can become very difficult. This growing phenomenon has prompted efforts to develop a national family leave policy that would require businesses having at least fifty employees to offer twelve weeks a year of unpaid medical or parental leave. In the early 1990s, Congress passed a bill under which employers would have had to continue health coverage for employees on leave and restore returning employees to their previous jobs or to equivalent positions. President Bush vetoed the bill and Congress was not able to override that veto, which the President justified by saying that he was in favor of time off for employees for a child's birth or adoption or for medical illness but that he did not believe that such a policy should be mandated by the federal government.

The Family Caregiver Support Act was introduced in the Senate in 1991 in an effort to assist states in providing services to support informal caregivers of individuals with functional limitations. This bill was important because it recognized the value of supporting family members whose ability to continue to provide care for dependent relatives was insufficient for assuming total responsibility for such care. Diminishing family size and the geographic separation of parents from children and other relatives had made it important to find ways to support the caregiver role if older persons were to be able to remain at home for as long as possible. This bill proposed to strengthen and facilitate informal support systems to maintain individuals with functional limitations within the community. Family caregiver support services were designed to cover the cost of care and services in the home or community on a temporary, short-term, intermittent, or emergency basis. Services were to include companionship, homemaker, personal assistance and day services in the community or temporary care in a licensed facility. This bill floundered in a period when the Congress was struggling with the concept of universal access to health care and the possible inclusion of chronic care services in the national health care scheme. However, its essence appeared in the mark-up of that year's Declaration of Objectives of the Older Americans Act, which called for " . . . support to family members and other persons providing voluntary care to older individuals needing long-term care services" (U.S. Senate Report 102-151, Sept. 10, 1991). The Family & Medical Act of 1993 (FMLA) was passed. See chapter 8 for discussion of the Act.

TRANSPORTATION

Availability of transportation for the elderly can make a major difference in their quality of life and oftentimes enables them to remain at home in the community by providing access to needed services. If an older person cannot drive, there is no family member to drive, and there is no accessible commercial transportation, the community should be able to offer transportation, especially in rural areas where small numbers of older persons live at greater distances from their destinations. In these circumstances, transportation can be relatively costly and less easily available.

Consequently, "in 1989, the area agencies on aging spent approximately $150 million on transportation services. The Older Americans Act portion of $67.7 million provided over 63 million trips to 1.2 million individuals, many of whom live in rural areas" (House of Representatives, 1991, p. 53). Transportation has become the third largest expenditure under Title III of the Older Americans Act programs and is the lifeline between the person in need of services and the availability of the services.

The Urban Mass Transportation Administration (UMTA), an agency of the United States Department of Transportation, is the principal source of federal financial assistance for public mass transportation. Its "section 16(b)(2) program provides capital assistance funds in both rural and urbanized areas to private nonprofit organizations to serve the transportation needs of elderly and disabled persons when planned mass transportation services are unavailable, insufficient, or inappropriate" (House of Representatives, 1991, p. 28).

Although funds from UMTA, primarily for the purchase of vehicles, coupled with AoA funds for the operation of the transportation service represent a major source of funding for this service, the total amount has been inadequate to provide needed transportation services, especially for frail older persons or rural residents.

In 1992, passage of the Americans With Disabilities Act recognized the importance of providing specially designed transportation for persons who use wheel chairs or are otherwise physically incapacitated by requiring transportation systems to operate vehicles which permit the disabled to maintain their involvement in the community.

SUMMARY

Housing and social service policies for the elderly have been discussed in the same chapter in order to illustrate the importance of coordinating these activities in the implementation of programs. It has become increasingly clear that experiences with aging in place have highlighted a negative consequence of developing housing policies without providing related social services. By disrupting the status quo of housing programs, aging-in-place has challenged housing programs to find ways to meet the changing needs of the tenants without forcing them to move to obtain the services they need. The best way to overcome this pervasive phenomenon is to provide a range of services that can be modified to respond to changing needs.

The importance of appropriate housing that serves as the base for services is nowhere more poignantly presented than in the plight of the homeless. Not having a place to call home deprives an individual of all the human and social services to which we have been accustomed. Lack of a place to eat, bathe, toilet, sleep with comfort or protect personal possessions represents a great human loss. A reasonable goal for our society should be the availability of housing and appropriate services for all residents, wherever they chose to live.

SUMMARY OF PART THREE

Ultimately, the intent of any public policy should be to advance quality-of-life issues for our population. This section explored several of the most significant policies directly affecting older persons. These policies collectively have had enormous influence on the lives of older persons and especially those who are dependent upon policies responsive to their age, income, living, and working experiences. It is our belief that if these policies are of great importance to older persons they are equally important to families and communities. By establishing these policies as entitlements by age or need we have minimized the adverse stigma attached to welfare policies in our society.

PART FOUR

The Advocacy Process in the Field of Aging: Policies for the Future

CHAPTER
11

Bonding the Generations

We the People of the United States, in Order to form a more perfect Union, establish Justice, insure domestic Tranquillity, provide for the common defense, promote the general Welfare, and secure the Blessings of Liberty to ourselves and our Posterity, do ordain and establish this Constitution for the United States of America.

(Preamble to The Constitution of the United States of America)

In reviewing two centuries of public policies affecting the elderly in our society this volume has described the growth of programs that have resulted from increased attention to the provision of significant services but also has noted mounting concern about the ways services are to be financed. It should be remembered, however, that the quantity and quality of health care services, employment opportunities, housing and other interventions designed to enhance the general welfare of all people in our society also have increased significantly.

Over the years, there have been great changes in the things American government is expected to do so as to promote public welfare. In particular, since the Great Depression of the 1930s the number, reach, and costs of government welfare programs have expanded enormously (Ladd, 1991, p. 520).

Nevertheless, our society does not provide an established minimal livable income for everyone, and there continue to be large numbers of impoverished people and a conspicuous lack of universal access to health care. Unquestionably, our "Union" is more perfect today than it was when the Constitution was written, but have we established "Justice" for all? Have we insured "domestic Tranquillity," promoted "the general Welfare" or secured for all of our inhabitants "the Blessings of Liberty?"

The debate on establishing a national goal for eliminating poverty goes on as we tentatively explore such alternatives to reducing poverty as ensuring a significant minimal income for all or making available subsidized services to augment personal income by paying all or part of the cost of housing, health care, transportation, etc.

The historical review in this text has identified patterns and trends in the evolution of complex public policies as well as obstacles to the implementation of additional policies. While deficiencies in our policies have been noted, no specific solutions have been advocated because solutions to problems can only evolve from clearly defined goals and the application of the policy process that has been described.

Exploration of the legislative histories of some of the most significant pieces of public policy that influence the way society deals with its older members has been complemented by some digressions into the philosophy of caring and balanced by presentation of some issues related to management of programs and policies. An unbiased presentation of the way policies have been developed does not provide much guidance on where they may need to go in the future, however, and any assumptions about future developments must take into consideration several realities.

One important reality is inherent in a policy process firmly grounded in the philosophy that too much power can lead to tyranny. Policy development in the United States is based on the sharing of power through checks and balances within the power structure, multiple congressional committee involvement and a high degree of dependence on the advocacy efforts of advisory and special interest groups. While the process has minimized tyranny, it has made it difficult to develop policy. But this is as it was supposed to be and it has worked.

At the same time, for the advocate interested in overcoming obvious social deficits, righting wrongs or fostering a favorite agenda item, it has made the road to success an often painfully slow and discouraging one. That is why it is so very important to understand the process, to anticipate delays and to be prepared for a long-drawn-out campaign whenever an attempt is made to effect major changes in the public policies of our nation. Only an advocate who has this knowledge base can understand the importance of building in a reserve of time and effort that is adequate to see the process to its successful conclusion.

Obviously, the task is made easier if the policy issue already appears on the nation's agenda, confirming an already established consensus regarding its importance and previous involvement of major forces in the policy process (i.e., chairpersons of the significant congressional committees). Major objections from within and outside of the government can be assumed to have been answered.

Another reality in the development of policy is the significance of special interest groups' advocacy activities. Support from advocacy groups implies that the interest of the electorate has been aroused and elevates the importance of the issue. Advocacy for policies that benefit the elderly can be expected from groups identified with aging-related issues. Advocacy from coalitions of more heterogeneous groups carries a more powerful message and should be encouraged. Such coalitions should evolve from a foundation of mutual recognition that the needed change will have effects beyond helping any single age or special interest group.

Generations United is an illustration of a coalition that advocates for both children and the elderly, recognizing that these two groups are equally vulnerable to the adverse impacts of poverty and lack of access to health care. A broad perspective on advocacy positions acknowledges that support for any one group's interests will be diminished unless an equal effort is mounted to overcome the same deficit for any other group in the society. Poverty is not restricted to any one age group, so the issue of poverty must be addressed and met for all. Access to health care is not the problem of any one age group, although some may have more restricted access because of income, place of residence or place of employment, if they are employed.

The temper of society has recently become less supportive of programs to benefit the elderly. Advocates on behalf of the elderly increasingly may encounter conflicting and sometimes negative public attitudes toward aging-related policies. The aged are no longer considered automatically to be among the needy poor, due in a large measure to the success of the Social Security program and its cost-of-living adjustments as well as to the increased earnings and savings of the elderly. In spite of these advances, poverty among the elderly continues, however, and is particularly severe for women and ethnic minorities.

Entitlement to benefits because of age or certain circumstances, such as is provided by Social Security, Medicare and Older Americans Act programs, has been represented by some to be a burden on our society because public expenditure for entitlements has been increasing so rapidly. Others argue that entitlement represents a bonding of generations through a generalized tax (i.e., on all wage earners) to provide support to those who earlier had been taxed to support a broadly accepted benefit (i.e., income for the preceding generation of workers). This is the social contract described by Locke.

> Societies are created for specific purposes by the contract which also provides rules by which members of the society agree to live. These rules, according to Locke, are needed to achieve the purpose for which the society was created (Dobelstein, 1990, p. 259).

Today's advocates for the elderly must be prepared to respond to a sometimes hostile public policy environment by being armed with a sound knowledge of the policy process, by having access to adequate data in support of any new program and by being ready to demand discussion of the issues, not merely the prejudices of opponents. For example, emotionally charged words such as socialized medicine, welfare, private enterprise and dependency all need to be understood in terms of the values associated with them before proceeding with any discussion of content for a proposed policy. The issue of health care cannot be simply an exchange of word-symbols but must address the goals of society, the limits of existing policies, the extent of coverage that should be provided, costs, and provision for future modification or amendment.

Our government has responded to the failure of savings and loan institutions by providing more than $500 billion to rescue the banks, their investors and depositors, arguing that the failure of the banks had major consequences for the economy of our society. In 1992, after major riots in Los Angeles with many deaths, looting of stores and businesses and widespread lawless behavior on the part of some people, the federal government was prepared to send large amounts of relief money to repair a disaster that might have been avoided had more careful attention been paid to the needs of the inner-city poor. In each of these illustrations public resources that were not available to meet a community need became available after a debacle. Absence of an understanding of the role of government in contemporary society or inability to grasp the important social and economic issues of the day often result in policy-making that responds to crises rather than in planning that is sensitive and responsive to needs.

There is widespread and sometimes angry debate about whether society has an obligation to support all people over a certain age or should specifically direct its support to those who have been determined to be in need of societal intervention. The issue of need versus age as the eligibility criterion for public support remains as far from resolution as when Ward (1984) asked the question, "When is age relevant?" Old age is variously perceived at different times and in different cultures, but aging often is associated with poor health, poverty, and diminished status and usefulness. Age-related entitlements have been seen as compensating for the dependencies of age or strategies to keep the elderly at arm's length from society (Shanas et al., 1968). There are those who insist that the elderly have been recipients of more than they need or more than their fair share, a point of view that has made older persons recipients of scorn and the scapegoats of a society plagued by social and economic problems. The common practice of attaching a stigma to being old has diverted our attention from some of the deficiencies in our society and engendered intergenerational conflict (Binstock, 1983). For as long as the elderly were seen as the deserving poor, society reacted with compassion toward them. When the elderly were perceived as competing for resources needed by others the compassion turned to competition. "The roots of scapegoating had been developed through decades of compassionate ageism. It was to be expected that a shrinking of resources would be accompanied by a shrinking of compassion" (Binstock, 1983, p. 140).

It appears likely that older people will feel better about themselves when being old is accepted as being of no great consequence. So, how are we to deal with the needs of older persons today without their being treated as a homogeneous group in need of government intervention? Societal responses should be made on the basis of collective responsibility toward everyone in our society. Ultimately we need to answer the questions raised by Binstock when he asks, "Do we wish to provide cash income transfers like Social Security to persons on the basis of their work histories? Or do we wish to provide income to them on the basis of their existential needs so that they can survive with some modicum of human dignity?"

In discussing need versus entitlement Rein (1983) said that what people receive from society may be considered "claims" or entitlements which result from individuals or groups pressing their bids for resources. This is an ongoing, incomplete process. When entitlements are given as a right—as in Social Security or Medicare—they must be seen as the outcome "of an earlier process of claim-pressing. It is kind of a truce in an ongoing struggle that has taken the form of requests, bids, bargains, or negotiations" (p. 26). Indeed, we see such an encroachment on the claim to Medicare in reductions in services and especially in proposals for rationing of services that are currently offered as an entitlement. According to Rein, claims can take at least two forms.

The first is a claim for stability and security or claims "directed at the continuity of life-style" (p. 27). This claim builds upon the success achieved in entitlements that have enabled individuals to achieve a life-style of security and comfort. The second is a claim for adequacy or negotiating for minimally secure income, health care and housing. We should be able to advocate for both stability and adequacy for everyone while insisting on the maintenance of gains made for the older population through Social Security and Medicare.

Nowhere are our claims for stability and security more threatened than in the current considerations for the rationing of health care. In the current situation, there appear to be ever-increasing costs for the provision of health care and no agreement on acceptable approaches to controlling them. Our current health care policies represent confusion and conflicting values. While some Americans have access to the best health care services in the world, many, probably in excess of 30 million persons, have no health care coverage and must either forego health care services or seek out the shortest line to some community charitable health care facility. Rationing exists for those who lack coverage or have only very limited access to health care services.

It also should be remembered that health care includes access to adequate nutrition, housing and the availability of a life-style that encourages good health. These components of health care are currently rationed to those with jobs, good pay and a suitable place to live. Programs that encompass private developments in expanded health care, government-sponsored services and various powerful groups which advocate on behalf of positions ranging from the maintenance of programs as they are to the complete reorganization of health care all attempt to influence health care policies.

In the midst of this chaotic scene there are proponents of solving the problem of costs by rationing services as being easier than the alternatives of reallocating our resources, increasing taxes, or reorganizing the health care delivery system in order to use available funds most productively. Relman (1990) said, "To avoid rationing, what we require most is not more money but the will to change those aspects of the present system that are responsible for the present crisis." A plan for rationing has to have more than economic justification. It must find justification in its ability to deal uniquely with individual needs, it must have a foundation in the ethics of our society that places a high value on an individual's life, and it must find acceptance in a political arena with conflicting values and pressures from the many advocacy groups.

Health care rationing in our society undoubtedly would ultimately, if not at the outset, include restrictions based on an individual's age. As Binstock and Post (1991) pointed out, "The potential moral and social costs of old-age rationing proposals are substantial." Would such rationing encourage mercy killing and assisted suicide as relief for abandoned older persons in need of health care? Would rationing restrictions be removed for favored members of the society, thereby rejecting the poor, the old, the homeless? Age-based rationing would imply that older persons have a responsibility to die when their health care costs exceed a predetermined factor and deny the individual freedom to choose to live or to determine how to live. If others are given authority to determine who shall live and who shall die, who is to protect individuals from choices based on issues of ageism or other discriminatory beliefs?

Our society is desperately in need of social and political leadership that strengthens the bonds between generations, that minimizes differences between groups, and that gives testimony to the idea that we are all responsible for the others in our society. We must believe that economics should not generate ethics but rather that ethics guide our use of all of our resources. Accepting the concept of rationing of health care, especially its implications for the elderly, crosses a moral divide from which there may be no return (Laster, 1990).

It should also be understood that all public policy "is part of a matrix of other related policies. Present policy builds on previous policy. No public policy stands alone" (Dobelstein, 1990, p. 5). Increased allocation of funds for domestic programs was anticipated as a potential benefit of the expected reduction in the defense budget resulting from the breakup of the Soviet Union. The Older Americans Act was an outgrowth of the successful implementation of humane social programs of the New Deal era.

Consequently, no public policy on behalf of the elderly responds solely to the elderly. The Social Security Act provides financial protection for dependent school-age children whose wage-earner parent has died. Benefits of the act are also provided without regard to the age of those who are severely disabled. Social Security support for older persons reduces the burden on their children or other relatives, giving them greater choice in the use of their assets. Medicare provides benefits for those who are disabled and, like Social Security, housing and other social programs, provides for families caring for their elders.

Dobelstein (1990) suggests that public policies serve the entire community in five ways because they have:

1) solved a social problem; 2) located the public interest; 3) identified and legitimized specific social goals with respect to the problems; 4) provided an environment for resolving conflicting values; and 5) established the direction for future social action with respect to the issues under consideration (1990, p. 6).

The use of this five-point paradigm to structure the presentation of a policy position on behalf of the elderly would encourage exploration of broader consequences of the policy, including impacts on other groups that may be adversely influenced by the policy as well as on those for whom the new policy would provide an advantage. Coalitions would emerge and regroup as the policies and their impact indicated the value of new alliances.

For example, although the issue of the large number of persons without access to health care coverage is a concern of persons of all ages, the issue of chronic care services is of special interest to the elderly, many of whom have chronic health problems. Part of the debate about implementing health care policies should include both meeting the specific needs of those who are chronically ill and giving support to their care providers. The provision of coverage through the Medicare and Medicaid programs has established an important level of societal intervention which set the stage for future social action, but lack of availability of health care remains a major social problem that has ramifications throughout the public and private sectors.

Lewin and Sullivan (1989) added another dimension to the discussion of policy development when they argued that

In formulating fresh policy approaches to these problems, we must not feel limited to options that are on the present agenda or to established ways of thinking. The current environment for policy-making—with wider recognition of the challenges facing us, as well as increasing pressure and ability to respond flexibly to changing economic and social conditions—makes fundamental reforms in our policies more feasible (1989, p. 5).

If we are to rethink our social welfare and health care programs, as these authors suggest, and reject past practices steeped in incrementalism in favor of fundamental reforms, all current policies must be subject to careful scrutiny and possible revision. Only then can we anticipate the bonding of the generations into a mutually responsible coalition to promote the welfare of the society and the social contract on which most of the public policies for the elderly have been developed.

APPENDIX
A

Congressional Committees and Subcommittees

Adapted from the *Seniors Guide to the U.S. Congress* (1987), with information on subcommittee jurisdiction provided by the *Congressional Yellow Book* (1990).

SENATE COMMITTEES

Committee on Agriculture, Nutrition and Forestry

Subcommittee on Nutrition and Investigations
This subcommittee is responsible for most of the legislation dealing with federal nutrition programs, such as: the food stamp program, and the women's, infant's and children's (WIC) program, commodities surplus program (which distributes food to low-income families), and nutritional programs for the elderly.

Committee on Appropriations

Appropriations is one of the most powerful committees in Congress due to its control over the flow of money to programs authorized by other committees. The spending decisions of the Congress are made through 13 separate appropriations bills which are the responsibility of each of this committee's subcommittees. The spending levels for Older Americans Act programs, low-income home energy assistance and social service programs, job training and employment programs and health research are all determined under the auspices of this committee.

Subcommittee on Agriculture, Rural Development and Related Agencies
Subcommittee on HUD-Independent Agencies
Subcommittee on Labor, Health and Human Services and Education
Subcommittee on Transportation

Committee on Banking, Housing and Urban Affairs

Subcommittee on Housing and Urban Affairs

The jurisdiction of this subcommittee covers Section 202 direct loans to sponsors of housing for the elderly and disabled, Section 8 rental assistance, and all other public and assisted housing programs.

Committee on Budget

The budget committee participates to some degree in all programs. It is responsible for establishing national priorities for taxing and spending through the annual drafting of the federal budget resolution. The committee is also in charge of reconciliation, requiring each of the authorizing and appropriations committees to pass legislation implementing the budget resolution.

Committee on Finance

The finance committee has jurisdiction over all tax issues as well as many entitlement programs. It also is specifically responsible for Social Security, Medicare, Medicaid, Supplemental Security Income, Title XX Social Services, private pensions and general taxation.

Subcommittee on Health
Subcommittee on Social Security and Family Policy

Committee on Labor and Human Resources

This committee is responsible for much of the legislation establishing federal programs for the elderly and the poor. Its jurisdiction covers such programs as private pension plans and railway retirement; public health and medical research on Alzheimer's and other diseases; emergency food assistance programs and low-income energy assistance; measures assisting the handicapped; Older Americans Act programs (including senior centers, in-home and congregate meals programs, legal and supportive services); the Senior Community Service Employment program and the Job Training Partnership Act; community services block grant and social services block grant programs; ACTION Agency Volunteer programs (including Foster Grandparents, RSVP, VISTA); and other initiatives and programs relating to public welfare.

Subcommittee on Aging
Subcommittee on Labor
Subcommittee on Employment and Productivity

Committee on Veterans' Affairs

The jurisdiction of this committee covers all matters pertaining to veterans, including: veterans' hospitals, medical care and treatment of veterans; veterans' pensions and insurance policies; compensation of veterans; and welfare and civil relief measures.

Special Committee on Aging

This is a non-legislative committee that specializes in developing research and legislative recommendations for the use of other committees. Its duties include conducting studies and holding hearings on all matters pertaining to problems and opportunities of the elderly. Due to its lack of legislative responsibilities the most important function of this committee is bringing specific problems of older people to public attention. It is required to report the results of its study and subsequent recommendations to the Senate at least once a year. The Special Committee on Aging has no subcommittees.

HOUSE OF REPRESENTATIVES COMMITTEES

Committee on Agriculture

Subcommittee on Domestic Marketing, Consumer Relations and Nutrition
This subcommittee is responsible for most of the legislation dealing with federal nutrition programs, such as: the food stamp program, and the Women's, Infant's and Children's (WIC) program, the Commodities Surplus program (which distributes food to low-income families), and nutritional programs for the elderly.

Committee on Appropriations

Appropriations is one of the most powerful committees in Congress, having control over the flow of money to programs authorized by other committees. The spending decisions of the Congress are made through thirteen separate appropriations bills, each of which is the responsibility of one of this committee's subcommittees. The spending levels for Older Americans Act programs, low-income home energy assistance and social service programs, job training and employment programs and health research are all determined under the auspices of this committee.
Subcommittee on HUD-Independent Agencies
Subcommittee on Labor, Health and Human Services and Education
Subcommittee on Rural Development, Agriculture and Related Agencies
Subcommittee on Transportation

Committee on Banking, Finance and Urban Affairs

Subcommittee on Housing and Community Development

The jurisdiction of this subcommittee covers Section 202 direct loans to sponsors of housing for the elderly and disabled, Section 8 rental assistance, and all other public and assisted housing programs.

Committee on Budget

The budget committee participates to some degree in all programs. It is responsible for establishing national priorities for taxing and spending through the annual drafting of the federal budget resolution. The committee is also in charge of reconciliation, requiring each of the authorizing and appropriations committees to pass legislation implementing the budget resolution.

Committee on Education and Labor

This committee is responsible for much of the legislation establishing federal programs for the elderly and the poor. Its jurisdiction covers such programs as private pension plans and railway retirement; public health and medical research on Alzheimer's and other diseases; emergency food assistance programs and low-income energy assistance; measures assisting the handicapped; Older Americans Act programs (including senior centers, in-home and congregate meals programs, legal and supportive services); the Senior Community Service Employment program and the Job Training Partnership Act; community services block grant and social services block grant programs; ACTION Agency Volunteer programs (including Foster Grandparents, RSVP, VISTA); and other initiatives and programs relating to public welfare.

Subcommittee on Human Resources
Subcommittee on Labor-Management Relations

Committee on Energy and Commerce

This committee has jurisdiction over all legislation relating to the Medicaid program and shares jurisdiction with the Committee on Ways and Means on Medicare Part B (physician services). The committee also has jurisdiction over energy pricing issues and consumer protection.

Subcommittee on Health and the Environment

Committee on Veterans' Affairs

The jurisdiction of this committee covers all matters pertaining to veterans, including: veterans' hospitals, medical care and treatment of veterans; veterans' pensions and insurance policies; compensation of veterans; and welfare and civil relief measures.

Committee on Ways and Means

Ways and Means handles all tax issues as well as Medicare Part A (hospital services); it shares jurisdiction over Part B of Medicare with the Committee on Energy and Commerce. It also has jurisdiction over entitlement programs such as Social Security, Supplemental Security Income and Aid to Families with Dependent Children.

Subcommittee on Health
Subcommittee on Public Assistance and Unemployment Compensation
Subcommittee on Social Security

Select Committee on Aging

The Select Committee on Aging was discontinued in 1993 and was replaced by a caucus on aging issues

APPENDIX
B

Statutes Establishing and Amending the Older Americans Act

1965   The Older Americans Act of 1965—Signed into law July 14, 1965 as Public Law 89-73.

1967   The Older Americans Act Amendments of 1967—Signed into law July 1, 1967 as Public Law 90-42.

1969   The Older Americans Act Amendments of 1969—Signed into law September 17, 1969 as Public Law 91-69.

1972   The Nutrition Program for the Elderly Act—Signed into law March 22, 1972 as Public Law 92-258.

1973   The Older Americans, Comprehensive Services Amendments of 1973—Signed into law May 3, 1973 as Public Law 93-29.

1974   Amendments to the Nutrition Program for the Elderly Act—Signed into law July 12, 1974 as Public Law 93-351.

1975   The Older Americans Act Amendments of 1975—Signed into law November 28, 1975 as Public Law 94-135.

1977   The Older Americans Act Amendments of 1977—Signed into law July 11, 1977 as Public Law 95-65.

1978   The Comprehensive Older Americans Act Amendments of 1978—Signed into law October 18, 1978 as Public Law 95-478.

1981   The Older Americans Act Amendments of 1981—Signed into law December 29, 1981 as Public Law 97-115.

1984   The Older Americans Act Amendments of 1984—Signed into law October 9, 1984 as Public Law 98-459.

1986   The Older Americans Act Amendments of 1986—Signed into law April 1, 1986 as Public Law 99-269.

1987   The Older Americans Act Amendments of 1987—Signed into law November 29, 1987 as Public Law 100-175.

1992   The Older Americans Act Amendments of 1992—Signed into law September 30, 1992 as Public Law 102-375.

Legislative History of the Social Security Act
Source Adapted From: Social Security Administration on the World Wide Web
http://www.ssa.gov - 1997

1700s

The Federal Government accepted the responsibility of providing pensions to disabled veterans of the revolutionary War.

Thomas Paine published his pamphlet, *Agrarian Justice,* in which he proposed a social insurance program for the young nation.

1800s

Civil War pensions were first paid to disabled veterans.

The first private pension plan in American industry was adopted by American Express. It provided benefits for employees 60 years of age or over who had 20 years of service with the company and were incapacitated for further performance of duty.

German Chancellor Otto von Bismark put forward his Prussian Plan for social insurance for German workers, making Germany the first nation to adopt a modern social insurance program.

1900s

Civil War Pensions were extended to elderly veterans.

A workmen's compensation system was established for civilian employees of the Federal Government.

The first Federal old-age pension bill was introduced in Congress.

1910s

The first workmen's compensation law to be held constitutional was enacted in Wisconsin.

The first contributory system of pensions covering all State employees was established in Massachusetts.

The first old-age pension legislation not challenged on the grounds of constitutionality was enacted in the Territory of Alaska.

1920s

A Civil Service Retirement and Disability Fund was established for Federal employees.

On March 5, 1923, Montana's Old-Age Pension Law was enacted. It was the first such State law to withstand the test of constitutionality.

1930s

Federal legislation to promote economic security was recommended in President Franklin D. Roosevelt's Message to Congress.

The Social Security Act was passed in the House of Representatives, 372 to 33.

The Social Security Act was passed in the Senate by a vote of 77 to 6.

The Social Security Act became Public Law 74-271 with President Roosevelt's signature on August 14, 1935.

Workers began to acquire credits toward old-age insurance benefits.

First applications for benefits filed. Ernest Ackerman, a retired Cleveland motorman, was among the first to apply.

First Social Security benefits paid (one-time payment only).

The Social Security Amendments of 1939 broadened the program to include dependents' and survivors' benefits.

1940s

Monthly benefits first became payable under old-age and survivors insurance to aged retired workers and their dependents and to survivors of deceased insured workers.

Ida May Fuller became the first person to receive an old-age monthly benefit check under the new Social Security law.

In a special message to Congress, President Harry S Truman proposed a comprehensive, prepaid medical insurance plan for all people through the Social Security system.

1950s

Social Security Act Amendments established a program of aid to the needy who are permanently and totally disabled.

The Federal Security Agency was abolished and its functions transferred to the newly formed Department of Health, Education and Welfare.

Amendments permitted reduced retirement for women at age 62.

The Social Security Act was amended to provide monthly benefits to permanently and totally disabled workers aged 50-64 and for adult children of deceased or retired workers, if disabled before age 18.

1960s

The Social Security Amendments of 1961 were signed by President John F. Kennedy, permitting all workers to elect reduced retirement at age 62.

President Lyndon B. Johnson signed the Medicare Bill in the presence of former President Truman who proposed this legislation in his message to Congress in 1945.

1970s

Social Security Amendments of 1972 were signed into law by President Nixon.

Supplementary Security Income went into operation as a result of the Social Security Amendments of 1972.

Eligibility extended to divorced persons aged 62 or older, previously married at least 10 years.

1980s

Department of Health, Education and Welfare became the Department of Health and Human Services.

Normal retirement age raised to age 67 on schedule from 2000-2022.

1990s

President William J. Clinton signed legislation to make SSA an independent agency, effective March 31, 1995.

President Clinton signed the Contract With America Advancement Act of 1996 (Public Law 104-121) which ends eligibility to disability benefits for drug addicts and alcoholics.

President Clinton signed the Personal Responsibility and Work Opportunity Reconciliation Act of 1996 (Public Law 104-193). This "welfare reform" legislation terminated SSI eligibility for most non-citizens and made it more difficult for children to qualify as disabled for SSI purposes. It also ended the federal entitlement to Aid to Families with Dependent Children that was part of the original 1935 Social Security Act.

Financing

"**Earnings Base**" is the amount of annual earnings subject to Social Security taxation, **OASI** is the Old-Age and Survivors portion of Social Security and **DI** is the Disability portion. Shown under these headings are the percentage of the Social Security tax rate allocated to each of these parts of the program. The total tax rate in a given year is shown in the OASDI column. The column labeled "Act" shows when the law was changed and the next column shows the Earnings Base and tax rate effective during those years. NOTE: This table does NOT include Medicare.

Act	Earnings Base	Employer and Employee			Self-Employed		
		OASI	DI	OASDI	OASI	DI	OASDI
1935-1947	$3,000	1.0					
1950	$3,600	1.5			2.25		
1961	$4,800	2.875	.025	3.125	4.325	0.375	4.7
1971	$9,000	4.05	0.55	4.6	6.075	.0825	6.9
1980	$25,900	4.52	0.56	5.08	6.2725	0.7775	7.05
1989	$51,300	5.6	0.6	6.2	11.2	1.2	12.4
1997	$65,400	5.35	0.85	6.2	10.7	1.7	12.4

Source: Adapted from: Social Security Administration from the World Wide Web: http://www.ssa.gov - 1997

Performance of Social Security Trust Funds 1937-1995
Includes Old-Age, Survivors and Disability Trust Funds
$ in Millions

Calendar Year	Net Interest	Total Income	Total Expenditures	Balance
1937	$ 2	$ 767	$ 1	$ 766
1940	43	368	62	2,031
1945	134	1,420	304	7,121
1950	257	2,928	1,022	13,721
1955	454	6,167	5,079	21,633
1960	569	12,445	11,798	22,613
1965	651	17,857	19,187	19,841
1970	1,791	36,993	33,108	38,068
1975	2,722	75,034	78,242	41,133
1980	2,330	119,712	123,550	26,453
1985	2,741	203,540	190,628	42,163
1990	17,245	315,443	253,135	225,277
1995	34,977	399,497	339,815	496,068

Note: This table provides historical data concerning the income and expenditures of the Old-Age Survivors and Disability Insurance Trust Funds. The series goes back to 1937, when the first benefits were paid. Keep in mind that Survivors benefits were first paid in 1940 and Disability benefits in 1957. This Table does not include Medicare.

Source: Adapted from: Social Security Administration from the World Wide Web: http://www.ssa.gov

APPENDIX
D

Major Activities of the Federal Council on the Aging

A brief overview of some of the major topics covered by the Federal Council over the years indicates the scope of issues dealt with by this body.

1974

Initially, Congress mandated that the Council undertake three specific studies. These included:

1. *A Study of State Formulae for Funding Older Americans Act Programs*, which was completed and submitted to the Commissioner on Aging, the Secretary of HEW, and to Congress on December 30, 1974. The major recommendation of the council was that the factor of "the population aged 60 or over who are living in poor households" should be added to the factor of the number of state residents aged 60 or older in all state allotment formulae for determining benefits under the Older American Act.
2. *A Study on the Interrelationships of Benefit Programs for the Elderly Operated by Federal, State and Local Government Agencies* to be carried out by outside contractors from a work statement prepared by the Council.
3. The third study mandated by Congress, concerning the impact on the elderly of all tax-supported programs, was assigned to a subsidiary unit of the Council, the Committee on the Economics of Aging.

1975

On December 29, 1975 the two studies in progress in 1974 (*A Study of the Interrelationships of Benefit Programs* and the *Study of the Impact of the Tax Structure on the Elderly*) were completed and submitted to the President. These two reports resulted in such recommendations as a call for government aid to be directed to the poorest among the elderly and all other age groups (in the form of cash or services) and that aid be more effectively and efficiently directed to its intended beneficiaries.

Other reports and subjects dealt with by the Federal Council in 1975 included:

1. A recommendation regarding the need for a national system of social care for the frail elderly. A justification for such a system was presented in this report under the title of a *National Policy for the Frail Elderly*. The essential thrust of the recommendation was that the "frail elderly" should receive first priority for services and that an assessment should be done to determine the basic core of social services that are needed.
2. A *Bicentennial Charter for Older Americans* was prepared upon the request of the Commissioner on Aging as a revision of the Senior Citizens Chapter developed by the 1961 White House Conference on Aging. It promulgated a series of rights which the Commissioner hoped would be considered at forums of older persons organized by advisory committees to the Area Agencies on Aging at the state and local levels.
3. *Focus on Older Women—International Women's Year.* A hearing on "National Policy Concerns for Older Women," held in conjunction with the annual meeting of the National Council on Aging, was organized in observance of International Women's Year to try to draw national attention to the particular needs and concerns of older women.

1976

1. In early 1976, *National Policy Concerns of Older Women: Commitment to a Better Life* was published by the Federal Council, containing the highlights of testimony presented in the 1975 hearings on "National Policy Concerns for Older Women." This report noted that one of the major problems identified for older women was a lack of adequate income.
2. Formulation of a new *National Policy on the Frail Elderly* continued apace. One of the priority activities of the Federal Council was to try to devise a federal response to the growing numbers of vulnerable elderly living at home. The Council stated its commitment to a national program that would assure the frail elderly of entitlement to a basic floor of defined social services, available nationwide regardless of income.
3. A *Study of Asset Testing* was started as a continuation of separate studies on benefits and taxes which were completed in late 1975.

1977

1. A grant was made to the Institute for Research on Poverty at the University of Wisconsin. In November of 1977, the technical papers which resulted from this grant were published in a report entitled *The Treatment of Assets*

and Income from Assets in Income-Conditioned Government Benefit Programs.

2. The council approved eight major elements of the *National Policy for Frail Elderly*. In sum, the Council's recommendation for providing systematized aid was described as a freestanding case assessment and case management service which would be offered as an entitlement to the frail elderly. It would be based on chronological age or identified functional need, on a universal and voluntary basis, providing a "floor" of social services upon which a skilled practitioner could build to develop a plan of care in conjunction with the older person and significant others, if available.

3. *Study of Minority Elderly*—In the course of the council's pursuing its mandated responsibility for reviewing and evaluating federal policies and programs affecting older persons, a number of problems confronting minority elderly emerged. These concerns were made especially apparent during the Council's work on a national policy for the frail elderly. It became obvious that age eligibility would be disadvantageous to minority elderly because their life expectancies tend to be substantially shorter than those of their white counterparts. Because of this, the Council undertook a study to examine the impact and equity of all major federal programs.

4. The Council continued its deliberations on *Personnel Needs in the Field of Aging*. In order to evaluate and plan for health care services for the elderly, the Council awarded a contract to analyze manpower issues in the delivery of health care services and to develop policy recommendations.

1978

1. Three reports concerning *Personnel Needs in the Field of Aging* were issued in 1978. These included: a) *Final Report Study of Health Manpower Needs for Services to Older Americans*; b) *Analysis of Quantitative Methods for Determination of Health Manpower Needs of Older Americans*; and c) *Supplemental Review of Literature and Bibliography*. A final report was entitled *Final Report for Study of Health Manpower Needs for Services to Older Americans* (with appendices).

2. *Public Policy and the Frail Elderly* was issued as an interim step in the Council's activities with regard to the frail elderly. Special concern for a focus on various subgroups whose longevity differs from that of the overall population continued. It was pointed out that methods were needed to assure that the same services as those available to the over-75 population could also be provided to those people from various ethnic/minority backgrounds whose needs may arise at an earlier age.

3. Evaluation of Older Americans Act programs, congressionally mandated through the 1978 Amendments to the Older Americans Act, was the major new project initiated in 1978. The study was designated *The*

Development of Procedures and Criteria for Evaluating Federal Policies on the Aging.

4. *The 1981 White House Conference on Aging*—After reviewing the legislation authorizing the conference the Council recommended to the Secretary of HEW that: a) the scope of the issues discussed at the conference be broad—having implications for all persons in our society; b) the theme of the conference should be "The Aging Society," echoing the first recommendation; and c) each Council member should be named to the Advisory Council of the 1981 White House Conference on Aging.

1979

1. *The Key Issues in Long Term Care*: A progress report was published in December 1979.
2. *Policy Issues Concerning the Elderly Minorities*—Fifteen policy recommendations resulted from this investigation.
3. The Council published *Mental Health and the Elderly: Recommendations for Action*, in recognition of the importance of the health and well-being of the nation's elderly. This publication contains the reports of the two major public advisory bodies existing in 1976-1978: The Secretary's Committee on the Mental Health and Illness of the Elderly and the Presidential Commission on Mental Health.
4. At its March 1979 meeting the Council decided to undertake a study concerning the employment of older workers. Preliminary investigation was undertaken and at the December 1979 meeting a summary of the preliminary findings and recommendations was presented to the members under the title "Toward a National Policy on Older Workers."
5. The preliminary findings from the Council's mandated study on evaluating the programs of the Older Americans Act indicated that Administration on Aging programs could be divided into four major categories: a) national policy development and issues advocacy; b) community services system development; c) financial social and nutrition services for the elderly; and d) applied research, demonstration, evaluation, and education. The schedule of this study provided for its completion by March of 1981.

1980

1. The largest portion of the Council's agenda was taken up with continuing work on the congressionally mandated study concerning the evaluation of the effectiveness of programs under the Older Americans Act.
2. Seven members of the Council were appointed to serve on the Advisory Committee of the White House Conference on Aging and others were

involved in technical committees. The advisory committee further asked the Council to assume responsibility for "monitoring and cooperating with others to implement recommendations" for the 1981 conference.

1981

1. *The Need for Long Term Care: Information and Issues.* A chartbook that presented essential information for determining current and future needs for long term care, was published. This was the third publication of the Council to deal with long term care and the frail elderly (the others being *Public Policy and the Frail Elderly* issued in 1978, and *Key Issues in Long Term Care: A Progress Report* issued in 1979). This report was developed with the hope that it would help frame the national debate on long term care and serve as an important resource document for the delegates at the 1981 White House Conference on Aging.

2. *Older Americans Act Programs—A Study by the Federal Council on the Aging* and *Toward More Effective Implementation of the Older Americans Act—Staff Report* were submitted to the Congress, reflecting the major work of the Council over the previous few years. The law mandating this study had required at least three activities: a) an examination of the fundamental purposes and effectiveness of programs conducted under the Older Americans Act; b) an analysis of the means to identify those elderly in greatest needs of services; and c) an analysis of the numbers and incidence of low-income and minority participants in such programs. At the conclusion of this study, the Council urged the reauthorization of the Older Americans Act and reaffirmed the central purposes of the act (namely, to serve the social needs of older persons and to give special attention to those with special needs), despite finding considerable ambiguity and conflicting goals within the law.

3. The Council's study on older workers was published by the Senate Special Committee on Aging in a condensed and revised form entitled Toward a National Older Worker Policy: An Information Paper.

1982

1. The Council adopted a theme for its activities, *Living Longer, the Critical Concerns of the Elderly*. This broad framework was utilized as a challenge to focus the Council's attention on issues that were most appropriate to its unique function. Under this umbrella the Council centered its efforts on committee meetings which focused on: a) housing issues of concern for the elderly; and b) recommendations for the reauthorization of the Older Americans Act in 1984.

1983

1. Major recommendations for 1983 were focused on the 1984 reauthorization of the Older Americans Act and housing for the elderly. Both the Housing and OAA Reauthorization Committees used the 1981 White House Conference on Aging recommendations extensively in developing the Council's 1983 recommendations, and a special committee dealing with conference recommendations concluded that the Council should continue to use these recommendations as reference points for deliberations in 1984.

1984

1. One of the most important activities of the Federal Council in 1984 was a symposium held in Washington, D.C. on *Increasing Support Services for the Frail Elderly*. This symposium reflected the Council's continuing concern for the problems and needs of the frail elderly, with the focus now centering on those charged with their care.
2. The Council held a panel discussion, *Aging in Place: Implications for Long Term Care*. The purpose of the symposium was to explore the feasibility of community-based long term care options from the point of view of federal, state, and local levels, and to help shape the developing Council agenda with regard to long term care issues.
3. Health care issues became the other major focus, with the concentration of study centering on the condition of hypothermia and its detrimental effects on the elderly.

1985

1. A staff report, *Health Care Study for Older Americans*, was used as the basis of a Council forum to try to clarify the mood of the nation, which the Council felt was sending contradictory signals—voicing support of decreased government while showing little willingness to give up government services.
2. On November 21, 1985 the Federal Council released the summary of a staff report entitled *The Relevance of Long Term Care Insurance for Family Caregivers*. This report dealt with extensive sociological research which shows that families of all types may present a strong market for private long term care insurance.
3. As evidence of the Council's support for the distribution of information concerning the elderly population, the Federal Council in conjunction with the Administration on Aging, the U.S. Senate Special Committee on Aging, and the American Association of Retired Persons, developed, published and distributed the second edition of *Aging America in 1985*. This publication

provided a broad overview of data on the health, income, employment, housing, and social conditions of the current older population.

1986

1. The Council undertook a special project to make recommendations to Congress which would be incorporated in the reauthorization of the Older Americans Act.

1987

1. *Health Care Study for Older Americans* was printed. This long-awaited report addressed the following issues: a) how and why health care costs have been increasing faster than general inflation; b) the current and future demographic trends which foretell a senior boom by the year 2010; c) a discussion of current public and private sources of health care payment and benefits for older Americans; and d) an analysis of possible strategies for addressing health care policy issues for present and future older Americans.
2. The May meeting of the Federal Council took place in Pierre, South Dakota, with the theme of *Methods and Practices for Serving Rural and Native Americans.*
3. The Council held a symposium on the subject of *Community Service Cooperation—A Mandate of the Older Americans Act.* Since the term "community service" appears frequently in Titles I, II and III of the act, the council wanted to gauge its interpretation under various settings and constraints.
4. The Council held a forum to address the issue *Impact of the AIDS Problem on the Elderly.* A number of witnesses from the public and private sectors addressed the following issues: a) maintaining quality health care; b) the economic effects on an epidemic-reduced younger generation; c) the actuarial effects on Social Security—Medicare and Medicaid; d) AIDS' sociological and philosophical effects on the older population.
5. The Federal Council, in cooperation with the Senate Special Committee on Aging, the Administration on Aging, and the AARP, helped to develop the third edition of the demographic study *Aging America: Trends and Projections.*

1988

1. The Council awarded a contract to develop a plan which would provide for an orderly, relevant and economically reasonable White House Conference on Aging in 1991.

2. *Intrastate Targeting of Federal Funds to Older Americans Act Designated Groups* was the subject of a forum held by the Council. Problems arising from the funding formulas in some states have led to legal actions against state departments on aging.
3. Through an Administration on Aging grant, a set of guidelines and standards on guardianship for state legislatures and law professionals was developed from testimony and material presented at the Council's May meeting focusing on *Elder Rights*.

1989

1. Following its forum on intrastate targeting in 1988, the Council held a briefing on the special tabulations system and the needs of the aging network for specifically designed special tabulations to assist in targeting.
2. The Council recommended that the method for assessing premiums to participate in the Medicare Catastrophic Act be postponed for one year. (The legislation was later repealed.)
3. The Council studied various aspects of the involvement of older persons in the workplace.
4. The Council issued a statement of commendation and tribute to the late U.S. Congressman Claude Pepper.

1990

1. Reviewed the various options and proposals being offered or developed to address the nation's growing crisis in long term health care.
2. Reviewed and discussed the Older Americans Act and issues related to the approaching reauthorization of the legislation and provided recommendations for reauthorization of the act.
3. Received a briefing on nutrition programs for the elderly.
4. Conducted a forum on mental health and the elderly.

1991

1. Participated in the development, printing and distribution of *Aging America: Trends and Projections, 1991 Edition.*
2. Forwarded to Congress recommendations for the reauthorization of the Older Americans Act of 1965.
3. Participated in developments of the National Eldercare Campaign.

1992

1. Monitored the authorization of the Older Americans Act.

2. Continued development of a comprehensive study of Mental Health and the Elderly.
3. Examined the issues of older persons living alone.
4. Helped to establish an Indian task force to serve as a liaison between IHS and FCoA, to closely examine issues of concern to elder Indians.
5. Took an active role in the National Eldercare Campaign, which was sponsored by AoA.

1993

1. Held a symposium on mental health issues confronting older individuals. The concept was to develop a book which could serve as a tool for health, behavioral and social sciences.
2. Reviewed information on gaps in the provision of long-term care.
3. Gathered information on the issue of income security.
4. Found issues of poverty and income security among older women to be a serious problem.

1994

1. Studied the area of home and community based services as alternatives to long-term care.
2. Worked with the National Institute of Mental Health on a book for clinicians in mental health. This was a continuation of previous mental health work by FCoA.
3. Studied the nutrition program sponsored by the Older Americans Act.
4. Started gathering data on the "special populations" that will make up for the 65 and older population in the future.

1995

The Council did not produce an annual report due to the loss of funding resulting in the termination of the Federal Council on the Aging.

APPENDIX

E

Federal Council on the Aging

Members	Staff	Chair/Vice Chair	Budget	President
1974 Bertha S. Adkins Nelson H. Cruikshank Dorothy L. Devereaux Carl Eisdorfer, M.D., Ph.D. Monsignor Charles J. Fahey Sharon M. Fujii, Ph.D. Frank B. Henderson John B. Martin Garson Meyer Bernard E. Nash Frell M. Owl Lennie P. Tolliver Charles J. Turrisi	*Executive Director* Cleonice Tavani	*Chair* Bertha S. Adkins *Vice Chair* Garson Meyer	None	Richard M. Nixon
1975 Bertha S. Adkins Nelson H. Cruikshank Dorothy L. Devereaux Carl Eisdorfer, M.D., Ph.D. Monsignor Charles J. Fahey	*Executive Director* Cleonice Tavani	*Chair* Bertha S. Adkins *Vice Chair* Garson Meyer	$500,000	Gerald R. Ford

Sharon M. Fujii, Ph.D.
Frank B. Henderson
Seldon G. Hill
Hobart C. Jackson
John B. Martin
Garson Meyer
Bernard E. Nash
Frell M. Owl
Lennie P. Tolliver
Charles J. Turrisi

1976
Bertha S. Adkins
Nelson H. Cruikshank
Dorothy L. Devereaux
Monsignor Charles J. Fahey
Sharon M. Fujii, Ph.D.
Frank B. Henderson
Seldon G. Hill
Harry S. Holland*
Hobart C. Jackson
John B. Martin
Garson Meyer
Bernard E. Nash
Frell M. Owl
Lennie P. Tolliver
Charles J.. Turrisi
Nat T. Winston, Jr., M.D.*

Executive Director
Cleonice Tavani

Chair
Bertha S. Adkins

Vice Chair
Garson Meyer

$575,000   Gerald R. Ford

353

Members	Staff	Chair/Vice Chair	Budget	President
1977 Bertha S. Adkins Nelson H. Cruikshank Dorothy L. Devereaux Monsignor Charles J. Fahey Sharon M. Fujii, Ph.D. Frank B. Henderson Seldon G. Hill Harry S. Holland Hobart C. Jackson John B. Martin Garson Meyer Bernard E. Nash Frell M. Owl Lennie P. Tolliver Charles J. Turrisi Nat T. Winston, Jr., M.D.	*Executive Director* Cleonice Tavani	*Chair* Nelson H. Cruikshank *Vice Chair* Garson Meyer	$575,000	Jimmy Carter
1978 *January 1 to June 25, 1978* Bertha S. Adkins Nelson H. Cruikshank Dorothy L. Devereaux	N. Alan Sheppard	*Chair* Nelson H. Cruikshank *Vice Chair* Garson Meyer	$450,000	Jimmy Carter

*New to the council.

354

Monsignor Charles J. Fahey
Sharon M. Fujii, Ph.D.
Frank B. Henderson
Seldon G. Hill
Harry S. Holland
Hobart C. Jackson
John B. Martin
Garson Meyer
Bernard E. Nash
Frell M. Owl
Lennie P. Tolliver
Charles J. Turrisi
Nat T. Winston, Jr., M.D.

Vice Chair
James T. Sykes

After June 26, 1978
Bertha S. Adkins
Nelson H. Cruikshank
Dorothy L. Devereaux
Fannie B. Dorsey*
Monsignor Charles J. Fahey
Harry S. Holland
Mary A. Marshall*
John B. Martin
Rev. Walter L. Moffett*
Bernice L. Neugarten, Ph.D.*
Frell M. Owl
James T. Sykes*
Fernando M. Torres-Gill, Ph.D.*

*New to the council.

Members	Staff	Chair/Vice Chair	Budget	President
Wesley C. Uhlman*				
Nat T. Winston, Jr., M.D.				
	N. Alan Sheppard	*Chair* Nelson H. Cruikshank	$450,000	Jimmy Carter
1979				
Bertha S. Adkins		*Vice Chair* James T. Sykes		
Cyril H. Carpenter*				
Nelson H. Cruikshank				
Fannie B. Dorsey				
Monsignor Charles J. Fahey				
Aaron E. Henry, Phar.D.*				
Mary A. Marshall				
John B. Martin				
Rev. Walter L. Moffett				
Mary C. Mulvey, Ed.D.*				
Bernice L. Neugarten, Ph.D.				
Jean J. Perdue, M.D.*				
James T. Sykes				
Fernando M. Torres-Gil, Ph.D.				
Wesley C. Uhlman				
1980	*Council Coordinator* Robert Foster	*Chair* Charles J. Fahey	$450,000	Jimmy Carter
Cyril H. Carpenter				
Jacob Clayman*				

*New to the council.

356

Nelson H. Cruikshank
Fannie B. Dorsey
Monsignor Charles J. Fahey
Aaron E. Henry, Phar.D.
Shimeji Kanazawa*
Mary A. Marshall
John B. Martin
Rev. Walter L. Moffett
Mary C. Mulvey, Ed.D.
Bernice L. Neugarten, Ph.D.
Jean J. Perdue, M.D.
James T. Sykes
Fernando M. Torres-Gil, Ph.D.
Wesley C. Uhlman

Vice Chair
James T. Sykes

$481,000   Ronald Reagan

1981
Cyril H. Carpenter
Jacob Clayman
Fannie B. Dorsey
Monsignor Charles J. Fahey
Aaron E. Henry, Phar.D.
Shimeji Kanazawa
Mary A. Marshall
John B. Martin
Rev. Walter L. Moffett
Mary C. Mulvey, Ed.D.
Bernice L. Neugarten, Ph.D.
Jean J. Perdue, M.D.

Council Coordinator
Robert Foster

Chair
Charles J. Fahey

Vice Chair
James T. Sykes

357

*New to the council.

Members	Staff	Chair/Vice Chair	Budget	President
James T. Sykes				
Fernando M. Torres-Gil, Ph.D.				
Esley C. Uhlman				
1982	*Council Coordinator*	*Chair*	$191,000	Ronald Reagan
Adelaide Attard	Edwin Marcus	Adelaide Attard		
Margaret L. Arnold				
Nelda L. Barton		*Vice Chair*		
Edna Bogosian		Charlotte Conable		
James N. Broder				
Sydney Captain				
Jacob Clayman				
Charlotte W. Conable				
Edmund T. Dombrowski, M.D.*				
Katie G. Dusenberry				
Monsignor Charles J. Fahey				
D. Anthony Guglielmo				
Aaron E. Henry, Phar.D.				
Frances Lamont				
Josephine K. Oblinger				
Edna Russell				

*New to the council.

1983

Adelaide Attard
Margaret L. Arnold
Nelda L. Barton
Edna Bogosian
James N. Broder
Sydney Captain
Jacob Clayman
Charlotte W. Conable
Edmund T. Dombrowski, M.D.
Katie G. Dusenberry
Monsignor Charles J. Fahey
D. Anthony Guglielmo
Frances Lamont
Josephine K. Oblinger
Edna Russell

Council Coordinator
Edwin Marcus

Chair
Adelaide Attard

Vice Chair
Charlotte Conable

$175,000

Ronald Reagan

1984

Adelaide Attard
Ingrid Azvedo*
Margaret L. Arnold
Nelda L. Barton
Edna Bogosian
James N. Broder
Sydney Captain
Charlotte W. Conable
Edmund T. Dombrowski, M.D.

Council Coordinator
Edwin Marcus

Chair
Adelaide Attard

Vice Chair
Charlotte Conable

$175,000

Ronald Reagan

*New to the council. Confirmed 12/21/81 by Senate.

Members	Staff	Chair/Vice Chair	Budget	President
Katie G. Dusenberry				
D. Anthony Guglielmo				
Frances Lamont				
Josephine K. Oblinger				
Edna Russell				
Albert Lee Smith, Jr.*				
1985				
Adelaide Attard	*Executive Director*	*Chair*	$200,000	Ronald Reagan
Ingrid Azvedo	James B. Conroy	Adelaide Attard		
Margaret L. Arnold				
Nelda L. Barton		*Vice Chair*		
Edna Bogosian		Charlotte Conable		
Oscar P. Bobbitt*				
James N. Broder				
Charlotte W. Conable				
Edmund T. Dombrowski, M.D.				
Katie G. Dusenberry				
D. Anthony Guglielmo				
Frances Lamont				
Josephine K. Oblinger				
Edna Russell				
Albert Lee Smith, Jr.				

*New to the council.

1986

Ingrid Azvedo
Nelda L. Barton
Edna Bogosian
Oscar P. Bobbitt
James N. Broder
Katie G. Dusenberry
D. Anthony Guglielmo
Jon B. Hunter*
Frances Lamont
Tessa Macaulay*
Mary Majors*
Russell C. Mills, Ph.D.*
Josephine K. Oblinger
Edna Russell
Albert Lee Smith, Jr.

Executive Director
James B. Conroy

Chair
Ingrid Azvedo

Vice Chair
Katie Dusenberry

$191,000   Ronald Reagan

1987

Ingrid Azvedo
Oscar P. Bobbitt
Virgil S. Boucher*
Mary S. Burdge*
Newton Dodson*
Katie G. Dusenberry
Jon B. Hunter
Frances Lamont
Tessa Macaulay

Executive Director
James B. Conroy

Chair
Ingrid Azvedo

Vice Chair
Katie Dusenberry

$200,000   Ronald Reagan

*New to the council.

361

Members	Staff	Chair/Vice Chair	Budget	President
Mary Majors				
Russell C. Mills, Ph.D.				
Josephine K. Oblinger				
Edna Russell				
Gloria Sherwood*				
Albert Lee Smith, Jr.				
1988				
Ingrid Azvedo	*Executive Director*	*Chair*	$191,000	Ronald Reagan
Oscar P. Bobbitt	James B. Conroy	Ingrid Azvedo		
Virgil S. Boucher				
Mary S. Burdge		*Vice Chair*		
Newton Dodson		Katie Dusenberry		
Katie G. Dusenberry				
Jon B. Hunter				
Frances Lamont				
Tessa Macaulay				
Mary Majors				
Russell C. Mills, Ph.D.				
Josephine K. Oblinger				
Edna Russell				
Gloria Sherwood				
Albert Lee Smith, Jr.				

*New to the council.

362

1989
Ingrid C. Azvedo
Oscar P. Bobbitt
June Allyson
Virgil S. Boucher
Newton B. Dodson
Frances Lamont
Tessa Macaulay
Mary J. Majors
Josephine K. Oblinger
Kathleen L. Osborne
Raymond Raschko
Patricia A. Riley
Gloria Sherwood
Norman E. Wymbs
E. Don Yoak

Executive Director
Kevin W. Parks

Chair
Ingrid Azvedo

Vice Chair
Oscar P. Bobbitt

$185,000   George Bush

1990
Ingrid C. Azvedo
Oscar P. Bobbitt
June Allyson
Virgil S. Boucher
Newton B. Dodson
Robert L. Goldman
Frances "Peg" Lamont
Tessa Macaulay
Mary J. Majors
Josephine K. Oblinger
Kathleen L. Osborne

Executive Director
Kevin W. Parks

Chair
Ingrid C. Azvedo

Vice Chair
Oscar P. Bobbitt

$185,000   George Bush

363

Members	Staff	Chair/Vice Chair	Budget	President
Raymond Raschko				
Patricia A. Riley				
Gloria Sherwood				
Norman E. Wymbs				
E. Don Yoak				
Virginia Zachert				
	Executive Director	*Chair*	$181,000	George Bush
1991	Kevin W. Parks	Ingrid Azvedo		
Ingrid C. Azvedo				
Bernard M. Barrett, Jr.		*Vice Chair*		
Oscar P. Bobbitt*		(Void)		
June Allyson				
Virgil S. Boucher				
Eugene S. Callender				
Robert L. Goldman				
Connie Q. Hadley				
Tessa Macaulay				
Mary J. Majors**				
Josephine K. Oblinger				
Kathleen L. Osborne				
Raymond Raschko				
Patricia A. Riley				

*Retired
**Deceased

364

Gloria Sherwood*
Norman E. Wymbs
E. Don Yoak
Virginia Zachert

1992

Ingrid C. Azvedo	*Executive Director*	$180,000 George Bush
Bernard M. Barret	Kevin W. Parks	
Virgil S. Boucher		*Chair*
Eugene S. Callender		Max Friedersdorf
Rudolph Cleghorn		
Stephen Franham		*Vice Chair*
Max L. Friedersdorf		(Void)
Robert L. Goldman		
Connie Hadley		
Charles W. Kane		
Josephine K. Oblinger		
Kathleen L. Osborne		
Raymond Raschko		
E. Don Yoak		
Virginia Zachert		

1993

Alice B. Bulos	*Executive Director*	$178,000 William Clinton
Eugene S. Callender	Brian T. Lutz	
William B. Cashin		*Chair*
Rudolph Cleghorn		(Void)
Stephen Franham		
		Vice Chair
		(Void)

*Retired

E (Cont'd.)

Members	Staff	Chair/Vice Chair	Budget	President
Max L. Friedersdorf Robert L. Goldman Connie Hadley Olivia P. Maynard Josephine K. Oblinger Myrtle B. Pickering Raymond R. Raschko Romaine M. Turyn E. Don Yoak				
1994	*Executive Director* Brian T. Lutz	*Chair* John E. Lyle *Vice Chair* Raymond R. Raschko	$177,000	William Clinton
1995	*Executive Director* Brian T. Lutz	*Chair* John E. Lyle *Vice Chair* Raymond R. Raschko	$176,000	William Clinton

APPENDIX
F

Major Interest Groups in the Field of Aging

MASS MEMBERSHIP ORGANIZATIONS

American Association of Retired Persons (AARP)
Washington, D.C.

Date Established: 1958

Purpose: To enhance the quality of life of older persons, to promote their independence, dignity and purpose, to provide leadership in determining the role and place of older persons in society, and to improve the image of aging.

Principal services provided by AARP include legislative advocacy, community involvement and membership services.

AARP is the largest of all interest groups in the field of aging and its publication, *Modern Maturity*, has the highest average circulation of any magazine in this country.

American Federation of Labor and Congress of Industrial Organizations
  (AFL/CIO)
Washington, D.C.

Date Established: 1955

Purpose: To improve federal legislation and assist state governments to meet applicable federal standards in federal programs that benefit workers, such as workman's compensation, unemployment insurance, welfare, Medicare, Medicaid, Supplementary Security Income, social services, national health proposals and federal policy relating to private pensions.

Chamber of Commerce of the United States
Washington, D.C.

Date Established: 1912

Purpose: To determine and make known to the government the recommendations of the business community on national issues and problems affecting the economy and future of the country. To work to advance human progress through an economic, political and social system based on individual freedom and initiative.

The Gray Panthers (GP)
Philadelphia, Pennsylvania

Date Established: 1970

Purpose: To bring together a coalition of the young, middle-aged and old to overcome the injustices of ageism, that is, the discrimination against and oppression of persons based on chronological age.

National Association of Retired Federal Employees (NARFE)
Washington, D.C.

Date Established: 1921

Purpose: To sponsor and support legislation, rules and regulations beneficial to federal employees eligible for voluntary retirement and to annuitants and potential annuitants of the civilian public service.

National Council of Senior Citizens (NCSC)
Washington, D.C.

Date Established: 1961

Purpose: To advocate on behalf of the elderly and to secure a better life for older persons, consistent with the national interest. Originally launched to help with passage of Medicare. Has close association with the union movement.

National Hispanic Council on Aging
Washington, D.C.

Date Established: 1980

Purpose: To provide an organization of individuals who work in administration, planning, direct services, research and education on behalf of the aging. Fosters the well-being of the Hispanic elderly through activities in all these areas.

Older Women's League (OWL)
Washington, D.C.

Date Established: 1980

Purpose: To provide the first grassroots membership organization to focus exclusively on the concerns of midlife and older women.

Silver Haired Legislatures

Date Established: 1973

Purpose: To invite elderly persons to hold a legislative session in their state. These sessions help legislators become more aware of policy interests among the aging, and they also help older persons expand their skills for influencing legislative decisions.

PROFESSIONAL ORGANIZATIONS

American Geriatrics Society (AGS)
New York, New York

Date Established: 1942

Purpose: To provide a professional society of physicians interested in problems of the elderly. Established to encourage and promote the study of geriatrics and medical research in the field of aging.

American Medical Association (AMA)
Chicago, Illinois

Date Established: 1847

Purpose: To disseminate scientific information to members and the public and inform members on significant medical and health legislation on state and national levels as well as to represent the profession before Congress and governmental agencies.

American Nurses' Association (ANA)
Washington, D.C.

Date Established: 1896

Purpose: To provide a national association for registered nurses. Sponsors subdivisions dealing with research, political action, economics and general welfare, human rights, education, and many nursing specialties, including gerontology.

Association of Gerontology in Higher Education (AGHE)
Washington, D.C.

Date Established: 1974

Purpose: To advance the development of gerontological education and training in institutions of higher education.

The Gerontological Society of America (GSA)
Washington, D.C.

Date Established: 1945

Purpose: To promote the scientific study of aging and to create a forum for the dissemination of the most current thinking and practice in the field of aging.

National Association of Social Workers (NASW)
Silver Spring, Maryland

Date Established: 1955

Purpose: To create practice standards for affiliated professional social workers and to advocate sound public policies through political and social action.

National League for Nursing (NLN)
New York, New York

Date Established: 1952

Purpose: To assess nursing needs, improve organized nursing services and nursing education, and foster collaboration between nursing and other health and community services. Provides tests used for selection of applicants to schools of nursing, evaluation of student progress and nursing service. Accredits nursing education programs and community nursing services.

INDUSTRY AND ADVOCACY GROUPS

Alzheimer's Disease and Related Disorders Association (ADRDA)
Chicago, Illinois

Date Established: 1980

Purpose: To promote research to find the cause, treatment and cure for the disease, and to provide educational programs for the public, the media and health care professionals. Represents continuing care needs of the affected population before government and social service agencies.

American Association of Homes and Services for the Aging (AAHSA)
Washington, D.C.

Date Established: 1961

Purpose: The American Association of Homes and Services for the Aging (AAHSA) is the national association of not-for-profit organizations dedicated to providing quality housing, health, community, and related services to older people. AAHSA's mission is to represent and promote the common interests of its members through leadership, advocacy, education, and other services.

American College of Health Care Administrators
Alexandria, Virginia

Date Established: 1962

Purpose: To provide an organization of persons actively engaged in administration of chronic care institutions, medical administration or activities designed to improve the quality of nursing home administration. Certifies members' ability to meet and maintain a standard of competence in administration and works to develop nursing home standards and a code of ethics and standards of education and training.

American Health Care Association (AHCA)
Washington, D.C.

Date Established: 1949

Purpose: To federate state associations of chronic care facilities. Promotes professional standards; focuses on issues of availability, quality and affordability. Conducts seminars and continuing education for nursing home personnel. Maintains liaison with government agencies, Congress and professional associations.

American Hospital Association (AHA)
Chicago, Illinois

Date Established: 1898

Purpose: To carry on research and education projects in such areas as health administration, hospital economics, hospital facilities and design, and community relations. Represents hospitals in national legislation. Offers programs for institutional effectiveness review and technology assessment.

American Medical Directors Association
Washington, D.C.

Date Established: 1975

Purpose: To provide an organization of physicians and allied personnel providing care in chronic care facilities. Sponsors continuing medical education in geriatrics. Promotes improved geriatric care.

American Society on Aging (ASA)
(Formerly Western Gerontological Society—WGS)
San Francisco, California

Date Established: 1954

Purpose: To improve the lives of older persons through education, training and policy analysis.

Association Nacional Por Personas Mayores (ANPM)
Los Angeles, California

Date Established: 1975

Purpose: To create an awareness among policymakers and the general public of the needs and status of the Hispanic elderly, and to meet those needs through direct services, research and information dissemination.

National Association for Home Care
Washington, D.C.

Date Established: 1982

Purpose: To develop and promote high standards of patient care in home care services, including that provided by home health aides. Seeks to affect legislative policies and regulatory processes, to increase visibility of home care services, and to gather and disseminate home care data.

National Association of Area Agencies on Aging (NAAAA)
Washington, D.C.

Date Established: 1976

Purpose: To represent the interests of the membership in the development of national aging policies; to serve as a communication link connecting area agencies and Title VI grantees with the administration and other national organizations.

National Association of Life Underwriters
Washington, D.C.

Date Established: 1890

Purpose: To support and maintain the principles of legal reserve life insurance and health insurance, to promote high ethical standards and to inform the public, render community service and promote public goodwill.

National Association of Mutual Insurance Companies (NAMIC)
Indianapolis, Indiana

Date Established: 1895

Purpose: To compile and analyze information on all matters relating to insurance and to the reduction and prevention of losses. Provides governmental affairs representation.

National Association of State Units on Aging (NASUA)
Washington, D.C.

Date Established: 1964

Purpose: To advance the capacity of state units on aging to execute their charge of ensuring that society's institutions and systems—social and economic, public and private—provide the equity, opportunity and benefits essential to guarantee the well-being of older Americans.

National Caucus and Center on Black Aged (NCBA)
Washington, D.C.

Date Established: 1970

Purpose: The National Caucus and Center on Black Aged is a nonprofit organization that works to improve the quality of life for older Black Americans.

National Council on the Aging (NCOA)
Washington, D.C.

Date Established: 1950

Purpose: The National Council on the Aging—a private, nonprofit organization—serves as a resource for information, training, technical assistance, advocacy, and leadership in all aspects of aging. NCOA seeks to promote the well-being and contributions of older persons and to enhance the field of aging.

National Hospice Organization (NHO)
Arlington, Virginia

Date Established: 1978

Purpose: To promote standards of care in program planning and implementation for hospices. Collects data for the purpose of demonstrating national trends in the hospice movement, encourages recognized medical and other health-education institutions to provide instruction in hospice care of the terminally ill and members of their families.

National Indian Council on Aging (NICoA)
Albuquerque, New Mexico

Date Established: 1976

Purpose: To promote the interests of elderly Native American Indians.

National Asian Pacific Center on Aging (NAPCA)
Seattle, Washington

Date Established: 1979

Purpose: The National Asian Pacific Center on Aging is a private organization that works to improve the delivery of health care and social services to older members of the Asian Pacific community across the country.

National Senior Citizens Law Center (NSCLC)
Washington, D.C.

Date Established: 1972

Purpose: To provide support to local representatives offering legal assistance to the elderly poor. Funded by the Legal Services Corporation.

GOVERNMENT ORGANIZATIONS

National Association of Counties (NACo)
Washington, D.C.

Date Established: 1935

Purpose: To provide research and reference service for county officials and represent county officials at the national level.

National Association of Manufacturers
Washington, D.C.

Date Established: 1895

Purpose: To represent industry's views on national and international problems to government.

National Governors' Association (NGA)
Washington, D.C.

Date Established: 1908

Purpose: To serve as a vehicle through which governors can influence the development and implementation of national policy and apply creative leadership to state problems. To keep the federal establishment informed of the needs and perceptions of the states.

National League of Cities (NLC)
Washington, D.C.

Date Established: 1924

Purpose: To develop and pursue a national municipal policy which can meet the future needs of cities and help cities solve critical problems they have in common. Represents municipalities before Congress and federal agencies.

APPENDIX
G

Medicare Fact Sheet 1999

The Medicare program helps to pay for health care services furnished to people 65 and over and for persons receiving Social Security Disability benefits after two years. Also served by Medicare are individuals of any age who have end-stage renal (kidney) disease (ESR) and need dialysis or kidney transplants. Medicare currently covers more than 38 million people, of whom approximately 5 million are disabled under Social Security and approximately 270,000 are ESR patients. The Medicare program has two parts: Hospital Insurance (Part A) and Medical Insurance (Part B).

HOSPITAL INSURANCE (PART A)

What's Covered?

- Inpatient hospital services, including room, meals, nursing care, operating room services, blood transfusions, special care units, drugs and medical supplies, laboratory tests, therapeutic rehabilitation services and medical social services.
- Skilled nursing facility care for continued treatment and/or rehabilitation following hospitalization.
- Home health care services prescribed by a physician for treatment and/or rehabilitation of homebound patients, including part-time or intermittent nursing services.
- Hospice care for the terminally ill.

What's Not Covered?

- Long-term or custodial care.

Paying the Bills

- For the first 60 days of inpatient hospital care in calendar year 1999, Medicare pays all approved charges except for a $768 deductible for which the beneficiary is responsible.
- For days 61 through 90, Medicare pays for all covered services except for $192 per day coinsurance payments for which the patient is responsible.
- From the 91st through the 150th day, the beneficiary coinsurance rate is $384 a day, but coverage beyond 90 days in any benefit period is limited to the number of lifetime days available.
- Each beneficiary has 60 lifetime reserve days that can be used only once. If a beneficiary has been out of a hospital or skilled nursing facility for 60 consecutive days, but is then readmitted to a hospital, a new benefit period begins and the beneficiary is again responsible for a $768 deductible for the first 60 days of inpatient care and coinsurance for days 60-90.
- If services in a skilled nursing facility are needed for continued care of a patient after at least three consecutive days of hospital inpatient care, not including the day of discharge, Medicare will pay for all covered services for the first 20 days. From the 21st through 100th day, the beneficiary is responsible for paying $96.00 a day in 1998. Medicare does not pay for skilled nursing facility care beyond 100 days in each benefit period.
- If a person is homebound and requires skilled care, Medicare can pay for medically necessary home health care, including part-time or intermittent nursing care, physical therapy, speech therapy, occupational therapy, medical social services, and medical supplies and equipment.
- For terminally ill patients, Medicare will pay for care from a Medicare-certified hospice, where the specialized care includes pain relief, symptom management and supportive services in lieu of curative services.

Financing Hospital Insurance

The Hospital Insurance Trust Fund is financed mainly from a portion of the Social Security payroll tax (the FICA) deduction). The Medicare part of the payroll tax is 1.45 percent from the employee and 1.45 percent from the employer.

MEDICAL INSURANCE (PART B)

Coverage

Medical Insurance helps to pay for physician services, outpatient hospital services (including emergency room visits when the patient is treated and released), outpatient surgery, diagnostic tests, clinical laboratory services, outpatient physical therapy and speech therapy services, medical equipment and supplies, rural health clinic services, renal dialysis, and a variety of other health services and supplies.

- Generally, Medical Insurance does not cover routine physical examinations, preventive care, services not related to treatment of illness or injury, and outpatient prescription drugs to be self-administered.
- Screening pap smear and mammography examinations are exceptions to the rule against Medicare coverage of routine physical examinations. Medicare covers screening pap smear tests at intervals of three years for detection of cervical cancer, or more frequently for women at high risk of developing cervical cancer. Medicare also covers screening mammography examinations every two years for women 65 and over. Medicare covers flu shots. The shots are free for those enrolled in Medicare Part B from physicians who accept Medicare payments as full payment. Medicare also covers vaccinations against pneumonia.

Paying the Bills

Medicare pays 80 percent of fee schedule amounts for most covered services after a beneficiary's payments for services have reached the annual deductible of $100. After meeting the deductible, beneficiaries can limit their out-of-pocket costs to the 20 percent coinsurance amount by choosing physicians and suppliers who accept Medicare assignment, which means they accept Medicare fee schedule amounts as full payment for their services.

- "Participating" physicians and suppliers agree to accept Medicare assignment in all cases. Directories listing participating physicians, and suppliers are available for examination in local Social Security offices, state and local offices on aging, and senior citizens organizations. Copies can be obtained from Medicare carriers.
- Physicians who do not accept assignment can charge up to 15 percent above the Medicare fee schedule amounts, and beneficiaries are responsible for the difference. Physicians who overcharge beneficiaries can be required to make refunds.

Funding Medical Insurance

Persons enrolled in Medicare Part B pay a monthly premium. The premium established by Congress for calendar year 1999 is $45.50. The general tax revenues of the federal government support approximately 75 percent of the program costs.

MANAGED CARE

Medicare beneficiaries may have lower out-of-pocket costs and added coverage if they choose to enroll in prepaid health care plans that participate in Medicare instead of receiving services under traditional fee-for-service arrangements. Most Medicare beneficiaries live in areas served by prepaid plans. Medicare contracts with Health Maintenance Organizations (HMOs) and Competitive Medical Plans (CMPs) to provide care to Medicare beneficiaries. Medicare prepays a fixed amount per member, per month for all Medicare-covered benefits. Many organizations offer additional benefits not covered by Medicare.

APPENDIX
H

A Guide to Medicare Plans — 1999

Medicare is changing. There are more Medicare plans to choose from. For the past several years, beneficiaries have enrolled in fee-for-service Medicare or a Medicare managed care plan. Now, while still enrolled in one of these plans, it is possible to privately contract with doctors. Also, five Medicare+Choice plan options are available:

Fee-For-Service

The beneficiary pays the $45.50 Part B premium to Medicare. An individual can go to almost any doctor, hospital, or other health care provider. Medicare pays its share of the bill. The beneficiary is responsible for the balance. The beneficiary receives an Explanation of Medicare Benefits (EOMB) regarding what portion of the bill he or she is responsible for paying. Medicare-approved fees generally are lower than those in the private sector. This protects seniors from exorbitant prices. Some 92 percent of Medicare's 38 million beneficiaries use this traditional fee-for-service system.

HMO (Managed Care)

Some HMOs offer Medicare managed care plans. Each plan has a network of doctors, hospitals, and other health providers. To be covered, the beneficiary must receive care from those in this network. If an individual goes outside the network, he is responsible for the whole bill. The beneficiary pays the Part B premium to Medicare. In turn, Medicare pays the HMO plan a fixed sum (based on the average annual cost of care per age group) for the coverage. In return, the HMO plan provides all of Medicare's benefits. The beneficiary does not pay Medicare's deductibles or co-payments. Depending on the plan, the HMO may charge a monthly premium and a per visit co-payment. About 8 percent of beneficiaries are enrolled in Medicare HMO plans.

Private Contracting

No matter which Medicare plan a beneficiary belongs to, he or she can enter into a private contract with any doctor or other health care provider at any time. A contract is signed with the doctor covering what services are involved and what they will cost. Beneficiaries are thus able to see doctors who don't participate in Medicare. The doctor is free to charge private rates, and the beneficiary pays the whole bill. Medigap supplemental insurance may not be used to help cover the costs. The beneficiary is still covered by Medicare for other services, however, under current law a doctor who accepts even one patient for one treatment under this arrangement may not participate in Medicare for 24 months.

PPO (Managed Care)

The key word in preferred provider organizations is "prefer." There is a network of health care providers the PPO prefers to be used by beneficiaries, however if others are used the full bill will not be paid by the individual. PPOs are a variation of managed care. They work like HMOs except that when a doctor is visited who is not in the network, the plan pays a percentage of this cost. This makes it easier to see a doctor or other health care provider who is not in the network, although the beneficiary may have to pay for the convenience.

PSO (Managed Care)

A provider-sponsored organization (PSO) is another variation of managed care. It works like a Medicare HMO plan, except that it is formed by a group of doctors and hospitals. Medicare HMO plans usually are offered by Insurance companies. The rationale for PSOs came, in part, from rural areas where sparse populations can't attract large companies to offer managed care plans. Beneficiaries in these rural areas haven't had the choice to join a Medicare managed care plan. Now, smaller networks of area doctors and hospitals may help fill that gap.

Private Fee-For-Service

A beneficiary shops for a private insurance plan that accepts Medicare beneficiaries. The individual pays the Part B premium to Medicare. Medicare, in turn, pays the private plan a lump sum (based on the average annual cost by age group) for coverage. A beneficiary may go to virtually any doctor, hospital, or other health care provider. The insurance plan reimburses them for each item or service received. The plan can charge premiums, deductibles, and co-payments, and it decides what to reimburse the doctors and hospitals for the health care services given.

Medical Savings Account

This is a test program for 390,000 seniors. An individual joins a private health plan with a high deductible of up to $6,000. Medicare pays the premium and then deposits into a special account the difference between the annual premium and the average beneficiary's cost to Medicare. The difference can be used to pay for medical expenses. Money left over may be added to the following year's account. An individual who stays healthy can save a lot of money. If a beneficiary gets seriously ill, money can be spent to meet the high deductible.

APPENDIX
I

National Institutes of Health
Department of Health and Human Services
9000 Rockville Pike
Bethesda, Maryland 20892
301-496-2433

Composed of thirteen research institutes:

National Cancer Institute
National Eye Institute
National Heart, Lung and Blood Institute
National Institute of Allergy and Infectious Diseases
National Institute of Arthritis and Musculoskeletal and Skin Diseases
National Institute of Child Health and Human Development
National Institute on Deafness and Other Communication Disorders
National Institute of Dental Research
National Institute of Diabetes and Digestive Kidney Diseases
National Institute of Environmental Health Sciences
National Institute of General Medical Sciences
National Institute of Neurological Disorders and Stroke
National Institute on Aging

and eight components:

National Library of Medicine
Warren Grant Magnuson Clinical Center
National Center for Nursing Research
National Center for Research Resources
Fogarty International Center
National Center for Human Genome Research
Division of Research Grants
Division of Computer Research and Technology

All are at the main center in Bethesda, Maryland except the National Institute of Environmental Health Sciences at Research Triangle Park, North Carolina 27709.

Bibliography

A Guide to Medicare Plans, *Secure Retirement*, January/February, 1998.

Achenbaum, W. Andrew, Historical Perspectives on Public Policy and Aging, *Generations, 12*:3, pp. 27-29, 1988.

Achenbaum, W. Andrew, Social Security: A Source of Support for all Ages, in *Social Security After Fifty: Successes And Failures*, Edward D. Berkowitz (ed.), Greenwood Press, New York, 1987.

Achenbaum, W. Andrew, *Social Security: Visions and Revisions*, Cambridge University Press, New York, 1986.

Achenbaum, W. Andrew, *Old Age in the New Land*, Johns Hopkins University Press, Baltimore, Maryland, 1978.

ACTION. *Foster Grandparent Program*, The Federal Domestic Volunteer Agency, Handbook #4405.90, Rev. 1/89.

ACTION. *Senior Companions*, The Federal Domestic Volunteer Agency, Handbook #4405.91, Rev. 8/88.

Administration on Aging, *Administration on Aging Annual Report*, Fiscal Years 1974, 1975 and 1976, U.S. Department of Health, Education and Welfare, Office of Human Development.

Administration on Aging, *Administration on Aging Regional Offices*, 1997. Addresses, Telephone Listings, and Hypertext Links: from the World Wide Web: http://www.aoa.dhhs.gov/aoa/pages.rolist.html

Administration on Aging, *Current Status of the Older Americans Act Reauthorization*, 1997. from the World Wide Web: http://www.aoa.dhhs.gov/oaa/98reauth/status.html

Administration on Aging, *The Administration on Aging and the Older Americans Act*, 1997. from the World Wide Web: http://www.aoa.dhhs.gov/aoa/pages/aoafact.html

Advocates Senior Alert Process, *Senior Guide to the U.S. Congress, 1987-1988*, National Council of Senor Citizens, Washington, D.C., 1987.

Altmeyer, Arthur J., *The Formative Years of Social Security*, University of Wisconsin Press, Madison, Wisconsin, 1968.

American Association of Homes for the Aging, *AAHA Provider News* (Newsletter), 7(2), February 1992.

American Association of Retired Persons, *A Profile of Older Americans: 1989*, Washington, D.C., 1989.

American Association of Retired Persons, *A Profile of Older Americans: 1996*, Washington, D.C., 1989.

American Association of Retired Persons, *After the Harvest: The Plight of Older Farm Workers*, Washington, D.C., 1986.

Anonymous, Editorial Introduction to Social Security: Continued Entitlement or New Means Test? An Issue of Program Stability, *Research Dialogues*, Issue No. 26, July 1990, TIAA-CREF External Affairs—Policyholders and Institutional Research.

Anonymous, Institute of Aging, *CQ Almanac, XXVI*, 92nd Congress, Second Session, pp. 425-426, 1972.

Anonymous, Institute of Aging, *CQ Almanac, XXIX*, 93rd Congress, First Session, pp. 516-517, 1973.

Anonymous, Institute of Aging, *CQ Weekly Report, XXX*(4), p. 2,852, 1972.

Anonymous, Institute of Aging, *CQ Weekly Report, XXXI*(28), p. 1,909, 1973.

Anonymous, Institute of Aging, *CQ Weekly Report, XXXII*(22), p. 1,444, 1974.

Anonymous, Institute of Gerontology, *CQ Weekly Report, XXX*(13), p. 683, 1972.

Anonymous, National Institute on Aging, *CQ Weekly Report, XXXII*(19), p. 1,241, 1974.

Anonymous, President Pocket Veto Statements, *CQ Almanac, XXVI*, 92nd Congress, Second Session, p. 82-A, 1972.

Anonymous, Problems of Aging, *CQ Weekly Report, XXIX*(24), p. 1,276, 1971.

Anonymous, Public Health Service Undergoes Reorganizations, *CQ Weekly Report, XXVII*(4), pp. 167-173, 1969.

Anonymous, Research On Aging Act of 1974 (PL 93-296; 88 Stat. 184), *U.S. Code Congressional and Administrative News*, pp. 209-211, 1974.

Ansak, Marie Louise, Consolidating Care and Financing, *Generations*, Spring 1990.

Anthony, W., M. Cohen, and W. Kennard, Understanding the Current Facts and Principles of Mental Health Systems Planning, *American Psychologist, 45*:11, pp. 1,249-1,252, November 1990.

Bandler, Jean T. D., Family Protection and Women's Issues in Social Security, *Social Work, 35*:4, pp. 307-311, 1989.

Bechill, William, White House Conferences on Aging: An Assessment of their Public Policy Influences, *Journal of Aging and Social Policy, 2*:3/4, 1990.

Berkowitz, Edward D., Introduction: Social Security Celebrates an Anniversary, in *Social Security after Fifty: Successes and Failures*, Edward D. Berkowitz (ed.), Greenwood Press, New York, 1987.

Berkowitz, Edward D., Wilbur Cohen and American Social Reform, *Social Work, 35*:4, pp. 293-299, 1989.

Bernstein, Barton J., The New Deal: The Conservative Achievements of Liberal Reform, in *Towards a New Part*, Barton J. Bernstein (ed.), Random House, New York, 1968.

Berry, Jeffrey M., *The Interest Group Society*, Little, Brown and Company, Boston, Massachusetts, 1984.

Bickman, L. and P. Dokecki, Public and Private Responsibility for Mental Health Services, *American Psychologist, 44*(8), pp. 1,133-1,137, August 1989.

Biegel, D., B. Shore, and M. Silverman, Overcoming Barriers to Serving the Aging/Mental Health Client: A State Initiative, *Journal of Gerontological Social Work, 13*:3/4, pp. 147-165, 1989.

Binstock, Robert H., The Aged as Scapegoat, *The Gerontologist, 23*:2, pp. 136-143, 1983.

Binstock, Robert H., Interest Group Liberalism and the Politics of Aging, *The Gerontologist, 12*, pp. 265-280, 1972.

Binstock, Robert H. and Stephen C. Post, Rationing and Ethics in Health Care, *Christianity and Crisis*, September 23, 1991.

Blumenthal, David, Medicare: The Beginnings, in *Renewing the Promise: Medicare and Its Reform*, D. Blumenthal, M. Schlesinger, and P. B. Drumheller (eds.), Oxford University Press, New York, 1988.

Bowen, Catherine Drinker, *Miracle at Philadelphia: The Story of the Constitutional Convention, May to September 1787*, Little, Brown and Company, Boston, Massachusetts, 1966.

Bremner, Robert H., *From the Depths*, New York University Press, New York, 1956.

Brickner, Philip W., *Home Health Care for the Aged: How to Help Older People Stay in Their Own Homes and Out of Institutions*, Appleton-Century-Crofts, New York, 1978.

Brickner, Philip W., Linda Keen Scharer, Barbara A. Conanan, Marianne Savarese, and Brian C. Scanlan (eds.), *Under the Safety Net: The Health and Social Welfare of the Homeless in the United States*, W. W. Norton and Company, New York, 1990.

Brody, E., *Long Term Care of Older People*, Human Science Press, New ork, 1977.

Brown, J. Douglas, *The Genesis of Social Security in America*. Industrial Relations Section, Princeton University, Princeton, New Jersey, 1969.

Bureau of National Affairs, *ERISA: Selected Legislative History, 1974-1986*, The Bureau of National Affairs, Washington, DC., 1988.

Chandler, R. C. and J. C. Plano, (eds.), *The Public Administration Dictionary*, 2nd Edition, ABC-Cleo, Inc.: ABC-Cleo, Inc., Santa Barbara, California, 1988.

Chelf, Carl P., *Public Policymaking in America: Difficult Choices, Limited Solutions*, Goodyear Publishing Co., Inc., Santa Monica, California, 1981.

Chen, Y., *Remarks for Plenary Session on Social and Behavioral Sciences*, 5th Asia/Oceania Congress of Gerontology, November 21, 1995, Hong Kong, 1996. With permission from the author.

CIS Index, *Legislative Histories*, Washington, DC: GPO, 1984, 1986, 1987, 1988.

Cohen, Elias S., The White House Conference on Aging: An Anachronism, *Journal of Aging and Social Security, 2*:3/4, 1990.

Cohen, Wilbur J., Reflections on the Enactment of Medicare and Medicaid, *Health Care Financing Review*, Annual Supplement, pp. 3-11, 1985.

Cohen, Wilbur J., *Retirement Policies under Social Security*, University of California Press, Berkeley, California, 1957.

Coll, B. D., *Perspectives in Public Welfare*, U.S. Government Printing Office, Washington, DC, 1969.

Commager, H. S., Introduction, in C. D. Bowen *Miracle at Philadelphia: The Story of the Constitutional Convention, May to September 1787*, Book-of-the-Month Club, Inc., New York, 1986.

Committee of the Institute of Medicine, *Responding to Health Needs and Scientific Opportunity: The Organizational Structure of the National Institutes of Health*, National Academy Press, Washington, DC, 1984.

Committee on Education and Labor, *Handbook to Title V of the Older Americans Act*, Prepared for the Subcommittee on Human Resources of the Committee on Education and Labor, U.S. House of Representatives, U.S. Government Printing Office, Washington, D.C., Serial No. 101-I, August 1989.

Committee on Education and Labor, No. 1792, 1969.

Committee on House Administration, *The Bill Status System for the United States House of Representatives*, p. 19, July 1, 1975.

Congress and the Nation: A Review of Government and Politics, IV, 1973-1976, Congressional Quarterly, Inc., Washington, DC, 1977.

Congressional Quarterly Almanac, XLIV (44), Congressional Quarterly, Inc., Washington, DC, 1988.

Congressional Quarterly Almanac, Selected articles from 1963 to 1987.

Congressional Quarterly Weekly, Selected articles from 1964 to 1987.

Congressional Quarterly Weekly, July 15 and July 22, 1989.

Congressional Quarterly Weekly, 47 (16), p. 891 and (24), p. 1,469.

Congressional Record, 74th United States Congress, 1st Session, U.S. Government Printing Office, Washington, DC, 1935.

Congressional Serial Set, Book No. 12061, S.R. 1440, 85th Congress, 2nd Session, *Welfare and Pension Plans Disclosure Act* (to accompany S 2888), April 21, 1958.

Congressional Serial Set, Book No. 12075, H.R. 2283, 85th Congress, 2nd Session, *Welfare and Pension Plans Disclosure Act* (to accompany H 13507), July 28, 1958.

Congressional Yellow Book, Spring 1990, Monitor Publishing Company, Washington, DC, 1990.

Consumer Reports, *Long-Term-Care Insurance: A Payment Option for Some*, September 1995.

Coombs-Ficke, Susan, *An Orientation to the Older Americans Act, Revised Edition, 1985*, NASUA, Washington, DC, 1985.

Corning, Peter A., *The Evolution of Medicare . . . From Idea to Law*, U.S. Department of Health, Education and Welfare, 1969.

Corporation for National Service, 1998. *The Senior Corps Home Page*: from the World Wide Web: http://www.cns.gov/senior/index.html

Corporation for National Service, 1998. *Summary of the President's Reauthorization Proposal*: from the World Wide Web: http://www.cns.gov/reauthorization/reauth_html

Cutler, Neal E., Demographic, Social-Psychological and Political Factors in the Politics of Aging: A Foundation for Research in Political Gerontology, *The American Political Science Review, 71*:3, pp. 1,011-1,025, 1977.

Cutler, Stephen J. and Jon Hendricks, Leisure and Time Use Across the Life Course, in *Handbook of Aging and the Social Sciences*, Chapter 9 in Robert H. Binstock and Linda K. George (eds.), Academic Press, Inc., San Diego, California, 1990.

David, Sheri I., *With Dignity: The Search for Medicare and Medicaid*, Greenwood Press, Westport, Connecticut, 1985.

Day, Christine L., *What Older Americans Think*, Princeton University Press, Princeton, New Jersey, 1990.

Deakin, James, *The Lobbyists*, Public Affairs Press, Washington, DC, 1966.

Denhardt, Robert B., *Public Administration: An Action Orientation*, Brooks/Cole Publishing Company, Pacific Grove, California, 1991.

Department of Health and Human Services, *Administration View on the Older Americans Act Reauthorization*, 1997. from the World Wide Web: http://www.aoa.dhhs.gov/oaa.98reauth/s97

Department of Labor, *Federal Register*, Part IV, Employment and Training Administration, Washington, DC, July 19, 1985.

Derthick, M., *Policymaking for Social Security*, Brookings Institution, Washington, DC, 1979.

Diamond, M., The Declaration and the Constitution: Liberty, Democracy and the Founders, *The Public Interest*, pp. 46-47, Fall 1975.

Dobelstein, Andrew W., *Social Welfare: Policy and Analysis*. Nelson-Hall Publishers, Chicago, Illinois, 1990.

Duncan, D., *The Life and Letters of Herbert Spencer*, Appleton and Company, New York, 1908.

Dunlop, Burton David, *The Growth of Nursing Home Care*, D. C. Heath and Company, Lexington, Massachusetts, 1979.

Durenberger, D., Providing Mental Health Care Services to Americans, *American Psychologist, 44*:10, pp. 1,293-1,297, October 1989.

Dye, Thomas R., *Understanding Public Policy*, 3rd Edition, Prentice-Hall, Inc., Englewood Cliffs, New Jersey, 1978.

Edison, G., *Annotated Bibliography of Nursing Home Resident Rights*, from the World Wide Web: http://www.ink.org/public/keln/bibs/edson2.html

Elder Facts, Administration on Aging, Department of Health and Human Services,

Elkins, B., Aging in Place: A Challenge for Assisted Living Providers, *Provider*, October 1997.

Equity Analytics, Ltd., 1996, from the World Wide Web: http://www.e-analytics.com

Estes, C., The Aging Enterprise Revisited, *The Gerontologist, 33*:3, pp. 292-298, 1993.

Evans, D., et al., Estimated Prevalence of Alzheimer's Disease in the U.S., *Milbank Quarterly, 68*, p. 267, 1990.

Evashwick, C., *The Continuum of Long-Term Care: An Integrated Systems Approach*, Delmar, Albany, New York, 1996.

Eyestone, Robert, *From Social Issues to Public Policy*, Wiley, New York, 1978.

Fahey, Charles, Housing for the Future, *Journal of Housing for the Elderly, 5*:1, pp. 3-5, 1989.

Fahey, Charles and David Tilson, Introduction, in *Aging In Place: Supporting the Frail Elderly in Residential Environments*, David Tilson (ed.), Scott, Foresman and Company, Glenview, Illinois, 1990.

Family and Medical Leave Act Basics, 1998. from the World Wide Web: http://hi-tec.tec.state.tx.us/employer/fmla-bas.htm

Federal Council on Aging report to the President, Washington, D.C., 1992, 1993, 1994.

Federal Council on the Aging, *Annual Report to the President*, Washington, D.C., 1990.

Fesler, James W. and Donald F. Kettl, *The Politics of the Administrative Process*, Chatham House Publishers, Inc., Chatham, New Jersey, 1991.

Fischer, David H., *Growing Old in America*, Oxford University Press, New York, 1977.

Fosler, R. Scott, in *Demographic Change and the American Future*, Fosler, Alonso, Meyer and Kern (eds.), University of Pittsburgh Press, Pittsburgh, Pennsylvania, 1990.

Freiman, M. and L. Sederer, Transfers of Hospitalized Psychiatric Patients under Medicare's Prospective Payment System, *The American Journal of Psychiatry, 147*:1, pp. 100-105, January 1990.

Fritschler, A. Lee, *Smoking and Politics*, Appleton-Century-Crofts, New York, 1969.

Frolik, L., *Elderlaw in a Nutshell*, West Publishing Company, St. Paul, Minnesota, 1995.

Fulghum, Robert, *Everything I Ever Needed to Know I Learned in Kindergarten*, Random House, Inc., New York, 1988.

Gelfand, Donald E., *The Aging Network: Programs and Services*, 3rd Edition, Springer Publishing Company, New York, 1988.

Ginzberg, E., *Tommorrows Hospital*, Yale University Press, New Haven, 1996.

Gollin, James, *The Star Spangled Retirement Dream*, Charles Scribners Sons, New York, 1981.

Graebner, William, *A History of Retirement*, Yale University Press, New Haven, Connecticut, 1980.

Grau, L., *Mental Health and Older Women*, Haworth Press Inc., 1989.

Green, Alan, *Gavel to Gavel: A Guide to the Televised Proceedings of Congress*, Benton Foundation, Washington, DC, 1986.

Haber, Carole, *Beyond Sixty-Five: The Dilemma of Old Age in America's Past*, Cambridge University Press, New York, 1983.

Hamilton, Alexander or Madison, James, (1787), The Federalist No. 51. in *The Federalist: A Commentary on the Constitution of the United States* (1888), Henry Cabot Lodge (ed.), G. P. Putnam's Sons, New York.

Hammond, P. Brett and Harriet P. Morgan (eds.), *Ending Mandatory Retirement for Tenured Faculty: The Consequences for Higher Education*, National Academy Press, Washington, DC, 1991.

Hardy, Carol and Judy Schneider, *An Introductory Guide to the Congressional Standing Committee System*, Library of Congress, Congressional Research Report No. 85-95 GOV, Washington, D.C., 1985.

Harris, Richard, *A Sacred Trust*, Penguin, Baltimore, Maryland, 1969.

HCFA Statistics: Populations, 1996. from the World Wide Web: http://www.hcfa.gov/stats/hstats96/blustats.htm

HCFA Statistics: Expenditures, 1996. from the World Wide Web: http://www.hcfa.gov/stats/hstats96/blustats2.htm

Health United States 1996-97 and Injury Chartbook, U.S. Department of Health and Human Services, Washington, D.C., 1996.

Hendricks, Jon and C. Davis Hendricks, *Aging in Mass Society: Myths and Realities*, 3rd Edition, Little, Brown and Company, Boston, Massachusetts, 1986.

Holahan, John and Joel Cohen, Nursing Home Reimbursement, *Generations*, Spring 1990.

Holtzman, Abraham, *The Townsend Movement*, Bookman Associates, New York, 1963.

House Report No. 93-906, Research on Aging Act of 1974 (PL 93-296), Legislative History, *U.S. Code Congressional and Administrative News*, pp. 3,242-3,249, 1974.

Housing and Urban Development Programs Guide, 1998. from the World Wide Web: http://www.hud.gov/local

Hudson, Robert B., Emerging Pressures on Public Policies for the Elderly, *Society, 15*, pp. 30-33, 1978.

Hudson, Robert B. and John Strate, Aging and Political Systems, in *Handbook of Aging and the Social Sciences*, Robert H. Binstock and Ethel Shanas (eds.), Van Nostrand Reinhold Company, Inc., New York, 1985.

Hyman, Herbert Harvey, *Health Planning: A Systematic Approach*, Aspen Systems Corporation, Germantown, Maryland, 1975.

Iglehart, John K., The New Law on Medicare's Payments to Physicians, *The New England Journal of Medicine, 322*:17, pp. 1,247-1,252, April 26, 1990.

Johnson, Coleen L. and Leslie A. Grant, *The Nursing Home in American Society*, The Johns Hopkins University Press, Baltimore, Maryland, 1985.

Johnson, Harold R., Three Perspectives on the 1981 White House Conference on Aging: Education, *The Gerontologist, 27*, p. 125, 1982.

Jones, Charles O., *An Introduction to the Study of Public Policy*, 2nd Edition, Duxbury Press, North Scituate, Massachusetts, 1977.

Kasschau, Patricia L., *Aging and Social Policy: Leadership*, Praeger Publishers, New York, 1978.

Katzoff, A., Allen, D., Cohen, F., and Hattendorf, G., *The Irwin Guide to Healthcare Benefits Management*, Irwin Professional Publishing, Chicago, 1996.

Keefe, W. J., H. J. Abraham, W. H., Flanigan, C. O. Jones, M. S. Ogul, and J. W. Spanier, *American Democracy: Institutions, Politics and Policies*, 2nd Edition, The Dorsey Press, Chicago, Illinois, 1986.

Kelly, Joan L., Employers Must Recognize That Older People Want to Work, *Personnel Journal*, pp. 44-47, January 1990.

Kelman, Steven, *Making Public Policy: A Hopeful View of American Government*, Basic Books Inc., New York, 1987.

Kennedy, E., Community-Based Care for the Mentally Ill: Simple Justice, *American Psychologist, 45*:11, pp. 1,238-1,240, November 1990.

Kennedy, John F., Special Message to the Congress on the Needs of the Nation's Senior Citizens, February 21, 1963, Public Papers of the Presidents: John F. Kennedy, 1963, U.S. Government Printing Office, Washington, DC, 1964.

Kingdon, John W., *Agendas, Alternatives, and Public Policies*, Little, Brown, Boston, 1984.

Kingson, Eric R., Misconceptions Distort Social Security Policy Discussions, *Social Work, 35*:4, pp. 357-362, 1989.

Kingson, Eric R., Barbara A. Hishorn, and Linda K. Harootyan, *The Common Stake: The Interdependence of Generations (A Policy Framework)*, The Gerontological Society, Washington, DC, 1986.

Kligman, Evan W., Health Care: Beyond Chicken Soup, Position Paper, Governor's Conference on Aging, Tucson, Arizona, December 7, 1990.

Koff, T., *Long-Term Care: An Approach to Serving the Frail Elderly*, Little, Brown & Company, Boston, Massachusetts, 1982.

Koff, T., Class Lecture Notes from November 3, 1986 (MAP 466).

Koff, T., *New Approaches to Health Care for an Aging Population*, Jossey-Bass, San Francisco, california, 1998.

Kravitz, Walter, The U.S. Committee System, *The Parliamentarian, 50*:3, p. 123, 1979.

Kutza, E. A., *The Benefits of Old Age*, University of Chicago Press, Chicago, Illinois, 1981.

Ladd, E. C., *The American Polity: The People and Their Government*, 4th Edition, W. W. Norton and Company, New York, 1991.

Lammers, William W., *Public Policy and the Aging*, Congressional Quarterly Inc., Washington, DC, 1983.

Laster, Leonard, Rationing Medical Care: A Second Opinion, *The Washington Post,* (LEGI-SLATE Article No. 114543), 1990.

Lawton, M. Powell, Three Functions of the Residential Environment, *Journal of Housing for the Elderly, 5*:1, pp. 35-50, 1989.

Lawton, M. Powell, The Relative Impact of Congregate and Traditional Housing on Elderly Tenants, *Gerontologist, 16*, pp. 237-242, 1976.

Lee, Charles R., Preface, in *Curing U.S. Health Care Ill*, Bert Seidman (author) National Planning Association, Washington, DC, 1991.

Legislative Report: Legislative Activity of Interest to SSA during the 104th Congress, 1998. from the World Wide Web: htt://www.ssa.gov/legislation/104congress_summary.html

Lewin, Mario E. and Sean Sullivan, *The Care of Tomorrow's Elderly*, American Enterprise Institute for Public Policy Research, Washington, DC, 1989.

Lindblom, Charles E., *The Policy-Making Process*, Prentice-Hall, Inc., Englewood Cliffs, New Jersey, 1968.

Lindblom, Charles E., The Science of Muddling Through, *Public Administration Review, 14*, pp. 79-88, 1959.

Lowy, Louis, *Social Policies and Programs on Aging: What Is and What Should Be in the Later Years*, D. C. Heath and Company, Lexington, Massachusetts, 1980.

Lubove, Roy, *The Struggle for Social Security 1900-1935*, University of Pittsburgh Press, Pittsburgh, Pennsylvania, 1986.

Maddox, George, Three Perspectives on the 1981 White House Conference on Aging: Research, *The Gerontologist, 22*, pp. 126-127, 1982.

Madison, James, (1787), The Federalist Nos. 10, 41, 47 and 48, in *The Federalist: A Commentary on the Constitution of the United States*, Henry Cabot Lodge (ed.), G. P. Putnam's Sons, New York, 1888.

Madison, James, (1787), Vices of the Political System in the United States, in *The Mind of the Founder: Sources of the Political Thought of James Madison*, Marvin Meyers (ed.), Bobbs-Merrill Company, Inc., New York, 1973.

Maidment, Richard A. and Michael Tappin, *American Politics Today*, St. Martin's Press, New York, 1989.

Marmor, Theodore, *The Politics of Medicare*, Aldine, Chicago, Illinois, 1970.

Mazmanian, Daniel A. and Paul A. Sabatier, *Implementation and Public Policy*, Scott, Foresman, Glenview, Illinois, 1983.

McElvaine, Robert S., *The Great Depression: America 1929-1941*, Times Books, New York, 1984.

McGuire, T., Outpatient Benefits for Mental Health Services in Medicare, *American Psychologists, 44*:5, pp. 818-824, May 1989.

Medicare Fact Sheet, 1996. from the World Wide Web: http://www.hcfa.gov/facts/f960100.htm

Medicare Program Information, 1997. from the World Wide Web: http://www.ssa.gov/medcare.html

Meehan, Eugene J., *The Quality of Federal Policymaking Programmed Failure in Public Housing*, University of Missouri Press, Columbia, Missouri, 1979.

Minois, George, *History of Old Age: From Antiquity to the Renaissance*, Polity Press, Cambridge, United Kingdom, 1989.

Montesquieu, Charles L., (1748), As quoted in The Federalist No. 47, in *The Federalist: A Commentary on the Constitution of the United States* (1888), Henry Cabot Lodge (ed.), G. P. Putnam's Sons.

Morehead, Joe, *Introduction to United States Public Documents*, 3rd Edition, Libraries Unlimited, Littleton, Colorado, 1983.

Myers, Robert J., *Medicare*, McCahan Foundation, Bryn Mawr, Pennsylvania, 1970.

Myers, Robert J., *Social Security*, McCahan Foundation, Bryn Mawr, Pennsylvania, 1975.

Myles, John, A Short History of Retirement, *Aging Today, XII* (1), p. 8, 1991.

National Association of State Units on Aging, *An Orientation to the Older Americans Act*, NASUA, Washington, DC, July 1985.

National Association of State Units on Aging, *An Orientation to the Older Americans Act*, NASUA, Washington, DC, May 1982.

National Council on the Aging, *Checklist for Candidates*, NCOA, Washington, DC, 1992.

National Council on the Aging, *Perspectives on Aging*, NCOA, Washington, DC, March/April 1990.

National Journal, 21:48, p. 2,960, December 2, 1989.

Nelson, Stephen D., *A Case Study of the National Institute of Mental Health*, National Academy Press, Washington, DC, 1984.

Nichols, J., and V. Harker, *Care Homes: Profiting from Despair*, The Arizona Republic, Phoenix, Arizona, 1997.

Nickels, Ilona B., *Guiding a Bill through the Legislative Process: Consideration for Legislative Staff*, Library of Congress, Congressional Research Service Report No. 86-58 GOV, Washington, DC, 1986.

Norman, J. William, The Older Americans Act: Meeting the Changing Needs of the Elderly, *Aging*, pp. 2-10, January-February 1982.

Norton, Thomas J., *The Constitution of the United States: Its Source and Its Application*, Committee for Constitutional Government, New York, 1943.

Older Americans Act Appropriation Information, 1997. from the World Wide Web: http://www.aoa.dhhs.gov/aoa/pages/97oaaapp.html

Older Americans Report, 16:3, Business Publishers, Inc., Silver Spring, Maryland, January 17, 1992.

Oleszek, Walter J., *Congressional Procedures and the Policy Process*, 2nd Edition, CQ Press, Washington, DC, 1984.

Olshansky, S. Jay, Mark A. Rudberg, Bruce A. Casrnes, Christine Cassel, and Jacob A. Brody, Trading Longer Life for Worsening Health, *Journal of Aging and Health, 3*:2, pp. 194-216, May 1991.

Olson, Lura Katz, *The Political Economy of Aging: The State, Private Power and Social Welfare*, Columbia University Press, New York, 1982.

Pearman, William A. and Philip Starr, *Medicare: A Handbook on the History and Issues of Health Care Services for the Elderly*, Garland Publishing, Inc., New York, 1988.

Peters, B. Guy, *American Public Policy: Promises and Performance*, 2nd Edition, Chatham House Publishers, Inc., Chatham, New Jersey, 1986.

Piven, Frances F. and Richard Cloward, *Regulating the Poor*, Pantheon, New York, 1971.

Pratt, Henry J., Politics of Aging, *Research on Aging, 1*:2, pp. 155-179, June 1979.

Pratt, Henry J., *The Gray Lobby*, University of Chicago Press, Chicago, Illinois, 1976.

Pratt, Henry J., Old Age Association in National Politics. *The Annals of the American Academy of Political and Social Science, 415*, 106-119, September 1974.

President's Committee on Corporate Pension Funds and Other Retirement and Welfare Programs, "Public Policy and Private Pension Programs: A Report to the President on Private Employee Retirement Plans," U.S. Government Printing Office, Washington, DC, January 1965.

Prud'Homme, Alexa, The Common Man's Tax Cut, *Time, 137*:13, p. 28, 1991.

Public Law 99-592, 99th Congress, Washington, DC, October 31, 1986.

Public Law 100-175, Washington, DC, 1987.

Pynoos, Jon, Housing the Aged: Public Policy at the Crossroads, Chapter 2, in *Housing the Aged: Design Directives and Policy Considerations*, Victor Regnier and John Pynoos (eds.), Elsevier Science Publishing Co., Inc., New York, 1987.

Quadagno, Jill S., From Poor Laws to Pensions: The Evolution of Economic Support for the Aged in England and America, *Milbank Memorial Fund Quarterly, 62*:3, pp. 417-446, Summer 1984a.

Quadagno, Jill S., Welfare Capitalism and the Social Security Act of 1935, *American Sociological Review, 49*(5), pp. 632-647, 1984b.

Quinn, J., and T. Smeeding, The Present and Future Economic Well-Being of the Aged, in *Pensions in a Changing Economy, Chapter 1*, Employee Benefit Research Institute, Washington, D.C., 1993.

Regnier, Victor and Jon Pynoos (eds.), *Housing the Aged: Design Directives and Policy Considerations*, Elsevier Science Publishing Co., Inc., New York, 1987.

Regulations to the Older American Act, Section 1321.27.

Rein, Martin, *From Policy to Practice*, M. E. Sharp, Inc., Armonk, New York, 1983.

Reischauer, R., Two Years that Make a Big Difference, *New York Times*, July 13, 1997.

Relman, Arnold S., Don't Ration Health Care, *Consumers' Research*, December 1990.

Rich, Bennett M., and Martha Baum, *The Aging: A Guide to Public Policy*, University of Pittsburgh Press, Pittsburgh, Pennsylvania, 1984.

Riley, M. W. and A. Froner, *Aging and Society*, Volume 1, Russell Sage Foundation, New York, 1968.

Roosevelt, Franklin D., Message to the Congress Reviewing the Broad Objectives and Accomplishments of the Administration (June 8), in *The Public Papers and Addresses of Franklin D. Roosevelt*, I. Rosenman, Vol. 3, Random House, New York, 1938a.

Roosevelt, Franklin D., Addresses to Advisory Council of the Committee on Economic Security (November 14), in *The Public Papers and Addresses of Franklin D. Roosevelt*, Samuel I. Rosenman, Vol. 3. Random House, New York, 1938b.

Rossum, Ralph A., James Wilson and the Pyramid of Government: The Federal Republic, *The American Founding: Politics, Statesmanship, and the Constitution*, Chapter 5 in R. A. Rossum and G. L. McDowell (eds.), Kennikat Press, Port Washington, New York, 1981.

Rossum, Ralph A. and Gary L. McDowell, Politics, Statesmanship, and the Constitution, in *The American Founding: Politics, Statesmanship and the Constitution*, Chapter 1, R. A. Rossum and G. L. McDowell (eds.), Kennikat Press, Port Washington, New York, 1981.

Rothman, David J., *The Discovery of the Asylum*, Little, Brown and Company, Boston, Massachusetts, 1971.

Roybal, E., Mental Health and Aging: The Need for an Expanded Federal Response, *American Psychologist*, pp. 189-194, March 1988.

Rushefsky, Mark E., *Public Policy in the United States: Toward the Twenty-First Century*, Brooks/Cole Publishing Company, Pacific Grove, California, 1990.

Sandell, S., and M. Rosenblum, Age Discrimination in Employment: Economic and Legal Perspectives, *Handbook on Employment and the Elderly*, Chapter 11, Greenwood Press, Westport, Connecticut, 1996.

Schiltz, Michael E., *Public Attitudes Toward Social Security, 1935-1965*. Social Security Administration Research Report No. 33, U.S. Government Printing Office, Washington, DC, 1970.

Schneider, D. M., *The History of Public Welfare in New York State 1609-1886*, University of Chicago Press, Chicago, Illinois, 1938.

Schottland, Charles, *The Social Security Program in the United States*, Appleton-Century-Crofts, New York, 1963.

Schottland, Charles, Presentation at University of Arizona, April 1991.

Schultz, J. H., *The Economics of Aging*, Auburn House, Dover, Massachusetts, 1988.

Schwarz, John E., *America's Hidden Success: A Reassessment of Public Policy from Kennedy to Reagan*. W. W. Norton and Company, New York, 1987.

Scull, Andrew T., *Decarceration: Community Treatment and the Deviant—A Radical View*, Prentice-Hall, Englewood Cliffs, New Jersey, 1977.

Seidman, Bert, *Curing U.S. Health Care Ills*, National Planning Association, Washington, DC, 1991.

Seidman, Harold, *Politics, Position and Power: The Dynamics of Federal Organization*, Oxford University Press, New York, 1970.

Senior Living Alternatives: The Nationwide Directory, 1997. from the World Wide Web: http://www.senioralternatives.com

Shanas, E., P. Townsend, D. Wedderburn, H. Friis, P. Milhoj, and J. Stehouwer, *Old People in Three Industrial Societies*, Atherton Press, New York, 1968.

Sharansky, Ira and George C. Edwards, *The Policy Predicament: Making and Implementing Public Policy*, W. H. Freeman and Company, San Francisco, California, 1978.

Sharansky, Ira and Donald Van Meter, *Policy and Politics in American Governments*, McGraw-Hill Book Co., New York, 1975.

Shephards Acts and Cases by Popular Names/Federal and State, 3rd Edition. Shephards/McGraw-Hill, Colorado Springs, Colorado, 1986.

Sherman, Susan R., Housing, *Handbook of Gerontological Services*, 2nd Edition, Chapter 18, Abraham Monk (ed.). Columbia University Press, New York, 1990.

Skocpol, Theda and Amenta, Edwin, Did Capitalists Shape Social Security? *American Sociological Review, 50*:4, pp. 572-575, 1985.

Skocpol, Theda and John Ikenberry, The Political Formation of the American Welfare State: In Historical and Comparative Perspective, *Comparative Social Research, 6*, pp. 87-148, 1983.

Smyer, M, Nursing Homes as a Setting for Psychological Practice, *American Psychologist, 44*:10, pp. 1,308-1,314, October 1989.

Snyder, D., The Economic Well-Being of Retired Workers by Race and Hispanic Origin, *Pensions in a Changing Economy*, Chapter 6, Employee Benefit research Institute, Washington, D.C., 1993.

Social Security: Key Dates, 1997. from the World Wide Web: http://www.ssa.gov/history/keydates.html

Social Security: A Brief History, 1997. from the World Wide Web: http://www.ssa.gov/history/history6.html

Social Security: A Brief History, 1997. from the World Wide Web: http://www.ssa.gov/history6.html

Social Security Administration, *Social Security Programs in the United States*, DHEW Publication No. (SSA) 72-11902). U.S. Government Printing Office, Washington, DC, 1971.

SOS Education Fund, *Supplementary Security Income*, Save Our Security, Washington, DC, June 1984.

Stern, L., can We Save Social Security? *Modern Maturity*, pp. 28-36, 1997.

Stevens, Robert and Ruth Stevens, *Welfare Medicine in America: A Case Study of Medicaid*, Free Press, New York, 1974.

Strauss, A., et al., *Chronic Illness and the Quality of Life*, Mosby, St. Louis, Missouri, 1984.

Streib, Gordon F., Congregate Housing: People, Places, Policies, in *Aging In Place: Supporting the Frail Elderly in Residential Environments*, Chapter 4, David Tilson (ed.), Scott, Foresman and Company, Glenview, Illinois, 1990.

Streib, G. F. and R. H. Binstock, Aging and the Social Sciences: Changes in the Field, *Handbook of Aging and the Social Sciences*, 3rd Edition, Chapter 1, Robert H. Binstock and Linda K. George (eds.), Academic Press, Inc., San Diego, California, 1990.

Swan, J., P. Fox, and C. Estes, Geriatric Services: Community Mental Health Center Boon or Bane, *Community Mental Health Journal, 25*:4, pp. 327-338, Winter 1989.

The Importance of ERISA Section 404(c), 1997. from the World Wide Web: http://www.rpg401k.com/erisa.htm

The National Chronic Care Consortium: An Overview of the Consortium's Purpose, Structure, Accomplishments and Future, 1993.

The Twentieth Century Fund, Social Security Reform: a Guide to the Issues, The Twentieth Century Fund Press, New York, 1996.

Thursz, Daniel, Principles for the White House Conference on Aging, *Perspectives on Aging, 28*:5, pp. 30-31, 1989.

Torrens, P., and S. Williams, *Introduction to Health Services*, Delmar, Albany, New York, 1993.

Toufexis A., From the Asylum to Anarchy, *Time*, pp. 58-59, October 22, 1990.

Trattner, W. I., *From Poor Law to Welfare State*, Free Press, New York, 1974.

Truman, David B., *The Governmental Process*, 2nd Edition, Alfred A. Knopf, New York, 1971.

United States Code Congressional and Administrative News, West Publishing Company, Legislative Histories, St. Paul, Minnesota, 1965, 1967, 1969, 1972, 1973, 1975, 1978, 1981, 1982, 1983, 1984, 1986, 1987, 1988, 1990.

U.S. Bureau of the Census, *Reported Voting and Registration by Single Years of Age and Sex*, 1994.

U.S. Committee on Economic Security, *Social Security in America*, Government Printing Office, Washington, DC, 1937.

U.S. Congress, Hearing before the Subcommittee on Early Childhood, Youth and Families of the Committee on Economic and Educational Opportunities, House of representatives, *Hearing on Older Americans Act*, Serial No. 104-42, 1996.

U.S. Congress, *Compilation of the Older Americans Act of 1965 as Amended through December 1988*, Washington, D.C., March 2, 1989.

U.S. Congress, *United States Code Congressional and Administrative News*, 93rd Congress, Second Session, 1974; 99th Congress, Second Session, 1986, West Publishing Co., St. Paul, Minnesota.

U.S. Congress: House Committee on Ways and Means, *Public Assistance Titles of the Social Security Act*, Hearings on HR 9120. 84th Congress, 2nd Session, 1956.

U.S. Congress: Select Committees on Aging, House of Representatives, *Transportation in the Nineties: Keeping America's Elderly Moving*, Hearing before the Subcommittee on Human Services, 102nd Congress, First Session, January 29, 1991, U.S. Government Printing Office, Comm. Pub. No. 101-792, Washington, DC, 1991.

U.S. Congress: Select Committee on Aging, House of Representatives, *U.S. Administration on Aging: The Mission and the Reality*, Hearing before the Subcommittee on Human Services, 102nd Congress, First Session, June 12, 1991, U.S. Government Printing Office, Comm. Pub. No. 102-811, Washington, DC, 1991.

U.S. Congress: Subcommittee on the Departments of Labor, Health and Human Services, Education, and Related Agencies, *Services, Education, and Related Agencies Appropriations for 1992*, Hearings before a Subcommittee of the Committee on Appropriations, House of Representatives, 102nd Congress, First Session, April 25, 1991, U.S. Government Printing Office, Washington, DC, 1991.

U.S. Department of Health, Education and Welfare, *Aging, 130*, August 1965 and other issues through August 1967.

U.S. Department of Labor, Pension and Welfare Benefits Administration, *What you should Know about your Pension Rights*, 1997. from the World Wide Web: http://www.nceo.org/library/pensions.html

U.S. Department of Labor, Pension and Welfare Benefits Administration, *What you Should Know about your Pension Rights,* Washington, D.C., 1995.

U.S. Senate, Departments of Labor, Health and Human Services and Education and Related Agencies Appropriation Bill, 1997, September 12, 1996, Report 104-368, 1996.

U.S. Senate, Hearing before the Subcommittee on Aging of the Committee on Labor and Human Resources, *Reauthorization of Senior Nutrition Programs under Title III of the Older Americans Act*, U.S. Government Printing Office, Washington, D.C., 1995.

U.S. Senate, Hearing before the Subcommittee on Aging of the Committee on Labor and Human Resources, *Reauthorization of the Older Americans Act: Maximizing resources in the Face of Growing Demands*, U.S. Government Printing Office, Washington, D.C., 1995.

U.S. Senate, Hearing before the Subcommittee on Aging of the Committee on Appropriations United States Senate, *Reauthorization of the Older Americans Act,* Senate Hearing 103-995, 1995.

U.S. Senate, *To Amend the Older Americans Act of 1995 to Improve the Provisions Relating to Indians, and for other Purposes,* report 104-335, August 27, 1996.

U.S. Senate: Special Committee on Aging, Chapter 5: Effective Organization of Federal Programs in Aging, *Developments in Aging, 1959-1963* (88th Congress, Report #8), Government Printing Office, Washington, DC, 1963.

U.S. Senate: Special Committee on Aging, *Developments in Aging: 1990, Volume I,* U.S. Government Printing Office, Washington, DC, 1991.

U.S. Senate: Special Committee on Aging, *Developments in Aging: 1989, Volume I,* Report 101-249, U.S. Government Printing Office, Washington, DC, 1990.

U.S. Senate: Special Committee on Aging. *Developments in Aging: A Report of the Special Committee on Aging,* Vol. I, U.S. Senate GPO, Washington, DC, 1977, 1980, 1981, 1982, 1988 and 1989.

U.S. Senate: Special Committee on Aging, *Developments in Aging,* 1968, 1980, 1981, 1987, 1988. Report of the Washington, DC: GPO.

U.S. Senate: Special Committee on Aging, *Lifelong Learning for an Aging Society,* An information paper, 102nd Congress, 1st Session, Serial No. 102-J, U.S. Government Printing Office, Washington, DC, December 1991.

U.S. Senate, *Action for the Aged and Aging,* Report by the Subcommittee on Problems of the Aged and Aging, January 27, 1961.

U.S. Senate, *Developments in Aging,* 1959 to 1963 and 1965 through 1988, Report of the Special Committee on Aging.

U.S. Senate, *The Older Americans Act of 1965: A Compilation of Materials Relevant to HR 3708,* As amended by the Special Subcommittee on Aging of the Committee on Labor and Public Welfare, U.S. GPO, Washington, DC.

U.S. Senate, *Older Americans Act Reauthorization Amendments of 1991,* 102nd Congress, 1st Session, Report 102-151, Washington, DC, 1991.

U.S. Senate Report No. 2363, 1958.

U.S. Senate Special Committee on Aging Report, Senate Resolution 33, February 9, 1961.

Victor, Kirk, Crying wolf?, *National Journal, 21*:43, pp. 2,630-2,633, October 28, 1989.

Vinyard, Dale, White House Conferences and the Aged, *Social Service Review,* pp. 655-671, December 1979.

Wagner, L., and K. Vickery, Assisted Living's Delicate Balance, *Provider,* October 1997.

Wais Document Retrieval. from the World Wide Web: http://www.acessgpo.gov/cgi-bin/waisgat...docID=751455598+0+0+0&WAISaction=retrieve: 29USCIA1001, 29USCIA1002; 29USCIA1003, 29USCIA1021, 29USCIA1025, 29USCIA1027, 29USCIA1031, 29USCIA1051, 29USCIA1053, 29USCIA1056.

Ward, Russell A., The Marginality and Salience of Being Old: When Is Age Relevant?, *The Gerontologist, 24*:3, pp. 227-232, 1984.

Webster's Ninth New Collegiate Dictionary, Merriam Webster Inc., Springfield, Massachusetts, 1987.

White House Conference on Aging, 1995. Final Report, Washington, D.C.

Williamson, John B., Judith A. Shindul, and Linda Evans, *Aging and Public Policy: Social Control or Social Justice?,* Charles C. Thomas, Springfield, Illinois, 1985.

Winslow, Susan, *Brother, Can You Spare a Dime?* Paddington Press, Ltd., New York, 1976.

Witte, Edwin, *The Development of the Social Security Act,* University of Wisconsin Press, Madison, Wisconsin, 1962.

Woll, Peter, *Behind the Scenes in American Government: Personalities and Politics*, Little, Brown and Company, Boston, Massachusetts, 1977.

Woll, Peter, *Public Policy*, Winthrop Publishers, Inc., Cambridge, Massachusetts, 1974.

Womens Voices for the Economy–Part II, 1995. from the World Wide Web: http://www.womenconnect.com.icpa11w.htm

Index

Other Titles in the
SOCIETY AND AGING SERIES
Jon Hendricks, Series Editor